A Colder Eye

A COLDER EYE

The Modern Irish Writers

HUGH KENNER

THE JOHNS HOPKINS UNIVERSITY PRESS
BALTIMORE

Originally published in 1983 as a Borzoi Book by
Alfred A. Knopf, Inc.
Johns Hopkins Paperbacks edition, 1989, published by
arrangement with Alfred A. Knopf, Inc.

The Johns Hopkins University Press
701 West 40th Street, Baltimore, Maryland 21211

Library of Congress Cataloging-in-Publication Data

Kenner, Hugh.
A colder eye.

Reprint. Originally published: New York: Knopf, 1983
Includes index.
1. English literature—Irish authors—History and criticism.
2. English literature—20th century—History and criticism.
3. English literature—19th century—History and criticism.
4. Modernism (Literature)—Ireland. 5. Ireland—
Intellectual life. I. Title.
PR8750.K46 1989   820'.9'89162   88-46119
ISBN 0-8018-3838-X

Acknowledgment of permission to reprint previously published
material is found on page 301, following the index.

In Memoriam
L. P. B.
Citizen, Husband, Father,
Wanderer
and Reincarnation of
Ulysses

The biological-historical fact is that *homo sapiens* is a species which uses oral speech, manufactured by the mouth, to communicate. That is his definition. He is not, by definition, a writer or reader.

ERIC HAVELOCK

CONTENTS

AUTHOR'S NOTE

This book tries, within reasonable limits of space, to tell a coherent story, which could be subtitled *Yeats and His Shadow*. That is one kind of book and not another kind; you'd no more consult it for a "balanced" treatment of anyone, even Yeats, than you'd consult *A Tale of Two Cities* for French history. It is not true that what I do not discuss I dismiss: Moore's fictions and Beckett's, Lady Gregory's plays, the work of James Stephens, the existence of Brendan Behan. They are part of a different story, or perhaps a different way to tell this one. I omit the living poets you may have expected—Kinsella, Montague, Heaney—because they seem to me the beginning of a new story entirely, the story of post-Yeatsian Ireland.

If a survey is what you were wanting I can recommend the one by Richard Fallis (*The Irish Renaissance,* Syracuse, 1977). For bibliographies, try Roger McHugh and Maurice Harmon (*Anglo-Irish Literature,* Dublin; 1982); it has a good text as well.

Do not be alarmed, finally, by vagaries of Irish spelling: Concobar, Conchubor, Conchubar; Padraic, Padraig; Beaslaoi, Béaslaí: I follow my source of the moment, in full awareness that systems were elbowing systems, dialects dialects, throughout the years of interest.

H. K.

ACKNOWLEDGMENTS

I haven't such a bad opinion of the
Jesuits. . . . They're an educated order.
I believe they mean well too.

Dubliners

If an intellectual community exists it is among the Irish scholars; a newcomer can only express delight at the generosity of those who really know. Brendan O Hehir has been entitled for years to wonder why his correspondents do not simply buckle down and learn some Irish. Their excuse must be that the more they learned the less pretext they would have for soliciting his wit. His highest moment must be the explication, at Richard Finneran's request, of a word Yeats wrote, "gluggerabunthaun." Gazing into its entrails, he divined "rattle-arse," a feat that made Theobald's "babbled of green fields" seem obvious.

Richard Finneran himself, Yeats's editor, has never failed to answer queries however naïve by return post, with Xeroxed evidence attached. In another incarnation I may hope for files of such adequacy, and for such patience. And the temptation to make an appendix of John V. Kelleher's letters needed serious resisting; I have merely pillaged them shamelessly, without quotation marks. "Saints and Scholars," runs the old motto; a scholar who set work aside to type single-spaced page after page for the use of a neophyte, on a machine moreover that chewed its best new ribbons, was earning his place in the company of saints.

Darcy O'Brien lent necessary and more general counsel, when tone and strategy were fluid still. He even encouraged me to persist in my stubborn courses. So study the chapter called "Warning." Do not regard what you read here as resting on any final authority save my own sense of what fits. If consultants disagreed I reminded myself that it was after all my book. I'm aware by the way that my spellings of Irish words can be inconsistent. Lacking the learning to harmonize them, I follow in each instance my source of the moment.

What I understand of Joyce is inextricable from Fritz Senn's conversation, Adaline Glasheen's inimitable letters, Tom Staley's archives. I've had help with specifics from Michael Groden and Hans Gabler, and Roland McHugh has answered spot queries from Dublin. Séan Golden and Conor Johnston were generous with linguistic details, W. M. Murphy with still more nuggets of Yeatsian biography than got into his splendid life of the poet's father.

For making a Dublin stay possible and profitable I am indebted to Vivian Mercier and Eilís Dillon, Elaine ní Chuilleánain and Macdara Woods, Sheila Norton and Pat Norton the Dayfather, Anne Yeats, Provost F.S.L. Lyons of Trinity, Katherine Kavanagh, Sean O'Faolain, Dr. J. B. Lyons, Ulick O'Connor, David Norris, Denis Donoghue; and whom have I missed? Some I never knew by name, notably the old man in the pawnshop who rattled about a friend "older than the Chinese" whose paid occupation should he find one would be "falling off of busses." You have to hear his kind of talk to believe it.

The librarians of the McFarlin Library, University of Tulsa, and the Interlibrary Loan staff at The Johns Hopkins University never failed to lay hands on whatever was wanted. Deans Owen and Suskind at Hopkins have been generous with research funds, Bill Buckley in New York with other assistance. Thank you too, Heath Co. and The Software Toolworks (Walt Bilofsky, Jim and Marrietta Gillogly) for technological acumen befitting a less stressful century. Though Joyce wrote every word of *Ulysses* by hand, I, contemplating a far slighter task, simply couldn't.

A Colder Eye

WARNING

I considered it desirable that he should
know nothing about me but it was even
better if he knew several things which
were quite wrong.

FLANN O'BRIEN, *The Third Policeman*

What an Irish Bull is we all know: when three cows are standing in a field
the one that is sitting down is an Irish Bull. These are encountered daily in
any part of the island where the hand of man has never set foot. Of more
consequence by far is the Irish Fact, definable as anything they will tell you
in Ireland, where you get told a great deal and had best assume a demeanor
of wary appreciation.

Thus chatting with the pastor of the Church of the Three Patrons, Rath-
gar, I asked him had he known that according to *Ulysses* it was in his
church the fictional Leopold Bloom had been baptized prior to espousing
the scrupulous Molly, who would countenance many things but not a mixed
marriage. He had not; and, one good tidbit deserving another, he confided
with husky emphasis, "And do you know who else was baptized in this
church?—*James Joyce!*"

An Irish Fact. Joyce was not baptized in Three Patrons at all. But he
ought to have been, for at least three reasons. (1) He was born nearby. (2)
He would surely have been baptized where his Bloom was. (3) Providence
in creating the Irish (finest of deeds) endowed them with a craving for
occasional emphatic assertions, lacking which the most mellifluous discourse

would be but as porter poured upon the floor. It is incumbent on each speaker to furnish these as the structure of discourse prompts, and that which it is structurally needful to say, and notably for men of God to say, wise Providence will surely underwrite.

In the first edition of Professor Ellmann's biography of Joyce you will read that our man was baptized on 5 February 1882 at the Church of St. Joseph, Terenure. Since that church was not built until 1904 this is another non-fact, though a better-grounded one since a footnote cites the baptismal record kept there. That the record pertains to a different church, now demolished, is something further inquiry can gather from still further records. So a trail of papers leads truthwards. There is comfort in written records; the very concept of "accuracy" derives from their mutual fit.

One document can accurately copy another, as we can check if we lay them side by side. Or a memorandum of spoken words, set down at the time, will continue to record them when speakers and hearers are long dead. Our faith is that it matched fresh memories when memories were there to match against it, hence its power to resurrect phantoms.

But in some pre-literate culture, for instance in Homeric Greece, unpestered by scribes, could it possibly occur to anyone to reject a narrative because it was inaccurate? For what could accuracy mean? Not only is what they'd need to match the tale against no longer there; the tale itself, once told, is no longer there either; and as recent a past as yesterday afternoon is no more than what the speaker of the moment says it was, and only so long as he's talking. Three different talkers, three different evanescing yesterdays, each one paced by a different sequencing of spoken flowers. (Hence the seven birthplaces of Homer.)

Though by no means pre-literate, in Ireland they remain on the whole unintimidated by literacy's pretensions, and notably by its pretense that it can attach impersonal value to getting things "right." Its *skills*, those are widely possessed, and deemed not without value; being forced to acquire them is what put the fear of the Lord and the leather into many a rapscallion, and galoots you'd have said would not amount to anything can get money writing yarns to be read in America. But black and white is tricky stuff entirely, the lad who scribbled it is not showing his face, you'd want your solicitor at your side before you'd be entangling yourself with it at all. What? Oh yes, as sure as I'm telling you.

A sinister disproportion between the free flow of gab and the bleached simulacrum a writer lays before us after a time of keeping unnatural silence upstairs, this is something that Swift discerned and his countrymen continue to suspect. Swift well knew how much you can get away with in print that nobody would tolerate face to face. You can even advertise—he did this once—that a pestilent man is dead, and put him to unspeakable trouble proving he is alive.

Though suspicious of paper instruments, they will take frigid pity on somebody entoiled in efforts to decipher one, and place Irish Facts in plenty at his disposal. Thus an old man explained—this was twenty-five years ago—what was needful to be known about one Mr. Hunter, concerning whom there is little public record save that in pre-1904 Dublin he lived in the Clonliffe Road and Jimmy Joyce and his brother Stannie both knew who he was. Jim once planned a story about Hunter, to be titled "Ulysses," but never wrote it, and we naturally wonder about Hunter's part in the *Ulysses* that did get written, the big book.

This old man's father had known Jimmy's father, they had used to sing together on Saturday nights, and Jimmy had put him into a story called "The Dead" under the name of "Bartell D'Arcy," which was nearly his name. But Mr. P. J. D'Arcy had not been flattered. The story had said he was not in good voice that night, hoarse as a crow in fact, something that was never true, and he went round to his solicitor, who told him he had no case. After that it was he took to drinking noticeably. The story, printed on all those sheets of paper bound into all those books, would not ever change nor go away, hoarse as a crow, D'Arcy, hoarse as a crow, and it was the cirrhosis killed him.

But about Mr. Hunter now; for the old man, son of long-dead "Bartell D'Arcy," knew from fifty years agone what it was Jim and Stannie would have known, and if I was as concerned as I professed to be I should know too.

We met by prearrangement near O'Connell Bridge. It was November, mid-afternoon, dusk falling, and if that causes surprise you've not reflected how far north Dublin is—the latitude of James Bay. He was short and wary-faced and overcoated. We strolled southward as he worked his way into his narrative.

"Hunter," he stated, "was his name, or rather it was not his name, if you follow me." I did not follow him, and he drew together his cheeks to expel an elucidation: "Jew." Hunter's wife, everybody knew about his wife, and the men she more than entertained, and Hunter knew about them too but for some reason was unable to control her. She was part-Spanish, that was known, and she sang. This singing was a handy pretext, what with the travelling.

Molly Bloom, you are thinking. Yes.

We had walked a couple of blocks, and the time had come for him to produce a Fact. "Her special man, the one who organized her tours and more than her tours, if you follow me, the one Joyce called Boylan, was a man named Creech, and he worked in the post office with my father. And to help you with him I have brought along a photograph."

Aid me, Muse, to say what it was he drew from his overcoat pocket: sepia, on cardboard, rather larger than a postcard, what they used to call half-plate size. We were near Kapp and Peterson's on the west side of Grafton Street, and I peered by the light from their window.

I recall a moustachioed Creech who regarded the lens, thus the world including posterity, over folded arms, unless that is an Irish Fact of my own contribution. So this was Blazes Boylan. (Boylan with impatience. That's the bucko that'll organise her, take my tip. Tipping her tepping her tapping her topping her. Tup.) You are wondering what he looked like. Chiefly, like a man in a photograph made about 1900, which was what he had become. That, and a theme for anecdote.

"I was present one day when Hunter was walking along this very path"— we had now crossed to Stephen's leafless Green—"and from around the bushes came Creech. They drew face to face. And I heard myself Hunter's very words to Creech."

The confrontation of Bloom with Blazes Boylan, an event outside the conception of *Ulysses*, this would be something to have come to Ireland to hear. He was facing me to make sure I heard it, and his voice dropped to a stage snarl: "You and your fuckin' concert tours!" A high-pitched laugh, and he savored the line anew. "You and your fuckin' concert tours."

Of this veritable kaleidoscope of Irish Facts we may say that some of it at least appears to be reliable. When the Ellmann biography of Joyce appeared three years later, one could read what Stannie, by that time himself an old man, had imparted independently about Mr. Hunter: ". . . a dark-complexioned Dublin Jew . . . who was rumored to be a cuckold." Prof. Ellmann has a different original entirely for "Bartell D'Arcy," on he does not say whose information, and lists several for Boylan, none of them called Creech, which is only to say that in his researches he encountered a different array of Irish Facts entirely.

As for Hunter's wife being part-Spanish, I could have been hearing about the factual nudge that gave Joyce's Molly Bloom her Spanish mother, or contrariwise it could have been Joyce's book nudging my man toward a little anecdotal creativity.

As for the concert tours and their epithet, a 1904 memory is perhaps less likely than a 1956 improvisation, meant to clinch to my satisfaction the identification of Bloom with Hunter, Boylan with Creech. For what happened in Stephen's Green that November dusk in 1956 was like many such Dublin happenings an inextricable mixture of reminiscence and performance. In time one learns caution, great caution.

One learns to be especially wary of profuse detail inessential to the narrative. This is apt to portend not documentation but invention. Oliver Gogarty was fond of retelling how young Joyce insulted the Yeats he'd only just met, and at a BBC microphone Gogarty once improved his story by claiming the immense authority of an eyewitness. He and Joyce, he said, were "going up Rutland Square, I think it was a horse-drawn tram in those days [*Careful! Not by 1905!*]. I happened to mention that thing that the newspapers were full of [*They weren't*] that it was Yeats's fortieth birthday and that Lady Gregory had collected from his friends forty pounds with which she bought a Kelmscott edition of Chaucer by William Morris [*The Chaucer is true*]. But when I told Joyce this, at the first tram stop he got out. Yeats was lodging in the Cavendish Hotel, in Rutland Square [*Careful! Yeats's habit was to stay at the Nassau*] and he solemnly walked in and knocked at Yeats's door. When Yeats opened the door of the sitting room he said, 'What age are you, sir?' and Yeats said, 'I'm forty.' 'You are too old for me to help. I bid you goodbye.' And Yeats was greatly impressed at the impertinence of the thing."

And Yeats would have been greatly impressed at the impertinence of this narrative, a splendid edifice of Irish Facts flawed by minor defects and destroyed by this main one, that when Yeats observed his fortieth birthday in Dublin, James Joyce was a thousand miles away in Trieste. Alas for that.

Another thing to be wary of is the neat fit they will often produce between accessible literature and remembered life. You are meant either to be impressed by the reminiscer's presence at some event now enshrined in libraries, or else to be disdainful of mere books that so wanly misrepresent what lives in spoken testimony, but you had best do neither of these and suspect your reminiscer of taking what prompts he chooses from the book.

Thus J. F. Byrne asks us to believe that when he was composing his memoir *The Silent Years* (1953) he remembered to the pound what a Dublin penny scale had said he weighed one evening in 1909: eleven stone and four pounds, exactly the weight moreover that *Ulysses* accords to Mr. Bloom; for we are also to believe that the author of *Ulysses*, who was present at that weighing, remembered the detail himself for the twelve years that elapsed before he inserted it into a page proof. You are moreover to judge that the pages of *Ulysses* in question are really about Mr. Byrne, who gets cross about details that don't jibe with his assertions. We might more wisely surmise that to help us believe he modelled for an escapade of Bloom's,

J. F. Byrne made use of a numerical datum he culled from *Ulysses*. We may observe also that fiction, a genre in which Irishmen indulge continually, obeys laws they seem incapable of acknowledging. They want it to have been written *the way they remember it*. How, demands Byrne, can his latch-key have been, as *Ulysses* states, upstairs "in the . . . pocket of the trousers he had worn on the day but one preceding," seeing that on the preceding day he was using it? But Joyce was writing of Bloom's fictional key and trousers. What is fiction, though, but the fabrication of a Great Peacock? And a peacock's consistency is with itself.

The type of the written Irish memoir is Lemuel Gulliver's. What Swift and Joyce did in frank fiction, Byrne, Yeats, Gogarty, Moore, O'Casey, even Lady Gregory, did in what they assure us are truthful accounts. No Irishman apparently addresses pen to paper with any intent save to produce a good yarn. What has spurred him to this exceptional scribal act is often someone else's yarn, an offense that wants neutralizing. After George Moore had published *Hail and Farewell*, his three-volume "history" of the Irish Literary Revival in which Moore figures as disappointed John the Baptist to Yeats's dreamy buffoon, Yeats in retaliation displayed his own superior mastery of the genre, leaving George Moore on record for all time, "insinuating, upflowing, circulative, curvicular, pop-eyed," "a man carved out of a turnip, looking out of astonished eyes," who did not know as late as middle life how to keep his underpants where they belonged.

> He said to a friend: "How do you keep your pants* from falling about your knees?" "O," said the friend, "I put my braces through the little tapes that are sewn there for the purpose." A few days later he thanked the friend with emotion.

It is in that last sentence we discern the master's touch.

" 'Tis manifest," wrote Swift, "what mighty advantages fiction has over truth," ministering as it does to happiness, which in turn is "a perpetual possession of being well deceived." Swift had spent years in seventeenth-century Dublin, a city that has since not altogether changed.

Its talkers cannot bear not to be in the know, and what peaceable man it was alive today that personally pulled the trigger on Kevin O'Higgins is one of the things they will tell you. That was in twenty-seven and it seems like yesterday; the whole Irish past seems like yesterday, one reason not to

---

*Semantic note: Irish "pants" are what go *under* trousers. An American showed me a laundry list he'd saved for the pedantry of it; they had marked it "Short" (by careful tally) "underpants, 2," and "Long" by an exactly corresponding "pants, 2."

let some upstart newcomer surpass their insight. Also they are pricked to creative embellishment of any event insufficiently attired. T. E. Lawrence—"of Arabia"—seemed to Yeats not repletely the stuff of legend, when he masqueraded as "Aircraftsman Shaw" and shrugged off his exploits as the busywork of a job he'd been given to do. "And I did it. . . . And that's all over. . . . And now I'm here." So when describing their encounter (Wyndham Lewis once told me), Yeats would draw back and sweep the air with his right or episcopal hand, his voice dropping to a register of spectral intonation:

> And I heard him say,
> "I was a poor Irishman.
> > *(Pause)*
> I rose from nothing,
> > *(upsweep of the hand)*
> I trod the heights of glory,
> > *(the hand planed downward)*
> And
> > to
> > > nothing
> > > > I
> > > > > returned."

There is also xenophobic delight in misinforming the stranger, whether from another land or another pub. For who is this that comes treading on my dreams? Brian O'Nolan, who made misinformation into an art form, so thoroughly led astray an investigator from *Time* magazine that the issue of 23 August 1943 presented as *Time*-checked fact such allegations as these:

—that O'Nolan spent his days "busy with many matters of state";

—that he had "informally beaten World Champion Alekhine" at chess;

—that on a quick visit to Germany in 1933 he had "met and married eighteen-year-old Clara Ungerland, blonde, violin-playing daughter of a Cologne basket-weaver. She died a month later. O'Nolan returned to Eire and never mentions her."

It is still unclear what taxonomists should do with this man. His achievement exceeded T. L. Peacock's (what does anybody do with *him*?) and in turn it seems exceeded by his abilities. He was Brian O'Nolan the minor civil servant ("matters of state"!), "Myles na gCopaleen"* the barfly columnist, "Flann O'Brien" in 1943 the author of one published novel, and, whatever his name, in the year of the interview a lifelong bachelor. He was

---

*Say "Gopaleen": this is called *eclipsis* and the "C" goes silent. It means "Myles of the Little Horses."

also, as *Time* editors did not suspect, the greatest living virtuoso of the Irish Fact. "Cologne basket-weaver," indeed. Des Moines oyster-shucker?

Later "O'Brien" claimed to have been the sole author of the "Interview" with John Stanislaus Joyce, father of the novelist, that turned up among James Joyce's papers and was published in Paris in 1949. "We could not wait to draw the corks, we slapped them against the marble-topped counter. . . . The Turkish bath came into my mind and there I went after having any God's quantity of champagne. Oh dear, dear God, those were great times." That "O'Brien" had the talent to write it is beyond doubt, though how in that case it found its way into the novelist's files has never been clearly explained. To have made the undisprovable *claim* to have written it would have been equally good fun, especially after it had begun to be cited, as it is to the extent of four footnotes in the standard biography. There dances before the mind an ideal academicism, manipulated from Ireland, founded wholly on items of fictitious data that have had their origin over pints of porter.

Though they have not so far as is known metastasized to that extent, the Irish Facts which infest all talk and all written memoirs have demonstrably effected some permeation into all areas of sober scholarship. There has been no way to exclude them from these pages. Let no one suppose that I vouch for every detail. In particular any such form of words as "They will tell you in Ireland" means that the next statement, though enlightening, is better not trusted. Any citation makes only the simple claim that the statements hereabouts have appeared in print previously. "The unfacts, did we have them," *Finnegans Wake* confirms, "are too imprecisely few to warrant our certitude."

As to why this maddening ostentation of the pseudo-fact should seem an Irish specialty, there is no better explanation of human variousness than Swift's, worth quoting verbatim:

There is in mankind a certain   *   *   *   *   *   *   *   *   *   *   *   *
*   *   *   *   *   *   *   *   *   *   *   *   *   *   *   *   *   *   *   *

*   *   *   *   *   *   *   *   *   *   *   *   *   *   *   *   *
Hic multa   *   *   *   *   *   *   *   *   *   *   *   *   *   *   *   *   *
desiderantur   *   *   *   *   *   *   *   *   *   *   *   *   *   *   *   *

*   *   *   *   *   *   *   *   *   *   *   *   *   *   *   *   *   *   *
*   *   *   *   *   *   *   *   *   *   *   *   *   *   *   * And this I take to be
a clear solution of the matter.

To which we need only append the no doubt accurately reported words of a possibly non-existent Dublin toper: "And so say all of us, says Jack."

POINTS TO PONDER

Out of Ireland have we come.
Great hatred, little room,
Maimed us at the start. . . .

W. B. YEATS, 1931

The hominid line was well preadapted for the development of speech, owing to the position of the larynx, the oval shape of the teeth row, the absence of diastemas between the teeth, the separation of the hyoid from the cartilage of the larynx, the general mobility of the tongue and the vaulting of the palate. . . . The transfer of the food-uptake function from the snout to the hands further facilitated the specialization of the mouth as an organ of speech.

ERNST MAYR, *Animal Species and Evolution*, 1963

Men are born liars.

LIAM O'FLAHERTY, 1934 (first sentence of his autobiography)

In trying to get at Euler's co-ordinates from Quaternions in Mountjoy, I noticed a rather curious theorem on rotations which I found very useful at times since.

EAMON DE VALERA, from Lewes Jail, 1917

A terrible beauty is borneo
Republicans once so forlorneo,
Subjected to all kinds of scorneo,
Top-hatted, frock-coated, with manifest skill,
Are well away now on St. Patrick's steep hill,
Directing the labour of Jack and of Jill,
In the dawn of a wonderful morneo.

SEAN O'CASEY, 1949, *in re* 1926

What the alleged poetry-lover loved was the Irishness of a thing. Irishness is a form of anti-art. A way of posing as a poet without actually being one.

PATRICK KAVANAGH, 1963

THE THREE PROVINCES

Do you know what it is? Do you
know what I'm going to tell you?

MYLES NA GCOPALEEN

You had better know what it is you are asked to trust: the hunches of a non-Irish observer whose pan-Celtic claim derives from one valued quarter of Welsh blood and one of Scottish. A portion of the remainder, nominally English, may be Cornish. I have visited Ireland a number of times, and once lived half a year there. A way in which I resemble most Irishmen is in wishing I could either read the official language or speak it.

Prefaced to another book such disclosures would be ludicrous, but when you propose to discuss the private affairs of the Irish, your (non)credentials may be called for. They can be a touchy people.

The management of a large part of the English language is now included among their private affairs. About 1890 they commenced to seize control of it, and to define the first of the literary dialects into which it has since been specialized. That was well before the better-publicized dustup in the Dublin post office, and has had less ambiguous effects. The conspirators who brought it off included Shaw, Yeats, Joyce, Synge, O'Casey . . . others, up to Beckett and beyond.

The other two main dialects of English are the *American* (Pound, Eliot, Williams, Stevens, Moore, Cummings, Faulkner, Lowell, Oppen, Zukofsky, more) and the *British* (Woolf, Waugh, Green, Bunting, Auden . . . more, and no list is free to exclude Charles Tomlinson).

Having said "dialects," three, I should lift the curse from the word "dialect." Irish, American, British, these are dialects in the light of a fourth phenomenon, *International Modernism*, which defined itself circa 1910–1930, and did its work out of grammars and dictionaries labelled "English." About 1900 anyone who foresaw International Modernism might have expected its language to be French; what would have been absent from his calculations was the birth in a Dublin suburb, 1882, of James Joyce.

Unlike Conrad, Joyce seems never to have considered French. English was quite foreign enough for him: the conqueror's tongue, at which he enjoyed a native speaker's aptness. Thus our century's pivotal book, *Ulysses*, came to be written (1914–1922) in English. So were two other works planned in its shadow by two other self-exiled native speakers of a regional English: Ezra Pound's *Cantos* (1917–1960) and T. S. Eliot's *The Waste Land* (1921). Like *Ulysses*, which has Greek and Latin on its first page, they were casual in citing other tongues; Eliot used four Sanskrit words in addition to quotations in German, French, Latin, Provençal, and Pound also ventured Chinese. These have seemed gestures of subordination: all the world's babble now encompassed by English.

Next, *Finnegans Wake* (1922–1938) was concocted, again by an Irishman, out of as many foreign word-lists as he could lay hands on, but according to English conventions of idiom and syntax. The little words that hold *Wake* sentences together are English words;* what guides its reader is a set of expectations trained, like its author's, on English. Though page after page this book seemed perfectly impenetrable, by 1959 it was selling in paperback (nineteen printings by 1977).

Paris, where *Ulysses* was published and *Finnegans Wake* composed, saw the next salient event in 1953: the production in the tiny Théâtre Babylone of *En attendant Godot*, a play by yet another Irishman, Samuel Beckett, sometime associate of Joyce's: a metallic-voiced upbeat pessimist and the last of the great International Modernists. It was written in a French its author had begun to acquire in Irish classrooms. It is not part of French Literature, nor yet of Irish; nor even, in the English to which he later transposed it, of English. It slips eel-like past idiosyncrasies of idiom; texts of *Godot* now exist in at least twenty languages.

---

*The same 141 common English words that make up 46 percent of the vocabulary of *Ulysses* also make up 46 percent of the vocabulary of the *Wake*. These are the words that "would be expected to make up something over sixty percent of normal English." [Clive Hart, *A Concordance to Finnegans Wake*, 1953, Introduction.]

Such are the masterpieces of International Modernism. None of them, and certainly not *Ulysses*, can be claimed for the literature of its author's native country: no, they define a tradition of their own, accessible to whoever will master the English necessary to read them; or, if skill with English be native, the detachment. What you must be detached from is the set of expectations you acquire in absorbing a national literature. If you chance to have grown up on Shakespeare, Milton, Wordsworth, you will need the knack of setting them aside. *Ulysses* is especially explicit about Bunyan, Pepys, Addison, Carlyle, Pater, Newman: the centuries-long march of English prose. It treats that as culture-bonded, hence alien to Dublin, though the mannerisms can be synthesized at will (pages of demonstration). This claims in effect that Saintsbury's *History of English Prose* need no longer be part of the seven centuries' nightmare from which Irish writers once felt powerless to awake: no, the ludicrous chronicle of a costume party.

Such a prospect affronted the soul of F. R. Leavis, who had no use for the *Cantos*, grew wary of *The Waste Land*, and for all his admiration of much of *Ulysses* excluded it (rightly) from the Great Tradition that had passed through George Eliot. Not having imbibed that tradition can offer advantages. Of the readers of *Ulysses* known to me, the one most at ease in what he reads is Swiss.

So one effect of the twentieth century's International Modernism was that "English" ceased to belong in its totality to a people resident on one storied island where they shared usages, intonations, hence memory, a history. Until recently it was they who had owned it all;* if you were not one of them and chose to write in English, you either courted assimilation, like Washington Irving, or remained a barbarian, like Herman Melville. Such American or Irish literature as mattered was just English Literature that by some accident has been written somewhere else. But now England's literature became a special case, the literature of one province among several. It is all like the separation of the French and Spanish literatures from Latin, which in turn mutated in its homeland into Italian.

And Modernism, whether defied or imitated, marked all that would thenceforth be done in any province: particularly in the three principal provinces, Ireland, the United States and England. You can tell when a

---

*American teaching anthologies like the Norton and the Oxford still subscribe to this definition of "English Literature," and fuss with technicalities to adjust the unreal twentieth century that results. Yeats, Joyce and Auden get admitted on the British passports they carried when they were young, Eliot on the one he obtained at forty. But nothing can be done about Pound (let alone William Carlos Williams), and students are left to imagine what is most idiosyncratic in twentieth-century poetry materializing mysteriously out of nowhere.

writer is scorning it, as Evelyn Waugh did, or toying with it, as Virginia Woolf did, and that is one of the most important things you can tell about these writers.

Thus Mrs. Woolf is no modernist at heart, but a twentieth-century English novelist of manners. She writes, like Jane Austen and George Eliot, for readers at home in England, at home in every sense: readers to whom her books show people like themselves. If they also notice something post-Victorian in her way of going about the novelist's business, that is because her work underwent much impress from *Ulysses*, scornfully though she dismissed the disturbing monster ("illiterate," "underbred"). (And her last book, *Between the Acts*, derives more than has ever been reckoned from what bright folk knew in the thirties about *Work in Progress*, as *Finnegans Wake* was long called.)

Nor is William Faulkner an International Modernist; he is as indigenously American as Mark Twain, as aware that if Americans don't understand him no one will. He too underwent the experience of *Ulysses* (a little later than Mrs. Woolf: about 1925). Its marks are everywhere on *The Sound and the Fury* (1929), whose husks of "technique," though, conceal an old-fashioned book. As early as 1936 Wyndham Lewis was shrewd in discerning no Mississippi Joyce, no, "A moralist with a corncob."

And in Ireland, the Third Province? The Irish story is more complicated. Plenty of the reading matter and acting matter they produce seems intended for natives alone, but Irish writers have always been naggingly aware that Irishmen do not as a rule buy books, have never bought them, have even inherited a tradition whereby to write when you might be talking is an unnatural act. Books in England are sacred objects, exempt from the 10-percent Value Added Tax: not (until 1 April 1982) in Ireland. And sensing that written words can even be *dangerous*, the Republic employs pretty active censors, who in addition to keeping out *Playboy*,* contraceptive advice, and tons of quick-turnover porn, have interfered with some poets and with nearly every major prose writer save, oddly, Joyce.

Such a large Dublin bookstore as Fred Hanna's prospers on American visitors. This points up a second fact, that Ireland keeps informal colonies beyond the seas, in such places as Boston on what used to be called "The New Island." Much of the Irish writer's public resides abroad, where it welcomes a look at him. Oscar Wilde went on display before Colorado miners, and Yeats earned "a roof for Thoor Ballylee" in New York, New Haven, Pittsburgh, Salt Lake City. A different public resides in England,

---

*No, not *The Playboy*; they had their fuss about that long ago.

where what is salable to connoisseurs of the quaint is sheer Irishness; to develop an idiom redolent of that was the earliest of the skills Yeats learned.

Finally, the management of English in Ireland is inextricable from on-going revolution, no end in sight. A faction has been holding for nearly a century that English wants not mastering but expunging, in favor of a native Celtic tongue. This tongue is called "Irish," and after fifty years' principled indoctrination through every school in the Republic (one of the first-reader words being *gunna*, "gun"; it's for instance on page 19 of a frisky primer called *Seo Leat*, by Máiréad Ní Ghráda, all about Dónall, Seán, Máire and dog Spota) Irish is now spoken by some tens of thousands out of five million. Still, it *is* the official language, sustaining Dubliners whose cause and recreation entail scenes in government offices where they demand to be served, as is their right, in Irish. Having engineered a satisfying fiasco, they write fervid letters to *The Irish Times*, in English.

Early in the century other factions included the Nationalists, who wanted Home Rule with no strings, and the Unionists, who thought the connection with England might be renegotiated but needed preserving. Nationalists derided any proposal to embellish the English leash with a rhinestone collar. Unionists were apt to echo genteel English literary opinion, especially when they were sure what it was. Extreme Nationalists thought you wasted your time and the nation's with anything save improving political consciousness, whether by marching-songs or by portrayals of the pure and holy folk in the Galway and Kerry fields.

Pure and holy folk were Catholic of course, as were most Dubliners, though in Dublin *Catholic* was apt to denote less a state of supernatural conviction than a web of secular allegiances. (Likewise *Catholic* and *Protestant* in the North today are shorthand for intricate sociologies, a thing the outside world comprehends imperfectly.) But public opinion—defined as what people think other people think—was manufactured in Dublin, where the newspapers came from, and public opinion could more or less identify the chief personnel of the Irish Literary Revival as (1) Protestant, (2) non-Dubliners, in fact (3) based at landed estates in the West; hence (4) identifiable as "Anglo-Irish": a Nationalist bête noire.

Lady Gregory, a flagrant case, was all of these. So was George Moore after he quixotically ceased to be Catholic. Moore's cousin Edward Martyn, though almost grotesquely Papist, otherwise filled the bill. W. B. Yeats was born in a Dublin suburb but identified his roots with Sligo in the West; gossip, moreover, could scatter him to the winds, situating him on Lady Gregory's estate at Coole, where rumor made him a virtually permanent houseguest, and in the same breath dismissing him as a Londoner since he always seemed to enter Dublin from that direction. J. M. Synge too was Dublin-born, but of a line of Protestant missionaries; he had moreover lived abroad, and in Paris, altogether too long for Nationalist tastes.

James Joyce though: Catholic; a Dubliner; non-landed; not by any stretch of the imagination Anglo-Irish: he ought to have filled the bill. But James Joyce, good God, had no manners, thought Ibsen was a dramatist, thought he himself was a genius, even thought Irish politics a waste of time. He'd also run off with a girl to Trieste or someplace. Every faction, including the small one around Yeats, excluded James Joyce, which was a mistake.

It's an intricate story, best entered, like the story of Troy, in the middle. No one knows where to find the beginning. A high point near the middle is nicely marked by the flourish of tin trumpets. We'll start with those.

A BAG OF CATS

O, but the mockers' cry
Makes my heart afraid,
As though a flute of bone
Taken from a heron's thigh,
A heron crazed by the moon,
Were cleverly, softly played.

W. B. YEATS, *Calvary*

Tin trumpets some of the omadhauns had brought along to bray with, but most came provided only with Irish lungs and booted Irish feet. Sitting together at one side of the pit, they caught Lady Gregory's eye because there wasn't a woman among the forty of them. She consulted with Mr. Synge, who was sweating with influenza, and suggested he telephone for some policemen to come by and make themselves handy. The police tramped over to the Abbey in greatcoats. Dublin's nighttime chill can catch the bone in January, and that Monday's drizzle—28 January 1907—concealed a moon just attaining to the full, the symbol, W. B. Yeats was later to think, of the passage from subjectivity to objectivity, from the proud assertions of the hovering soul to the exactions of the feral world where beasts run in packs.

Yeats would also be adducing flutes of bone, as though the curtain had not risen on a tinplate era.

Just at present Mr. Yeats was still in Scotland, preaching some aspect of his multifaceted gospel. In Aberdeen two nights before—that was Saturday night, the opening night of the play—he had been handed a telegram,

= PLAY GREAT SUCCESS =

But it had been sent prematurely, and at past one in the morning his host had brought to his bedroom a second telegram dispatched as soon after the final curtain as a phone could be reached amid the calamities:

= AUDIENCE BROKE UP IN DISORDER AT THE WORD SHIFT =

That had been, Lady Gregory was to remember, "a very large audience," and it had commenced by laughing and applauding, albeit "a little shocked at the wild language": the language of a wild play in which a man kills his father, twice, but at the end walks off behind him towards "a romping lifetime." It was called *The Playboy of the Western World.* Mr. Yeats himself had told the author there was "far too much 'bad language.' " Parricide was enough without the name of God invoked rather often in dubious connections.

—Don't strike me. I killed my poor father, Tuesday was a week, for doing the like of that.
—Is it killed your father?
—With the help of God I did, surely, and that the Holy Immaculate Mother may intercede for his soul.
—There's a daring fellow.
—Oh, glory be to God!

A few such invocations (not enough) were cut in rehearsal. Saturday's audience had found much to be uneasy about in the second act, and a shocker in the third, the wild man overwhelming a peasant girl of but twenty with his rush of pagan talk. Let her only wait

till we're . . . making mighty kisses with our wetted mouths, or gaming in a gap of sunshine with yourself stretched back unto your necklace in the flowers of the earth.

That is no decent posture for courting, as she does not seem to reflect. No, from her dazzled soul comes breathed "(*In a low voice*)" her most alarming line of the play:

—I'd be nice so, is it?

Recumbent, a sweetmeat, delicious. In Ireland! Worse: mitred bishops would vie to admire her.

—They'd be the like of the holy prophets, I'm thinking, do be straining the
bars of Paradise to lay eyes on the lady Helen of Troy, and she abroad,
pacing back and forward with a nosegay in her golden shawl.

Peasants were by definition strict and pure, bishops and prophets sacred.
Fortunately the words were moving too fast for outrage to collect itself. The
Lady Helen, though a bad lot if you've been to school, at least moves the
onus away from Irish girlhood, and is not availably recumbent but pacing
back and forth. Still there was murmuring and hissing. Values were awry.

Before long, an offstage murder: a blow, a yell. The wild man re-enters;
he has done it this time. They will hang him! But he'll not run off, so he
tells the Widow Quin. "What good'd be my lifetime if I left Pegeen?"

Nonsense. "Isn't there the match of her in every parish public, from
Binghamstown unto the plain of Meath? Come on, I tell you, and I'll find
you finer sweethearts at each waning moon."

Girlhood traduced wholesale! By now disorder was teetering on a brink,
and Willie Fay, playing the wild man, was acutely anxious. The next line of
the playscript required him to conjure up glories to be set at naught against
Pegeen: "a drift of chosen females . . . from this place to the eastern world."
"Drift" is a word used of cattle; Fay made a rapid substitution, "Mayo girls"
for "chosen females," hoping to avert the suggestion of a fleshly market.
That may have been the worst thing he could have done, or it may not have
mattered, since he failed to elide the one word that sufficed to catalyze
outrage. What was spoken and heard was this:

—It's Pegeen I'm seeking only, and what'd I care if you brought me a drift of
Mayo girls, standing in their shifts itself, maybe, from this place to the
eastern world?

"Audience broke up in disorder at the word shift": of all words. (It means
an item of underwear: approximately, slip.) Part of the disorder was hissing,
part applause.

Could it have been only that word? In the street afterwards Lady Gregory
put the question to a first-night regular, Joseph Holloway. What did he
think was the cause of the disturbance? "Blackguardism." On which side?
" 'The stage' came from me pat." By the time he was at home with the
journal that obsessed him for fifty years Holloway was milking satisfaction
from his own surliness, putting on record how he returned "monosyllabic"
answers to fatuous questions, indeed angry enough not to notice that he was
counting *Blackguardism* among the monosyllables. He adduced support for

his outrage. "Many gentlemen such as D. J. O'Donoghue and McNamara, the architect, said to me afterwards that they were delighted they had not taken their wives to the show. The latter said he never was so taken aback in his life and hissed for all he was worth. What did Synge mean by such filth? Was there no one to supervise the plays?"

Holloway set down the moral. "Synge met with his deserts from the audience and I hope he will take the lesson to heart. . . . Synge is the evil genius of the Abbey and Yeats his evil lieutenant. Both dabble in the unhealthy."

So the first night had gone. And tonight, the lads with the tin trumpets in the pit. Word was around that *The Playboy of the Western World* was a play to skelp, squelch, scuttle.

Of the eleven "first nights" it had weathered in its first two years, the Abbey had scheduled seven for Saturdays. Saturday gave the critics a weekend to prepare their notices, and word-of-mouth a weekend to travel, before the play settled in Monday for its run. This time outrage had had a weekend to organize itself.

It did not achieve unanimity. The Ascendancy (= King & Country) *Irish Times* merely deplored indiscretions that had wrecked a potentially "brilliant success." The *Evening Mail* castigated an author "stupid enough to suggest that the Irish people are cannibals or gorillas," but declined to be baited by his "preposterous theory that Irish peasant girls fall in love at first sight with the worst kind of murderers." The Nationalist (= Home Rule) *Irish Independent* found the conception dramatically impossible. "Peasants who look and act like omadhauns don't suddenly develop a passion for killing their fathers as easily as Mr. Synge would have us believe," and the "crisp and sparkling, sometimes rather coarse dialogue" was what kept the audience from noticing this.

It was the equally Nationalist *Freeman's Journal*, a paper now chiefly remembered for an advertisement canvasser it employed in 1904, that elected to rant without let against "this squalid, offensive production," of which "the barbarous jargon, the incessant and elaborate cursings" were such as could not be conveyed in chaste print. A letter from "A Western Girl"—an office fabrication?—expressed astonishment that Molly Allgood, playing Pegeen, "is forced to use a word indicating an essential item of female attire which the lady would probably never utter in normal circumstances even to herself." (Only "A Western Girl" seems to have heard Pegeen say "shift" in Act II; it was when Christy said it in Act III that the howling broke out.*) With "Western Girl" covering his flank the *Freeman* reviewer plunged forward flailing. "The hideous caricature would be slanderous of a Kaffir kraal." (Such denunciations tend toward an asymptote; fourteen years later the *Sporting Times* of London would declare *Ulysses* "enough to make a Hottentot sick.") "Everything is b——y this or b——y that." (We in fact find the word "bloody" just four times in the uncut text, two of these times denoting actual blood.) Purporting to exhibit the mores of "Irish peasant men and, worse still . . . Irish peasant girlhood," the play was "an unmitigated, protracted libel." The sky was now bidden to fall. "It is clear that there is need for a censor at the Abbey theatre."

Logic, if it mattered, would have forced the *Freeman* to reject a censor as tantamount to an abortionist. Nationalists eschewed all English customs, and (Yeats had shrewdly pointed out when the Abbey opened) censorship of plays was one English vulgarity Ireland was happily spared. Londoners were even forbidden *Oedipus Rex*, though "the great American Catholic University of Notre Dame" had performed it not long ago.† The perfect expression of Sassenach mentality, "a censorship created in the eighteenth century by Walpole, because somebody had written against election bribery, has been distorted by puritanism, which is not the less an English invention for being a pretended hatred of vice and a real hatred of intellect."

In suavely aligning "Catholic" with Sophocles, "English" with "puritanism," W. B. Yeats was doing one of the things he did best, pre-empting the terms of discourse before opposition should lay hands on them. He confronted, though, lengthening odds. An expert intriguer in a city of intrigues, Yeats was committed to strategies fast becoming unworkable, depending as they did on Nationalist support for an Irish National Theatre Society that so long as he was running it had no patience for Nationalist tactics.

He and Lady Gregory and pious Edward Martyn had founded the Irish *Literary* Theatre in 1899, and despite his political sympathies he had no intention now of compromising what the word "literary" still entailed: not even though, with new directors including the Nationalist seer AE, the Nationalist Jezebel Maud Gonne and the Gaelic propagandist Douglas Hyde, it had been reorganized in 1903 as the Irish *National* Theatre Society. He had sanctioned that not to further a revolution but to enlist available ener-

---

*Though Willie Fay's account twenty-eight years later contradicts everyone else's in asserting that "the row was just as bad" when Pegeen said "shift." Or was he remembering one of the other performances?

†Yeats thought to reinforce this point with an Abbey version, and went so far as to commission from a young Hellenist named Oliver Gogarty a crib on which it might be based. But the Yeats *Oedipus* didn't get done until 1928.

gies, which happened to be patriotic ones, and in so doing to get the service of the Irish amateur actors that Frank and Willie Fay were collecting, Yeats having perceived that English professionals were wrong for the plays he wanted to present. (Irish professionals? There were none. Dublin's big theatres were played by touring companies from England.)

The amateurs, soon to become the Abbey Players, were a great success from the start, though their extra-theatrical passions and those of their supporters made trouble early. Within a few months Dudley Digges had resigned from the company rather than countenance the production of its fourth play, let alone act the lead, and Maud Gonne had attacked in print the "foreign thoughts and philosophies" she and her revolutionizing colleagues detected in the playscript. The play was *In the Shadow of the Glen*, by J. M. Synge, one of whose offenses was to have lived five of his thirty-two years abroad, while another was the traduction of Irish womanhood, in its pure state a revolutionists' utility like gunpowder.

Bruised sensibilities were never the point with these desperadoes. The point, as much when *In the Shadow of the Glen* aroused ire in 1903 as when *The Playboy of the Western World* summoned out police in 1907, was that propaganda required an impeccable peasantry, not least because news out of Dublin was sure to reach England, where they already confused Irish peasants with comical monkeys. So no nonsense about a nice morsel on her back or about the titillations of parricide.

That was the molten core of opposition to *The Playboy*, its failure to provide what it was the country needed to come awake. Much else, though, was troublesome, commencing with that anomalous presence, the Abbey Theatre itself.

The Abbey had been named, and what with such goings-on we may think named somewhat incongruously, for its address on Lower Abbey Street, just north of the Liffey and a few hundred yards off Sackville Street, the main thoroughfare of North Dublin, where all the lines of the most advanced electric tram system in Europe converged at Nelson's Pillar. Abbey Street (Upper, Middle and Lower) is a district of pubs and small shops, so a short walk would get you a drink at intermission though there was no bar at the Abbey.

It was unlicensed because existing theatres had opposed yet one theatre more. Though among them they commanded ten times the seats it was proposing, still the managers of the Gaiety, the Queen's and the Royal hired lawyers to block the Abbey on principle. (The English love a lord, the Irish a lawyer.) The lawyers with their beaks together at last agreed on how it should serve no drink and also restrict itself to what the big three had no use for anyway, "plays in the Irish or English language, written by Irish writers on Irish subjects and selected by the Irish National Theatre Society." That being understood, a patent (i.e. permission) was granted on 20 August 1904. The Patentee also agreed not to put on the stage any exhibition of wild beasts, "or to allow women or children to be hung from the flies or fixed in positions from which they cannot release themselves."*

The Patentee of record was Dame Augusta Gregory, of Coole Park, near Gort, in County Galway, Ireland's remote Western World. It would have accorded closer with potent realities to name Miss Annie Horniman of London, whose Hudson's Bay Company shares were underwriting the venture, but the law would have the papers for a Dublin theatre in Irish hands, and Miss Horniman was not resident in Ireland.

Nor, technically, was Mr. Yeats, whose address had been London since 1887; it was presently 18 Woburn Buildings, near St. Pancras Church, where Miss Horniman, a fellow theosophist with a habit of consulting the Tarot, served him as amanuensis and secretary. How many of his 26,891 days on earth Ireland's foremost man of letters spent in Ireland would be laborious to estimate: perhaps, counting numerous brief trips, about one-third, and in that case a lesser fraction even than James Joyce, the professional exile, who got out of the country for good in 1904 but spent twenty-two all-but-unbroken years there first.

Yeats's pattern of cyclic estrangement commenced when he was three and the family moved to Regent's Park in London because his father did not want all Dublin looking over his shoulder while he mastered his new profession, painting in oils. They were back when Willie was fifteen, left again when he was twenty-two; whereupon London claimed him for nearly a third of a century. He was fifty-three when he settled briefly in Dublin that his first child might be born there; promptly removed to Oxford for two years; was a Dubliner six years while serving in the Senate; in his last decade was much abroad for his health; and died near Roquebrune in the south of France where they interred him not far from Aubrey Beardsley and were nine years bringing him home to be buried beneath an arrogant epitaph near Sligo. (The Tower? Ah yes, the Tower: Thoor Ballylee in the West, four miles from Gort. It was a symbolic address, uninhabitable save in

---

*Was Sam Beckett remembering this sixty-eight years later when he arranged to have the heroine of *Not I* immobilized on a dark stage throughout the performance, in a harness with her head in a clamp? But *Not I* is unlikely to be coveted by Abbey management.

summer and uncomfortable then; he had it fixed up and used it for several summers in the 1920's, whereafter all was soon ruin once again.)

So in January 1907, at the time of the troubles over J. M. Synge's new play, it was common knowledge in Dublin where they know everything that the Abbey Theatre was funded by an English scold with no love at all for Irish politics ("Wicked politics," Miss Horniman would say; and one hiss she was told of during the *Playboy* riots—a hiss from the stage, moreover—she had no difficulty identifying as a *political* hiss); moreover that her motive in going to so much expense, beginning with the patent which had cost her £455, was neither Ireland nor theatre but her sponsorship of—the unkindly said her infatuation with—Mr. Yeats, who lived in London where he dressed as elaborately as the late Mr. Wilde, of unmentionable repute.

It was not, moreover, much of a theatre: a building like a little grey stone bus station, seating a mere 562 and with a stage only twenty-one feet wide by fifteen deep, clearly an outpost for fanatics with designs on something or other. You had to suspend disbelief a good deal to suppose, in that exiguous box, that when the curtain rose on *The King's Threshold* you were seeing displayed a king before his palace, when just a few actors made the stage look crowded and you were so close you could see the stitching on the costumes.

The costumes were made of a kind of burlap called hessian that got boiled in a tubful of dye on the greenroom stove. At just sixpence the yard in a full six-foot width this stuff was one thing they could afford much of, and one girl in hessian looked to a catty visitor as though about to give birth to a grand piano.

You'd expect to get inside a place like that for sixpence, but the Abbey had opened without sixpenny seats: something else to enrage the Nationalist clubs, which perceived in the sixpenny crowd revolution's God-given constituency and demanded to know why non-possession of a shilling should shut a man out of the National Theatre. Maud Gonne had nagged Willie Yeats on that theme too. She thought he'd be crushed when she told him the clubs held him lost to Nationalism.

Outside, the Abbey had an art-nouveau canopy like a Paris Metro entrance for patrons to let down their umbrellas under. Above that it said "Abbey Theatre," and if you craned higher you could see carved on the front cornice the words "Savings Bank," that being what part of the building had been used for formerly. Those words have been retouched out of a good many photographs. Another part had been the Mechanics' Institute Hall—that was what had been turned into an auditorium—and another part had been the City Morgue, where they'd once mislaid a body before the inquest and found no trace of it till workmen fitting up the Abbey dressing-rooms came upon human bones. It would one day please Yeats to write to Lady Gregory how a player had been stopped in mid-speech for a moment or two, feeling that "his shoulder had suddenly been grasped by an invisible hand."

Yeats's interest in spooks was notorious; so were his raven cowlick, his billowing stock, his pince-nez on a ribbon, his cape, his languid stance, the knees and spine curved forward. Frequently cap-à-pie in black, he reminded the local Aristophanes, George Moore, of a large umbrella forgotten at a picnic. He had troubled the orthodox eight months before the century's turn, when thirty-three students at the Catholic university (U.C.D.) had signed a manifesto against his play *The Countess Cathleen*.

That was 8 May 1899, at the Antient Concert Rooms in Great Brunswick Street, for which a one-time permit had been obtained. The play was about a noblewoman who sold some devils her soul to get bread for her people. There had been demonstrations in the gallery, police on the floor, a cry, "One boo for Yeets," from an Ulsterman, and much bewilderment over what had stirred up the whole brouhaha, a pamphlet called *Souls for Gold* which a fellow named O'Donnell had stuffed into letterboxes all over Dublin, misleading Cardinal Logue into stating that "an Irish Catholic audience which could patiently sit out such a play must have sadly degenerated."

A dozen or so U.C.D. boys read this as official bidding to go anyway and jeer. Years afterward the one student who made an issue of not signing their manifesto described, through his *alter ego* Stephen Dedalus, how the night had seemed:

> He was alone at the side of the balcony, looking out of jaded eyes at the culture of Dublin in the stalls and at the tawdry scenecloths and human dolls framed by the garish lamps of the stage. A burly policeman sweated behind him and seemed at every moment about to act. The catcalls and hisses and mocking cries ran in rude gusts round the hall from his scattered fellowstudents.
> —A libel on Ireland!
> —Made in Germany!
> —Blasphemy!
> —We never sold our faith!
> —No Irish woman ever did it!
> —We want no amateur atheists.
> —We want no budding buddhists.

(The actress James Joyce saw play the Countess was May Whitty, long afterward the old lady in Alfred Hitchcock's *The Lady Vanishes*.)

Abbey ways of acting too had a certain notoriety. Much subtle Yeatsian injunction had gotten reduced by Frank and Willie Fay, the installed *cory-phaei*, to a two-part rule: not to move while speaking, not to speak while others were moving. This meant that nobody moved except between speeches, when nobody moved much. The effect was so novel it could either annoy English critics ("pleasant but in no way remarkable amateur theatricals"— *St. James's Gazette*) or enchant them ("As a rule they stand stockstill. The speaker of the moment is the only one who is allowed a little gesture. . . . When they do move it is without premeditation, at hap-hazard, even with a little natural clumsiness, as of people who are not conscious of being stared at in public."—*Times Literary Supplement*). The opinion of Henry James is unrecorded, though he was in a London audience the same day as those reviewers. Irish playing had curiosity value in England, where the company went from time to time to raise funds.

To play so was to reject the English way of playing Shakespeare, which breaks up the long speeches with busy-ness; to reject too everyone's way of playing the inconsequential, by trying not to seem to be acting.

One must act, *and* be seen to be acting. In 1909 Yeats would think worth recording in his diary a glimpse of a man in a train who moved awry, "from his head only." The man seemed vulgar. "His arm and hand, let us say, moved in direct obedience to the head, had not the instinctive motion that comes from a feeling of weight, of the shape of an object to be touched or grasped. There were too many straight lines in gesture and in pose. The result was an impression of vulgar smartness, a defiance of what is profound and old and simple."

Such a man would one day seem a portent:

> Constrained, arraigned, baffled, bent and unbent
> By these wire-jointed jaws and limbs of wood

—anti-art, mere "visible history, the discoveries of science, the discussions of politics": a puppet-people. The posturing recommended by the Fays seemed by contrast "profound and old and simple."

Its simplicities were reinforced by certain physical constraints—as that, the proscenium arch not being opposite stage center, nothing of importance could take place upstage right, an area invisible to a third of the audience; or that, the stage being so shallow, its rear wall was apt to be the back of the set, leaving nothing to walk behind, so that a character who needed to get to the other side before his next entrance had to "leave the theatre by the scene-dock door, hurry down a lane and ring a bell to get in by another door at the corner of the street. No harm was done if in the meantime there were sufficient lines in the play to keep things going during any delay caused by conversations with casual acquaintances whom one usually met in the lane." After much trotting just to get onstage, you might think the separation between Art and Life best served by standing fairly still once you were there.

All this had come about because Willie Yeats yearned to write plays. His earliest work, dating from 1885 when he was twenty, is *The Island of Statues*, an unactable play, and his first book (1886, when he was twenty-one) is *Mosada*, "a dramatic poem" but typographically a play. In 1894 his *Land of Heart's Desire* was performed in London on a double bill with Mr. Shaw's *Arms and the Man*. The first night there were "chuckers-out" in case the Shaw caused a disturbance, as it did.

In 1896 Yeats and a fey Welshman, Arthur Symons, cicerone of *symbolisme*, had called on Edward Martyn, who admired Ibsen and wanted to write plays, and they met Augusta Gregory, who was to write many plays. (Martyn, whose scrupulous piety was a theme for cartoonists, would a decade later sit in the Abbey stalls that first night of the *Playboy*, cringe at shock after shock, and tell George Moore he would never enter the place again.)

It was in 1897 that Yeats confided in Augusta Gregory his interest in a theatre for Irish plays, perhaps in London? No, Lady Gregory thought, in Dublin. Plays ensued; never mind the metamorphoses and the politics, by 1904 thanks to Miss Horniman the two of them had the Abbey, which opened in December of that year with a play by her and a play by him.

"Be bold," Yeats had chanted from the stage that first night, to Dublin at large, quoting Spenser. He was in black as usual, and conjuring with his right hand. "Be bolder still! Be yet more bold! *But not too bold!*" Nobody knew what he meant by this.

Their earliest statement of purpose deserves reproducing:

We propose to have performed in Dublin, in the spring of every year, certain Celtic and Irish plays, which whatever be their degree of excellence will be written with a high ambition, and so to build up a Celtic and Irish school of dramatic literature. We hope to find in Ireland an uncorrupted and imaginative audience trained to listen by its passion for oratory, and believe that our desire to bring upon the stage the deeper thoughts and emotions of Ireland will ensure for us a tolerant welcome, and that freedom to experiment which is not found in the theatres of England, and without which no new movement in art or literature can succeed. We will show that Ireland is not the home of buffoonery and of easy sentiment, as it has been represented, but the home of an ancient idealism. We are confident of the support of all Irish people, who are weary of misrepresentation, in carrying out a work that is outside all the political questions that divide us.

Quite so. And they had the great and by no means incidental advantage that Shakespeare was not sitting on their shoulders the way he sat on English shoulders. Within a tradition defined by Shakespeare's inheritors the available ways to write a play were these:

1. You could set down tushery as Tennyson had from 1875 till the year he died, blank-verse tushery with Shakespeare on its curved horizon, but mediated by the Keats of *Otho the Great*; it is difficult to guess what might have become of verse drama save for the legend that Keats very nearly wrote some.

2. You could emulate Ibsen and be realistically prosaic. Or

3. You could start from a knowledge of stagecraft like Ireland's own Dion Boucicault, explode a river-boat, tie your heroine to railway tracks, and pack houses. (There was also the Théâtre Francaise where they went in for "construction," but only George Moore knew about that.)

It was Boucicault who packed the houses in Dublin. Joyce records a Boucicault *Rip Van Winkle* that tugged heartstrings: Rip "*in tattered moccasins with a rusty fowlingpiece, tiptoeing, fingertipping, his haggard bony bearded face peering through the diamond panes*" at his re-wed wife. Dubliners didn't read the book, they saw the play.

Yeats knew (in those first years) little of stagecraft, did not wish to pack houses, disliked Ibsen, and would be thought by English critics to have followed the Shakespeareanizing example of Tennyson. But no, it was possible for an Irishman simply to succeed the Romantic blank-verse masters as though there had been no Shakespeare. That was much.

> Bend down your faces, Oona and Aleel;
> I gaze upon them as the swallow gazes
> Upon the nest under the eave, before
> She wander the wide waters.

That is not fake Shakespeare. It is from the 1895 revision of *The Countess Cathleen*, a play Yeats first wrote as early as when he was twenty-six, with Maud Gonne on his mind. That had been 1891, the first year she declined to marry him, and he had imagined her selling her soul to the devil to free the Irish from bondage. Giving statement to her whims would be one of his lifelong burdens. At fifty-four he would put the barter more sharply:

> Have I not seen the loveliest woman born
> Out of the mouth of Plenty's horn,

> Because of her opinionated mind
> Barter that horn and every good
> By quiet natures understood
> For an old bellows full of angry wind?

All his plays grew out of brooding about something that mattered; that was one thing that kept them from being willed exercises in stage versification.

When *The Countess Cathleen* was at last performed in 1899, it was Arthur Griffith,

> afterwards slanderer of Lane and Synge, founder of the Sinn Fein movement, later first President of the Irish Free State, and at that time an enthusiastic anti-cleric, [who] claimed to have brought "a lot of men from the Quays and told them to applaud everything the Church would not like."

—so Yeats phrased *that* event thirty-six years later.

And the boys from University College had come to counterdemonstrate, and Yeats had seen to it that some big burly (English) policemen were in attendance.

English? In the pay of England; of Irish stock, by regulation five foot nine or taller, half a foot above the average Irishman; much resented as symbols. They were country boys, ran the story (that is where bosthoons grow tall, *hic sunt monstra*), and not being urban nor urbane they were reputed to have their provender thrown at them from a spoon the like of a shovel: "Number 65, catch your cabbage!" Their symbolism, like most local symbols, was lost on the Anglified Yeats at that time. ("In using what I considered traditional symbols I forgot that in Ireland they are not symbols but realities"—thus his comment on the detail of the first version of the *Countess*, where an evil peasant trampled on a Catholic shrine. It is amazing what he asks us to believe he forgot.)

Anyhow, tonight, in 1907, the tin trumpeters assembled for the second performance of a play word-of-mouth had been disimproving all weekend. They got going partway through the first act of *The Playboy*. Soon, reported the *Freeman's Journal*, "the uproar assumed gigantic dimensions, stamping, booing, vociferations in Gaelic, and the striking of seats with sticks were universal in the gallery and pit. Amidst this Babel of sounds the refrain of 'God Save Ireland' was predominant."

> "God Save Ireland!" said the heroes,
> "God Save Ireland!" said they all.

> "Whether on the scaffold high
> Or on the battlefield we die,
> O, what matter when for Ireland dear we fall!"

It will bellow richly, and to the same tune you can sing "Tramp, tramp, tramp, the boys are marching," a cadence for boots to stamp to. A dozen big policemen filed in and were booed. In their solemn presence the first act was played out, but nobody heard a word of it.

The next police move was toward the exits, in state. Lady Gregory had given them the sign, thinking the disturbers might best be let tire themselves out. They did not. A "hurricane of hissing," a tootling of tin, belaboring of seats and walls with blackthorn sticks, shouts in English and Irish and full-lunged choruses of "The West's Awake" and "A Nation Once Again" obliterated every word of the second act, and then of the third. And there were few words to obliterate. The actors were going through the play in dumb show.

> But—hark!—some voice like thunder spake
> *"The West's awake, the West's awake"*—
> "Sing oh! hurra! let England quake
> We'll watch till death for Erin's sake!"

"Sinn Fein, Sinn Fein Amhain!"* and "Kill the Author!" were among the shouts noted down by gleeful journalists.

The author? Backstage a man from the *Evening Mail* had cornered him, taken note of his feverish brow, perhaps thought him merely excited.

Did he think himself holding up the mirror to nature?

(*To himself*): "The devil hang you by your own guts." (*Aloud, emphatically*): "No, no."

Then what was his object?

"Nothing. . . . The idea appealed to me and I wrote it up."

Had he not thought how it might displease others?

"I never thought of it."

(*An interruption, one of many. Synge was to recall the pressman's hectoring as going on for two hours, on the trot upstairs and down, backstage and front, the audience in its frenzy all the while.*)

"I wrote the play because it pleased me, and it just happens that I know Irish life best, so I made my methods Irish."

---

*(Say *shin fayn, shin fayn avawn*): "Ourselves, ourselves alone!", the rallying-cry of Griffith's ultra-separatists.

So, far from serving the Irish National Theatre, he had simply been pleasing himself?

"Exactly so."

(*The reporter was not ashamed of being too simpleminded for this. Not art for art's sake was the new word, but art for the artist's sake. Ha.*)

But was it probable that simple honest people of the West would idealize a parricide?

"No, it is not; and it does not matter. Was Don Quixote probable?"

(*The way Synge remembered that bit, "The interviewer got in my way—may the devil bung a cesspool with his skull—and said, 'Do you really think, Mr. Synge, that if a man did this in Mayo girls would bring him a pullet?' The next time it was, 'Do you think, Mr. Synge, they'd bring him eggs?' I lost my poor temper [God forgive me that I didn't wring his neck] and I said, 'Oh well, if you like, it's impossible, it's extravagant, it's extravgance [how it's spelt?]. So is Don Quixote!' "*)

And what had ever suggested such an idea?

" 'Tis a thing that really happened. I knew a young fellow in the Arran Islands who had killed his father. And the people befriended him and sent him off to America."

And did the girls all make love to him?

"No. Those girls did not, but mine do."

And why did the girls in his play do that?

"It is a comedy, an extravaganza, made to amuse."

(*Here the lights went out.*)

In summary, then, Mr. Synge had simply no object in the play save gratification of his own artistic sense?

"Yes. I don't care a rap how the people take it."

And what of the rest of the week?

"We shall go on with the play to the very end, in spite of all." (*Snapping his fingers*): "I don't care a rap."

God forgive him indeed that he had not wrung that man's neck. In the paper he sounded a fool. My play had nothing to do with real life. It is credible because it actually happened. I was simply pleasing myself. I made it to amuse people. I do not care if they are displeased. Still, I am made impatient by your displeasure. In short, it is true that I murthered my father and my mother, but please to remember that I am but a poor orphan.

* * *

Here and there patriots met in upstairs rooms, with rhetoric Sean O'Casey has done us the favor of conflating.

"Some blasted little theatre or other has put on a play by a fellow named Singe or Sinje or something, a terrible play, helped by another boyo named Yeats or Bates or something, said to be a kind of a poet or something, of things no one can understand, an' he was to blame for it all, assisted by some oul' one or another named Beggory or something, who was behind the scene eggin' them on in their foul infamity. A terrible play, terrible! There was ructions in the theatre when th' poor people staggered into the knowledge of what was bein' said! What was th' play about? Amn't I after tellin' you it was a terrible thing; a woeful, wanton play; bittherin', bittherin', th'n, th'n th' bittherest thing th' bittherest enemy of Ireland could say agin' her!"

Sinje had "made a go at every decent consignment left living in th' country," and resolutions were moved and seconded for the suppression of his tirade of sulfurious infamity against among other things the chastity of Ireland's chaste womanhood, the whole world knowing as it did that wings grew from the shoulders of every thrue Irish lady.

Tuesday night now, the boyos in place again in the pit, someone had even brought along a bugle, and for the honor of God and was that Holy Willie? All black like an old jackdaw it was himself, with the eyeglasses on the ribbon and the necktie on him like a poodle-dog's ruffle. Ireland's poet, back at last from Scotland. Get on, he was no kind of poet at all. A notable gluggerabunthaun. The very word. Whisht, here he is now.

He was nearly upstaged by a man in a smart-fitting overcoat who called on anybody to fight because he would wipe the streets with them, announced in addition that he was a little bit drunk, and also attempted to play the pit piano. Still it was Yeats who commanded the attention when he sidled onstage before *The Playboy* commenced to make mention of "a difference of opinion that had arisen between the management and some of the audience," and when someone got up to say "I have one word to say: it is this," Yeats did not so much as permit him to say what it was.

If he seemed in command it was because he felt himself to be so, having detected a strategy and devised a counterstrategy. The opposition, Yeats had decided, was not spontaneous but organized, and organized moreover by his old Nationalist friends, beginning with Arthur Griffith who had been ready enough to help break up protests against *The Countess Cathleen* because those had the clergy behind them and the grip of the clergy on Ireland was something to break, but would not be caught tolerating *The Playboy* because the myth of Irish peasant saintliness was something to foster. Eight years ago, in the days of *The Countess*, Griffith had got wind of the Catholic university claque and offered a counter-claque. Tonight if Griffith had a claque in the pits, it was Yeats, his apt pupil, who had a counter-claque ready in the stalls. It had been recruited at the other university, Trinity, the one known for loyalty to the Crown, and Yeats would have relished the symmetry, the more so knowing, if he knew, that Griffith himself was in the house tonight. There were extra policemen too.

"We have put this play before you," Yeats now stated, "to be heard and be judged. Every man has a right to hear and condemn it if he pleases, but no man has a right to interfere with another man who wants to hear the play. We shall play on and on, and I assure you our patience will last longer than their patience." (*Applause and groans.*)

About now there was a shuffling of sturdy lads as a new contingent from Trinity entered the stalls. Lady Gregory had made the mistake of asking a nephew to bring them, thinking they might be of ablebodied use in case there was an attack on the stage. There was not and they were not. In fact it was one of them, named Moorhead, who soon had most spectacularly to be carried out, a deportation effected by Synge himself and by the big fellow Ambrose Power who would not be needed on stage until late in the second act, playing as he did Christy Mahon's "murdered" da.

The hullaballoo resumed from last night as per script, augmented by the bugle. Jeers from the pit had the Trinity boys up and waving their sticks. A young doctor could hardly restrain himself, he told Synge, from jumping onto a seat and pointing out in the mob the men he was treating for venereal disease. The drunken fellow in the overcoat got shoved out, and Yeats next appealed to all who were sober to listen to the play. No one listened. *But hark some voice like thunder spake THE WEST'S A WAKE THE WEST'S A WAKE.* And the police filed in as before, only more of them and this time with W. B. Yeats at the head of the file. That calls himself a poet. Tell me this now, can anyone at all remember one verse of his poetry without the book? And Trinity jackeens, insult to Ireland. *God Save Ireland said the heroes.* The bluecoats were ranged along the walls of the pit endeavoring to look massive, but anybody who supposed that patriots true would whisht for those spying louts had a head on him the four winds would blow into. *Where thereon the sky fold high.* And all at once *trampatrampatrampa DIE* it was Willie Yeats himself running up and down the aisle pointing out disturbers for them to arrest. O, as sure as I'm telling you. Willie and who was that other chap in the moustache? Lane, Hughie Lane. In pictures wasn't he?

Picture postcards likely. In the picture trade in London that was it. Yes and wasn't he the old hake Gregory's nephew and telling the peelers to light into decent people.

When it was all over not half a dozen consecutive sentences of *The Playboy* had been heard by anyone, the pit was singing *A Nation Once Again*, and the Trinity lads in a final insult to Ireland were up on stage shaking rafters with *God Save the King*. The police had to shove them out and march them back to the college, and one of them got fined £5 for assaulting an officer. PERFORMANCE CONCLUDES WITH "GOD SAVE THE KING" ran a headline next morning, accurate in divining the most outrageous detail.

Mr. Yeats had also been talking to the *Freeman*.

When I was a lad, he said, Irishmen obeyed a few leaders, and one or two of them were men of genius; he mentioned Parnell. But now we must obey the demands of commonplace and ignorant people. They do not persuade, for that is difficult; they do not expound, for that needs knowledge; they rule a mass which only understands conversion by terror, threats and abuse, a mob that have been so long in mental servitude that they cannot understand life if their head is not in some bag.

Larger and more important than Mr. Synge's play was the question he called The Freedom of the Theatre. Art, as some French writer had said, was "exaggeration apropos," and was Lady Macbeth a type of the Queens of Scotland, or Falstaff of the gentlemen of England? As far as he could see, the people who formed the opposition had no books at all in their houses.

The *Freeman* soon let him know it had enough of a book in the house to dispose of his Scots analogy. "Mr. Yeats asks if Lady Macbeth is a type of the Queens of Scotland? The question is puerile. It might have some relevance if Lady Macbeth danced a Highland fling after the murder of Duncan, and if she was congratulated all round on the murder."

Mr. Yeats made no reply to this. He was busy swearing in the Northern Police Station that he "distinctly heard a Boo." Those charged with "offensive behaviour between 10 and 11 o'clock on the previous night" included Patrick Columb, clerk, whose son Padraic Colum would one day undergo notice from anthologists, and a little man named Pearse Beasley who would one day write the biography of the gunman's gunman Michael Collins and today was requiring that the spelling "Piaraos Beaslaoi" be used on the charge sheet: the first overt incursion of Gaelic League patriotism.

MR. YEATS (*corroborating Constable 170C*): "I saw the defendant at the performance last night in the Abbey Theatre. There was an organized disturbance by a section of the pit to prevent the play being heard. I saw the defendant arrested, and saw him before the arrest rise up and yell at the top of his voice."

MR. MAHONY (*from the bench*): "Did he say anything?"

MR. YEATS: "He addressed some words to me in Irish."

MR. MAHONY: "Were they complimentary or the reverse?"

MR. YEATS: "I am sorry to say I understand no Irish."

MR. MAHONY: "Well, I know some Irish, and I know that one can say very scathing things in Irish."

The defendant on his own behalf testified that he was no part of any organized gang. Mr. Yeats had stood over him and said he would give in charge the next man who booed. Mr. Yeats then pointed him out to the constable and he was taken in charge. No threats or penalties would deter him from protesting what he considered an outrage on the Irish people. Previous to this he had been an admirer of the Abbey Theatre and a regular supporter of it. He had made his protest and he considered that every true Irishman would act in the same way.

MR. MAHONY: "I must fine you 40s. or a month's imprisonment."

Asked later why he had singled out Beaslaoi, Yeats said that he did not want to charge a rowdy like some of those who were then making a noise (*groans and boos*). He chose a man he could respect (*"Oh, oh," and hisses*), knowing that the dispute that lay between them was one of principle (*A voice: "That won't wash"*). As for Columb, Lady Gregory offered to pay his fine, a tactical error, rejected as patronizing.

Wednesday night, police everywhere: over fifty in the theatre to control a house of perhaps four hundred twenty. Though one man kept yelling "Shut up!" and one fistfight got going, patrons who had come for the rioting felt ungratified. Yeats in a nervous frenzy ran continually up and down aisles, in and out doors, but ignored requests for "a cake walk." Following the inaudible performance there were pro- and anti-*Playboy* processions in the streets. The police stood by.

Thursday night much of the play was audible. Over two hundred police stood guard inside and out, and arrested two people on the bizarre charge of attempting to leave before the program was ended. Yeats now decided that his point was made. The run would end in two days.

Friday night things were calmer: just one arrest.

Saturday, amid police "thick as blackberries in September," a sullen public sat through *The Playboy*'s first uninterrupted performance.

The press did not let up.

Belfast Morning News, 31 January: "A torrent of execration has been the nightly reward of the actors who strive to represent a murderer, an idiot, some vulgar, shameless, unnatural viragoes with the souls and tongues of strumpets, and a medley of drunken mindless brutes, as typical peasants of the Gaelic County of Mayo. . . ."

United Irishmen, 2 February: "The father of the hero refers to his son in one place as 'a dirty——lout'. The word omitted is so obscene that no man of ordinary decency would use it."

This drew a letter: "Dear Sir: I am the actor referred to as having spoken the word you mention. The word which you indicate by a dash was in the text, and as I spoke it on the stage, 'stuttering'. I fail to see anything obscene in the word. I demand an immediate public withdrawal and apology. — Ambrose Power."

The Sinn Fein weekly retracted as to this point alone. Griffith on Tuesday night had thought something he heard amid the din was "scuttering," a bad word.

And nothing odder appeared anywhere than the letter to the *Freeman* from Alice L. Milligan, who herself had written a play and would live to hear herself described by Thomas MacDonagh, subsequently an Easter Rising Martyr, as "the best living Irish poet." From what she claimed was an insider's knowledge of Abbey ways, Miss Milligan, who had not seen *The Playboy*, alleged that the trend toward indecency had started with Yeats. "We must fill the house at all costs," she had him saying to himself. "Let us be audacious; let us shock."

"Mr. Yeats began it himself in *Deirdre*. Of this no more need be said than that, as the most brazened playgoers and play actors require acting expurgated editions of Shakespeare, acting expurgated editions of Yeats will be called for. . . ."

Searching the text of Yeats's *Deirdre* (1906) we may marvel at the lady's hallucinations. Was "the tumult of the limbs" the phrase that inflamed her?

Monday night, the fourth of February, the run being over, they opened the theatre for a discussion of principles to which they cannily charged admission, so filling the Abbey for the first time all week and netting £16 at half prices. The familiar allegations got made, as that Mr. Synge's play was "the result of brutal ignorance, born almost of idiocy (*great noise and cheers*)."

But speaking of idiocy, a medical student was ruled in order. He alleged that Synge had drawn with great accuracy that predominant Irish type, the sexual melancholic. In any country town in Ireland, he said, you would find types like Christy Mahon. "He would refer them to the lunacy reports of Ireland (*disorder*) and to Dr. Connolly Norman's lectures at the Richmond Lunatic Asylum (*some laughter and great disturbance*). When the artist appeared in Ireland who was not afraid of life the women of Ireland would receive him (*cries of 'Shame!' and great disorder. Many ladies whose countenances plainly indicated intense feelings of astonishment and pain, rose and left the place.*)"

Nineteen-year-old Mary Maguire, years later Mary Colum, was stubborn in not joining them. She and a friend were "surrounded by a group of angry males ordering us, if we were virtuous girls, to leave the theatre." Yeats, who "in spite of his well-publicized dimness of vision could always see well when it suited him," had them escorted to the stalls among the men in evening dress, who if not hospitable were at least not threatening. Three decades later Mary Colum still marvelled: "I never witnessed a human being fight as Yeats fought that night, nor knew another with so many weapons in his armory."

Timid and evasive though he might be by temperament, Yeats that night was sustained by a player's role. He was Cuchulain, fighting the waves: cold in his frenzy, defying the ungovernable sea; and when he had imagined Cuchulain's defiance just three years ago, in his play *On Baile's Strand* with which the Abbey opened, he had had in mind Charles Stewart Parnell whom the mob had dragged down, Parnell who had known though how to deal with a mob, and particularly the mob-mind of his own parliamentary party. "He was the only man that could keep that bag of cats in order," recalls one of the men James Joyce recalled. " 'Down, ye dogs! Lie down, ye curs!' That's the way he treated them." These words were spoken to document the proposition that Parnell was a gentleman. He was also "the uncrowned king," and like Cuchulain died sword in hand: mortally exhausted, so legend ran, by howling hatred that swirled round the hustings in the 1891 election. A shift, to emblematize his paramour Kitty O'Shea, was something mobs had used to wave at him.

So it was sustained by Cuchulain and Parnell, and through them by the strength which flows from a role, from a mask, that Yeats that winter night on the Abbey stage, confronting the seething pit, fought the battle of the shift.

One weapon, which quieted a spell of disorder, was his theatrical cry, "The author of *Cathleen ni Houlihan* appeals to you" (*cheers*). That play, as no one present could forget, had been, with Maud Gonne in the title role (1902), the chiefest success ever of nationalist propaganda.

But his most remarkable weapon was his sixty-eight-year-old father, John Butler Yeats, painter and raconteur. As J.B.Y. mounted the stage people shouted at Willie, "Kill yer father!" J.B.Y. ignored such nonsense, and was surely too clear-headed to be musing that Cuchulain in his son's play had fought the waves after learning that the man he had just killed was his own son. (Filicide, parricide, what a country.) He had not read the Synge play, he said. He had seen it, twice. But, he added, he had not *heard* it. (*Unrest.*) He knew, he said, that Ireland was the Land of Saints (*cheers*)—"of plaster Saints" (*disorder and groaning*). His beautiful mischievous head was thrown back. It was the peasants of applauded hacks like William Carleton,* he said, who were an insult and a degradation. Synge's peasant was "a real vigorous vital man, though a sinner" (*groans*). Then something more popped into his head, and he could not resist saying it: "Unfortunately, in this country people cannot live or die except behind a curtain of deceit." After that he could not proceed for the noise.

Ten months later J. B. Yeats left the country for New York, where he spent fifteen years full of joy and mischief, dying there quietly on 3 February 1922. Just the day before, in Paris, an *ad hoc* firm called Shakespeare & Co. had published a big book called *Ulysses*.

Sinn Fein rage moved the same way as J. B. Yeats, westward. To *An t-Oilean ur*, the New Island, a greater Ireland whose hub was Boston/New York, went all the Dublin papers by slow boat, and in Fenian cells a slow dull fury kindled. After four years it was self-sustaining, so when the Abbey Players finally came to America in 1911 ("Ever since we were the height of a table," said one girl, "America it was always our dream") the United Irish Societies of New York greeted the announcement of *The Playboy* in Boston with a resolution to "drive the vile thing from the stage." Nothing happened in Boston. In Washington sermons denounced them, and Catholics received at the church door a pamphlet which cited "hell-inspired ingenuity and a satanic hatred of the Irish people." In New York one congregation was told it would be a mortal sin to attend, and another was advised to attend and bring eggs to throw. They threw a good many potatoes, and an old watch, and a tin box with a cigar in it. The owner of the watch later asked for it at the stage door.

In Philadelphia there was something more like a riot, though (Lady

---

*1794–1869: author of *Traits and Stories of the Irish Peasantry*, of which Willie Yeats had edited a selection.

Gregory wrote) "Nothing was thrown but a slice of currant cake, which hit Sinclair, and two or three eggs, which missed him—he says they were fresh ones." Before long an outraged fellow had everyone placed under technical arrest and held on bail for five days. He had been thrown out for rowdiness when Act I had been playing five minutes, during which time he had noticed enough indecency to demoralize a monastery. He had a brother, a priest, who had stayed right through and could not begin to list the sins to which *The Playboy* incited Philadelphians. Had anything immoral happened on the stage? a witness was asked. Not while the curtain was up, was his reply.

Gyres turned, and in 1968 the Abbey company toured all the way to Rome, where Pope Paul VI received them in audience. They presented him, sixty-one years after the much-remembered opening, with a copy, bound in white leather, of *The Playboy of the Western World*. This was not the play's first experience with exalted company. On the 1911 tour they had encountered both Yale and Harvard professors who had it on their curricula. Would professors have heard so quickly of a mere unbooed Irish play? It was the rioting had launched John Synge into seminar immortality, like, as the man said of someone else altogether, a shot off a shovel.

A TALE OF A POT

It resembled a pot, it was almost a pot,
but it was not a pot of which one could
say, Pot, pot, and be comforted.

SAMUEL BECKETT

The Pot of Broth, written more or less by W. B. Yeats though most of its
talk has the cadence of Lady Gregory, is a play about a foolish woman who
bought a stone to make broth with, the blarney of a tramp having caused
the willing suspension of ordinary sense.

He said he had the stone from one of the Little People, and he boiled it
in her pot with only water, and sure enough in a short time there was a
broth thick and rich despite difficulties. For you ought to boil the stone with
a little sprig of herb to stop the enchantment slipping away from it, and she
had neither a bit of Slanlus that was cut with a black-handled knife, nor a
bit of the Fearavan that was picked up when the wind was from the north,
so he had to make do with a handful of cabbage and onions. And she had
no cover for the pot would ward off the bad luck the stone would put on
anyone who might catch sight of it boiling, and again he made do, throwing
in a handful of meal that would make the water turn cloudy. None of that
interfered either with another of its virtues, for this stone that will turn meat
black on a Christian Friday is tested with a chicken put into the pot, and
sure enough on this day that is not a Friday the chicken is not altered at all.

Despite all these irregularities the stone's powers have made plain water taste of cabbage and onions and meal and even fowl, and this woman so close she would skin a flea for its hide has made one more very good bargain in getting the stone for herself. For she gave the tramp nothing for it only the chicken and a bottle of whiskey, and what use would either of these ever be now that she has a stone will make stew or poteen or stirabout or wine itself when you only boil it in a little water? He is a very gifted man, the tramp.

And a gifted man Mr. Yeats, the malicious say, since he did but drop this anecdote into Lady Gregory's pot and out it came after a bit in the likeness of a little play, and in dialect cadences too, at a time when, as he recalled twenty years later, "I had no mastery of speech that purported to be of real life."

He was talking of 1902. "I hardly know how much of the play is my work," he acknowledged, and soon he was even thinking it might be more Lady Gregory's than his. "I remember once urging her to include it in her own work, and her refusing to do so." If in 1922 he went on to find the dialect not quite the right temper, that need imply no aspersions on her, for was he not now incorporating *The Pot of Broth*, defects and all, into his own arcane canon? He was, and you will find it there today, and allotted twenty pages of the *Variorum Plays*, with a diligent record of variants.

It was "the first comedy in dialect of our movement." It takes only about fifteen minutes to perform and enjoyed a long life as a curtain-raiser. Also it needs only three actors and not much in the way of a set. You need a first-rate tramp, though, as good as Willie Fay. The part is not trivial. Yeats was doing something he did in his imagination many times, entrusting the likes of the Philosopher's Stone to a vagabond, with the difference on this occasion that it was not even the real Philosopher's Stone at all, only something picked up to throw at a dog, but (the play shows) as efficacious as the real thing if you put the right style on the speaking you do while you're boiling it.

In that respect it is a parable of the Theatre itself, in which we see with our eyes everything the actors do and yet are hoodwinked by their rites of glory. We need to know how to lend ourselves to the deception. One time in 1903 Willie Fay and Maire Quinn and P. J. Kelly played *The Pot of Broth* before a house that did not know how and were greeted with stony silence. That was in Foynes, County Limerick, where the Social Improvement Society was improving the locals, a houseful of whom made nothing of the play at all.

"We were holding an inquest," Fay remembered, "to find out how the play had been killed (our gloom deepened by the sound of the applause that greeted the singers who followed us), when in comes my Lord Monteagle to ask could we do another turn, as the night was still young. 'We've only the one play,' I said, 'and they didn't like it.'

" 'What do you mean?' said he.

" 'They never laughed,' said I.

" 'Oh, is that all?' said his Lordship. 'Don't you know that probably not one of them ever saw a play before? And besides they'd be thinking it was disrespectful to laugh at the swell actors from Dublin.' "

The swell actor addressed, who in Dublin had demonstrated the knack of surviving a week on under a pound when necessary, was able to think as quickly as the tramp in the play, and he devised exactly the way to bring the Foynes folk round. He stepped out and explained to them how it was, that this was the story of a foolish woman and a stone, a funny story, and that the clever tramp was deceiving her, and how the deception was done. Then he and Miss Quinn and Kelly played it all through again, and this time "they laughed at every line whether it was funny or not. The scene at the fall of the curtain was tremendous."

For that is how a play works. There must be agreement about what kind of reality is being alembicated, otherwise the swell actors from Dublin will be perceived as reciting prepared statements at one another, stone perceptibly stone. Had not "God-appointed Berkeley" proven all things a dream, *esse est percipi*, the folk then united by their perceived world which is simply a common dream? (Dr. Johnson, enraged at this thought, thought to kick a stone—"Thus I refute him"—but in hitting the stone had he not missed the point?)

Always, it seemed, in Ireland, the ideal preceded the pragmatic, things came to be as they were perceived to be, noble talk foreran noble deeds (or ennobled what deeds it foreran). Life, a notorious Irishman remarked, imitates art. In 1926 the Agricultural Ministry of the Free State of Ireland believed this, and requested the Commission on a National Coinage, through its chairman, Senator Yeats, to arrange alterations in the effigy of a pig because in its submitted state it would affect the agriculture of Ireland. Circulated from hand to hand beneath eye after eye, this image on the halfpenny piece would become the Platonic Idea of the Irish Pig, toward which selective breeding would swerve; and its chops were unsuitable. The design was altered, though the cancelled pig survives in Yeats's noble threnody:

I sigh, however, over the pig, though I admit that the state of the market for pig's cheeks made the old design impossible. A design is like a musical composition, alter some detail and all has to be altered. With the round cheeks of the

pig went the lifted head, the look of insolence and of wisdom, and the comfortable round bodies of the little pigs. We have instead querulous and harassed
animals, better merchandise but less living.

To permit an artist to be dictated to by the Agricultural Ministry was not
his normal way, still less to consent to relay the dictation, but he was
charmed by their acknowledgment of the mind's power over piggeries, and
a few months later he was writing of

> . . . God-appointed Berkeley that proved all things a dream,
> That this pragmatical, preposterous pig of a world, its
>   farrow that so solid seem,
> Must vanish on the instant if the mind but change its theme.

These were always plausible themes on John Bull's Other Island, where
even now anything at all tends to look as though it might just as well have
been otherwise, had whim taken people differently. Irish roads seem tenta-
tive and often unfenced, huge flocks of dreaming sheep wandering by and
across them, whereas English country lanes, sunken by millennial feet,
guarded by hedgerows and overarched by deep foliage, are part of the
immemorial order of things. Dig down two feet in England and your spade
strikes history, but in Ireland limestone if not a bog. An Irish village,
sometimes four or five roadside structures, seems indifferent to additions or
excisions. It is not always clear whether somebody was building a stone
cottage or simply heaping the stones he'd cleared from his field. In tracts of
the West you can wander for hours and meet nobody, sight nobody, see no
sign even that anybody was ever here before yourself. What settled order
would a massive reforming unsettle? Revolution is *always* thinkable. Have
the people around dull Gort, or amid the lunar Burren stone, settled in their
minds that they belong amid their land, are staying, are living with calm
assurance the way they live? A tourist's eye is not convinced of it. (Yeats's
was a tourist's eye.)

It can be felt profoundly otherwise in England, where a villa that had
affronted the benign powers moved Pope to prophecy:

> Another Age shall see the golden Ear
> Embrown the Slope, and nod on the Parterre,
> Deep Harvests bury all his Pride had planned,
> And laughing *Ceres* reassume the Land.

For Ceres, immune to our whims, knows how things human and natural
must cohere, and in the long run will tolerate no upstart's disharmony.

There are men in England who are at peace with Ceres, and their increase is blessed. She came north from Tuscany through Touraine all the way to Hampshire of the hogs, and she presided till recently over all the practices by which, in a mind older than ours, things rural and permanent were meant to be.

But she stopped short of Ireland, where the Irishman does as he does, and might as well do otherwise, except that otherwise is not just now the way it is being done, by him. It is like living in a fit-up stage. In such a setting three or four generations may pass for immemorial tradition. But let a single will once falter and we shall have nothing save a long unremarkable time

> When nettles wave upon a shapeless mound
> And saplings root among the broken stone.

That, Yeats foresaw, would be the state of Augusta Gregory's Coole, and he foresaw rightly. It was so within a dozen years of his poem: not Ceres reassuming the land, not even wildness reasserting ancient rights, but uneventful casualness waving and rooting once the mind had changed its theme, for the Gregory grandchildren were casually uninterested in staying there. (They sold it to the Forestry Department of the Land Commission, and after Augusta Gregory had died in 1932 it stood empty nine years until a man bought it for the price of the stones his workmen could decompose it into. That man was born under an acquisitive moon.)

Coole's transience is not an uncharacteristic story. Ireland displays untended ruins of every century from the fifth to the twentieth. Even Leopold Bloom's house on Eccles Street, Dublin, is a ruin. And the story of many waste places has been quite short. From Robert Gregory, chairman of the East India Company, who built it in the eighteenth century, to the gallant Major Robert Gregory (1881–1918) whose death in "that tumult in the clouds" made its sale in 1927 inevitable, there had been but five generations of Gregorys at Coole, Robert, William, Robert, Sir William, Major Robert. The house stood rather less than two centuries, a mere Irish episode.

Similarly Thoor Ballylee, built in the sixteenth century or by some accounts the fourteenth, soon dropped out of Irish history and by 1917 was so decrepit (rotten floors, no roof) that W. B. Yeats was able to buy it with its two cottages for £35. As he set about the never-finished work of restoration he was well aware that should his own children lack his romantic will the tower would rapidly again

> Become a roofless ruin that the owl
> May build in the cracked masonry and cry
> Her desolation to the desolate sky.

(He did not foresee its becoming a Yeats Museum where nice ladies sell mementoes.)

For history has long flowed to and fro over the conquered people in their occupied land, where "the seven centuries" has connotations as grim as "the six million" elsewhere: a nightmare from which no one can awake and salient with the discontinuities of nightmare. It can even be difficult to specify who were the occupiers, who the occupied; the first Gregory on the Irish scene was a Warwickshire man who came over with Cromwell. We need not be surprised that in this ancient land man and a house and ground and rock and hill are nowhere united with the intimacy fields and lanes proclaim in Umbrian towns or even Yorkshire villages, nor that Nature seems not to utter Wordsworthian directives, nor that it should be implausible to speak as if autochthonous tutelary powers governed Irish intercourse with place. All turns on willfulness, and proclaims the quality of transient will.

> Some violent bitter man, some powerful man
> Called architect and artist in, that they,
> Bitter and violent men, might rear in stone
> The sweetness that all longed for night and day,
> The gentleness none there had ever known.

This land has no gods as Mediterraneans understand gods, gods assimilable, as the English language records, to the understanding of northern poets, whose sense of the numinous was if anything strengthened when they dropped the Augustan habit of naming classical deities. So though English was nineteenth-century Ireland's literary language, in Ireland the conventions of English Romanticism, its blessings in the gentle woods, its brooks that murmur and its winds that cry, were simply implausible. They correspond to no Irish sense of things. "Flora! Pomona!" cries Samuel Beckett's Hamm, his eyes on a desolation like an ash-heap. The physical is no more than can be seen in it: if Coole's walls were one generation's "dance-like glory," they were another's vendable stone. Ruined castles, ruined houses, ruined towers round or square, mark achievement that flared briefly and flamed out, whereupon a few more stragglers shifted their ground.

The land *is* alive, yes, but with malicious ancient people, the *Sidhe* (say

"Shee") who steal wits and whose gold proves a bag of leaves, whose stone a stone. They journey in whirling leaves, Yeats reported, and "when the country people see the leaves whirling on the road they bless themselves, because they believe the Sidhe to be passing by. . . . And the great among them, for they have great and simple, go much on horseback." (Ceres moved afoot.) If you see them overmuch they strike you with anomie, and some of them that are in the waters "beckon to men, and drown them in the waters."

> And if any gaze on our rushing band,
> We come between him and the deed of his hand,
> We come between him and the hope of his heart.

There was also something wicked that flapped itself up into a Mayo woman's face in the likeness of a newspaper, no less, "and she knew by the size of it that it was *The Irish Times*," an Ascendancy organ and an ominous thing to be blinded by in Mayo. It turned into a young man she'd the sense to rebuff, and he vanished. So you had best see to your wits: remembering, though, that it is the Irish way to exchange civilities with the world beyond, men and spirits only ill-treating each other within reason. It is very likely, if you were a civil tramp, that one of them might impart a stone that made broth; likely too, if you were the kind of niggard woman would starve the rats, that the tramp who passed the stone on to you was codding you.

THE CONQUEST OF ENGLISH

> ... he would wipe alley english spooker,
> multaphoniaksically speaking, off the face
> of the erse.
>
> *Finnegans Wake*

Civility is what you exchange with a potential enemy; that is the famed Irish courtesy, not owed only to the Sidhe. Stephen Dedalus about 1902 may be heard exchanging civilities with his Jesuit Dean of Studies, an English convert, while his silent mind reflects that they have in fact no common language at all. So how can they partake in the one reality?

> The language in which we are speaking is his before it is mine. How different are the words *home, Christ, ale, master,* on his lips and on mine! I cannot speak or write these words without unrest of spirit. His language, so familiar and so foreign, will always be for me an acquired speech. I have not made or accepted its words. My voice holds them at bay. My soul frets in the shadow of his language.

The list repays glossing:

Home. An Englishman's was his castle, an Irishman's the shelter from which he might momentarily be evicted.

Christ. When he cuts his thumb on a bottle an Irishman does not cry "Chroist!" but "Jaysus!"

Ale. Metonymy for wholesome English custom, scattered through the language as in *bridal* (bride-ale); but in Ireland they prefer a porter allegedly discovered in the eighteenth century by a man named Guinness who had burned the hops by mistake.

Master. In England your teacher, your Saviour, or one before whom you are pleased to touch your forelock; in Ireland the owner of a pack of hounds or the racker of a pack of tenants. (The word bobs through Maria Edgeworth's 1800 *Castle Rackrent*: "My new master"; "Pity my poor master.")

Joseph Conrad, a distinguished pioneer in the twentieth-century enterprise of subduing English from without, used to complain that no English word was a word, so entangled was it apt to be in historical, social, moral half-assertions. His example was "an oaken table," where "oaken" does so much more than specify a wood. Some attributes of an oaken table are moral.

That seems not easy to appreciate in England, and as late as 1973 an English amateur of linguistics could find Stephen Dedalus's fret "sentimental and self-pitying, not even forgiveable in an undergraduate." This was Anthony Burgess, whose novel *A Clockwork Orange* is peppered with made-up words like *droob* and equipped with a glossary; but Burgess reasoned that despite a few local words such as *crubeen, drisheen, oxter, plain* (pig's foot, black pudding, armpit, beer) "we need no special dictionary to read Joyce's plainer works." True, we do not think we do, and so may not know if we are reading askew.

Burgess next makes the interesting suggestion that what Stephen is really concerned about is sounding queer. "He feels the inferiority of the provincial in the presence of a metropolitan or ruling-class accent," and Joyce "has cunningly chosen words that demonstrate very well the main phonic differences between the speech-systems of the English and Irish capitals." Thus the Dean diphthongizes *home* whereas Stephen utters a long open vowel; in his *Joysprick* (page 28) Burgess transcribes both ways of saying all four words into the International Phonetic Alphabet, surely something Joyce hoped somebody would one day do.

Still Joyce has never just one intention, and we may decide that semantic as well as acoustic chords will concern a poet who must install himself in an alien system of words. Joyce might have been describing some of W. B. Yeats's early difficulties.

> The woods of Arcady are dead,
> And over is their antique joy

—so run the first lines in Yeats's *Collected Poems,* verses he wrote at eighteen in the course of inserting himself in all innocence into the English literary tradition. The fingerprints of his reading are everywhere. "Arcady" would be a word he had from Keats, who found it in Milton. "Antique joy" remembers Marlowe's "antic hay," the way annotators gloss it. In pairing this poem, "The Song of the Happy Shepherd," with one called "The Sad Shepherd," he is following Milton's "L'Allegro," as decades later he would go to "Il Penseroso" for strong confirmation of his myth of the Tower. As for melodious shepherds, young Willie would have met them in "Lycidas," and further down on the page the phrase "optic glass" assures us he's looked a few pages into *Paradise Lost,* where he found Satan's shield likened to "the Moon whose Orb / Through Optic Glass the Tuscan Artist views."

There is even an Irish Connection of a sort. Yeats's opening words echo a stock Nationalist complaint that Ireland's woods too are dead: destroyed by the English, ran the tale, to deprive Gaels of concealment, though what in fact finished them off was a seventeenth-century frenzy for exporting barrel-staves and fueling iron-mills. Never mind, the melancholy fact of deforestation will nestle snugly into a rhythm of Milton's and a phrase of Keats's, who invented Arcady's "groves": at this cost, though, that hardly a reader will recognize the vanished woods of Ireland.

So while W. B. Yeats was forming his first style, English stylists were determining what he could say with it. One result was to suffuse his Irish Eden with unreality. "Noon a purple glow," indeed!—not a Lough Gill noon, that noon, an *aesthetic* noon. In "The Lake Isle of Innisfree," a poem about his intense desire to be home instead of in London, Yeats makes his theme explicit to English Bible-readers by taking his opening words, "I will arise and go," from St. Luke's account of the homesick Prodigal Son (Luke xv.18), but seven years have made him warier, and this familiar poem avoids the word "home" entirely. He will arise and go now, and go to Innisfree, and he will build there "a small cabin," the Anglo-Irish word for what a tenant farmer lives in, and build it "of clay and wattles," the local way.

"Wattles" are stakes interlaced with twigs, which clay would make fairly windproof; English usage associates such a technique either with primitive ancestors or with backward contemporaries such as the bog-Irish. The *OED* cites in succession the 1510 *Galway Archives,* Hooker's 1586 *History of Ireland,* Stafford's 1633 *Pacata Hibernia: Ireland Appeased and Reduced*: works in which Tudor or Stuart observers are saying how the rude folk of the western island do things: "and there they cast a trench, and builded a little castell or hold, with turffes and wattell." "Wattell" is not a native word: those natives would have spoken Irish. It is an English word, in use since the time of the Venerable Bede. In 1867 it helped Tennyson evoke an appealing early simplicity—

And there he built with wattles from the marsh
A little lonely church in days of yore.

So wrote the Laureate in *The Holy Grail*, which may even be where Yeats came across the word, not then knowing, perhaps, its role in the long story of English condescension to things Irish.

Yeats had written in an 1888 draft of "Innisfree" that he would "live in a dwelling of wattles, of woven wattles and woodwork made," but by two years later, when at twenty-five he finally published the poem, he had learned about the use of clay, also called "wattle-daub," and changed the line to its well-loved form. "Innisfree" was, he came to think, "my first lyric with anything in its rhythm of my own music," and from its first appearance in W. H. Henley's *National Observer* it stood virtually immune to his notorious penchant for tinkering with the way he had put things when he was younger.*

"Innisfree" was instantly admired; it drew a fan letter from Robert Louis Stevenson in Samoa; by 1901 Yeats was wishing his other poems were liked as well; in 1916 Robert Bridges wanted to put it into an anthology along with Homer, Shelley, Augustine, Gregory the Great, Wordsworth, Aristotle, to comfort people in wartime and also show them what poetry meant. At sixty-four he was begging a young admirer, "Please don't think 'The Lake Isle of Innisfree' is better than all the rest, for I don't." Audiences would never permit him not to read it, he would sometimes anticipate them by offering to recite "the only poem of mine that you know," and it is the text for two of the four recordings of his voice that have survived. It was, the whole world came to agree, "Celtic." His Celtic identity was the stone he had dropped into the pot.

He had also dropped in, before all eyes but unnoticed, three other things: (1) a surefire myth of country *vs.* city ("pavement grey" has no chance against "lake water"); (2) an unorthodox but scannable rhythm,

dactyl		trochee		spondee		iamb		iamb		iamb
I will a		rise and		go now		and go		to In		nisfree;

and (3) a large number of English words that can exploit our uncertainty whether the long vowel overrules the stress, as when we are pleasantly

---

*Twice, in 1921 and 1935, the change to "a small cabin buil*t* there" withdrew the claim that his own hands would actually "build" it, but in the Definitive Edition his Thoreauvian fantasy won out. The poem recalls his father reading Thoreau to him, and he'd not have been thought inadequate to that.

doubtful if we should say "rows will I" or "rows will I," a dubiety we may be pleased to deem Celtic.

And he read it as he read everything, in a peculiar half-chant in which Ezra Pound heard keening, and other Americans heard Celtic melancholy, and Dublin heard Willie Yeats putting on airs. A no-nonsense American lady asked him to kindly infarm the audience (he recalled the sound she made as "infarm") why he read his poetry in that fashion. He replied that every poet since Homer had read in that fashion. She asked him to further infarm them how he knew that Homer had read in that fashion. He replied that the ability of the man justified the presumption.

He might also have speculated whether Homer of Chios recited to audiences who spoke a different-sounding Greek from his own, and made a style that subsumed the difference. He himself had achieved such a bewilderment of cadence and such an overwhelming of bardic presence that no one was likely to question his vowels in home, Christ, ale, master. It was not even noticed how closely the "Celtic" measure of "Innisfree" followed the six-beat iambic of his English friend Ernest Dowson: so much so that if you dropped just the word "now," what was left,

> I will arise and go, and go to Innisfree

was indistinguishable in its rhythm from

> Last night, ah, yesternight, betwixt her lips and mine,

a Rhymer's Club measure to which Yeats had been faithful in his fashion.

It is vowels that worry taxonomists of regional speech. "Are you not somewhat bulgar in your bowels?" asks an insolence in *Finnegans Wake*, the word *bleak* having just previously been pronounced *blake* prior to some confusion about *black*. These are habits which in London would get their possessor called Paddy, a thing by the way that happened regularly to Sam Beckett during a miserable period in his life. Beckett's vowels stayed tense, and as late as 1964 he could be heard crying "But he's wrang! Wrang!" (He was rejecting an opinion of Charlie Chaplin's.) Long before that he had switched over to writing in French, and commenced treating English as the foreign tongue into which he translated his works.

The spectacle of Yeats getting into an alien tradition only to be put to great trouble getting out of it again may have stiffened the resolve of James Joyce to be his own man from the start. By 1914 he was exhibiting English (to the English) as a system in which early on you say things like "When you wet the bed first it is warm then it gets cold," and having by 1922 made himself its greatest master since Milton (T. S. Eliot's judgment) he devoted for seventeen years his full powers to a big book in which you have a constant sense it is English you are hearing though the odd words that stumble you are never in the dictionary. *It darkles, (tinct, tint) all this our funnanimal world. . . . We are circumveiloped by obscuritads.*

When an O'Casey persona is telling you home truths they go down on the page like this: "I don't envy yeh, Sean, for I wouldn't like to be alone with him long. His oul' mind's full of th' notion of oul' kings and queens the half of us never heard of; an' when he's talkin', a fella has to look wise, pretendin' he's well acquainted with them dead an' gone ghosts. It's a terrible sthrain on a body whenever he stops to talk."

Which is none of it Standard English, and is about Yeats, who for his part made great Paycocks in a way Ezra Pound remembered:

> . . . so that I recalled the wind in the chimney
>   as it were the wind in the chimney
>   but was in reality Uncle William
>   downstairs composing
>   that had made a great Peeeeacock
>   in the proide of his eiye
>   had made a great peeeeeeeacock in the . . .
>   made a great peacock
>   in the proide of his oyyee
>
>   proide ov his oy-ee
>   as indeed he had, and perdurable
>   a great peacock aere perennius

That was in the 1913–1914 winter, in Stone Cottage in Sussex, where Yeats made "The Peacock"—

> What's riches to him
> That has made a great peacock
> In the pride of his eye? . . .

—and made it in his normal manner, which was to chant his phrases over and over, "lettin' powerful moans and groans out of him" as Lady Gregory's coachman remembered other occasions, pulling vowels this way and that until vowels and rhythm and syntax, the whole intricate network of tensions, would settle into a taut integrity. His own eyes being troublesome, he had

brought Pound there to read, and they were likely sampling the Pennells'
Life of Whistler, where on page 301 we find the master's tart appraisal of
riches ("It is better to live on bread and cheese and paint beautiful things
than to live like Dives and paint pot-boilers") and five pages later his proposal
for "a great peacock ten feet high."*

Pound read to him too, that winter, much of Doughty's *Dawn in Britain*
and ("for the sake of his conscience") "nearly all Wordsworth," and we are
free to conjure, since no Max ever limned it, Yeats in his forty-ninth year
between solicitations of the Great Peacock half-attending to the stage-Phila-
delphian tones in which Pound in his twenty-ninth year made travesty of
what Wordsworth, *aetat.* seventy-six, had composed by his normal method,
which was to shout aloud in Northumbrian: the fervors, say, of a dank
invective against Illustrated Books and Newspapers—

> Avaunt this vile abuse of pictured page!
> Must eyes be all in all, the tongue and ear
> Nothing? Heaven keep us from a lower stage!

The Three Provinces have seldom been so nicely conjoined.

English to be written well, T. S. Eliot wrote, needs writing with a certain
animosity: a withholding of assent from all the things its words want to say
unbidden. These are island-things, things bespeaking a people, a climate,
and a local history self-congratulatory like all histories. Late in the twentieth
century since Christ and the eleventh since the Venerable Bede, speaking
and reading a dialect of what has become the worldwide language of air-
control towers, we easily forget how rooted its simple words once seemed.
Conrad's *oaken*, for instance: an oaken table, unlike a French *table du chêne*,
is understood to be substantial, well and truly constructed, old enough to
have been cherished by one's grandfather. Oaks grow very large in England,
live a thousand years. The hull-timbers that repulsed Armada balls were
oak. The young Yeats was briefly fond of *oak* and *oaken*, words intrinsic to
a Victorian poet's vocabulary. But in the final text of his *Poems* you will find
no use of *oak* later than the 1889 *Wanderings of Oisin* save for one "blasted
oak" where Crazy Jane has a tryst with a ghost, and the "oak and beechen
bough" of "Lullaby." (These poems were written within three weeks of
each other, in 1929.)

---

*Never executed; it was to have gone on a stairhead panel of the new (1892) Boston library.

Or savor *home* as Rupert Brooke exploited it:

> A body of England's, breathing English air,
> Washed by the rivers, blest by suns of home.

It is the noted ill-luck of the French that they must do without such a word, hence without such an emotion. *Chez soi* will not serve. The German *Heimat* is less far off:

> *Frisch weht der Wind*
> *Der Heimat zu. . . .*

Home receives nearly eight columns in the *OED*. One's *ham* was at first one's village, as we now remember only from its diminutive, *hamlet*, but was early transubstantiated to mean one's house and one's family circle. Moreover if we do not say "a home" the way we say "a house" (except frigidly—"Poor man, he is in a home") that is because, as some vigilant *OED* editor reasoned, we feel about *home* as we do about *youth*, *wedlock*, *health*, words which take no article because they are nouns of condition, not of place ("They enjoy health"; "They are home").

"A place, region or state to which one properly belongs, in which one's affections centre, or where one finds refuge, rest, or satisfaction": so runs *OED* entry *Home* I.5, cadenced with a feeling absent from most entries on those 4100 pages. Home keeps off the continual rain, keeps out the fogs, the chill (the word is less potent in Florida). Home is inviolate as though English bowmen protected it. The Queen herself may not enter your home uninvited. The Englishman's home is his castle, and when James Joyce transposed this formula he was accurate in altering both key words: "The Irishman's house is his coffin." The long womb-like vowel too Joyce perceived and devalued. "Safe home!" calls an undertaker late in *Ulysses*, and it is his horse that neighs the *responsus*, "Hohohohohome."

For such words—*home*, *Christ*, *ale*, *master*, *oak*, a thousand others—require close watching. "With a certain animosity" an Irishman picks his way past sticky places. Thus

> The young
> In one another's arms,

and

> . . . birds in the trees,

even piscine teeming,

> . . . the mackerel-crowded seas,

—all of these W. B. Yeats collapsed into "fish, flesh and fowl," and farewell Romeo and Juliet, the nightingale, Hakluyt. Though it is true that he was playing at being too old for amative delight, he was also playing at being too Irish, and the capital to which he proposed to cross the seas was not London nor yet Boston but Byzantium, where not even an Oxford man would feel at ease condescending.

That is the way the Irish writers work, and you can watch them do it, the way you watch the tramp's business with the stone. It goes into the pot, and whatever else comes out is also something you saw go in (something you do not see happen as you read Keats or Tennyson), and when it is all over you are to recall that the stone was in fact a stone, the word a mere word.

> . . . Being by Calvary's turbulence unsatisfied. . . .

It is unforgettable, and yet we saw Yeats drop that dictionary word into place, "turbulence." Contrast Tennyson's

> A cry that shivered to the tingling stars.

English evasiveness: we don't quite see how "tingling" fits there, shielded by an unwritten "twinkling."

They work from the outside, these Irishmen, and sometimes even use dictionaries (whence Joyce fetched ". . . Acardiac *foetus in foetu*, aprosopia due to a congestion, the agnatia of certain chinless Chinamen . . ."). He'd checked in Skeat the descent of *wit* from *witan*, "to know," and wrote "witty Aristotle"—master of those who know—in fine disregard of any English usage that associates "wit" and tavern gaiety.

Beckett is chillier still. In *All That Fall*, a play for radio, the old cracked voice of Mr. Rooney speaks of having been in the Men's, "or *Fir*, as they call it now, from *vir*, *viris*, I suppose, the *v* becoming *f* in accordance with Grimm's Law." Amid the wind and rain he fears being wet "to the buff. From buffalo." Hearing a voice fondle pedantries like these is like watching a face in a photograph disintegrate into dots, human urgency and human discomfort obliterated alike by a system of signals as elaborate and as arbitrary as the rules of chess.

Yeats too, pedant in passion, has "the uncontrollable mystery," he has "the entire combustible world," he has "this pragmatical, preposterous pig": not simply big words, though it is true that you will hear bigger words used casually in Dublin than you will most other places, but big Latinate adjectives joined to Saxon substantives as though in defiance of the great English moral distinction between Saxon and everything else.

For it is an English conviction that the strong Saxon words, the little English words, are the bone and muscle of discourse. This was an especially widespread conviction when Yeats was young; it informs Doughty's *Dawn in Britain*, read to him by Pound in 1914. Another man thought Latinisms and Hellenisms like "dormitory" and "photograph" nearly immoral, and proposed replacing them by Saxon coinages, "sleepstow" and "sunprint." That was William Barnes, of Dorsetshire, and his name for "grammar" was "speechcraft." Then Gerard Manley Hopkins wrote (1885)

> My cries heave, herds-long, huddle in a main, a chief
> woe, world-sorrow; on an age-old anvil wince and sing,

where only "cries" and "chief" are not Saxon; and four decades later the impressionable Ernest Hemingway was judging that "abstract" (i.e. Latinate) words such as glory, honor, courage, were "obscene." They were not rooted and sensual, not Saxon.

In Yeats the little Saxon words can be strong:

> Those that I fight I do not hate,
> Those that I guard I do not love

or

> And is their logic to outweigh
> MacDonagh's bony thumb?

—where that thumb is on the scales like a cunning grocer's and the "logic" on the other pan is something to associate with Hellene glibness.

But time and again, on Yeats's page, it is the abstract word, the polysyllable, that detonates, and this by Saxonist theory should not happen.

> the worst
> Are full of passionate intensity

or

> Out of the murderous innocence of the sea

or

> Their magnanimities of sound

or

> All complexities of mire and blood. . . .

and even

> . . . that discourtesy of death.

For we are to believe that this poet from Sandymount and Sligo has taken possession of the language, and in so doing has disengaged it from English history. Moving between small words and magniloquent words he does not move between the rooted speech of the shires and Renaissance abstractions, between Anglo-Saxon bloodedness—*dust, fire*—and Latinate specters—*pulverisation, conflagration*: no, he moves among notes on a keyboard all accessible alike to his convenience: *discourtesy, death*. Hence, whatever the vocabulary, the look of *performance*, of a virtuoso way with words that appeals to no commonality of usage.

He continues the performance from the grave, for when his tombstone in Sligo enjoins us,

> Cast a cold eye
> On life, on death. . . .

each of these monosyllables needs redefining by Yeatsian usage, as though a ghost, and not sixty million living Englishmen, had the tongue still in its keeping.

Cast. The verb of indifference. "When such as I cast out remorse." (1929)

Cold. Austere. ". . . cold / and passionate as the dawn." (1916)

Eye. The focus of aloofness. ". . . the lidless eye that loves the sun." (1910)

Life and *Death.* Juggler's contraries. "We have naught for death but toys." (1917) "Death and life were not / Till man made up the whole." (1927) "What is life but a mouthful of air?" (1934)

These are no longer "English" words but *his* words, almost accidentally coincident with English ones. To take possession of polysyllables in this way is less difficult since they tug at no one's heart. So T. S. Eliot could make *dissociation* and *correlative* his own. But to reverse the connotations of a homefelt word like *cold*, to turn coldness into a bracing quality, neither the death of affect nor the absence of living warmth, would seem an impossible defiance of what Keats invoked—"When this warm scribe, my hand, is in the grave"—or Emily Brontë in the poem she called "Cold in the Earth."

Yeats accomplishes it with no visible effort. "The cold and rook-delighting heaven," he wrote in 1912, installing life in the cold, an alien life but one capable of delight. Two years later,

> . . . 'Before I am old
> I shall have written him one
> Poem maybe as cold
> And passionate as the dawn.'

We are no longer to doubt that a cold poem is the right kind of poem, and it is explicitly not passionless. He then makes *cold* a moon-word—"The pure cold light in the sky"—and more than once a dawn-word—"The first cold gleam of day." And he has a girl infatuated with someone because

> . . . his hair is beautiful,
> Cold as March wind his eyes.

So in adjuring us from his gravestone to "Cast a cold eye," he can be sure of our agreement that no other eye is worth casting, and confident in his triumph over one of the seeming absolutes of English. It is a less equivocal victory than the Pyrrhic one the rebels won in the post office.

Nor was Yeats alone in this act of appropriation. Joyce too when he went into exile—his essential symbolic gesture—made as if to kidnap the language and take it away with him. English prose would henceforth be something contrived in Trieste and other remote places. It is into his private word-hoard that Joyce dips his hand, not into the store of common English speech, as much for the components of a sequence like

> Clean to see: the gloss of her sleek hide, the white button under the butt of her tail, the green flashing eyes. . . .

as for one like

> Assuefaction minorates atrocities (as Tully saith of his darling Stoics) and Hamlet his father showeth the prince no blister of combustion.

For one of these is not to be thought plain English, the other fancy: they are equally Joycean contrivances. English, Joyce will have you know, is good for nothing at all unless there is a contriving. Left to itself or to its native speakers, the English language not only cannot describe the gloss of a cat's sleek hide (has it ever before so much as accorded a cat a "hide"?), it cannot even tell you a simple a thing like what a cat says (one of the things she says is "Mrkrgnao!"). And as for style, much nonsense is talked about style, as though you needed the shaping forces of English civilization working their slow ferment to generate after many centuries a Browneian prose, after decades more a Pepysian: whereas it is plain to be seen that specimens of either can be fabricated on demand in 1920 by an Irishman in Zurich with an anthology or two and some dictionaries.

For watch him do it. Here is a Restoration diarist:

> So Thursday the sixteenth June Patk. Dignam laid in clay of an apoplexy and after hard drought, please God, rained, a bargeman coming in by water a fifty mile or thereabout with turf saying the seed won't sprout, fields athirst, very sadcoloured and stunk mightily, the quags and tofts too.

A date, a name abbreviated (diarists write for their own eyes), homely events (the rain), anecdotal focus (the bargeman), unliterary words like *stunk* and *quags* and *tofts* (which are all in the dictionary), a practice of stringing out elements paratactically on the way to a convenient fullstop: drop these into your pot and stir, nothing simpler; and do not omit to drop in also the stone called by some Celtic humor, acquired in pubs or from the blood, and by others macaronic learning, had from the Jesuits. And let no analyst henceforth presume to root English idiom in the speaking habits of Englishmen.

THE LORE OF IRISH

These were sounds that at first, though
we walked glued together, were so much
Irish to me.

SAMUEL BECKETT

As for the speaking habits of Irishmen, these are much complicated by the fact that there is another language besides English to worry them. It is called *Gaedhealg*, Irish, and when tourists these days mention Gaelic they will be told that though truly *Gaedhealg* is pronounced, approximately, "Gaelg," what is called Gaelic in English is only what they misspeak in Scotland. It is correct to remember how when the native tongue, *an teanga Gaedhilge*, was to be promoted, the new organization to promote it was christened The Gaelic League, but that was in 1893 when racial claims were at stake, the lilt and richness of coursing pan-Gaelic blood against anemic Saxon chatter. Politics has triumphed over blood and the correct word now is Irish.

Like many nineteenth-century heroines Gaedhealg (*f.*) underwent a long decline. This fact has aroused suspicion (would a Celt abandon his mother?) and you will be told with great circumstantiality how the Board of Commissioners of National Education were plotting her extinction in Dublin Castle in the 1830's. Occam's Razor makes this improbable. The most Anglophile of commissioners had no call to take action against a tongue that was being abandoned. By 1892 Douglas Hyde was reporting a queer thing—parents speaking in Irish, children in English, each of them understanding the other's speech though not able to speak it, and many of the children not even aware two tongues were in play. He said this went on in "thousands upon thousands of houses" and did not explain how the schools he excoriated could have brought it about if the parents did not concur.

They saw reason to concur, since after the Union—that had been 1800—your one way to get ahead and often the only way not to starve was to master English, and by 1851 the census-takers could find only 320,000 natives in the whole country who had not begun to do this at all. These speakers of nothing but Irish were about 5 percent of the population, and another 23 percent had something of both tongues. This counts both *Gaeltochta* who were forgetting their Irish and the handful of *Sasanacha* who were learning some, and it means altogether that already in the year before Tom Moore died (and George Moore and Lady Gregory were born), only half a century since one man in three spoke the language, nearly three Irishmen in four had no Irish whatsoever.

After that the decline was precipitous. George Moore by 1894 felt safe in thinking that "nobody did anything in Irish except bring turf from the bog and say prayers," since during the second post-Union half-century, 1850–1900, while the entire population was dwindling by 2 million, the proportion with only Irish went down to 0.48 percent (21,000) and the number with "some" Irish to 14.4 percent, many of the latter stumblers in improvised classrooms. So by 1901 the count of Irishmen with any pretense to their ancestral tongue stood at a mere 660,000 out of 4.4 million: a spectacular half-century's loss.*

Also during that half-century Irish underwent the advantage of any tongue that was perceived to be on its way to extinction: like the American Indian languages, it was studied. It is not an easy speech to pick up by ear; Frank O'Connor distinguished two dialects, Back-of-the-mouth and Toothless. Many found its intricacies beyond them, and one man even pronounced them beyond the power of the human brain. That was Yeats's mentor John O'Leary, which may help excuse the poet's willingness to merely dabble.† It is a language in which you cannot so much as say "yes" and "no," but instead the equivalents of "It is that" and "It is not." There were amateurs to be charmed by such details, and philologists, often German, to be fasci-

*By 1980 there were estimated to be 40,000 Irish speakers in the entire officially bilingual country: down from 70,000 in 1950.
†Brendan O Hehir makes the more interesting suggestion that Yeats's "dominion over English"—a lord of which can compel any word at all to do the office of any part of speech—"was the root cause of his inability to learn any other language whatsoever."

nated. Both classes of enthusiast might be encountered hallooing after natives among the Inishmaan rocks.

Or you could study Irish more formally (J. M. Synge did) at Trinity College, where they were not encouraging anybody to talk to *Gaeltochta* peasants unless for the purpose of converting them from Romish superstition, Trinity's reason for situating its Irish classes in the Divinity School. Synge's principal text was *An Soisgeul do reir Eoin*, the Gospel of St. John, a 1602 version distributed by the Irish Society gratis, and its idioms were of limited applicability. Though at Trinity he was an Irish (also Hebrew) prizeman, his encounter with living speech in 1898 on the Aran Islands drove him at once to engage an Irish tutor.

His academic interest in the language was more than casual. Besides the Gospel he had been reading *The Children of Lir,* also, very slowly, *Diarmuid and Grania*, texts not written in the modern Gospel idiom but in a version of the language as remote as Spenser from anything actually spoken. What these were like is instructive.

Oidheadh Cloinne Lir, the Fate of the Children of Lir, tells how the four of them were bewitched by their wicked stepmother into swans, so to remain until Christianity should come to Ireland; when they were released after centuries they were of immense age and decrepitude, but on being baptized entered heaven in the form of radiant children again. It is of medieval origin as can be guessed, and in 1892 would have appealed to tastes Wagner had molded (and Synge's passion was music). The Society for the Preservation of the Irish Language had printed it, with notes and vocabulary, in 1883.

As for *Toraidheacht Dhiarmada agus Ghráinne*, the Flight of Diarmuid and Grania, it is part of the *Fionn Mac Cumhail* (Finn MacCool) cycle, and tells how Grania who was betrothed to old Finn became enamored of young Diarmuid and put a spell on him, so that he fled with her through the woods and across Ireland, and came at last to a bitter end. It had an 1889 reprinting, with vocabulary, from an 1857 edition. Its pertinence to Romantic tastes needs no comment, nor its resemblance to the similar story Wagner picked up, of Tristan and Isolde.

For just as, when philology was recovering Provençal texts, the troubadour preferred by both learned and lay tastes was apt to be the one least unlike Tennyson, Giraut di Bornelh, so when patriots and folklorists edited and translated the inchoate materials of the Red Branch Cycle and the Fionn Cycle, attention was fixed on whatever would be enhanced by dim lights and music: tales of downdrawing women and of pathos, the story of Grania, the story of Deirdre, and of doomed heroism, the story of Cuchulain. So it was natural for Yeats's and Synge's generation to suppose that the Irish imaginative heritage was much like what cultivated Europeans prized, only more authentic.

The recovery of even these exemplars was no exception to the rule that in Ireland nothing moves forward unjeered at. The work had been under way since before 1785, the year of the foundation of the Royal Irish Academy; it was commanding by mid-century able intelligences, journals, sponsors, societies; yet as late as 1899 the Professor of Comparative Philology at Trinity, Robert Atkinson, was informing a government commission that the Irish manuscripts contained mostly folklore, that all folklore was "at bottom abominable," and that in ancient Irish literature it would be difficult to find a book "in which there is not some passage so silly or so indecent as to give you a shock for which you would not recover for the rest of your life."

Atkinson's credentials included familiarity with the difficult Irish verb system. Though his colleague the formidable classicist John Pentland Mahaffy knew barely any Irish save what was useful to a man fishing for salmon or shooting grouse in the West, occasions on which he "had found a few words very serviceable," Mahaffy did not hesitate to endorse these literary opinions concerning what he did not deem literature: it was all, he testified to the same commission, either silly or indecent when it was not merely religious. The commission, which had been charged to investigate the advisability of introducing Irish into the schools, duly reported, to the fury of the Gaelic League, that there was no imagination nor idealism in the whole range of Irish literature.

They were right about the presence of indecency. Yeats would be wicked and wild and old indeed before his verse could assimilate it; his praise of "great-bladdered Emer"—queenly in her powers of retention—was not printed until he was seventy-five. But from very early in life Yeats had no difficulty in admiring what he could find in the Irish sagas that was neither silly nor indecent but pathetic or heroic.

Yeats found such things where anybody save specialists found them, in translations and retellings. Not only had he no Irish—to the end of his life, in fact, he had no Irish, not even spoken, let alone Old or Middle—he had also no more than any other amateur a hope of penetrating archives so vast it would be a life's work reading through them all attentively once. The Cuchulain materials alone were estimated by one scholar at two thousand octavo pages; another was to guess that even the exclusion of what is repetitious and dull would not bring fourteen centuries of writing in Irish much below five hundred to a thousand printed volumes. And names recur, and themes, and variations, in a wilderness of tilted textual mirrors.

The contrast with, for instance, Anglo-Saxon could not be more marked. The student of Beowulf has only one *Beowulf* to cope with, recorded in just one manuscript. The student of Deirdre must recover the Deirdre theme from a plethora of inconsistent retellings. The version Thomas Kinsella rendered in 1969 from an eighth- or ninth-century source runs to fewer than four thousand words. Lady Gregory's version of 1903 was nearly four times that length, because she wrote diffusely but also because she gathered the details she liked from numerous sources including Scotch Gaelic ones, all scrutinized through translations into some language she knew better. An amateur might reasonably set out to read the entire Anglo-Saxon corpus. An amateur of Old and Middle Irish would get lost within days in a hundred-acre labyrinth were it not for the guidance of indexers and selectors and conflators. The Irish heritage as it stood by 1900 was accordingly something *shaped* by a sequence of enthusiasts.

There had been an early concentration on Ossian son of Finn, by 1889 the hero, "Oisin," of Yeats's first major poem. This was because when the Scotsman James Macpherson published his "Ossianic" fustian in 1763 and started a craze, he had been at pains to deny any Irish connection, having worked, he said, from epic poems written in Scotland in the third century.[*] So when the first wave of Celtic enthusiasm swept across Europe (and Napoleon took his *Ossian* with him to St. Helena) Ireland was excluded from the glory.

No Irishman with learning or without it proposed to take such an insult lying down, and by mid-century enough philological expertise was available, much of it German, to sustain the activities and the publications of learned bodies in Dublin, which sponsored many pages of dogged translating. The Irish Archaeological Society (founded 1841), the Celtic Society (founded 1847), the Ossianic Society (1854–1861), and their roster of scholars—O'Donovan, O'Curry, O'Daly, Walsh, Conellan, O'Looney, Standish Hayes O'Grady—had their work cut out for them. For if it was not true that, as one Englishman had asserted, the mythology of the Celts resembled that of the Hottentots, or that the Irish in particular had no tincture of civilization till the Normans did them the favor of subduing them, then Irishmen needed this knowledge as much as the world at large.

By custom the scholars wrote for one another. Thus the *Silva Gadelica* of

---

[*]Though Macpherson and his books have faded away, Boswell's Johnson denouncing a scoundrel stays vivid, and it's arcane knowledge now that Macpherson's folly went up on a scrabbly foundation of real Gaelic ballads. (His Dar-thula and Nathos are Deirdre and Naisi.) We may connect his need to fake a Celtic Homer with the exactions of a public that would not have known how to get interested in fragments.

Standish Hayes O'Grady (2 vols., London, 1892) is a repellent place to be seeking enlightenment. His normal prose, as exhibited in his preface, reads like a hasty exercise done from Bulgarian (". . . the thing itself falls into divers kinds of all which one only variety can be valid here"), and Middle Irish so tormented clunks balefully.* "O tiny wren most scant of tail!" (page 59) is his effort at part of a poem, and as for narrative technique, while he can rise to this:

> To him enters now a burly wizard of great daring, and from the direction of his rear impinges on him with a kick. (page 302)

he can sink to this:

> . . . thrice fifty high-mettled men-at-arms with their suitable allowance of gentle women, forby a white-toothed rosy-cheeked delicate-handed and black-eyebrowed maiden that sat against a castle wall: a silken mantle, a tunic netted of gold threads she had about her and, on her head, a queen's rightful decorated wimple. (page 303)

The foremost parodists of two generations, James Joyce and Flann O'Brien,† struggled without success to attain such depths.

As materials accumulated, more varied diction was luckily placed at their service. During several decades, 1857–1880, Sir Samuel Ferguson (1810–1886) published sprightly volumes of "versions from the Irish" which had an effect, though many no longer sound Irish at all. Ferguson tantalizes. Away from Irish he can seem to parody Gray:

> Delicious Liffey! from thy bosoming hills,
> What man who sees thee issuing strong and pure,
> But with some wistful, fresh emotion fills,
> Akin to Nature's own clear temperature?

Close to Irish, he can be stage-Irish jaunty, as in the version of "Pastheen Finn" Yeats twice rewrote—

*Save for Yeats, who scorned the "eighteenth-century frenzy" of O'Grady's diction, this is not received opinion; thus readers of Aodh de Blácam's *Gaelic Literature Surveyed* (1929) are told (page 375) that *Silva* contains "the most spirited translations ever made from Gaelic prose," into English "flexible, whimsical, vivid." Let each find delight where he can; "The Siamese eat puppydogs."

†Fans of O'Brien's saga of Dermot Trellis will be glad to have O'Grady clarify "At Swim-Two-Birds": "Where Dermot in his banishment was just then was at *snámh dá én* (that is to say: two birds that Nar son of Conall Cernach's son Finncha killed there on Eistine the Amazon's shoulder, whence it is named *snámh dá én*, i.e. 'two birds' swimming-place')." (page 76)

Oh, my fair Pastheen is my heart's delight,
Her gay heart laughs in her blue eye bright,
Like the apple blossom her bosom white
And her neck like the swan's on a March morn bright!
   Then, Oro, come with me, come with me, come with me!
   Oro, come with me, brown girl sweet!
   And oh, I would go through snow and sleet,
   If you would come with me, brown girl sweet! . . .

But once, in "The Fairy Thorn"—written, so Malcolm Brown tells us, in his twenty-third year—Ferguson virtually invented what soon passed on Yeats's page for the verse effects peculiar to an Irish soul. Though Yeats for some reason omitted "The Fairy Thorn" from his 1900 *Book of Irish Verse*, he had quoted it with enthusiasm, almost entire, in his first published piece of prose, an appreciation of Ferguson he did for *The Irish Fireside* when he was twenty-one and Sir Samuel Ferguson just two months dead. Both he and AE (so Austin Clarke reported on AE's authority) got their best music from the way of its "internal assonances," in which Ferguson was imitating a complex of Irish verse effects:

"Get up, our Anna dear, from the weary spinning-wheel;
   For your father's on the hill, and your mother is asleep;
Come up above the crags, and we'll dance a Highland reel
   Around the Fairy Thorn on the steep."

This haunts with its density of consonance and assonance—*hill* for instance is part of the *wheel-reel* cluster, and if *dear* and *weary* echo one another from the second and fourth strong beats in their line, so do, less obviously, *crags* and *dance*. Later *Fairy* remembers *dear* and *weary*. And that hypnotic, elusive rhythm with its arrested fourth line—has anything like it been heard in English before? Only music can explain such seeming invention on the part of a minor though industrious poet. Ferguson had, as the Celts say, "a chune in his head," not anything counted by syllables. More than once he lost its spell and lapsed into doggerel, but not in a stanza like this:

. . . They're glancing through the glimmer of the quiet eve,
   Away in milky wavings of neck and ankle bare;
The heavy-sliding stream in its sleepy song they leave,
   And the crags in the ghostly air. . . .

The enchantment seizes them; the four girls all in green stay entranced through the night, immobile, bowed beside the Fairy Hawthorn in its lonely rowan grove. By morning the four are three. No more than the child in W. B. Yeats's *The Land of Heart's Desire* will gay truant Anna be seen by mortals again.

Yet as such versification can elide into doggerel (and Ferguson's more than once does, within this very poem), so such material, even when infused by the substantial genius of Yeats, can deliquesce into the quaintness that prompted Max Beerbohm to caricature "Mr. W. B. Yeats, presenting Mr. George Moore to the Queen of the Fairies." *The Land of Heart's Desire* itself is an instance. For years Yeats seemed to think access to the *Sidhe* the note of a proper Irish imagination.

But no wee folk, no faery elusiveness distracted Standish James O'Grady (1846–1928), who sought "the reconstruction by imaginative processes of the life led by our ancestors in this country," hoping "to make this heroic period once again a portion of the imagination of the country." His *History of Ireland: The Heroic Period* appeared in 1878, crammed with vigorous murk. Joyce parodies with matching vigor. Which of the two wrote the following?

> Then all at once, on a sudden impulse, they sang the battle-song of the Ulto-
> nians, and shouted for the war so that the building quaked and rocked, and in
> the hall of the weapons there was a clangour of falling shields, and men died
> that night for extreme dread, so mightily shouted the Ultonians. . . . The trees
> of Ulster shed their early leaves and buds at that shout, and birds fell dead
> from the branches.

Save for a certain adjectival paucity, it is nearly worthy of the "Cyclops" episode.

O'Grady also singled out Cuchulain and Finn and retold their stories as adventure novels, though he had not Rider Haggard's skills. Yeats and AE when young read him gladly. "I was as a man who, through some accident, had lost memory of his past," AE recalled in old age. "When I read O'Grady I was as such a man who suddenly feels ancient memories rushing at him, and knows he was born in a royal house, that he had mixed with the mighty of heaven and earth and had the very noblest for his companions." Assured of that royal house, neither he nor Yeats likely reread what they were still praising when they were older; why complicate glowing memories?

The influence of Standish James O'Grady presents an instructive compli-cation. In part out of ready confusion with his cousin Standish *Hayes* O'Grady (1832–1915) he was widely supposed to be a Gaelic scholar. In point of fact he had little grasp of the language, which he insisted on tackling in disregard of folderol like eclipsis, syncope, broad and slender vowels; the spirit, that was the thing. In this he resembled some enthusiast for French who should expedite encounters with that tongue by not fussing over such trivia as grammatical gender (water and trees masculine? what nonsense!), and by the time Standish James had become a living symbol for the vivification of the nation's heritage, ironies aplenty were clustering. "Paradise of pretenders then and now," wrote Joyce with his mind on a different lot of people. With such experts as Standish Hayes so manifestly deficient in literary skills, the Revival was a paradise of amateurs.

One of these, Victor O'D. Power, saw cash in printed Irishness and cashed in. Weekly pulps still reprint his concoctions, e.g.:

> Wisha, faith, 'tis time for us to have a good laugh tonight, imbeersa! So I'm going to tell ye all about Nannie Ryan's matchmaking, and 'tis worth your while to listen to old Kitty, for 'tis a droll story enough, so it is.

And on and on, and you could write it in your sleep, as Victor O'Donovan Power doubtless did, waking hours being surely insufficient for the quantity of stuff he put his name to. The trick is to drop in many a *'tis* and *wisha* and *imbeersa*, and always spell "yellow" *yella*, faith an' begorra, and though you've no ear at all for the tune of a sentence 'tis *Ireland's Own* and *Our Boys* will have ye into print so fast they'll not even read proof, awonomsa, and yer young compathriots thimselves it is will put out their pennies to make believe yer the voice of the oul' sod itself, mossa, the same that is watered wi' th' blood o' saints, begannies, and it rich too with the spuds, the Lord save us all.

Power has his reward, which is to be reprinted seemingly forever and like Homer to have his very dates forgotten; "fl. late nineteenth and early twentieth centuries" is the best the *Dictionary of Irish Literature* can do. One pathetic fact he highlights is the starvation of mind young Irish people faced once their elders, to help them get on, had left them with English for their sole tongue. If there was a storyteller—*seanachie*—in the place they could understand no word of his. Pennies for *Ireland's Own* brought them "Kitty the Hare" instead, to tell them in blotchy print "the finest of all my poor mother's fireside stories" or some such imposture.

But the most gifted of amateurs, a man who by sheer dedication earned professional status and a chair of Irish, was Douglas Hyde, five years Yeats's senior and the son of a Protestant rector in Roscommon. Hyde provided the National Literary Society with one of its most famous occasions when he addressed it (25 November 1892) on "The Necessity for De-Anglicising

Ireland." This was to be accomplished chiefly by way of the old language, to which English should be no more than a helpful auxiliary. He was soon a platform evangelist for this cause; George Moore describes his look when he "stood bawling," "the great skull, its fringe of long black hair, . . . the droop of the moustache through which his Irish frothed like porter," and adds cryptically that "when he returned to English it was easy to understand why he desired to change the language of Ireland."

When the Gaelic League got founded (1893) Hyde was its first president, and it's startling to hear that his Irish was self-taught and never freed from solecisms at which native speakers snickered.

In 1893 he published *Love Songs of Connacht*, a thin book with English pages facing the Irish ones. This must rank among the most influential fascicles of our age, and the part that had the influence was what he'd spent least pains on, the connecting prose and the footnotes. His notes meant to offer merely literal cribs to the verses he'd laboriously put into imitations of their original forms, since in contorting "Mala Néfin" into lines like these—

> Did I stand on the bald top of Néfin
> And my hundred-times loved one with me,
> We should nestle together as safe in
> Its shade as the birds on a tree. . . .

he was aware of having had to let go precisions his conscience wanted to acknowledge. Also he was helping beginners with the language, and a lot of the words in that stanza they'd search the Irish in vain for. So at the bottom of the page he offered:

> If I were to be on the brow of Nefin and my hundred loves by my side, it is pleasantly we would sleep together like the little bird upon the bough. It is your melodious wordy little mouth that increased my pain, and a quiet sleep I cannot get until I shall die, alas!

That has charm and so has this:

> 'Tis the cause of this song—a bard who gave love to a young woman, and he came into the house where she herself was with her mother at the fall of night. The old woman was angry, him to come, and she thought to herself what would be the best way to put him out again, and she began twisting a suggaun, or straw rope. She held the straw, and she put the bard a-twisting it. The bard was going backwards according as the suggaun was a-lengthening, until at last he went out of the door, and he ever-twisting. When the old

woman found him outside she rose up of a leap and struck the door to in his face. She then flung the harp out to him through the window, and told him to be going.

Douglas Hyde arrived at this artless English quite artlessly; on the left-hand page was what he had written in Irish, and the English, to help learners, was following as exactly as it could, almost as "Qu'est-ce que c'est?" might be turned into "What is it that it is?" It seemed a new and charming kind of English; Yeats called it "a mountain stream of sweet waters," and "the coming of a new power into literature."

If this many years later his enthusiasm seems excessive, still we can understand it. By an unlikely route, Douglas Hyde's pedagogic transpositions into the *Beurla* of sundry poets' Irish and his own, a new quality was being made available for some writer of English who might know what to do with it and not be carried away by the opportunity to create a newly fey Stage Irishman. In another decade J. M. Synge would qualify, and what would keep Synge from coy charm (to the rage of patriots) would be his knowledge of Irish itself.

One of the poems Hyde collected had the distinction of inspiring as fine a lyric as ever came even out of Ireland, Padraic Colum's "I Shall Not Die for Thee." It is a miracle of courteous self-possession, the kind Englishmen lost the knack of after Marvell. "O woman, shapely as the swan . . .": based on Irish of unknown age that had been remembered by the people, it stuck in as un-Hibernian a memory as Ezra Pound's, who wondered in the Pisan stockade

> Whoi didn't he (Padraic Colum)
> keep on writing poetry at that voltage

Here is Hyde's crib, and Colum's poem:

I shall not die for thee, O woman yonder, of body like a swan. Silly people (were they) thou hast ever slain. They and myself are not the same. Why should I go to die For the red lip, for the teeth like blossoms; The gentle figure, the breast like a swan. Is it for them I myself should die. The pointed (?) breasts, the fresh skin; The scarlet cheeks, the undulating cool; Indeed, then, I shall not die For them, may it please God. Thy narrow brows, thy tresses like gold, Thy chaste secret, thy languid voice, Thy heel round, thy calf smooth. They shall slay none but a silly person. Thy delightful mien, thy free spirit, Thy thin palm, thy side like foam, Thy blue eye, thy white throat!—I shall not die for thee. O woman of body like a swan, I was nurtured by a cunning man, O thin palm, O white bosom—I shall not die for thee.

O woman, shapely as the swan,
On your account I shall not die:
The men you've slain—a trivial clan—
Were less than I.

I ask me shall I die for these—
For blossom teeth and scarlet lips—
And shall that delicate swan-shape
Bring me eclipse?

Well-shaped the breasts and smooth the skin,
The cheeks are fair, the tresses free—
And yet I shall not suffer death,
God over me!

Those even brows, that hair like gold,
Those languorous tones, that virgin way,
The flowing limbs, the rounded heel
Slight men betray!

Thy spirit keen through radiant mien,
Thy shining throat and smiling eye,
Thy little palm, thy side like foam—
I cannot die!

O woman, shapely as the swan,
In a cunning house hard-reared was I:
O bosom white, O well-shaped palm,
I shall not die!

As for Hyde, he had no *literary* future; President of the Gaelic League from the day it was founded, he was not interested at all in renovating English, only in letting it take what course it might in due subordination to the historic tongue. So his Muses' blade, as Yeats put it, got beaten into prose: serviceable polemic prose, no longer enchanting. He also wrote plays, but in Irish: the tale of the poet and the twisted rope became *Casadh an tSugáin*, famous as the first play in Irish produced at a professional theatre (by the Gaelic League Amateur Dramatic Society, at the Gaiety, Dublin, 21 October 1901). The unzealous were later given access in a printed translation done by Lady Gregory, *The Twisting of the Rope*.

So we come to Lady Gregory. Dumpy, in widow's black, a Victorian's imperturbable Victoria, driven for long years by duties self-imposed, stolid in the confidence she shared with Ascendancy noddies and Yeats that English however modified would continue to be the language of Irish cultivation—

they were right— it was she who contrived and imposed an "Anglo-Irish" anybody with half an ear could imitate. For decades it was the idiom of stock plays at the Abbey, where the irreverent gave marks for "PQ" (Peasant Quality). It is as formulaic as pseudo-Yiddish and any funny man can still drop into it. In her hands her belief in what she's doing keeps it far from contemptible.

Her decisive work came about thanks to the report of the commission that heard about silliness and indecency. What that required was some retelling of Irish tales that could not but command respect. W. B. Yeats was the evident man for it, and a scholar offered to supply cribs he could put his English on, but he was busy. So it was Augusta Gregory that undertook it—" 'We work to add dignity to Ireland' was a favourite phrase of hers," Yeats remembered—and contrived when she was about it the way of writing English that still imitates to Anglo-American ears the fluent idiosyncratic speech of Ireland.

Open *Cuchulain of Muirthemne* at random: " 'I swear by the oath of my people,' said Cuchulain, 'I will make my doings be spoken of among the great doings of heroes in their strength.' "

"My deeds will be remembered," that is, "with the great deeds heroes performed when they were in their prime"; but we have here an idiom which habitually prefers the verb-like form—*doings* for *deeds,* the immediate form—*spoken of* for *remembered,* and the concrete form—*strength* for *prime.*

We have also a syntactical mannerism which we may notice as early in the book as Lady Gregory's explanation of how she shaped her language. "I have told the whole story in plain and simple words, in the same way my old nurse Mary Sheridan used to be telling stories from the Irish long ago, and I a child at Roxborough."

Since Lady Gregory commenced learning Irish only when she was past forty, we are to understand that her old nurse Mary Sheridan used to be talking to her in English, an English moreover that had been strained and stressed by Irish habits of thought. "And I a child at Roxborough" is a symptom, and the way it differs from "When I was a child" merits pondering, with a valuable exposition by Maire Cruise O'Brien to guide us. We shall find that the English sense of things works from verb to verb like Latin, and arranges verbs in systems of subordination, chronological or causal. "She told me that when I was a child" is a normal English sentence, the "was" clause subordinated to the "told" clause. But Irish centers on *states*, represented by nouns and noun-like constructions. "She used to be telling me" recreates her telling as a stable, ongoing process, she telling and telling, in a vivid pocket of time, something to picture; "I a child" locates my condition as that telling proceeded; the "and" does no more than link these, the child put into the picture with the storyteller.*

Such a language shapes, is shaped by, a view of life that proceeds frame by frame, in vivid static scenes. Mrs. O'Brien states the principle a little more technically:

> Irish syntax concentrates on the expression of states rather than actions; its verbal system is highly aspective, with the subject of the sentence as the focus of the utterance and all occurrences relating back thereto. It shows a marked predilection for the substantival cast of sentence, i.e., a sentence where the noun carries the main burden of content. It has a highly developed prepositional system widely employed; prepositions in Irish supply many of the functions of the verb in English.

When these Irish habits are strong, as in the speech of first-generation bilinguals, they produce such violations of idiom as "If it is a thing that he do come." This means "If he should come," and the word "thing" is trying to anchor it to the aspective. But under pressure from English idiom more accurately sensed that kind of pidgin tends to vanish, "and only Gaelicisms inherently amenable to the recipient structure are retained in mono-lingual Anglo-Irish." So an English comes to be spoken that has nothing grammatically wrong with it but with still something strange about it, a strangeness frequently obtained by the Irish habit of concentrating on states but supplementing the feeble English verb "to be" with verbs like "put," "leave," "have," which are used to indicate how a state of things has been effected: "She has him crying" (she has made him cry); "I put the fear of God on him" (I frightened him severely); "Have it off him" (take it from him).

Writers who know Irish well can make wonderfully free with this principle. Any page of Sean O'Casey is alive with a baroque jostle of aspectives: "Give us a glass o' malt, for God's sake, till I stimulate meself from th' shock o' seein' the sight that's afther goin' out!" That sentence halts and turns on the nouns "shock" and "sight." Here is one doing the same on "way" and "fact": "Th' safest way to hindher her from havin' any enjoyment out of her spite, is to dip our thoughts into th' fact of her bein' a female person that has moved out of th' sight of ordinary sensible people."

---

*Pepys and Jane Austen are among the English writers who have once in a while found this construction comfortable, but that does not mean their minds have such a habit: only that English will take the syntax without strain.

Then there is the custom of beginning each sentence, straight off, with a verb, be it only a sort of " 'Tis." "Went we to Galway yesterday" would be a paradigm, and "It's we went to Galway yesterday," "It's yesterday we went to Galway," "It's to Galway we went yesterday," would be various alterations of emphasis, with "is"—Irish "is"— for that ineluctable head-verb; hence Synge's "It's cold he is surely," or "It's many a lone woman would be afeard," or "It's soon he'd be falling asleep." What's done with syntax needn't be done with voice, and the Irish voice accordingly is free to play its equable tune, under no responsibility for assigning emphasis.

In the light of all this we may revert to Cuchulain's "I will make my deeds be spoken of," and appreciate Lady Gregory's firm sense of the statal aspect: I will bring it about that this speaking-of will go on. From that arises the peat-brown flavor: from that lingering on states achieved. Everywhere in *Cuchulain of Muirthemne* instances leap to the eye.

With that they got up upon the floor, and put on their shields and took hold of their swords, and they attacked and struck at one another till the one half of the hall was as if on fire with the clashing of swords and spears, and the other half was white as chalk with the whiteness of the shields. There was fear on the whole gathering; all the men were put from their places, and there was great anger on Conchubar himself and on Fergus, son of Rogh, to see the injustice and the hardship of two men fighting against one, Conall and Laeghaire both together attacking Cuchulain.

All those "ands" divide the discourse into scenes, and we see how the fighting brings it about that the hall is divided into a red half and a white half. And this narrative of hewing and slashing and shouting does its business with a minimum of vivid verbs. Its underlying structures are mutations of the verb *to be*, each one stating a newly shifted mental scene.

And here is Cuchulain's lament after he learns that it is his son he has killed:

"Och! It is bad that it happened; my grief! it is on me is the misfortune, O Conlaoch of the Red Spear, I myself to have spilled your blood.

"I to be under defeat, without strength. It is a pity Aoife never taught you to know the power of my strength in the fight.

"It is no wonder I to be blinded after such a fight and such a defeat.

"It is no wonder I to be tired out, and without the sons of Usnach beside me.

"Without a son, without a brother, with none to come after me; without Conlaoch, without a name to keep my strength.

"To be without Naoise, without Ainnle, without Ardan; is it not with me is my fill of trouble?

"I am the father that killed his son, the fine green branch; there is no hand or shelter to help me.

"I am a raven that has no home; I am a boat going from wave to wave; I am a ship that has lost its rudder; I am the apple left on the tree; it is little I thought of falling from it; grief and sorrow will be with me from this time."

This stately cascade of aspectives—I myself to have spilled your blood, I to be under defeat, I to be blinded, I to be tired out—moves toward four culminating predicatives, all nouns: I am a raven, I am a boat, I am a ship, I am the apple. It is so formal we may barely notice how minimal is its intercourse with verbs, and it struck many ears with the force of poetic revelation.

There were mockers who found the language vulnerable, and it got called "Kiltartanese" after the Kiltartan villagers to whom she'd dedicated the retellings. George Moore thought she did it by formula, dropping the occasional "Irish" nut onto acres of bland prose patchy with genteelisms such as "lawn" or "courting." (Did bronze-age savages tend lawns? Did they "court"? Moore judged them savages.) Her bowdlerizing of savagery distressed others, who forgot Professor Atkinson's charge that the old stories were "intolerably low," and that Lady Gregory's need had been to rebut it.

Certainly her prose is mannered, better for battles and orations than for reflecting or simply telling, and today, its first spell long dissipated, *Cuchulain of Muirthemne* can seem tedious, a book to sample and excerpt from. Still, she had provided an idiom, and if you could parody it you could also base stronger things on it. After two years Synge called her book "still a part of my daily bread." The 1902 edition was reprinted in 1903, 1907, 1911, 1915, 1919, 1926, 1934. As a "Celtic" resource it rivalled the *Ossian* which Napoleon had taken to St. Helena. That detail too has its cognate. President Theodore Roosevelt, required to spend much time on trains, used to carry *Cuchulain of Muirthemne* for reading in about wielders of the big spear, as American telegraph poles flickered by.

To an exhaustion that was beginning to be perceived in standard English, Modernism early in the twentieth century brought two remedies that seem at first diametrically opposed. One was recourse to the Saxon hoard of strong verbs; the other was this Celtic habit of vivid static images. Gerard Hopkins offers extreme examples of the former—catching a Falcon

> . . . at his riding
> Of the rolling level underneath him steady air, and striding
> High there, how he hung upon the rein of a wimpling wing
> In his ecstasy! then off, off forth on swing . . .
> . . . the hurl and gliding
> Rebuffed the big wind.

Here a diagram discloses but two formal verbs. But a diagram understands a verb as nothing more than the transitional word between subject and predicate—"he hung upon"; "the gliding rebuffed. . . ."—and what interests Hopkins is not this syntactic expedient but the action in the word of action: riding, rolling, striding, wimpling, hurl-and-gliding. "Underneath him steady," even, has verbal force—we feel that air as an equilibrist feels his rope—and "off, off forth" releases into the sentence the energy of a catapult. So the Hopkins lines are crammed with phantom verbs.

It was potentials such as these in language that Ernest Fenollosa sought to unlock with his famous analogy of the Chinese Written Character, which Ezra Pound did not say was about Chinese, no, "on verbs, mostly on verbs." "The Chinese Written Character as a Medium for Poetry" depends not at all on its sinology, being concerned with notions Fenollosa took with him to the Orient and clarified while gazing into ideograms: that all words act, enact, verbwise, the very prepositions channellers of force, that "things" are "cross-sections cut through actions, snap-shots." He thought that writers should hone a sense of language on practice pages containing "no use of the copula."

Seeing that to Irish ways with language the copula is indispensable and the pattern sentence is the one that finds you in a state of having-been-done-to, we may wonder how it is that early-twentieth-century Modernism can be any kind of cohesion with both Fenollosa and Irish, Pound and Yeats, contained in it. A way toward accepting this is to reflect that Pound's first modern master was Yeats, and that at Stone Cottage in 1913–1914 he was undergoing the impact of Fenollosa's papers in Yeats's very presence without any division occurring. Quite the contrary: Fenollosa's *Noh* notebooks, on which Pound was then working, were suggesting to Yeats the way of his own later drama. And Pound divulged a great many years later that what had drawn him to Yeats in the first place was Yeats's skill with syntax: especially his ability, repeatedly demonstrated, at fitting a sentence very snugly into a stanza of any length. "He had made lyrics of a single sentence, with no word out of natural order."

Yeats had sensed the need of this, and begun learning the trick of it, as early as the ballads he was writing in his twenties before he knew anything of Irish constructions, responsive as he was so early to a need for some way to shape and bound the Victorian verse sentence: such a sentence as any of Tennyson's:

> O brother, had you known our Camelot
> Built by old kings, age after age, so old
> The King himself had fear that it would fall,
> So strange, and rich, and dim; for where the roofs
> Tottered toward each other in the sky,
> Met foreheads all along the street of those
> Who watched us pass; and lower, and where the long
> Rich galleries, lady-laden, weighed the necks
> Of dragons clinging to the crazy walls. . . .

—which is looking for no particular place to stop and meanders ten more lines before it finds one. Whereas here is a boxed and bounded Yeats sentence, in his mature manner as perfected by 1898:

> THE FISH
>
> Although you hide in the ebb and flow
> Of the pale tide when the moon has set,
> The people of coming days will know
> About the casting out of my net,
> And how you have leaped times out of mind
> Over the little silver cords,
> And think that you were hard and unkind,
> And blame you with many bitter words.

The effect of such a sentence, with its "Irish" layering of "and" clauses, is to make not just one clause but the whole poem aspective, held in place for the looking: here is how things habitually, recurrently are. This formal composition is the means by which posterity will know my casting and casting, your leaping and leaping, and the poem you are reading now contains posterity too, endlessly reprobating. It is all one timeless endlessly enacted thing, and my syntax can lasso it in a single ceremonious gesture:

> Although you hide
> They will know
> > about the casting
> > about the leaping
> and they will judge
> and they will blame.

Their "many bitter words," moreover, are excluded from the scope of my poem, which has but sixty words, and those courtly. Blocked and boxed, it is all there, stabilized in one inviolate frame of rhymed and measured words, and the title fixes our minds on a noun: The Fish. It contains no fewer than eight verb forms, all of them frequentative, designating what goes on and on, as permanent in issueless activity as was, in those years, the poet's pursuit of Maud Gonne.

Beneath such a poem runs an Irish feel for the aspective of which Yeats may not have been conscious. And shaping the poem's sense of what it is about is an Irish genre he knew very well, the Curse.

> May none of their race survive,
>   May God destroy them all,
> Each curse of the psalms in the holy books
>   Of the prophets on them fall.
>   Amen
> Blight skull, and ear, and skin,
>   And hearing, and voice, and sight,
> Amen! before the year be out,
>   Blight, son of the Virgin, blight.
>   Amen!

That version from a nineteenth-century original is by his friend Douglas Hyde. And here is the folk muse in the genre:

> . . . May every buck flea* from here to Bray
>   Jump through the bed that he lies on,
> And by some mistake may he shortly take
>   A flowing pint of poison. . . .

And James Stephens:

> May she marry a ghost and bear him a kitten, and may
> The High King of Glory permit her to get the mange.

For the bards of old were retained to do two main things, praise the king's friends, curse the king's enemies, and if they knew their business their curses were efficacious; there are tales of rats rhymed to death. When the bard Senchan Torpest spoke quatrains against rodents who'd eaten his

*Say "flay."

dinner, ten of them dropped dead from the rafters of the house. That was about A.D. 600, in King Guaire's palace in Gort, near Coole where Yeats did much work.* In some moods Yeats thought the curse the only honest Irish genre:

> . . . All that was sung,
> All that was said in Ireland is a lie
> Bred out of the contagion of the throng,
> Saving the rhyme rats hear before they die.

Now if a curse is efficacious, like a gunshot, it is also aspective, like a gargoyle. On Paris churches sinners turned to stone must discharge waste water from church roofs through their open mouths for ever, and likewise as long as there are people to read or hear a fine elaborate curse it holds the victim contorted in its torments.

> May the devil grip the whey-faced slut by the hair,
> And beat bad manners out of her skin for a year.

—As he does, he still does.

Yeats was often closest to the traditions of Irish when he was least ostentatious about trying to be: when he was doing homage to the wavering unemphatic sound its speakers make, or permitting a bardic convention to configure like a skull some fetching rhetorical skin of his contrivance. That is his Irishness. Himself, he had the sense not to write in Kiltartan, save in the prose dialogue of several plays. There Lady Gregory was a necessary collaborator, since Yeats well understood his own powerlessness to write speeches that sounded like anyone but himself.

What made Yeats Yeats was not what made Shakespeare Shakespeare: he is most himself when he sounds like only himself. It is when he sounds like himself that dead bardic ancestors somehow speak through him. To recognize the Curse beneath "The Fish" is to gain new respect for—for what? For the tenacity of a genre? Perhaps rather for the inextinguishability of tutelary ghosts.

---

*My thanks to Mr. Terence Ross, who tracked these facts down to a place Yeats could have found them, the notes to *As You Like It* (Act III) in James Halliwell's 1856 edition of Shakespeare. That snapper-up of trifles could in turn have heard the story from a man who was much in Ireland, Spenser.

IRISH WORDS

... the continually more and less intermis-
understanding minds of the anticollaborators,
the as time went on as it will variously inflec-
ted, differently pronounced, otherwise spelled,
changeably meaning vocable scriptsigns.

Finnegans Wake

Irish spelling has been stumbling outsiders for centuries. Thus *Hamlet*, an improbable name as most will agree for any Dane, let alone a Prince of Denmark, becomes intelligible when we learn that it is the French form of *Amlethus*, which was what Saxo Grammaticus in his *Historica Danica* inherited from someone who had copied it out in Latin with his eye on *Amhlaoibh*, the Irish spelling of a decent Scandinavian name, *Olaf*. (In Ireland, Olafson, *Mac Amhlaoibh*, lingered as a surname: thus MacCauliffe and Macauley and even Cowley.) Since Ireland's was a literate culture when the Olafs and their crews first impinged on it yelling, it was natural for Viking names to enter Latin through an Irish door. And the Irish scribes had heard "Olaf" and said "owlayv," and then written by their usual system *Amhl* = owl, *ao* = ay, *(i)bh* = v. So *Amhlaoibh* and, ultimately, Hamlet.

They wrote *bh* for *v* because they were short of letters: only eighteen letters for an array of phonemes still more numerous if possible than those of English, where even twenty-six letters do not suffice. Why *mh* should also say *v* before a vowel but elsewhere *w* is a darker question than there is space here to illuminate, but it does, and *aoi*—more than a diphthong, a tripthong—is something close to the vowel in "weigh" (and pray ponder

82

the *gh* in "weigh" before casting stones), so by a process perfectly logical to an Irish scribe *Caoimhghin* tells you to say "kayv(y)in,"* anglicized "Kevin." Likewise Ó hAonghusa is more or less Hennessey, and Ó Fionnmhacá is Finucane, and Mag Aonghusa has long since become (M')Guinness. You've begun to guess that *Samhain*, the old autumn festival Yeats felt the Abbey's fall season commemorated, sounds like anything but "Sam-hane." Right. You'd come close with "Saw-wen."

The reverse has occurred also. Dublin district and street names since the revolution have all been posted in Irish, and whereas *Stighlorcain* does but undo the absurdity whereby *(s)tigh*, the church, of St. Lawrence, *Lorcain*, became anglicized as "Stillorgan," *Cnoc na fuiseoigh* (Hill of the Lark) performs an absurdity of its own, turning Larkhill near Dublin into mock-Irish: "Larkhill" had nothing to do with larks but was a misunderstanding of *Lár Coille*, Center of the Wood. Like the kudzu-weed in Mississippi the orthography obliterates what it cannot absorb, but obliteration is seldom necessary since the underlying language is rife with enzymes to disassemble and reconstitute foreign bodies.

Century by century borrowed words—from Scandinavian, from Church Latin, even from English—have been absorbed with barely a noticeable trace. Latin *devotus*, "devout," became *devóideach*, which looks Irish but still sounds Latin; whereupon a fake-Irish etymology was fitted to it, the elements *deagh* (good) and *móid* (vow) being inserted to yield *deaghmhói-deach* which sounds nearly the same as before but proclaims that its roots are Hibernian and moral at that: "good vow," "devout."

A word obtruding a fake etymology, that is like *Finnegans Wake*, where *fadograph* pretends to tell us that photographs are so named because they fade (English) or else because *fadó* means "long ago" (Irish); never mind any talk about *photos* (Greek for "light"). The language Joyce devised for his last book is like Irish in its capacity for assimilating anything at all, likewise for being open to infinite misinterpretation. ("Soft morning, sor," said Paddy, knowing what his landlord did not, that *sor* means "louse.") As for devising a language sure to addle the zealous and defeat the casual, Joyce was free to reflect when he was first doing it in the mid-1920's that the government of *Saorstát Éireann* was doing pretty much the same thing, renaming for instance Kingstown *Dún Laoghaire* (*Dún* = "fort," *Laoghaire*, a name they'd not mind you connecting with the High King in St. Patrick's

---

*I take this transcription, like much of the lore hereabouts, from Brendan O Hehir. His *(y)*, standing for Irish *gh*, says to make "a roughened *y* deep in the throat," which you'll not want to risk in the absence of a teacher.

time), and permitting visitors to discover by trial and error that to get there you must know to say "Dunleary." They had the excuse of restoring the place's old name, and the satisfaction of strewing stumbles before Sassenach tongues.

Elsewhere the old names are beside the point. The bus for Dolphin's Barn says *Carnán* because nobody knows how Dolphin's Barn got named. *Cáirn Uí Donnchadh*, Donnchadh's Cairn, was implausibly suggested, and being too long for the bus signs this academicism got shortened to *Donnchadh carnán*, then just to *Carnán*.

The opening conventions of *Finnegans Wake* are topographical, with a "we" that is the "we" of guidebooks, and we are touring a place of perpetual misunderstanding. We may overhear something seemingly about cakes (bannocks), and not understand that "the bannocks of Gort and Morya and Bri Head and Puddyrick, your Loudship" was not a recommendation of the lovely cakes (bannocks) of four places including Bray Head but the blessing (*beannacht*) of God and Mary and Bridget and Patrick. On the other hand an Irish dictionary seems called for by "mhuith peisth mhuise as fearra bheura miurre hriosmas" but gives no help, whereas if someone tells us how to pronounce these "words" by Irish convention—"wit pesht wishi as fare vére mwiri hrismos"—our ears may catch "With best wishes for a very merry Christmas." We may soon feel like echoing the tonguetied Jute: "Boildoyle and rawhoney on me when I can beuraly forsstand a weird from sturk to finnic in such a patwhat as your rutterdamrotter." This permits the supposition that Baldoyle and Raheny, Dublin districts, have something to do with oil and honey, and also says that ears attuned to *Beurla* (foreign talk) can understand Pat's what-is-it (patwhat, *patois*) no more than barely.

Natives can sometimes beuraly forsstand a weird either. "Myles na gCopaleen,"[*] whose column in *The Irish Times* was as frequently in Irish as in English in the early 1940's, would occasionally vex his *Gaedhealach* following with passages like:

TAIDHGHIN: Thí bhas tócuing abamht boots, Sur.
SUR THARBHAIGH: Iú cean téil dat tú de Diuds. Éabharaighbodaigh thiar ios undar airést. Aigh bhil títs iú tú bí dioslógheal. Cbhuic meairts!

—which is English spelled by Irish rules, and says,

*Also alias "Flann O'Brien," and known to his Civil Service bosses as Brian O'Nolan. "gCopaleen" tells you to say "Gopaleen," the *gC* marking an inflection called eclipsis whereby only the first consonant is pronounced. Joyce plays with eclipsis here and there: "What a mnice old mness it all mnakes!" (*FW*19) says "What a mice old mess it all makes." As it does, especially as *n* is not an eclipsible letter.

TEAGUE: They was talking about boots, Sir.

SIR HARVEY: You can tell that to the judge. Everybody here is under arrest. I
  will teach you to be disloyal. Quick march!

His Irish readers would have grinned knowingly too at the *bod* in "Éabharaighbodaigh," which means "penis"; also at *bodaigh*, the plural of *bodach*,
"prick." The paper they were grinning over is the staidest in the country.
"O'Brien"/O'Nolan, an old hand in the bureaucracy, was indulging what
may be an unexamined genre, Civil Service Humor. A petit, mildmannered
priest in the government offices (by law, bilingual) was made to blush daily
at the sound of his name, Frederick Doyle, being pronounced by co-workers
as its Irish homophone, *Fear dorcha an dúil*, The Dark Man of Desire.

W. B. Yeats, as external to these wonders as most of us, was not above
inventing the name Ribh, which he thought looked Irish and presumably
meant us to pronounce Reeve, and he was certainly willing to put upon his
page, in his poem "At the Abbey Theatre," the line

> Dear Craoibhin Aoibhin, look into our case

without giving us a hint at all about what sounds to make (krayvin eevin).*
He wanted, certainly, in his early poems the glamorous look on the page of
Irish names, but was perpetually uncertain how to spell them.

"I copied at times someone's perhaps fanciful phonetic spelling, and at
times the ancient spelling as I found it in some literal translation, pronouncing the words always as they were spelt." "Perhaps fanciful" implies that as
little knowledge exists as the little that amateurs possess, and "as they were
spelt" would make *Amlaoibh* say neither "Olaf" nor even "Amlethus" but
"Am-loyb." If Yeats cannot have been that innocent then he is assuming
that innocent a reader. "I do not suppose I would have defended this system
at any time, but I do not yet know what system to adopt. . . . If I ever learn
the old pronunciation I will revise all these poems." So he wrote in 1895,
and the note stood, with revisions, as late as 1929.

The poems were never overhauled as promised, though in 1933 he did
commence, he said, to adopt what he called "Lady Gregory's spelling."
Having died the year previously, she could not blush. Yeats in his prose
always tended to make a mare's nest look Euclidean, and it is misleading to
affirm anything systematic of his waverings between Usheen and Oisin,

---

*His annotators do no better, telling us merely that *an Craoibhin Aoibhin* was Douglas Hyde's pen-
name and means "little flowering branch." Anybody who knows how to pronounce the line knows
that already.

Almhuin and Allen, Conchubar and Conhor and Conor, not to mention disasters like Clooth-na-Bare where he fiddled a little with hyphens without touching on the root difficulty, that in attempting to anglicize *Cailleach Béara* (the Hag of Beare) he'd made a thing with no discernible meaning.

In particular it is difficult to feel certain what sounds he wanted us to utter. Thus "Niam" in the 1889 *Wanderings of Oisin* seems to have been picked up from the "Niamh" of a printed page, perhaps even from an old-style "Niaṁ" with a dotted *m*, and pronounced as if it were English. (We have no way to be quite sure of this, since he never let the word fall in a rhyming position.) By the time of the 1895 *Poems* he's been told about *mh* = *v*, and changes "Niam" to "Neave." "Oisin" at the same time becomes "Usheen," and a reader in London would now in both cases be likely to say something pretty nearly correct by the lights of the Royal Irish Academy. But in the 1899 reprint of *Poems* "Oisin" and "Niam" are back, to show us he's over being cowed by scholarship. Thereafter "Neave" never recurs. In reprint after reprint usage wavers between "Niam" and "Niamh," from which it seems safe to infer that Yeats had reverted to hearing the word as "Nee-am" and was willing to regard the terminal *h* as Celtic decoration. Between "Oisin" and "Usheen" he continued to oscillate on a less evident principle. "Usheen" appears as late as 1929, and we may guess that although "Usheen" was what he said,* he was unwilling to give up "Oisin"'s eye-rhyme with Macpherson's "Ossian." "Oisin" is the final form, in what his death just after approving it enables his publishers to call the Definitive Edition.

His susceptibility to high-sounding words was enhanced by a visit to Stratford after which he steeped himself in Elizabethan history-plays. That was 1901, the same year Lady Gregory was working on *Cuchulain of Muirthemne*, and blood newly shaken with onomastical splendors—

> Is it not brave to be a King, Techelles!
> Usumcasane and Theridamas,
> Is it not passing brave to be a King
> And ride in triumph through Persepolis?

—was unlikely to resist "Muirthemne," a glowing word. Yeats was soon writing his royal tragedy, *On Baile's Strand*, and in 1904, two days after

---

*A manuscript from the time of the change to "Usheen" (between 1889 and 1895) at least once spells "Osheen," as it were O'Sheen, and another time "Ussheen." An 1886 draft of "Oisin Part I" almost consistently uses "Oison." [Information from Prof. George Bornstein.] But the spelling of the man whose handwritten "distains" (for "disdains") crept into the first printing of "Byzantium" was atrocious in any language, and we'd best stay content with a gross distinction between his "Oisin" and "Usheen" tendencies.

Christmas, George Roberts in the robes of Concobar designed by Annie Horniman herself declaimed before the Abbey Theatre's very first audience the following lines:

> I have called you hither, Kings of Ullad, and Kings
> Of Muirthemne and Connall Muirthemne,
> And tributary Kings, for now there is peace—
> It's time to build up Emain that was burned. . . .

If Irish speakers heard this there were shudders. Though "Muirthemne," now the plain of Louth on the seacoast sixty miles north of Dublin, is ambiguous of pronunciation like many place-names, no one disagrees about where the stress goes: in the middle. "Muir-<u>them</u>-ne" will get you by, "Muir-<u>hev</u>-na" for extra credit. But Yeats's meter forced Roberts to distribute the accents as in "<u>Mick</u>-ey-<u>Mouse</u>." Time's curtain has fallen on the ensuing remonstrances; but in his 1905 rewriting of the play Yeats avoided entirely a word he'd used six times.

We can be pretty sure how he pronounced it himself, since in "Baile and Aillinn" (1903) he was so incautious as to place it in a rhyming position. Its stresses are <u>Muir</u>-them-<u>ne</u> and it rhymes with "happily." He did not revise this line, which would not be declaimed at the Abbey. Dublin's know-it-all playgoers were one thing; readers of the silent page, most of them foreign, could share the dream of words sounding the way they looked.

An intricate instance is the old king's name which in 1889 Yeats spelled "Conor" and by 1895 had dressed up slightly as "Conhor":*

> And the names of the demons whose hammers made armour
> for Conhor of old.

"Conhor," two syllables, the second *o* long, is someone's effort to improve on the more commonplace "Conor" by getting a kind of guttural into it; and why was that?

We begin with something Yeats knew (an 1895 note assures us so), that we are dealing with the same name that is often spelled "Conchubar," better still "Conchobhar." (It means "Hound-lover."†) If you are now prompted to recognize *bh* = *v* and say <u>Con</u>-chov-er and if you've also kept all vowels short and the stress up front you are fairly close to the way the name would

---

*I paraphrase and condense what follows from a letter of John V. Kelleher's.
†If like many scholars you derive it from *Con*, "hound." But a dictionary of Irish names gives "high will" or "high desire," as a man named Conor was quick to point out to me.

have sounded in the ears of the Old Irish scribes who first wrote it down. (Old Irish is dated A.D. 750–900; do not suppose that you know what King Conchobhar called himself if he existed, since that was a thousand years earlier.)

But by Yeats's time and ours, talkers fluent in "Back-of-the-mouth" had squeezed out half a syllable or so, nearly dropping the word's first vowel and contracting its middle syllable to a kind of cough. So in the West, where Lady Gregory and his other mentors heard Irish, folk said (we'll write X for the guttural) something like *K'nX-oor*. Toward the north the *K'n* sound became *K'r* and they said K'rX-<u>ore</u>, second syllable accented, a sound somehow picked up in the south by Michael Banim of Kilkenny, whose story "Crohore of the Bill-hook" (1825) Yeats knew without likely knowing that "Crohore" hid "Conchobhar."

The *h* in Banim's "Crohore" is an effort to acknowledge the guttural, and likewise the sound of *K'nX-oor* was what prompted someone to fix up "Conor" by writing "Conhor," the compromise spelling Yeats inserted into the 1895 *Wanderings of Usheen*. "Conhor" rode out the reprintings till 1933, when Yeats in a fit of exoticism made the change to "Conchubar." By then he seems to have decided either that the great name ought to have three syllables as in the old days or that anyway his readers would think it had, even if, heaven help them, they said Con-chew-bar. He accordingly re-worded the line:

> And the name of the demon whose hammer made Conchubar's
> sword-blade of old.

So it stands to this day, in *The Wanderings of Oisin*, part III, line 80, an entrapment for innocent eyes. Yet for forty-four years he'd had the King's name sounding a little more right, only looking a little less fancy.

Yeats will likely often have been pulled three ways: toward (1) the erroneous anglophone sounds he had heard in his mind when he looked at Irish words as a very young man; toward (2) authentic Irish sounds Augusta Gregory and Douglas Hyde urged on his attention; toward (3) a compromise which should offer non-Irish readers (his principal audience) both the sound of (1) and the look of (2): hence Niamh, pronounced Niam, not Neave. One would like to know what he *said* when he read "Niamh," "Oisin," "Aedh," "Ribh" aloud, just as one would like to know whether, when as often he placed "wind" in a rhyming position, he pronounced it "win'd" or "wined."

But we have only a few minutes of his recorded voice, in no case coinciding with a test word. They will tell you in Dublin how a BBC engineer charged with weeding out the archive for wartime storage smashed discs left and right but saved "Innisfree" because he'd heard of it. The truth seems less dramatic. Such recordings as there were disappeared along the way because there seemed no obvious reason to keep them, and there were never many to begin with; Yeats's days at the BBC were the days before tape; acetate discs were costly and troublesome and took up room; his voice was allowed, like most voices, like Vergil's in the ear of Dante, to vanish on the air.

YOUNG YEATS

... Unvisited by tempest or by sun,
Immortal ladies tread the ground
Dizzy with harmonious sound. ...

"Colonus' Praise"

W. B. Yeats, George Moore thought, did not look sufficiently at landscape; all the stranger, then, that Moore himself does not describe the tunnel of shade and greenery that conducts to Coole Park: a prolonged astonishing overarching of great trees. Moore's mind is not on these but on not falling off his bicycle. He has come to collaborate with Yeats on a play. It is 1899 or thereabouts.

Lady Gregory, fiftyish, was thought to have kidnapped Yeats a couple of years previously, and at Coole he was rumored to be a permanent guest, like Tannhäuser under the mountain. Carpets muffled the corridor outside his door; maidservants tiptoed along it to bring him beef tea. Eight lines was a good morning's work, and when not working he ate a great deal. He was struggling with something he called *The Shadowy Waters,* perhaps a play, perhaps a poem, perhaps rhymed, perhaps not: its conception was not less vague in reality than in the blandly malicious account George Moore gives us in *Ave,* where the fancies of seven years are said to have accumulated on "the pirate ship ranging the Shadowy Waters, ... laden to the gunnel with Formorians, beaked and unbeaked, spirits of Good and Evil of various repute," who "accompanied a metaphysical pirate of ancient Ireland cruising in the unknown waters of the North Sea in search of some ultimate kingdom."

And now the two of them envision a play, why God knows, save that Moore (born in west Ireland, long an adopted Parisian and Londoner) feels summoned by an Irish vocation. He understands the stage too, better than Yeats.

Collaboration is thinkable because in Moore's judgment Yeats, though still a marvel of "style," has ceased to create; the work for which he will be remembered is done. (Yeats nearly came to think so himself. So did AE, who told Moore, "We go to see him as we go to see the tomb of Shakespeare.")

That work was but 288 pages, the contents of *Poems (1895)*. This went on being reprinted (with revisions) as late as 1929, and it contained what most readers persisted in thinking of when they thought of Yeats: one unread "epical" narrative, *The Wanderings of Oisin;* two dramatic efforts, *The Countess Cathleen* and *The Land of Heart's Desire;* most prizeworthy, some forty lyrics including "Innisfree": the ones we now find in the big *Collected Poems* under the headings "Crossways" and "The Rose."*

Epical, dramatical, lyrical. On 19 May 1893, Yeats had told the National Literary Society (a Mr. George Casey in the chair) that a literature grew steadily like a tree by "a constant sub-division of moods and emotions": and for each nation and each race its *own* tree, a blossomer invariably growing by the same pattern and always manifesting three successive stages. These were: "First, the period of narrative poetry, the epic and ballad period; next the dramatic period; and after that the period of lyric poetry."

So in Greece behold first Homer, next Aeschylus and Sophocles, finally "the lyric poets, who are known to us through the Greek anthology"; likewise in England first Chaucer and Malory, then Shakespeare, then "that lyrical outburst of which Byron, Shelley and Keats were the most characteristic writers." And in Ireland—? In Ireland "We are still in our epic or ballad period."

Epic was simple stuff: racial and national, like the patriotic ballads of the 1840's. Drama next subdivided such themes into characters. Then Lyric analyzed characters into moods. At the inception of a lyric age, "The great personages fell like immense globes of glass, and scattered into a thousand iridescent fragments." (Yeats was speaking nineteen months after the death of Parnell.) Lyric poets consequently "must express every phase of human

---

*Yeats never issued volumes with these names. They were an 1895 expedient for separating what he regarded as two periods, what he'd done before age twenty-four and what he'd done after: in short, before and after Maud Gonne entered his life.

consciousness no matter how subtle, how vague, how impalpable," and their poetry, emerged from "the general tide of life," becomes "a mysterious cult as it were, an almost secret religion made by the few for the few." Ah, that explains something.

The Rev. J. F. Hogan proposed a vote of thanks, inviting those present to "pay all possible honour to those who were distinguished in literature in Ireland in the past, especially to those who were faithful to the country (applause)." The proceedings then terminated, no one having said how sketchy was the literary history proposed. That is what George Moore would have said if he had been there, but this was six years before Moore felt the call to return to Ireland and help out with its destiny: arriving, it will be noticed, just in time to give the Dramatic period an aiding shove.

Sappho and Alkman, for one thing, made songs long before Aeschylus made plays, and for subtleties of human consciousness you'd look in Sappho before the Greek Anthology. So much for subtle Lyric near the end of time. But what Yeats was up to is not served by straightforward history. Address-ing one of the societies he'd helped found ("The Great Founder," Sean O'Casey was to call him), he needed to (1) disencumber Irish urgency from the models patriots were advocating; (2) rationalize his own progression, epical *Oisin* (1889), dramatic *Kathleen* (1892), and the satellite lyrics of the *Kathleen* volume: in this way justify his present lyrical-"symbolist" phase as something sanctioned by organic history; finally (3) give reassurance to anyone who might dream that Ireland's imaginative future was before it, but England's terminated. There's no tidy way to do all that at once, espe-cially if you reflect that the Yeatsian lyric of the Mauve Decade is only something for which the tree is ripe if it's the English tree you're looking at, not the Irish. Time was running out in England; it was in the last stage. But time was beginning in Ireland. It would take the interlocked cones of *A Vision,* three decades and more in the future, to show how a man could exist in two cycles at once, living one another's death, dying one another's life.

That is really what *A Vision* is about, the experience of living in two tempo-ral processes at once. Its complications are like those of Ptolemaic astron-omy, which out of fidelity to data that seemed intractable had multiplied eccentric and tilted wheels till the heavens clanked. What was clear to Yeats in 1892, when he delivered the epic-dramatic-lyric lecture, was his commit-ment to both an English tradition, dying, and an Irish one, seemingly powerless to get born save amid distressing racket from the patriots. The patriots refused to understand that if one of an Anglo-Irish poet's historical burdens was the history of Ireland, another was the history of the English language, implicit in every use of every word. There was no disowning Spenser, Marlowe, Shakespeare, Milton, Shelley, Keats. (If today John Montague and Seamus Heaney disregard them, that is because they can profit from Modernism's disengagements, and Montague especially from *American* Modernism.)

A thing not clear to Yeats at all was the way his sense of poetic tradition, being English, pertained wholly to *writing*, hence to *readers*. Introspection, which was what he meant by "lyric," was the mauve flower of a pen-and-paper culture after many centuries of which a Shelley could write "I arise from dreams of thee" and be talking to no one at all, needed have no one in mind at all, might be no more than conjuring up a mood with the help of first- and second-person pronouns. That is the act of a man accustomed, like most writers, to manipulating language while all alone.

But the mind of Ireland is held by the realities of talk, the most notable reality of which is the presence of others. If you were to say "I arise from dreams of thee" when there was no "thee" and you were not in your night-clothes, the chief thing you'd do is let people know you were daft.

There's a story—Yeats tells it in "The Tower"—of how the blind bard Raftery celebrated Mary Hynes so effectively that men "maddened by those rhymes" rushed off to behold her (one got drowned in a bog). They understood that there *was* a Mary Hynes, by whose perfections Raftery's praises were checkable: a fact you'd not mistake even today or even from Douglas Hyde's translation, though it follows the music for but a single stanza before lapsing into a crib.

> Going to Mass of me, God was gracious,
> The day came rainy and the wind did blow,
> And near Kiltartan I met a maiden
> Whose love enslaved me and left me low.
> I spoke to her gently, the courteous maiden,
> And gently and gaily she anwered so:
> "Come, Raftery, with me, and let me take you
> To Ballylee, where I have to go." . . .

That has the feel of something happening. But if you read in the Yeats of 1892,

> A girl arose that had red mournful lips
> And seemed the greatness of the world in tears,

not even assurances about Maud Gonne would persuade you that you ought to see for yourself. "Arose," for one thing, pertains to a world of books; not a girl getting for instance out of a chair, but a phenomenon like the rise of pre-Raphaelitism. Literary convention shaped the diction of those lines, and Maud herself (to her chagrin) entered literary convention in entering Yeats's life.

Though his audience that night included people who were notable for the reading they did—AE, Dr. Sigerson who translated Gaelic poetry, his daughter Dora Sigerson who wrote poems, the editor of *United Ireland* and the editor of *Irish Theosophist*—Yeats had not the terminology, nor they the sophistication, to shake their notions of literature free from literacy: to reflect, as Professor Havelock teaches us to do, on the measure of cultural literacy: the size of the reading public within the total population, where "reading public" pertains not at all to the number who can read, indeed read easily— by that standard urban Ireland is a modern literate state like Germany— but to the number whose habit is to turn to print for information and opinion.

In Ireland they'd rather turn for these to one another; they prefer the way you'll hear stories *told* to the way the O'Connors, the O'Faolains or the Joyces wrote them down; and the poetry they care for is the kind men keep at hand for reciting: hence the durability of marching songs from 1848, and the reduction of even Yeats to a few sturdy lines like "A terrible beauty is born."

So writing and reading, however fluently practiced, remain exceptional acts. We are told that when James Joyce's father wrote a letter all noise had to cease in the house and if possible in the street outside. As for reading, I have handed a page to a man so far from illiterate he made his living setting type, and seen him step behind a door to glance at it, quite as though it was not decent to be reading in somebody's presence. These are marks of some- thing not unlike a pre-literate consciousness. Yeats was more right than he knew in placing it at the epical stage, and Joyce obliquely right in rhyming the Dublin he knew with Homer's Greece.

The part of his mind that obscurely sensed all this was turning Yeats toward words living voices might speak. Plays, therefore.

Not seeing any choice when very young, Yeats had set out to be a late-Victorian English poet; we've noticed how "The Song of the Happy Shep- herd," published when he was twenty, accretes details from books by

Spenser, Marlowe, Milton, Keats: the High Romantic tradition as then defined.

Other details pertain to the 1880's. "O, sick children of the world" evokes that wellspring of Victorian pathos the Children's Hospital, and "the wandering earth" draws the etymology of "planet" (*planetes*, wandering) from such a book of popular astronomy as marked the time's most confident ventures in adult education. Leopold Bloom, who had Sir Robert Ball's *Story of the Heavens* on his shelf, might have been the man to appreciate ". . . dishevelled wandering stars . . ." in the song his guest Stephen Dedalus loved to sing; that phrase, which Yeats set down before 1892, collects from some book such as Ball's not only *planetes* but also the "dishevelled" star called "comet" (*aster kometes*, long-haired star).

"Words alone are certain good," sings the Happy Shepherd, since Truth, being "grey," inheres in a "painted toy" (made in Germany) sick children might play with: a wheel kept spinning by a thumb-driven plunger, a little tin wheel on which seven painted colors blur before your eyes into grey as Newton prescribed. That was Truth. Color is but a local event in the eye. Fuse the "objective" colors, and it vanishes.

But, the eye once undeceived, we still have the word "color," which stays behind in the language. Red, orange, yellow, blue, are not to be unsaid; no Newton can eradicate their "certain good." (Yeats decades later would elevate the Irish Berkeley, who held that things *are* as they seem; so if saying is faithful to seeming, things are as they are said.)

Poetry, meanwhile:

> Where are now the warring kings,
> Word be-mockers? . . .
> An idle word is now their glory,
> By the stammering schoolboy said,
> Reading some entangled story. . . .

The perdurability of the Word is a cliché out of Shakespeare's sonnets, reaffirmed recently by Paul Verlaine (*Le buste / survite à la cité*). The lines remember too Yeats's time in the Erasmus Smith High School, on Harcourt Street in Dublin (which he entered in the fall of 1881, the year after Leopold Bloom left it to take up the family business of peddling; thus the two most celebrated alumni never met). "Entangled story" was originally "the verse of Attic story," the schoolboy "stammering" because called on to translate. (At Erasmus Smith Willie "held his own" in classics, though he did best, he'd not have had us know, in science.)

His adolescent copiousness astonishes. By age nineteen he had written *The Island of Statues*: long, symbolical, Shelleyan. This "Arcadian Faery Tale" of 828 rhyming lines was headed by a list of *Dramatis Personae*:

> Naschina, ... *Shepherdess.*
> Colin, ... *Shepherd.*
> Thernot, ... *Shepherd.*
> Almintor, ... *A Hunter.*
> Antonio, ... *His Page.*
> Enchantress of the Island.
> *And a company of the Sleepers of the Isle.*

He found Colin and Thernot (Thenot), musical swains, in *The Shepherd's Calendar*, the eighth eclogue of which also prompted their duel of song (I.1,1–100); he'd been looking too at Crashaw's "Music's Duel," which in 1881 Coventry Patmore called "the most wonderful piece of wordcraft ever done." His place is the woods of Arcady, his time the time before their antique joy was over, his plot about enchantment and release from enchantment, bringing to life sleepers that fell silent before Dido was dust. As they resume their lives, the shepherd girl who freed them turns immortal, and stands on the island with them in the moon's light "shadowless." Immortal ladies, all his life Yeats would dream of immortal ladies: Oisin's Niamh, the Guardian of the Well, the woman Homer sung. Of wonderful islands too; his only poem that everybody knows is about an island. This first time he scatters rhymes headlong, "a poisèd lily," "a cellar chilly," a gifted schoolboy's shards of sparkling glass.

Yet how gifted! Whatever we make of the plan, he completed it, his joy in the pulse, in the rhymes, in the very inversions refracted everywhere.

> Oh, more dark thy gleaming hair is
> Than the peeping pansy's face

—there is pleasure, not desperation, in that backward syntax. Parts are better than parts of *Endymion*, and four 1885 issues of the *Dublin University Review* contained proof that co-linguists of the aging Tennyson might yet once more own a poet.

The man who converted Yeats to a better ambition than being an English poet was John O'Leary, the old Fenian who took, as Yeats later thought, "Romantic Ireland" with him to the grave. O'Leary, who had been imprisoned in 1865 for the non-violent crime of publishing a newspaper, did not forbid violence but warned against such futile violence as inflamed the wits of Fenian dynamiters. That was what allowed W.B.Y. to honor him as a fellow pacifist whose injunction about "things that a man must not do to save a nation" pointed patriots toward the high path of stoical nobility.

When Yeats met him in 1885 (at age twenty), O'Leary had just finished a twenty-year sentence, five in jail, fifteen in exile. At fifty-five he displayed a head "worthy of a Roman coin," one of a lifetime's five "beautiful lofty things" Yeats would feel moved to enumerate a half-century later. And in the youth who had been alive just a few months longer than he himself had spent beneath harsh law, O'Leary recognized (and said so) "genius." He introduced Yeats to the ravening emotions of Ireland, and to books unread in England. He'd brought back with him from Paris trunkloads of books.

Yeats read them avidly. He had spent most of his life in London, never dreaming of so much literary passion rooted in the country of his birth. A year later readers of *The Irish Fireside* encountered amid its lore on cooking and sewing the first published prose of William Butler Yeats: "The Poetry of Sir Samuel Ferguson." It began as one would wish, by reprinting almost the whole of the magical "Fairy Thorn," that poem utterly inconceivable within the comparatively Augustan tradition of the English lyric. Adieu, suddenly, Spenser, Crashaw. Welcome Ireland. And O'Leary symmetrically brackets Yeats's prose career; it was in his last published essay (1938) that he divulged how when Kegan Paul, Trench & Co., London, published five hundred copies of *The Wanderings of Oisin* in 1889, they required advance subscribers and John O'Leary found most of them.

Had the books in O'Leary's trunks been able to disclose more poets like Samuel Ferguson at his rare best, more poems like "The Fairy Thorn," the rest of the story would be simpler. But the Anglo-Irish tradition entailed burdens as well as opportunities, including as it did the matter of Young Ireland, some fifty years past. That was what Yeats was dismissing, that night in 1893, as Ireland's primitive or epic stage: his cunning way of including the Young Ireland poets in literary history just sufficiently to get rid of them.

Young Ireland was a cluster of patriots whose mission in a paper called *The Nation* had been to smite Britain hip and thigh. Their energumen was Thomas Davis (1814–1845), to whose verses feet would be stamping as late as the *Playboy* riots:

> But—hark!—some voice like thunder spake
> *"The West's awake, the West's awake"*—
> 'Sing oh! hurra! let England quake,
> We'll watch till death for Erin's sake!"

Never mind that the rhetoric has been to school to Macaulay; that was the way for Irish poets to go, and no blather about the bee-loud glade.

> . . . Lead him to fight for native land,
>   His is no courage cold and wary;
> The troops live not on earth would stand
>   The headlong Charge of Tipperary!
> . . . Let Britain brag her motley rag;
>   We'll lift the Green more proud and airy;—
> Be mine the lot to bear that flag,
>   And head the Men of Tipperary! . . .

And here he is again if you can stand it:

> We hate the Saxon and the Dane,
>   We hate the Norman men—
> We cursed their greed for blood and gain,
>   We curse them now again.
> Yet start not, Irish born man
>   If you're to Ireland true,
> We hate not blood, nor creed, nor clan—
>   We have no curse for you.

This says that as long as you got yourself *born* in Ireland and manifest the right allegiances, we of the chanting mob'll not probe your ethnicity. (The Yeatses were of British mercantile stock, come to Ireland just before the start of the eighteenth century.)

Though Thomas Davis was long dead (scarlatina, age thirty-one), *The Nation* survived until 1892, and one of its founders, Sir Charles Gavan Duffy, was around, amazingly, until 1903. Duffy could play the Seniority card, also, with authority, the Patriotic card, and a tussle with him, over a New Irish Library of cheap books to improve Irish consciousness, was one of the few Yeats lost. Duffy seized control of the series and commenced a resuscitation of Young Ireland, beginning with a pamphlet by Davis which sold "ten thousand copies before anybody found time to read it." It was full of particularities about the Parliament of 1689, and its chances of real popularity, Yeats thought, might have been greater on the planet Neptune, where it's so cold they'll read anything.

There seemed no escaping Young Ireland's incubus, unless by drawing attention (Yeats and Joyce did this separately) to its least typical bard, James Clarence Mangan (1803–1849), who on account of booze and opium and early death is conventionally called the Irish Poe.

> . . . O! the Erne shall run red
>   With redundance of blood,
> The earth shall rock beneath our tread,
>   And flames wrap hill and wood,
> And gun-peal, and slogan cry,
>   Wake many a glen serene,
> Ere you shall fade, ere you shall die,
>   My Dark Rosaleen!
>   My own Rosaleen!
> The Judgement Hour must first be nigh,
> Ere you can fade, ere you can die,
>   My dark Rosaleen!

This is "Róisín Dubh," the dark rose, *aliter* Cathleen ni Houlihan, shapely as a swan, in time not wholly to be distinguished from the Secret Rose of William Butler Yeats. And note the fine "redundance," to which "abundance" is as close as most poets would have come; Yeats would learn that trick of the arresting abstraction: "the *ceremony* of innocence"; "*magnanimity* of light."

That poem, and among four of five other Mangan poems "O'Hussey's Ode to the Maguire"—

> . . . Though he were even a wolf, ranging the round green woods,
> Though he were even a pleasant salmon in the unchainable sea,
> Though he were a wild mountain eagle, he could scarce bear, he,
> This sharp, sore sleet, these howling floods. . . .

—display a break with taTUM taTUM iambic you'd attribute to absorption in Gaelic save that Mangan had no Gaelic and "translated" (from it and from several other tongues) out of cribs prepared by others.* Like Poe again, he thought to mystify provincials with the sham-exotic. But whatever the state of his Arabic or his German, to Gaelic he'd *listened*, that's clear.

---

*The crib from which he worked up the "Dark Rosaleen" stanza would have looked something like this: "The Erne shall be in strong flood, the hills shall be torn down, and the sea shall have red waves, and blood shall be spilled, and every mountain valley and every moor shall be on high, before you shall perish, my little black rose."

"Though he were a wild mountain eagle, he could scarce bear, he . . .": that fourfold internal rhyme on "he," that assonantal "scarce bear," that hovering unassignable rhythm: the author of "Innisfree" (1890) was attending.

But the instance of Mangan, a lesser Ferguson, indicates how tenuous was a usable native tradition for a poet with no Irish. Young Ireland and Thomas Davis were what Irish readers expected of a national bard. To further disconcert such readers, the case of Yeats presented a complication called Maud Gonne.

She belongs to his English inheritance, not his Irish: in his own terms, the "lyric," not the "epic." From Keats's Belle Dame sans Merci to Swinburne's Dolores, Lady of Pain, Romantic England had shaped and reshaped its dream of a heartless beauty, Siren, Lorelei, the burden of man's fate, whose eyen two wold slee you sodenly, but to possess whom was to possess a phantom. She persists as late as T. S. Eliot's early years, stands on the highest pavement of the stair, weaves, weaves the sunlight in her hair, and it is her smile we see vanish beneath caricature's mocking waters as her voice dismisses Prufrock, woeful knight, with "That is not what I meant at all."

Among Yeats's immediate precursors, the English pre-Raphaelites, for whom the poet's destiny was to live The Poet, life as well as imagination required a Maud Gonne: an Immortal Lady incarnate, such a "stunner" as Rossetti's Elizabeth Siddal in whose coffin poems were tempestuously inhumed only to have to be exhumed again—a macabre episode of spades and lanterns — or as Morris's Jane Burden, tall, prognathous, his "Guinevere."

But there was a complication, since Maud Gonne came to Yeats as part of his O'Leary legacy, and fancied herself in a different scenario entirely. Not hers to ornament a poet's hours; she was an Irish patriot, a woman with a cause like Young Ireland's, whom John O'Leary, spinning revolutionary webs, saw fit to put in touch with such eminent Irishmen domiciled outside Ireland as J. B. Yeats Sr., father of the young poet. Accordingly in London on 30 January 1889 she came to call on the Yeatses at 3 Blenheim Road, Bedford Park, and, said W.B.Y., "the troubling of my life began." After twenty-six years he drafted (but did not publish) an elaborate paragraph whose rituals might rise to the occasion:

I had never thought to see in a living woman so great beauty. It belonged to famous pictures, to poetry, to some legendary past. A complexion like the blossom of apples, and yet face and body had the beauty of lineaments which

Blake calls the highest beauty because it changes least from youth to age, and a stature so great that she seemed of a divine race. Her movements were worthy of her form, and I understood at last why the poet of antiquity, where we would but speak of face and form, sings, loving some lady, that she paces like a goddess. I remember nothing of her speech that day except that she vexed my father by praise of war, for she too was of the Romantic movement and found those incontrovertible Victorian reasons, that seemed to announce so prosperous a future, a little grey. As I look backward, it seems to me that she brought into my life in those days—for as yet I saw only what lay upon the surface—the middle of the tint, a sound as of a Burmese gong, an overpowering tumult that had yet many pleasant secondary notes.

Pictures, poetry, Blake, divinity; a sudden insight into a poet (he later said Vergil) by whom it is doubtful that Yeats was greatly worried in 1889; Victorian truth esteemed as but grey (". . . a painted toy"); the middle of the tint, a Burmese gong: a compendium, she, of aesthetic notes and qualities.

A model for that piece of writing is Walter Pater's 1869 homage to the Mona Lisa, the passage every aesthete had by heart, the one Yeats would one day arrange into cadenced lines to open *The Oxford Book of Modern Verse*. Pater's "presence . . . expressive of what in the ways of a thousand years men had come to desire," who is "older than the rocks among which she sits . . . and as Leda, was the mother of Helen of Troy, and, as Saint Anne, the mother of Mary," an eternal woman all of whose experience "has been to her but as the sound of lyres and flutes," exemplifies an odd but persistent mid-century node, where the notion of a *femme fatale* intersects occult themes of reincarnation. Pater's paragraph for instance seems akin to lines Swinburne wrote in 1860, whose speaker says she has been Helen, Cressida, Guenevere. The roots of that eerie conception, the composite eternal female of whom this or that exceptional woman may present but the fleshly mask, reach long fingers through the loam of the century. Joyce plays with it: Molly Bloom was once Penelope. Throughout *Ulysses* he is having sport with Yeats, one of his less likely models for Bloom, a dark-suited non-belonger—Yeats wore black and never entered pubs—with "a touch of the artist" about him. Among his first spoken words is a short exposition of how we may have "all lived before on the earth thousands of years ago or some other planet."

Yeats in 1889 was already an adept occultist, a man who took reincarnation seriously: hence one of the quick themes await in his mind for Miss Gonne's stirring: "the troubling of my life," indeed. She was twenty-three, he six months older. As for her preternatural height, we have a measurement: five feet ten inches.

Yeats's sister Lily, twenty-two, thought the apparition very la-di-da, smiling upon her "a sort of royal smile" she hated. Lily looked down as well as up, and noticed slippers!* The great lady and Willie had dinner in Belgravia the very next evening, her pet monkey making "little melancholy cries on the hearthrug." Lacking the shilling cabfare, he walked home.

O'Leary had briefed her well; she had read *The Island of Statues*, and gave Yeats pause by hating the triumphant Shepherdess, preferring the Enchantress of the island whose loss of power turns her into a dead green frog. *Active* power fascinated her. She wanted to talk about politics; she wanted a play in which she could stir Irish audiences. The one he promised became *The Countess Cathleen*. The one she eventually appeared in (3 April 1902) was *Cathleen ni Houlihan*, with consequences that troubled Yeats's mind for the rest of his life.

> (Did that play of mine send out
> Certain men the English shot?)

But in those first days, the days he never got over, she was the Immortal Lady of nineties poetic, the "Modern Beauty" his friend Arthur Symons celebrated:

> "I am the torch," she saith, "and what to me
> If the moth die of me? . . .
>
> .   .   .
>
> "I am Iseult, and Helen, I have seen
> Troy burn, and my most fondest knight lie dead;
> The world has been my mirror, Time has been
> My breath upon the glass. . . ."

How soon did he learn that "Maud" anglicizes the name of Queen Maeve? Soon Col. Tommy Gonne's English-born daughter was Helen, and Deirdre:

> Who dreamed that beauty passes like a dream?
> For those red lips, with all their mournful pride,
> Mournful that no new wonder may betide,
> Troy passed away in one high funeral gleam,
> And Usna's children died.

He was a lord of language, none living more gifted. She was all for results and haranguing meetings, and thought him tiresome save as he might be

---

*It is to Lily's amused eye we owe many such details. She recorded Willie "in the throes of another lyric" in the street, passers-by thinking him mentally afflicted; also a Chaplinesque encounter between Willie's fine new coat and some kitchen flypaper.

useful. He would even come to think her "an old bellows full of angry wind," but not soon. One day in 1891 they walked the cliff paths at Howth, high above the sea, the same place Molly told Poldy that yes she would, Yes, with a nannygoat looking on; and they gazed down on the seagulls always flying and W.B.Y. unlike Poldy had no satisfaction at all save the satisfaction of arranging his cry:

I would that we were, my beloved, white birds on the foam of the sea!

Enough. She was the theme of half his life. Most say that nothing ever came of it all; others say something did, as late as about 1909, but unfulfillingly. It is certain that she refused marriage with him again and again; certain too that the girl, Iseult, whom she introduced as her niece, was her natural daughter by a French politician named Millevoye. In 1903 she married a redheaded "drunken, vainglorious lout" named MacBride, Major John MacBride, Boer War veteran. It lasted two years. Long afterward the Nobel people were to certify their son Sean a man of peace. A squad's volley in 1916 knocked Major MacBride dead at the stake. Yeats proposed marriage once more to Maud (negative), in desperation to young Iseult (also negative). In 1917 Georgie Hyde-Lees ended his solitude: a half-cousin of Dorothy Shakespear's who had married Ezra Pound. Dorothy's mother Olivia, hostess, novelist, was the woman who'd moved in with Yeats a while in 1895 and solaced him when the torment of Maud had been at its most intense. Iseult? In 1920 she married an eighteen-year-old named Francis Stuart, later a novelist, who tells us in his *Black List, Section H* how he learned of *droit de seigneur* over his bride having been exercised by Ezra Pound. Enough.

He had met O'Leary at the Contemporary Club, a discussion group informally associated with Trinity. Men at the club ran the first journal to publish his verse: the new *Dublin University Review*. In its March 1885 issue his name was appended to this:

A man has a hope for heaven,
But soulless a faery dies,
As a leaf that is old, and withered and cold,
When the wint'ry vapours rise.

Soon shall our wings be stilled,
And our laughter over and done. . . .

Such bric-à-brac Yeats could toss off with his left hand while his right was engaged on what seemed to matter, *long* poems.

The Romantic Long Poem seems not to have been studied: the genre to which belong *Endymion, Hyperion, Alastor, The Triumph of Life, Prometheus Bound*: visionary narratives and plays not for players. They bear the genetic impress of *The Faerie Queene*, a narrative of which we cannot doubt that it has more on its mind than telling a story the way *Hero and Leander* ornately tells a story. Some parable seems intended of the mind's movements: by Romantic times, of the movement of a Poet's mind. Wordsworth, always miraculously literal, made the *Prelude*, longest of Romantic Long Poems, into an almost frank poet's autobiography. Blake exploded the genre into a political allegory inextricable from a poetic one: *America, The Book of Urizen, Jerusalem*.

It was just a few weeks before Maud Gonne commenced troubling his life that W. B. Yeats published his first real book of poetry, named *The Wanderings of Oisin* for its chief poem, his own contribution to Ireland's epical phase. What he thought a long poem was he told a correspondent disarmingly:

> There is a thicket between three roads, some distance from any of them, in the midst of Howth. I used to spend a great deal of time [there]. . . . The thicket gave me my first thought of what a long poem should be. I thought of it as a region into which one should wander from the cares of life. The characters were to be no more real than the shadows that people the Howth thicket. Their mission was to lessen the solitude without destroying its peace.

Oisin was also an effort to do something authentic with the title figure, "Ossian," of Macpherson's celebrated fabrication. Accordingly, Yeats undertook something quite un-Romantic: close work in a library from anti-quarian texts, perhaps in the British Museum or perhaps at home from journals O'Leary supplied. In the *Transactions of the Ossianic Society, for the Year 1856* he found "The Lay of Oisin on the Land of Youth," fifty pages translated by Brian O'Looney from an eighteenth-century poet named Michael Comyn. Other volumes of the society's *Transactions* contained the traditional dialogues between Oisin and St. Patrick. All these versions were in verse of a sort, and what he took from them he put into verse of an exceptional sort:

> Her eyes were soft as dewdrops hanging
> Upon the grass-blades' bending tips (I, 41–42)

was a transmutation of

> Her eyes, blue, clear, and cloudless,
> Like a dew drop on the top of the grass.

Yeats's story (we'll not labor the differences from Comyn's) entails an immortal hero, Oisin, a faery bride, Niamh, and three islands, on each of which they stay a hundred years. Yeats explained in an 1889 letter, "There are three incompatible things which man is always seeking—infinite feeling, infinite battle, infinite repose—hence the three islands." "Vain gaiety, vain battle, vain repose" was the way he put it in a poem decades later, a poem with the line "What can I but enumerate old themes?" For some themes of *Oisin* never left him. That certain human desires are incompatible was a ground note of his lifelong thought, and also one secret of his staying power, since the questions he rotated, being irreconcilable, could not be used up.

The story of the faery bride and the three islands he enclosed in another story: Oisin the old pagan justifying himself to the Saint. His justification is a simple one: pagan Ireland exhilarates, Christian does not. "On the flaming stones, without refuge, the limbs of the Fenians are tost," St. Patrick warns, and Oisin ends the poem by retorting,

> I will go to Caoilte, and Conan, and Bran, Sceolan, Lomair,
> And dwell in the house of the Fenians, be they in flames or at feast.

Caoilte and Conan were companions, Bran, Sceolan and Lomair were hounds. The Catholic Heaven has no provision for dogs. And he will go where they are because on earth he is immortal no longer, having broken the injunction of the faery bride by touching the soil of Ireland with his foot.

Yeats may have meant by this that dreams require guarding from the daylight, and old stories from any effort to discern their historical truth. But foot-on-the-ground, that was the contact from which, according to his thought of fifty years later, "Everything Antaeus-like grew strong": one more antinomy, since the verse of *Oisin*, in touch with nothing in particular save the strong rhetoric of Romantic dream, portended no future, whereas writing that touched ground in evanescent speech, his late writing and Lady Gregory's and Synge's, proved the durable stuff.

Yet how powerfully he commands the Romantic rhetoric!

> "I hear my soul drop down into decay,
> And Manannan's dark tower, stone after stone,

> Gather sea-slime and fall the seaward way,
> And the moon goad the waters night and day,
> That all be overthrown.

> "But till the moon has taken all, I wage
> War on the mightiest men under the skies,
> And they have fallen or fled, age after age.
> Light is man's love, and lighter is man's rage;
> His purpose drifts and dies."

He got it by labor, not by spontaneous overflow; that is his 1895 rewriting of two inferior 1889 stanzas, with a third deleted. He has in his blood the beat of Spenser's strong line, and a sure sense of how stanza and syntax may shape one another. Taken all together, 1889–1895 with subsequent retouchings, *The Wanderings of Oisin* is an astonishing debut. He was one of the poets who start out strong: Pope drafted the *Essay on Criticism* in his teens, Eliot "Prufrock" at twenty-one, Keats *Endymion* at twenty-three, Yeats *Oisin* at twenty-two. And polish though he would, his first drafts in those days were copious. He was not yet managing just seven or eight lines at a sitting. Such costiveness came later, as did the turn toward plays in his effort to inform the Irish public mind.

For *Oisin* could not do that. Not all his desire to restore the old stories to Ireland could lift it from the plane of "literary" myth, to hearten a John O'Leary by no more than the ability it showed. Unlike the old tale, which had a tribal function—keeping in memory what was communally important—*Oisin* emerged from a library, and from the poet's dreams.

To *The Countess Cathleen*, then, and to the Maud Gonne cycle of lyrics he collected in 1895 as *The Rose*. The play, which he rewrote any number of times—its five published versions overtax the apparatus of the *Variorum Plays*—contained unforgettable verse from its earliest version: for instance the intricately sounded lyric of Fergus, which Stephen Dedalus sang to his dying mother, "holding down the long dark chords":

> *Who will go drive with Fergus now*
> *And pierce the deep wood's woven shade,*
> *And dance upon the level shore?*
> *Young man, lift up your russet brow,*
> *And lift your tender eyelids, maid,*
> *And brood on hopes and fears no more. . . .*

Fergus, the father of Conchobar, was once King of all Ireland, a note tells us, "but gave up his throne that he might live at peace hunting in the woods"; another note adds that he gave it up for love.

William Empson has not failed to discern a fine mare's nest of ambiguities. Is it a happy song or a sad? (Yeats often leaves us unsure; "The Song of the Happy Shepherd" seems a melancholy affair.) Are we summoned to freedom with Fergus, or does a sad voice ask "Who will go drive with Fergus now?" because there is no Fergus anymore nor anyone to follow him?

There's another blur shortly. "Brood on hopes and fears no more" seems to summon young man and maid to carefree certainty, hope and fear irrelevant alike. But in 1933 Yeats or someone deleted the *s* from "fears," making "fear" an imperative verb that attaches "no more" to itself—we're to fear no more—but also leaves us, apparently, to "brood on hopes," which is different perhaps from hoping. The song has been printed that disorienting way ever since.

In the play its melancholy is richer still. Old Oona who sings it sings in Christian times, when supernature drives bargains (the famine will end if Cathleen sells her soul).

> SHEMUS: God and God's mother nod and sleep—at last
> They have grown weary of the prayers and candles,
> And Satan pours the famine from his bag,
> He does not nod, nor sleep, nor droop his eyelids;
> I am half mindful to go pray to him
> To cover all this table with red gold. . . .

For lack of red gold men turn bestial and rob one another's flocks and orchards, and devils are abroad buying souls. (Those devils, an Irish audience would think, are very mercantile, very English.) It is amid such troubles, in her great hall before a tapestry

> . . . where Oisin and young Niam ride
> Wrapped in each other's arms, and where the Finians
> Follow their hounds. . . .

that the Countess calls for a song:

> Sing how King Fergus in his brazen car
> Drove with a troop of dancers through the woods.

After she has sung the first verse, Oona says,

> You have dropped down again into your trouble.
> You do not hear me.
> KATHLEEN: Ah, sing on, old Oona,
> I hear the song of Fergus in my heart.
> OONA: I do not know the meaning of the song.
> I am too old.   ˙
> KATHLEEN: The horn is calling, calling.
> OONA: *And no more turn aside and brood*
>   *Upon Love's bitter mystery;*
>   *For Fergus rules the brazen cars,*
>   *And rules the shadows of the wood,*
>   *And the white breast of the dim sea*
>   *And all dishevelled wandering stars.*

Amid these vague promptings we may think that "Love's bitter mystery" is Christian, the brazen cars uncomplicated and pagan, and "Who will go drive with Fergus now?" means simply, "What hope is there of getting those better times back?" When she says "I do not know the meaning of the song. I am too old," Oona speaks like an old Catholic woman; in a less tormented culture it is age like hers that would possess the lore of meanings.

After 1908 he took the song out of the play altogether, and put it with the lyrics he called *The Rose*, some of which are obliquely addressed to Maud Gonne. A few of these toy with a sentimental Catholicism—

> Bow down, archangels, in your dim abode:
> Before you were, or any hearts to beat, . . .
> He made the world to be a grassy road
> Before her wandering feet.

That note is even stronger in the 1899 collection, *The Wind Among the Reeds*: "When the flaming lute-thronged angelic door is wide; / . . . Our hearts endure the scourge, the plaited thorns. . . ." He even asks for prayers to release him and her from a purgatory he puts no belief in:

> O Colleens, kneeling by your altar rails long hence,
> When song I wove for my beloved hides the prayer . . .
> Bend down and pray for the great sin I wove in song,
> Till Maurya of the wounded heart cry a sweet cry. . . .

This sweet pitying religion was, he presumably told himself, part of the matter of Ireland; under national color he could continue to be pre-Raphaelite and exquisitely self-pitying. That was a bad sign, and another was that by the time he was writing *The Wind Among the Reeds*, lyric verse was coming very slowly. Much of it was contrived at Coole, protected by Lady Gregory, by closed doors, by tiptoeing maids. Though it's exquisitely wrought—"wrought" seems the word—something is gone, the inimitable lyric flow he'd managed in so much of *The Countess*:

> Impetuous heart, be still, be still,
> Your sorrowful love can never be told,
> Cover it up with a lonely tune. . . .

That was when he had known so surely how such verse should sound he'd had Florence Farr put it into notation for the psaltery.

Yeats's ear was not as it has been represented. In particular, the ritual statement that he was "tone-deaf" names a condition unknown to otological science. It merely alludes to the fact that he could not sing, much as others cannot compose verses the like of these:

> At the grey round of the hill
> Music of a lost kingdom
> Runs, runs and is suddenly still.
> The winds out of Clare-Galway
> Carry it: suddenly it is still.

"I have," so he said himself, "the poet's exact time-sense, only the vaguest sense of pitch." This does not mean that he did not hear pitches, but that he could not make his voice repeat them: hence his uncertainty about recognizing tunes, recognition entailing as it does silent repetition.

Such nuances so elude criticism's terminology that it turns with relief to his later systems of idea and symbol. If, as we've been being told for decades, the *great* Yeats was getting ready to be born, a considerable Yeats had also died: been taken away, it may be, by malignant fairies called Duty and Middle Age. By 1902, in "Adam's Curse," the changeling is making a virtue of newly shouldered toil.

> I said, "A line will take us hours maybe;
> Yet if it does not seem a moment's thought,
> Our stitching and unstitching has been nought. . . ."

The New York Public Library's Berg Collection preserves one mark of unstitching and stitching, in a typescript of "Adam's Curse" itself. The phrasing of that seamstress's metaphor is an emendation entered by hand;

and though we can't know she didn't write it at the poet's dictation, the handwriting is Lady Gregory's.

Yeats used up the last of his heart, George Moore thought, when he wrote *The Countess Cathleen*. He had become a monster of calculation, doing his day's few lines with endless erasing, and the play on which he and Moore proposed to collaborate, a treatment of the legend of Diarmuid and Grania, would receive its style by a contorted process indeed. For Yeats, if we are to believe Moore, which is perilous, burst into Moore's bedroom at Coole— about 1898, that would have been—with this proposal: that Moore should draft the play in French; that Lady Gregory should put the French into English; that Taidhg O'Donoghue should then put the English text into Irish for Lady Gregory to reconvert to Kiltartan English, on which Yeats would then put style, "a last and immortal relish." This makes a kind of crazy sense: the French for construction, the first English only for Taidgh O'Donoghue's eye, the Irish for root idiom, the second English for "PQ" (Peasant Quality), the "style" to give Yeats after all something to do. (It is Moore's continual suggestion that Yeats's prose plays are his by virtue only of the "style" he put on pages of Lady Gregory's, and that does seem to be true of *A Pot of Broth*.)

In *Hail and Farewell*, where this tale is spun, Moore even offers what he says is a specimen of his French draft. Its pair of bronze-age thugs, named in the approved French manner "Ier Jeune Homme" and "2ème Jeune Homme," behave with Gallic method, and the excerpt in general reads suspiciously like parody:

> IER JEUNE HOMME. Nous venons de Finn.
> DIARMUID. Et vous venez pour me tuer?
> IER JEUNE HOMME. Oui. . . .
> GRANIA. Qui de vous attaquera Diarmuid le premier?
> IER JEUNE HOMME. Nous l'attaquerons tous les deux à la fois. . . .

Other than by displaying these strange speeches, the underpinnings of an Irish Heroic Play, Moore says he saw no way to convince his reader "that two such literary lunatics as Yeats and myself existed, contemporaneously, and in Ireland too, a country not distinguished for its love of letters."

More lunatic if possible was the only production, in October 1901, in Dublin. For however *Diarmuid and Grania* got written—it assuredly did not pass to and fro among three or four languages, though the job seems to have involved Lady Gregory and even Arthur Symons—it was by intent an

Irish Heroic Play, and it got played, at the Gaiety, by a company of touring actors with English accents.

The principal characters bore names like Caoelte and Niall, and the land was called Eire. Someone at the last minute persuaded Yeats that the Englishmen were pronouncing such words all wrong. Yeats hastened to interfere; they restudied, hastily, uncouth sounds from his amateur renditions. One actor, Matheson Lang, who'd played Niall, remembered the ensuing chaos for thirty-eight years.

> For instance, the name of the country Eire he wanted pronounced something like "Oorchah" (to us it sounded much more like a sneeze!). A character which was played by Henry Ainley was named "Caoelte." This we had been pronouncing at rehearsal "Kaoltay," but Yeats said no, it ought to be "Wheelsher." So it went on right through the cast. . . . Everyone was in a panic. . . . Harry Ainley went through the evening being called successively "Wheelchair," "Coldtea," and "Quilty." Poor Eire, that distressful country, suffered another injustice by being called every kind of name but its proper one.

Sense can be made of this. Brendan O Hehir writes me (13 March 1980) that "Caoilte" (a better spelling than "Caoelte") makes a sound for which "Queelcher" wouldn't be too far off. That helps explain both "Wheelchair" and "Quilty." As for "Eire," "If Yeats was proposing the Old Irish form of the name, Eriu, something reasonably sneezelike is possible. Palatal -r- sounds something like -rzh- or -rz- so Eriu could be represented by 'Errchuh' in the crudest possible phonetics."*

That was Yeats's lowest hour, and possibly George Moore's also. They never published *Diarmuid and Grania*, of which our knowledge comes from a sole surviving typescript. Moore's 650-page *Hail and Farewell* is his account of what he came to regard as the Irish Literary Fiasco. Yeats's *Autobiography* retaliates. Susan Mitchell, AE's longtime secretary and an expert thorn in Moore's flesh, makes Moore speak both concisely and like the man of the world he hoped to be taken for:

> We have reformed the drama, myself and Yeats allied,
> For I took small stock in Martyn, and less in Douglas Hyde.
> To bow the knee to rare AE was too much for my pride.

---

*Still, in *Variorum Poems* 129–130, two lines never changed after 1895 tell us that when Yeats *said* "Eire" he rhymed it indifferently with "Faery" and with "weary." Matheson Lang by the way remembered imperfectly; it was E. Harcourt Williams, not Ainley, who played Caoelte/Wheelchair. He also recalled the prose text as blank verse, which hints at the reverence Yeats encouraged them all to show it.

> But W. B. was the boy for me—he of the dim wan clothes;
> And—don't let on I said it—not above a bit of pose;
> And they call his writing literature, as everybody knows.
>
> If you like a stir or want a stage or would admired be,
> Prepare with care a naughty past and then repent like me.
> My past alas! was blameless, but this the world won't see.

Yeats went on staying at Coole as long as he could manage, part of every year. Robert Gregory's wife, who thanks to the descent of land through the male line was titular mistress of the seven-wooded demesne, came to think him a pest. Never one not to finish, he struggled with *The Shadowy Waters*, year in, year out, till he'd made both a stage version that didn't work and a reading version no one ever reads. It is his Pyrrhic victory of the high-falutin' symbolical. Indifferent to the destiny his symbols would have coerced for her, Maud Gonne married, separated, lived in France, while, thick as thieves with Lady Gregory, Yeats bent his creative mind to the theatre: after 1904, the Abbey, where they were fortunate enough to flush a genius: Synge.

Yeats never printed his paper on Ireland's three stages, epic, lyric, drama, but the meeting he addressed in 1893 was elaborately reported in the Parnellite *United Ireland*, the same paper whose forcible reclamation by friends of the Uncrowned King occasioned the brouhaha in which Parnell's hat was knocked off and young Leopold Bloom, for picking it up, was told "Thank you." The adamant Parnellite James Joyce, who was eleven when Yeats spoke, may later have found the speech there. However he came by them, those Yeatsian categories were surely what Joyce reordered as lyric-epic-drama, for his Stephen Dedalus of 1902 to use in a veiled polemic against Yeats.

In Stephen's version lyric is no complex flower but early man's primitive cry; it was Ibsen's drama that was the subtle culmination, something Joyce would gladly have demonstrated had he had access to a theater like the Abbey and also been as gifted a dramatist as Yeats. His destiny instead was to write "our national epic," in fact two of them like Homer, the night one as well as the day one. What with him and Synge and Yeats, a constellation truly incredible, as it were a Homer, a Sophocles and a Pindar, the rocky little country was adequately stocked with genius.

Buck Mulligan thought, puzzled.
—Shakespeare? he said. I seem to know the name.
A flying sunny smile rayed in his loose features.
—To be sure, he said, remembering brightly. The chap that writes like Synge.

Ulysses

A rattletrap metal Sphinx, an absurdity with serried levers like the knees of iron grasshoppers and interchangeable typewheels, J. M. Synge's No. 5 Blickensderfer ("Made in U.S.A.") stayed in its wooden box when he dealt with his mail, for which task it was too slow, but clacked on his worktable when something deliberate needed picking out letter by letter. The sentences he stood by were the ones he typed, with excruciating slowness. For instance:

The only truth a wave knows is that it is going to break. The only truth we know is that we are a flood of magnificent life, the fruit of some frenzy of the earth.

—So ran a draft he typed in Paris at thirty, something to be spoken in a 'prentice play that was never produced. In Ireland, his spokesman went on to say, was no life like a great wave: only a melancholy degeneration. "Every one seemed to be taking his friends to the asylum or bringing them back from it."

Ireland's incidence of insanity, measured by admissions to mental hospitals, was twenty-seven per thousand before Synge died, "the highest figure on the earth" as he observed, and it is the highest still. What the figures mean gets controverted. Are they inflated, perhaps, by counting readmissions as separate cases, some depressive drawing the statistical strength of ten from sidling in and out of custody every five weeks? Or do they not reflect the great charity with which God's most blessed people look after one another? Or is it that the figures from the rest of the world cannot be trusted, whereas in Ireland, as readers of Beckett know, to count and calculate accurately is a mania? Such debate is as melancholy as the withdrawal and derangement it would minimize. "On a given census day in 1971, two out of every hundred males in western Ireland were in a mental hospital," wrote an American social scientist, Nancy Scheper-Hughes, who called her book *Saints, Scholars, and Schizophrenics* and remarked on a society's unwillingness to recognize itself in the suffering individuals it rejects or locks up. True, the less catatonic even get bussed out to vote in national elections, and if you ask why you'll be asked why not.

The title of Synge's aborted play, *When the Moon Has Set,* touches on the etymology of "lunacy," and its protagonist is surnamed Sweeney after the king in the twelfth-century Irish story who is driven mad by a cleric's curse. Synge brings on stage a woman long ago crazed from learning her fiancé did not believe in God. Before she went out of her mind she threw him over.

> SISTER EILEEN: She did what was right. No woman who was really a Christian could have done anything else.
> COLM SWEENEY: I wish you had seen her tonight screaming and crying out over the bogs.

He drafted this play and redrafted it, as late even as when he was working on *The Playboy of the Western World,* and after he was dead his executors were obliged to weigh his request that they publish a version of it. Yeats dissuaded them (rightly), and *When the Moon Has Set* was not accessible until Synge's reputation had been long secure.

His numb persistence is intelligible. His own irreligiousness was what had turned away his first love, and shaped his difficult relations with his Protestant family. Ireland's well-publicized Catholicism was not the only desiccant of feeling Synge perceived.

Somewhere, somewhere, somewhere there needed to be an abounding glittering life. W. B. Yeats in 1894 had located such a life no nearer than faeryland,

Where nobody grows old and godly and grave,
Where nobody grows old and crafty and wise,
Where nobody grows old and bitter of tongue.

You got there by lending ear to "a voice singing on a May eve like this,"
and following "half awake and half asleep." Then like "a Princess Edain, a
daughter of a King of Ireland," you might expect to stay beyond time
forever,

busied with a dance
Deep in the dewy shadow of a wood,
Or where stars walk upon a mountain-top.

So intent an alienation might be called derangement of a sort, and Sam
Beckett would one day hint that mental patients were escaped into a system
of benefits out of the howling fiasco called civic life. It is the padded cells in
Beckett's *Murphy* that are bowers of bliss, and his lunatic Mr. Endon (Greek
for "in one's own country") is busied with a chess-game: a queer sort of
game in which he takes no offense in any sense of that phrase, but simply
plods his pieces out and then back again. This so disorients Murphy he
cannot collect his wits for the ready win.

The rituals of early Yeatsian verse, forty years before W. B. for his part
had come to situate wisdom in Crazy Jane, accommodate no such sardonic
viewing. These rituals hint at a languorous lovely world, and in *The Land
of Heart's Desire,* which he wrote in London upon being asked to create a
fairy-child part for Florence Farr's niece, he opposed such a world of wistful
dream to a Sligo peasant-world of a century past.

Yeats was twenty-nine, it was his first real play for actors to speak, and
he later excused the unreality of its dialogue by saying that the characters
were supposed to be speaking Gaelic. He had nothing to say about the
implausible setting, a very solid prosperous interior with a settle, a large
dresser, a great bowl of primroses on the sill and a crucifix on the wall. The
house commands a hundred acres of good land, and a stocking stuffed with
yellow guineas will be the portion of the young folk when the old folk are
gone. This is not, in the time of food riots, a plausible peasant cottage. It is
an English Victorian household refreshed by Celtic charm, and with its
Vicar transmuted into that Protestant fantasy, an amiable priest with a
palate for wine.

Prosperity plus Father Hart sums up all by which the young bride Maire

Bruin is repelled, and in the short play's last moments her soul is torn from her body between Father Hart pointing her the way to Heaven and the faery child pointing her the way she can

> ride upon the winds,
> Run on the top of the dishevelled tide,
> And dance upon the mountains like a flame.

Where her soul goes we cannot be sure about from a play that gives Father Hart the last spoken words—

> Thus do the spirits of evil snatch their prey
> Almost out of the very hand of God;
> And day by day their power is more and more,
> And men and women leave old paths, for pride
> Comes knocking with thin knuckles on the heart.

If we like we may accord these words more credence than those of the faery song on which the curtain falls:

> The wind blows out of the gates of the day,
> The wind blows over the lonely of heart,
> And the lonely of heart is withered away;
> While the faeries dance in a place apart,
> Shaking their milk-white feet in a ring,
> Tossing their milk-white arms in the air. . . .

Or if we prefer believing that faeries dance somewhere we may believe that instead. For who knows whether they exist, save in song? We may want to trust song, or not.

Was the other world real and if so were its beings benign? On such matters Yeats's mind was never settled. In 1890 he had disrupted the Theosophical Society by "experiments" that included organizing a committee to raise if it could the ghost of a flower from its ashes. What might be metaphor ought to be established, what might be credulousness, what might be *so*. His resignation was formally asked for. The devout of theosophy did not understand that Yeats persisted in his testing of their truths because he hoped they were true. Much eloquence of song flowed into *The Land of Heart's Desire*'s faery world because he wanted that to be real and good likewise. Yes he did. And yet might Father Hart's "spirits of evil" be the right words? Yeats vacillated.

Within a decade James M. Barrie, later Sir James, would show what lucrative success a dramatist might get by not vacillating; audiences had to shout out their belief in fairies before Tinker Bell could be saved and *Peter Pan* happily ended. A heartless audience might let Tinker Bell die, but this seems never to have happened.

Another working of the theme is Henry James's, who followed Yeats in permitting a victim to die when he wrote *The Turn of the Screw* four years after Yeats's play.* His hapless Master Miles did not die into faeryland; no, into, so far as we can tell, mere death, destroyed like Maire Bruin by a tug-of-war between the undead and the living. The undead are not pretty dancing children but a spectral pair with aberrant names we are not to trust, Quint and Jessel, and the living are represented not by mild Father Hart but by a frantic governess; and the supernatural, we understand, is apt to be nasty: nothing to solicit lyrical assent.

And yet another working is Synge's, who (as no one remarked before Denis Johnston in 1965) commenced his own career as a stageworthy dramatist by addressing himself to Yeats's theme of escape and grounding it in peasant earth. Unlike Yeats or James, John Synge was undivided about the otherworldly. His first finished play, *In the Shadow of the Glen* (1903), caused the outcry about foreign nastiness by presenting an option so immediate it might tempt any housewife. Nora Burke walks out of her marriage in company with a tramp: "You've a fine bit of talk, stranger, and it's with yourself I'll go": just like that.

They will walk, he has promised her, where nobody gets old and godly and grave because there will simply be no talk of age. She'll be hearing

> the grouse, and the owls with them, and the larks and the big thrushes when the days are warm, and it's not from the likes of them you'll be hearing talk of getting old like Peggy Cavanagh, and losing the hair off you, and the light of your eyes, . . . and there'll be no old fellow wheezing the like of a sick sheep close to your ear.

Old age—Synge was thirty-one and may have begun to suspect he'd be dead in seven years—is a queer thing surely.

> —It's a queer thing to see an old man sitting up there in his bed, with no teeth in him, and a rough word in his mouth, and his chin the way it would take

*Which it's hard to think the inveterate playgoer James didn't see, since it played on the same bill with the first run of *Arms and the Man*, and even the Prince of Wales got around to attending. But Professor Leon Edel tells me there's no surviving evidence.

the bark from the edge of an oak board. . . . We'll all be getting old, but it's a queer thing surely.

All the tramp has to offer is deliverance from a life of "sitting in this place, making yourself old with looking on each day and it passing you by." There will be cold, and frost, and great rain, and—a detail Synge struck out of one of the drafts—she'll have less worry about one day having no teeth in her head than about what to put between them when the sun comes up. If thanks to her tramp's skills she'll "not be sitting up in a wet ditch," it's in no fine house she'll be sheltered either but likely in a shed or haystack.

Though none of this is "to dance upon the mountains like a flame," still it seems a life within the grasp of the living, and a more fulfilling one than loveless marriage contains: not like the offer of Yeats's faery child either, thin hypnotic poetry to conceal the disagreeable stipulation that en route to The Land of Heart's Desire you must die.

In a 1907 poem Synge put the distinction clearly, waving literary fairies (the *Sidhe*) aside:

> Adieu, sweet Angus, Maeve and Fand,
> Ye plumed yet skinny Shee
> Our poets walked with hand in hand
> To learn fine ecstasy.
>
> We've learned to cherish Kerry men
> The ditches lovers know
> The badger, salmon water hen
> The weazel lark and crow.

It was a much rewritten version he printed, but this draft is sharp. It dismisses such a world as Yeats dreams of in "Under the Moon" (1901), which mentions both Aengus and Fand but no dirty things like badgers. The badger, the weazel help us know exactly what life is the tramp's life, the one Nora Burke has opted. It was no life for Michael Dara who was flirting with her, Michael Dara who at the play's curtain is drinking a glass with the grotesque old husband she has left, and the husband saying to his long-time rival, "But you're a quiet man, God help you, and I don't mind you at all." This is well imagined. Dan the husband was Michael Dara once; Dan is the old age of Michael Dara; together, drinking there, they epitomize the first and last of all she has walked out of with her tramp.

Synge's was the generation of the Tramp. There was a cult of Villon in those years, and Synge shared it, and made translations ("The man I had a love for—a great rascal would kick me in the gutter—is dead thirty years and over it, and it is I am left behind, grey and aged"). Robert Louis Stevenson had travelled with a donkey; W. H. Davies would soon write *The Autobiography of a Super-Tramp;* in 1902 Hilaire Belloc made a well-praised picaresque book out of scorning trains and walking from Paris across the Alps almost to Rome. That was the same year Yeats wrote *The Pot of Broth,* a play about a clever tramp. And had not Homer gone about begging his bread? The tramp is a *poète maudit,* but since he takes no absinthe a healthy one.

Tramps, tinkers, vagabonds, Ireland has them in plenty. They will thrust on you handwritten accounts of their misfortunes. Synge idealized them, never from a fastidious distance. He had been on the road himself, in Europe where he sometimes earned a loaf with his fiddle, and in Wicklow and Kerry. Intimate letters were signed "Your Old Tramp," and notebook pages describe vagabond encounters. "I have met an old vagrant who believes he was a hundred years old last Michaelmas. Though now alone he has been married several times and reared children of whom he knows no more than a swallow knows of broods who have flown to the south. . . . If you do not follow his sometimes mumbled phrases he will call a blight from heaven on your head though your silver is only warming in his pouch."

And: "Man is intellectually a nomad, and all wanderers have finer intellectual and physical perceptions than men who are condemned to local habitations."

He believed that this was true, and *In the Shadow of the Glen, The Tinker's Wedding, The Well of the Saints, The Playboy of the Western World*—four of the six Synge plays—all end with a pair setting forth upon a future of wandering: not as at the end of *Paradise Lost,* exiles from a garden, but as at the beginning of *The Prelude,* liberated into a wilderness of possibilities and leaving behind them people who in being condemned to local habitations are in every sense less than they.

Those left behind include two or more people on the stage and several hundred in the audience, who if the play works as it should will be brought to recognize that beyond the stage door through which the wanderers have departed extends a hard free frenzied life they do not know how to imagine. For the truth of that life is "the only truth we know," that we are "a flood of magnificent life, the fruit of some frenzy of the earth," but if we are Irish Christians we have allowed ourselves to be persuaded that we are the deposit of some whim of heaven's, our lives therefore apt like Shawn Keogh's in *The Playboy* to contain much "waiting these days on Father Reilly's dispensation from the bishops, or the court of Rome." Father Reilly would have us think the vagabonds are likely mad, but it is the stay-at-homes are apt to become that way: 2 percent of all males in the West on any one census day.

And "the only truth the wave knows is that it is going to break," so when the next sentence commences with "The only truth we know . . ." we think we see its ending: "that we are going to die." That is not the way the sentence ends, but it is a contrapuntal truth to what the sentence does go on to affirm, the truth of vital magnificence. For if "magnificent life" is "the fruit of some frenzy of the earth," then like all earthly fruits it will wither and drop, and Synge wrote two other plays, *Riders to the Sea* and *Deirdre of the Sorrows,* which end when the best and most vital people have finished their vagabondage and lie dead: Bartley after his last ride with the horses to the wild sea, Deirdre and Naisi after their flight from Conchubor the High King.

—The stars are out, Deirdre, and let you come with me quickly, for it is the stars will be our lamps many nights and we abroad in Alban, and taking our journeys among the little islands in the sea.

That is from the end of the first act of *Deirdre,* which takes Deirdre and Naisi just as far as the one-act *Shadow of the Glen* took Nora and the tramp, as far as the door. Had two more acts been appended to *The Shadow,* they could only have traced the course of Nora and the tramp as far as the end of *Deirdre*: through vagabondage under the stars to death. Synge, it may be, handled but the one story six times, a story of setting out and then dying, in which those who set forth have chosen better than those who choose to stay. That is what lies, grim and simple, behind the brilliant extravagance of the language, and when John Synge seemed to be himself enacting his story in making his recurrent departures to the glens and to the islands and then dying in mid-career, was he not offering his own life as an emblem to be completed by another's imaginative act? W. B. Yeats came to think so.

Yeats too had one main story on his mind all his life, in which people who do some not wholly fulfilling thing possess the mind of a poet who turns them into symbols to fill the imagination of the living. Cuchulain fighting the waves, Maud Gonne on her soapbox, Robert Gregory obeying that lethal impulse of delight, the sixteen begetters of the "terrible beauty," all of these were completed only when he had emblematized them in strong verse. For this story he needed only two characters, a thwarted hero and a poet. In late life he commenced to combine them, and the last man he would make into a symbol was his mortal self:

> Under bare Ben Bulben's head
> In Drumcliffe churchyard Yeats is laid. . . .

Never did he labor longer to transubstantiate another man than he labored over Synge, nor ever achieve his end with more authority. Especially because the reticence of Synge's family prevented any biography of their black sheep till as late as 1959,* we can still hardly glimpse past the Yeatsian emblem to the man: the man for instance who could curse so ably "the ungodly ruck of fat-faced sweaty-headed swine" known to the circumspect as the Catholic Middle Class.

Part of Yeats's way toward creating and fixing the emblem was to seek some single plenary epithet, and he sought it in public for nearly twenty years, leaving us to rotate and balance his attempts.

> (1918)   And that enquiring man John Synge comes next . . .
> (1929)   . . . and that slow man
>   That meditative man John Synge . . .
> (1937)   And here's John Synge himself, that rooted man,
>   "Forgetting human words," a grave deep face . . .

"Enquiring," "slow," "meditative," "rooted," these entail a density of particulars they refrain from specifying. If we resist the iambic magniloquence we can fill them out. Thus "forgetting human words" remembers a poem of Synge's about his wanderings far from cities:

> . . . I knew the stars, the flowers, and the birds,
> The grey and wintry sides of many glens,
> And did but half remember human words,
> In converse with the mountains, moors, and fens.

When Yeats calls him in the same breath "that rooted man" we may think that what converses with mountains, moors and fens is likely a tree, and allow our minds to be touched by another poem of Synge's, the grim "To the Oaks at Glencree" which celebrates his hierogamous union with his coffin-wood.

> My arms are round you, and I lean
> Against you, while the lark
> Sings over us, and golden lights, and green
> Shadows are on your bark.

---

*They abhorred theatres and thought lymphatic cancer as disgraceful a thing to die from as syphilis.

> There'll come a season when you'll stretch
> Black boards to cover me:
> Then in Mount Jerome* I will lie, poor wretch,
> With worms eternally.

"That rooted man," indeed. But in extrapolating so many allusions from a few words of Yeats we are but testing for resilience the intricate Syngean net he had been weaving in the deeps of his mind for three decades, and did not ever wholly disclose to his readers. As early as 1905, in his Preface to *The Well of the Saints,* he had stated how Synge's plays evade the schoolroom habit that looks for Character and Motivation.

> The ordinary student of drama will not find anywhere in *The Well of the Saints* that excitement of the will in the presence of attainable advantages, which he is accustomed to think the natural stuff of drama. . . . If he see *The Shadow of the Glen,* he will ask, Why does this woman go out of her house? Is it because she cannot help herself, or is she content to go? Why is it not all made clearer? And yet, like everybody when caught up into great events, she does many things without being quite certain why she does them. She hardly understands at moments why her action has a certain form, more clearly than why her body is tall or short, fair or brown. She feels an emotion that she does not understand. She is driven by desires that need for their expression, not "I admire this man," or "I must go, whether I will or no," but words full of suggestion, rhythms of voice, movements that escape analysis.

Acutely observed, this is prompted by the troubles Yeats himself was having with audiences who desired a vulgar clarity, and when he evokes on a neighboring page the writer plunged into "some beautiful or bitter reverie" by his "dream of an impossibly noble life," he is portraying the melancholic poet he kept in his own mind's repertory company. Synge would qualify for that role in dying unfulfilled, and Yeats's first sketch of a mythologized Synge was composed ten days after the rooted, taciturn man had turned to the wall and died (of Hodgkin's Disease, long suffered) on 24 March 1909. This was the thirteen-hundred-word Preface to the Synge *Poems and Translations* Elizabeth ("Lollie") Yeats was passing through her hand press at Dundrum. It was the initiating gesture of a process that would continue for many years, the incorporation of John Millington Synge into the myth of modern Ireland. It ended memorably: "He was but the more hated because he gave his country what it needed, an unmoved mind where there is a perpetual Last Day, a trumpeting and coming up to judgement."

*The Protestant cemetery in Dublin.

That fine sentence was based on something Yeats wrote in his diary about four days after Synge died. Further pages from that 1909 journal underlie an aphoristic and meditative complexity called *The Death of Synge* which he polished and published after nineteen years and annexed to his *Autobiography* a decade after that, having perhaps pondered how James Joyce rounded off *A Portrait of the Artist as a Young Man* with the artist's diary excerpts.

It is among the diary's 1909–1910 night thoughts that elements of the Synge Myth begin to reach toward one another. While their ink was still black Yeats drew on them for a long essay called "J. M. Synge and the Ireland of His Time," having meanwhile followed Maud Gonne to Normandy and had out with her again the old quarrel that had come to a head with *The Playboy,* between art and patriotic duty. It remained the one difference about which she still felt strongly. They spent a rainy afternoon arguing; Yeats's thought suddenly clarified; the next day, a day in mid-May 1910, he set down at last—for his own use, in his journal—the elements of a perfectly lucid statement that risked no vacuities about hierophantic Art.

> Practical movements are created out of emotions expressed long enough ago to have become general, but literature discovers; it can never repeat.

That was the central truth, too clear almost for publication. And:

> It is the attempt to repeat an emotion because it has been found effective which has made all provincially political literature . . . so superficial.

That is worth rereading: "It is the attempt to repeat an emotion because it has been found effective which has made all provincially political literature . . . so superficial." So of stirring words written to agitate, words such as Thomas Davis's by which Yeats himself had once been stirred—

> The troops live not that could withstand
> The headlong charge of Tipperary*

—he now had the adequate dismissal. "Had this been true it would not have been necessary to write it."

Quite. It is never necessary to write what anyone can see is true: that the sod is green, that our boys are invincible (if they are). So when such things are affirmed, and men take heart in repeating the affirmation, that is apt to

---

*Slightly misquoted (see page 98 above), hence quoted from memory; the heavy iambic feet of Davis still marched across Yeatsian dreams as late as 1910.

be because they are *not* true, though some purpose will be served if we can be made to believe it.

Literature discovers; it can never repeat; and what *is* necessary to be written is "the vision of the naked truth." He uses "vision" like Blake, trans-optically. The test of vision is emotional freshness: "entirely spontaneous emotion . . . that headlong plunge into the future, that rage to create that comes from delight in emotional discovery." (Blake: "Energy is Eternal Delight.") Synge had worked out of vision, and Yeats himself and Lady Gregory too—he seemed embarked on a list of names but checked himself: "no, there is no other than these"—and the three of them had created "an Ireland which will remain imaginary," i.e. indestructible. Twenty-seven years later he recapitulated in strong verse:

> John Synge, I and Augusta Gregory, thought
> All that we did, all that we said or sang
> Must come from contact with the soil, from that
> Contact everything Antaeus-like grew strong.
> We three alone in modern times had brought
> Everything down to that sole test again,
> Dream of the noble and the beggar-man.

The beggar-man comprises the Synge tramp and Homer; "contact with the soil" looks toward the lines about "that rooted man" that will open the very next stanza.

Such a literature would take a long time to ripen, and a longer time still, Yeats foresaw in 1910, to enter the unconscious premises of action. Writers who then seemed patterns of the national, men like Scott and Burns, "with their lack of ideas, their external and picturesque view of life" (the external view is not the view of *vision*) had by contrast created in Scotland "not a nation but a province with a sense of the picturesque": just "kilts and bagpipes, newspapers and guidebooks." Likewise plays acceptable to Sinn Fein could have done no more for the Irish nation than endow it with an up-to-date sort of stage Irishman, connoisseur very likely of wolfhounds and round towers, harps and shamrocks.

(Cold water: there is no shamrock. Any three-leafed weed at all will qualify: *Trifolium repens,* or *Trifolium minus, Trifolium pratense,* even *Medicago lupulina.* There is no wolfhound either; what is now called that is a breed reconstituted in the nineteenth century out of mongrel disjecta. So much for received symbols.)

By confronting his old symbol, Maud Gonne, with his new symbol,

Synge, Yeats in 1910 had managed to clarify much. Unfortunately when he came to put style upon the journal pages a few months later he only succeeded in making "J. M. Synge and the Ireland of His Time" opalescent of surface and labyrinthine of argument, unlikely to convince any patriot who already knew how out of the mouth of Yeats came but cadences of the empty priesthood of art. Style often gave him that trouble.

Nor was style the whole of the essay's poor luck. When he wrote it he'd expected its intonations would be balanced by J. M. Synge's whole gamy text, since it was to have introduced the four-volume Maunsel edition of his friend's *Works*. At the last minute he withdrew it for less conspicuous publication, having entered the honorable list of quarrellers with Maunsel & Co., the same firm which would soon be guillotining Joyce's *Dubliners* on account of words such as "bloody." Not that they were deleting words from Synge's text. Their offense this time was opportunistic *inclusion*: Maunsel's George Roberts sweeping together newspaper work unworthy of the reputation Yeats was sponsoring for Synge. Roberts did not balk at "shift," nor at *The Playboy*'s four "bloody"s, and it is odd that his rows with Joyce were just then beginning, over words he was printing in Synge's plays without demur. If Joyce sometimes seems paranoid we can understand.

It would be 1918 before Yeats had resolved all these matters including the essential treacherousness of George Roberts, and he was ready for an iconic presentation of Synge. The catalyst, as so often a bout of anger, had been working in his mind for some years. One evening in 1912 the infinitely forgiving AE had defended Roberts as merely muddle-headed, and Yeats, stung by the ease with which AE preached charity toward mischief-making and incompetence, "got angry and described the dishonesty of the muddle-headed whose darkness has always one light, that of self-interest; there, though there alone, attention does not wander." That light guides them toward the paradise of lined pockets which is their heart's desire. But Synge, enquiring man, had journeyed differently, and the first appearance of his name in Yeats's poetry heads one long finely definitive sentence.

> And that enquiring man John Synge comes next,
> That dying chose the living world for text
> And never could have rested in the tomb
> But that, long travelling, he had come
> Towards nightfall upon certain set apart
> In a most desolate stony place,
> Towards nightfall upon a race
> Passionate and simple like his heart.

Knowing nothing of Synge, what might anyone make of that? A farer upon some emblematic journey, some quester, some Childe Roland come to some dark tower where desolation can yield mysterious fulfillment: no mention of playscripts many times written over, nor of actors nor riotous crowds, nor Arthur Griffith drawing across the trail green herrings from his limitless supply: no, a subdual of turbulent particularity to the romantic image that still enfolds Synge's name: enquiring, dying, living, travelling, and with a passionate simple heart.

In not choosing a dead world for his text Synge had rejected not only Sinn Fein counsels but Yeats's own example from his days of writing verses liked by people who liked William Morris. Yet it was Yeats who claimed to have sent him on his journey, having found him (1896) in a students' hotel in the Latin Quarter. ("I said: 'Give up Paris. . . . Go to the Aran Islands. . . . Express a life that has never found expression.' ") That is mythical even if it happened. Synge's folklore studies were impelling him that way anyhow.

The desolate stony place he came to was Inishmaan, a mere nine square miles of ocean-beaten rock "where men must reap with knives because of the stones" and "have a peace and dignity from which we are shut for ever." He spent there and on the larger island Aranmore a total of four and a half months during the summers or autumns of five years, 1898–1902, and listening to the talk of these bilingual people taught him the dialect he was to use in his plays. "I have been sitting all the morning over a great turf fire in the kitchen where an old man had been brought to tell me stories while the family drew round on their stools and the daughter of the house in her wonderful red garments span her wheel at my side." In his first weeks he heard the stories on which he would base two plays; he was also taken to see the miraculous well he remembers in *The Well of the Saints,* and was told moreover that the islands seemed overrun with students of the old language.

"I have seen Frenchmen and Danes and Germans," said one man, "and there does be a power of Irish books along with them, and they reading them better than ourselves. Believe me there are few rich men now in the world who are not studying the Gaelic".

And there was a "dark" (blind) man who spoke of another old man: "But he's walking about with two sticks under him this ten year. Did you ever hear what it is goes on four legs when it is young, and on two legs after that, and on three legs when it does be old?" J. M. Synge (A.B. Trinity, 1892) gave him the answer. "Ah, master, you're a cute one and the blessing of God be on you. Well, I'm on three legs this minute, but the old man beyond is back on four; I don't know if I'm better than the way he is; he's got his sight and I'm only an old dark man."

To have a blind man ask you Sophocles' Riddle of the Sphinx with Sophocles twenty-four centuries dead, that would feel like falling down a hole through time. And how did the riddle get to Aranmore? By the learning of a hedge-schoolmaster? Or was it perhaps a folk-memory, shunted everywhere else into literature that gets forgotten save by the few who read, but here alive on quick lips? These might be (as Synge's Paris professors had suggested) the only truly primitive people left anywhere in Europe, and the patriots who thought Synge's stories smelled barbarously of Greece may have guessed righter than they deserved to.

The plays he started writing in 1902 came from stories he had been told. He set them in places he had visited and made up the dialogue, laborious sentence by sentence, out of phrases he had heard. It was the way James Joyce worked too, though not Yeats, and it was a check against vagueness. Though a time would come when Yeats's verse could describe a piece of lapis lazuli with museum-catalogue accuracy, on the whole his aversion to particularity, save for sudden effect, seemed constitutional. "I have read in some old book," he would intone, or "A friend of my father's used to say . . . " When he and Lady Gregory received Synge's *Aran Islands* typescript, a lively prose account of four visits, it was Yeats's immediate counsel that details should be blurred, even the names of the islands omitted, in the service of "a curious dreaminess" Synge had no interest whatever in attaining: Synge who held the setting of *In the Shadow of the Glen* so clearly in mind his biographers have had no trouble identifying Nora Burke's actual cottage, inhabited when Synge was up there in 1897 by two brothers and their sister, name of Harney. When Willie Fay would ask during rehearsal, "Was Dan standing where he is on the right, behind the table, when he said those lines?" Synge would say, "No, he was on the right-hand side of the table with his hand on it." Not for him the indifference that could let whole orderings of the visible vanish on the instant at whim, or envisage the setting and groupings of *The Land of Heart's Desire* in two quite different ways and vacillate between them from reprinting to reprinting.

Not for him either the rapid poet's pen to catch fleeting thoughts for reworking. Taking a play through a dozen drafts or more, he composed with much premeditation on the queer little typewriter with twenty-seven keys and shifts for FIG and CAP. He bought it in 1899 for his Aran Islands book, and because each keystroke had first to rotate the printwheel and then slam it forward it was not a machine on which you could get up speed: transcribing thirteen hundred words was a day's work. We must assume that he welcomed its slow staccato, its stubborn interposition between brain and paper, forcing deliberate attention to every preposition, every mark of punctuation. "Good evening kindly, stranger" differs substantially from "Good evening, kindly stranger," which was how a London printer in 1905 commenced Nora's first speech in *Shadow*. Though other printers have followed him, the first version is what Synge typed at least twice.

Unlike most of the Abbey playwrights, he was a writer at heart, not a talker; the commonest perception of Synge in company was that he hardly ever spoke. The speech in his plays is as synthetic as Shakespeare's, something Thomas MacDonagh was wincing at when he found it "too full of rich phrases." You might say the same of any speech of Falstaff's, if what you expected was to hear the way English knights talk. In a time with poetic conventions so introspective they were all but useless on stage, and a prose of no more interest than a polished plate-glass pane, Synge had glimpsed a way to stylize words for speaking aloud, and it got mistaken for malicious misreporting.

When John Quinn, in New York, thought of buying the *Playboy* manuscript Synge described what it was like.

> I work always with a typewriter—typing myself—so I suppose it has no value? I make a rough draft first and then work over it with a pen until it is nearly unreadable; then I make a clean draft again, adding whatever seems wanting, and so on. My final drafts—I letter them as I go along—were "G" for the first act, "I" for the second, and "K" for the third! I really wrote parts of the last act more than eleven times, as I often took out individual scenes and worked at them separately. The MS., as it now stands, is a good deal written over, and some of it is in slips or strips only, cut from the earlier versions—so I do not know whether it has any interest for the collector.

It had; and the typescript Quinn bought is now at Indiana University. Later Synge made two more drafts of Act II, so the Indiana copy is "K."

The plays gained density slowly. A notebook draft of what was still called *The Fool of Farnham* has the pubkeeper's daughter writing out an order: "Three barrels of porter with the best compliments of the season." (Synge disliked using any but authentic phrases, and "wishing you the best compliments of this season" was a flourish from a letter a girl on Aran wrote him.)

By typescript "D" this had become "Two dozens of Powers Whiskey. Three barrels of porter. And soda as before." In the margin of draft "E" (23 May 1905) he prompted himself: "Open out? Try making her order her trousseau?" and flipping the page he jotted a trousseau: "Six yards of yellow silk ribbon, a pair of long boots, bright hat suited for a young woman on her wedding day, a fine tooth comb to be sent. . . ." His pen hovered over this. "Long boots" became "pair of shoes with English heels"; then "English" became "big," "big" became "long," "long" became "lengthy," and in the printed text that copies typescript "G" *The Playboy of the Western World* begins:

> PEGEEN (*slowly, as she writes*): Six yards of stuff for to make a yellow gown. A pair of lace boots with lengthy heels on them and brassy eyes. A hat is suited for a wedding day. A fine tooth comb. To be sent with two barrels of porter in Jimmy Farrell's creel cart on the evening of the coming fair to Mister Michael James Flaherty. With the best compliments of this season: Margaret Flaherty.

Sharp eyes will notice that "the season" became "this season," exactly the wording of the letter of the girl from Aran. No detail was too minute for pondering. As late as the final typescript of Act III the "drift of chosen females" was standing "stripped itself," and when Synge at the last minute draped them in the notorious shifts he thought he had adjusted an outrageousness. His model was the thirty virgins arrayed in the old story, to quench Cuchulain's bloody rage with the sight of their stark nakedness: the hero paid them nearly Victorian courtesy.

Some elements were never changed at all. One of the things he knew from the first about his playboy hero was that his name was Christy: a mock-Christ who puts an end to crucifixion by killing the Father. Brought up in a Scriptural family which had even preceded him to the Aran Islands in the person of a reverend uncle with a mission to reform papists' ways ("I have succeeded in putting a stop to the ball match that used to go on here every Sunday"—1851), the sardonic John Millington Synge made free in his plays with Scriptural motifs. *The Well of the Saints* is about a canonical miracle, blindness cured, which proves unwanted ("It's a power of dirty days, and dark mornings, and shabby-looking fellows we do have to be looking on when we have our sight"). *In the Shadow of the Glen* turns on a resurrection, also unwanted; when the "dead" husband leaps from his bed no one present, including his wife, is anything but chagrined. And *The Playboy* has a resurrection too, for good measure a pair of them, the slain and risen figure both times not the son but the father, whom Synge after several deleted tries surnamed Mahon, pronounced Ma'on, approximately Man: not a "meaning," no, an agnostic author at play.

In this topsy-turvy gospel Christy the Son of Mahon was as abstemious as you'd want ("poor fellow would get drunk on the smell of a pint") and so chaste he ran from the sight of a distant girl (when "you'd see him shooting out his sheep's eyes between the little twigs and the leaves") and indeed had every virtue you can list save being any use; and when his old rascal of a father instructed him that his next move in life, after these potatoes were dug, should be to wed the Widow Casey, Christy would have none of that idea at all. For the Widow Casey was "a walking terror from beyond the hills, and she two score and five years, and two hundredweights on her, and a blinded eye, and she a woman of noted misbehaviour with the old and young." In all but not being skinny she was the Sheela-na-gig, the old Irish effort at a fertility goddess, a skeleton with huge pudenda, grinning like death.*

So Christy banged his father with the spade, saying later he'd split his skull to the knob of his gullet and still later that he'd split him to the breeches belt; but in fact by the word of the resurrected father, "Weren't you off racing the hills before I got my breath with the start I had seeing you turn on me at all?"

That was in Kerry, where the Kerrymen come from about whom the Irish tell their Polish jokes; the way the Kerryman broke his leg was he fell out of the tree raking leaves, so you know murder is a thing he'd botch. Christy next ran and walked for eleven days all the way north to the mean bleak country toward Belmullet in County Mayo. (Did it amuse Synge, as it would have amused James Joyce, that to get there he must have trudged past Lady Gregory's Coole?)

Northwest Mayo was a sinister overpopulated wilderness, bogs, stones and hovels, the heart of the Congested Districts that stretched down the Atlantic Coast from Donegal to Dingle and were the special concern of a Board charged with bureaucratic countermeasures to starvation. This blind corner of Ireland stunned even the optimistic AE. It was from Belmullet itself AE had written to Synge in 1897 how he was disheartened out of words. There was nothing to write about save the distress and that was "a disgrace to humanity" and "not cheerful subject matter for a letter."

Synge was first in Belmullet in September 1904, and made there the first sketches for all three acts of The Murderer (A Farce), four titles later The

---

*See Vivian Mercier, The Irish Comic Tradition, 53–56.

Playboy of the Western World. The people thereabouts, his journal recalls, were "debased and nearly demoralized by bad housing and lodging and the endless misery and rain." Any girl's usual costume was "a short red petticoat over bare feet and legs, a faded uncertain bodice and a white or blue rag swathing the head," and the town was "squalid and noisy, lonely and crowded at the same time and without any appeal to the imagination." It was in a like place he heard an old boatman's lament: "I don't know what way I'm going to go on living in this place that the Lord created last, I'm thinking, in the end of time; and it's often when I sit down and look around on it I do begin cursing and damning, and asking myself how poor people can go on executing their religion at all." That was the Western World, so called to contrast it with the Dublin or eastern side of the island, and Christy Mahon fetches up there. Nowhere was it less likely that the pure and exalted peasantry of Nationalist myth might be found, chaste in action, chaste in speech, united in simple love of Ireland and Holy Church and Father Reilly.

That was true even if Synge had been content to depict them naturalistically. The region had a long history of strife. It was there in 1880 that Captain Boycott got boycotted, and that was a mild dealing. Reprisals were normally brutal. Twenty-nine Mayo men, by a story Synge heard there and made a ballad of, once decided it was high time to deal with a hell-raiser named Danny, 'd capsize the stars:

> "But we'll come round him in the night
> A mile beyond the Mullet;
> Ten will quench his bloody eyes,
> And ten will choke his gullet."

W. B. Yeats's sister Lollie declined to set this in type. Synge's ballad particularized what damage Danny did the lads who ambushed him, but it was dozens to one, and

> . . . seven tripped him up behind
> And seven kicked before,
> And seven squeezed around his throat
> Till Danny kicked no more.
>
> Then some destroyed him with their heels,
> Some tramped him in the mud,
> Some stole his purse and timber-pipe,
> And some washed off his blood.

. . .

> And when you're walking out the way
> From Bangor to Belmullet,
> You'll see a flat cross on a stone
> Where men choked Danny's gullet.

The pious X-marks-the-spot is a fine touch. And between Belmullet and Bangor, that would not be far off from where we might look for the *shebeen* (low pub) Christy Mahon, reputed murderer, stumbles into after getting his wind in a ditch.

Synge's first thought had been to dramatize a story he was told on Aran, about how folk in a remote place will shelter a fugitive. When W. B. Yeats himself first visited Aran in 1896 there were islanders who thought from his oblique eye he was a killer in need of refuge instead of a tourist with a skew cornea. "If any gentleman has done a crime we'll hide him," Yeats was told meaningfully. And an old man, the oldest on Inishmaan, more than once told Synge a story out of living memory "about a Connaught man who killed his father with the blow of a spade when he was in a passion, and then fled to this island and threw himself on the mercy of some of the natives. . . . They hid him in a hole—which the old man has shown me— and kept him safe for a week, though the police came and searched for him, and he could hear their boots grinding on the stones over his head." Then they got him off to America. Synge reflected:

> This impulse to protect the criminal is universal in the west. . . . Such a man, they say, will be quiet all the rest of his life, and if you suggest that punishment is needed as an example, they ask, "Would any one kill his father if he was able to help it?"

But the first sketches he set down in Belmullet in late 1904 already eschew this sententious note. He had commenced to amuse himself with the notion of a folk who might not simply shield a murderer but glorify him. For whom did Irishmen glorify? Looking round at their current heroes he saw Fenians, the Phoenix Park murderers—thugs, dynamiters, knifers; also the literary cult of Cuchulain the skull-basher.*

So in Act I we should see the bang on the head itself, out in that Kerry potato-field. Then in Act II—this was pivotal—the murderer would be a

---

*Declan Kiberd (*Synge and the Irish Language,* 109–121) lists impressive correspondences of detail between Christy's exploits and Cuchulain's. Thus like Cuchulain in borrowed armor, it is in a borrowed suit Christy wins himself three trophies; they correspond to "the triple headship of warriors, poets and musicians" Cuchulain was awarded on another occasion, being a blackthorn stick to bash with, a fiddle (the poet's emblem), and a bagpipes.

feisty talker; himself it was would dictate the terms of glory. He would tell of the deed at every provocation, and his eloquence would boss the show. They would elect him county councillor! (When Synge was feeling sardonic his thoughts turned ritually to politicians, though never did any of these windbags survive into a finished play.) In Act III the father—not dead after all—would turn up to spoil the victory speech by calling his son a liar. "Son attacks father and is handcuffed. . . ." This was *The Murderer (A Farce)*, and whether Synge judged it more farcical to disgrace this politician or reinstate him we cannot know, since the next leaf is torn from the notebook.

It is trivial, but so are all Synge's projects in the notebook stage beyond which most of them were never carried. His way, in four of the six plays he finished—the exceptions are *Deirdre* and *Riders to the Sea*—was to start from something like a sophomore's joke and endow it slowly with human range and weight: blind folk who treasure their blindness, dead men who will not stay dead, tinkers who crave the blessing of the parish priest and end up tying him in a sack. It was while *The Playboy* was still a *jeu d'esprit* that he let a simple point of stagecraft impose a crucial decision. The opening scene, the killing in the potato-field, was deleted. For to keep an audience from seeing the blank side walls of the Abbey's box a set-dresser would have to arrange canvas frames, called wings, on which he would have painted—what but trees? So, as Yeats explained to an audience at Harvard, "Synge gave up the intention of showing upon the stage a fight between 'The Playboy' and his father, because he would not have six large trees, three on each side, growing in the middle of a ploughed field." That was impeccable Irish logic.

Consequently *The Playboy* has but the one set, the *shebeen* Pegeen helps her father run, and now Synge was able to get interested in an idea he might otherwise have dropped, since we in the audience no longer know what happened in the field as we listen to Christy, so his eloquence can work on us the way it does on the men and girls of Mayo. This greatly alters the effect envisaged in *The Murderer*, where we'd have seen a braggart inflaming silly folk we were free to feel superior to. Now Christy's talk can create an heroic world.

> CHRISTY (*impressively*): With that the sun came out between the cloud and the hill, and it shining green in my face. "God have mercy on your soul," says he, lifting a scythe. "Or on your own," says I, raising the loy.
> SUSAN: That's a grand story.
> HONOR: He tells it lovely.

CHRISTY (*flattered and confident, waving bone*): He gave a drive with the scythe, and I gave a lep to the east. Then I turned around with my back to the north, and I hit a blow on the ridge of his skull, laid him stretched out, and he spilt to the knob of his gullet. (*He raises the chicken bone to his Adam's apple*).

GIRLS (*together*): Well, you're a marvel! Oh, God bless you! You're the lad surely!

Indeed it's a grand story and he tells it lovely, guided by a playwright who knew with what ceremonies of formal speech and specificity of clinical detail *The Iliad* tells such things, or how Ulysses, famous for his lies, entranced the Phaiacians over drinks with wondrous tales. The equipoise between language and heroics in Homer would eventually occupy Joyce, and Synge had no doubt that eloquence the like of Nora Burke's tramp's could limn for the deprived some land of heart's desire. *The Playboy*, one of the first self-cancelling plays, is a great iridescent bubble we watch blown, and admire till the moment it bursts, and regret after. It is we, and not only Pegeen in that forlorn last speech, who have lost the only Playboy of the Western World. We shall have him back as surely as the curtain can be persuaded to rise on another performance.

But tucks will appear in a fabric however well woven. If on the opening night the wrongness that offended the patriots was not wrong with the play but with their ideology, still there was something else wrong, to be sensed as dogs sense ozone far from thunder, and that was a subtle wrongness with Synge's whole sense of even the most brutalized Catholic peasantry. Though he used, he said, barely a word that he hadn't heard, still it was by him the words were arranged, and the oaths and invocations seem not so much over-numerous as disconcertingly placed. They bubble at the crests of good-humored vigor; and a cheerful vigor in that continuum of poverty is the daydream of a scion of Bible-readers who trusts that elsewhere, despite all, there exist people the rhythm of whose "Providence and Mercy, spare us all!" bespeaks chthonic energies.

Among such people there will be poltroons of course, afeard of Father Reilly and fussing about a dispensation to marry; that was a way to characterize Shawn Keogh, and it did not trouble Synge that there was no intelligible reason why a dispensation should be needed. Prof. Henn thinks it is necessary because Pegeen and Shawn are being married in Lent, but Lent is in March and Synge's note beneath the list of characters states plainly that the play is set in the autumn.* No, "dispensation" for Synge is a piece of Papist rigmarole Father Reilly can worry Shawn Keogh with: a trivial detail but indicative of a surface beneath which his knowledge of Kerry and Mayo did not penetrate.

Or cast a cold eye on the speech with which Pegeen's father greets Christy in Act III:

> —The blessing of God and the holy angels on your head, young fellow. I hear tell you're after winning all in the sports below; and wasn't it a shame I didn't bear you along with me to Kate Cassidy's wake, a fine stout lad, the like of you, for you'd never see the match of it for flows of drink, the way when we sunk her bones at noonday in her narrow grave, there were five men, aye, and six men, strained out retching speechless on the holy stones.

That is not the talk of the Congested Districts but of a fantasy land as like Mayo as Shakespeare's bear-plagued seacoast of Bohemia is like the Adriatic strand. Shakespeare had the advantage over Synge, that no one from Bohemia was likely to be at the Globe.

The speech assembles much verifiable detail: that spirits flow at a wake, that one measure of a spirituous deluge is the body-count of the prostrate, that these if conscious will retch, that a grave is narrow, that God and the holy angels may get ceremonially invoked. Yet as the utterance of a Mayo pubkeeper it is implausible, and Synge though he defended his local accuracies ("one or two words only that I have not heard") never claimed a play made of such speeches was plausible. "An extravaganza," he said, and we'd best believe him, noting how like are its mechanics to those of well-made French farce, abundant in contrivances to hustle someone—in France the deceived husband, here the aggrieved father—back and forth through doors so he'll not meet someone else.

Synge's extravagances are propelled by his love of dizzying contrasts:

> MAHON . . . (*With hesitation.*) What's that? they're raising him up. They're coming this way. (*With a roar of rage and astonishment.*) It's Christy, by the stars of God! I'd know his way of spitting and he astride the moon.

This has literary analogues more cogent than the dubious folk ones Synge half-claimed. The stars of God, spitting, the moon: heterogeneous ideas yoked by violence together: a taste for such effects was coalescing, and we may reflect that the play was finished only six years before Grierson's edition

---

*Prof. Henn may have been misled by Christy's reference to gaming when Good Friday's by, but Christy has also said that'll be "in four months or five."

of Donne inaugurated the new century's resurrection of that yeasty poet. "Metaphysical" qualities have since been noted in the way Jimmy Farrell tells how madness is a fright:

—It's a fright, surely. I knew a party was kicked in the head by a red mare, and he went killing horses a great while, till he eat the insides of a clock and died after.

Horses, an indigestible clock: if we think of lovers and a pair of "stiff twin compasses" we spot something astir in the sensibility of that decade, that would soon welcome "A Valediction, Forbidding Mourning," despised nearly two hundred years. Or "The Relique":

> When my grave is broke up again
> Some second guest to entertain
> —For graves have learned that woman-head
> To be to more than one a bed—
>   And he that digs it, spies
> A bracelet of bright hair about the bone. . . .

Soon T. S. Eliot would marvel at the "telescoping of images," "the sudden contrast of associations of 'bright hair' and of 'bone,'" and in a similar connection would adduce "that surprise which has been one of the most important means of poetic effect since Homer," poetic effect having been delivered from Tennyson. Yeats concurred. "Donne could be as metaphysical as he pleased . . . because he could be as physical as he pleased." And Synge:

—Did you ever hear tell of the skulls they have in the city of Dublin, ranged out like blue jars in a cabin of Connaught?
—And you believe that?
—Didn't a lad see them, and he after coming from harvesting in the Liverpool boat? "They have them there," says he, "making a show of the great people there was one time walking the world. White skulls and black skulls and yellow skulls, and some with full teeth, and some haven't only but one."
—It's no lie, maybe, for when I was a young lad there was a graveyard beyond the house with the remnants of a man who had thighs as long as your arm. He was a horrid man, I'm telling you, and there was many a fine Sunday I'd put him together for fun, and he with shiny bones, you wouldn't meet the like of these days in the cities of the world.

He labored through many drafts of a poem for his fiancée Molly Allgood that evokes near a churchyard full of whitening bones a sexual resurrection of the body. In verse, though, he was too near the Victorians to attempt direct speech save at the bony lines. In one draft we find,

> . . . With what new gold you'd gilded all the moon
> With what rare anthem raised the river's tune
> Where bees fetch honey for their swarming cribs
> And we're two skulls and backs and forty ribs. . . .

Meter, until the skulls and ribs poke through, confines him in Georgian diction; he was right to give up his early fumblings toward verse drama. It was out of rhythms the pentameter does not permit that his idiosyncratic effects arose.

Yet a governing rhythm, which entails a convention for speaking, was one ground of Elizabethan stage success, and Synge's high ambitions left him soon uncontented with anything less than a modern equivalent. Yeats noted as early as *The Well of the Saints* that "all his people would change their life if the rhythm changed," and *The Playboy,* so often rewritten in quest of a form for its verbal designs, offers one audacious experiment, the presence from the opening words to the closing of a persistent recurrent tune, an Irish tune with remote Gaelic credentials, marked by a rhythmic figure that troubles actors because its jaunty beat can be neither obeyed nor suppressed. When Yeats wrote that Synge "made word and phrase dance to a very strange rhythm," difficult for players "till his plays have created their own tradition," *The Playboy* was still in the making, and no actor had yet confronted the challenge of delivering Christy Mahon's exit-speech, that summation of a romping future with his da:

> CHRISTY: Ten thousand blessings upon all that's here, for you've turned me a likely gaffer in the end of all, the way I'll go romancing through a romping lifetime from this hour to the dawning of the Judgement Day.

Something wants to force the last clauses into a quatrain:

> The way I'll go romancing
> through a romping lifetime
> from this hour to the dawning
> of the <u>Judge</u> ment <u>Day</u>.

Nor is that unique; more are easily collected.

> I did not then.
> Oh, they're bloody liars
> in the naked parish
> where I grew a man.

Each of the following is within a page of the next:

> It should have been great
> and bitter torment
> did rouse your spirits
> to a <u>deed</u> <u>of</u> <u>blood</u>.
>
> .   .   .
>
> That was a sneaky
> kind of murder
> did win small glory
> with the <u>boys</u> <u>it</u> <u>self</u>.
>
> .   .   .
>
> And that there isn't
> my match in Mayo
> for thatching, or mowing,
> or shearing a sheep.
>
> .   .   .
>
> Till I'm thinking this night
> wasn't I a foolish fellow
> not to kill my father
> in the <u>years</u> <u>gone</u> <u>by</u>.

These are all from Act I, and once we have picked up the pattern—three syncopated measures, then a thudding three-stress termination—we may come to think it omnipresent. We may even find its elements, with free interpolation dividing them, in Pegeen's opening words:

> Six yards of stuff
> for to make a yellow gown
> A pair of lace boots with lengthy
> heels on them and brassy eyes.
> A hat is suited
> for a <u>wed</u> <u>ding</u> <u>day</u>.

"For a <u>wed</u> | <u>ding</u> | <u>day</u>"; "in the <u>years</u> | <u>gone</u> | <u>by</u>"; "of the <u>Judge</u> | <u>ment</u> | <u>Day</u>"; that triple terminal beat: where can we have heard it before? It is possible we are remembering its debasement in the anthology piece about the bells of Shandon on the <u>ri</u> | <u>ver</u> | <u>Lee</u>.

> On this I ponder
> Where'er I wander

> And thus grow fonder,
>> Sweet Cork, of thee:
> With thy bells of Shandon
> That sound so grand on
>> The pleasant waters
>>> Of the river Lee.

Those over-familiar lines of Francis Mahony (1804–1866) dance to a persistent tune indeed: they echo "The Groves of Blarney" by Richard Milliken (1767–1815), who was parodying something anonymous called "Castlehyde," which went to Irish music that once had Gaelic words, now lost. Synge was a fiddler. Did he somewhere pick up the old tune? Was it merely "The Bells of Shandon" that rang in his head?

Surely not. Fiddle-music or no, he could have found Irish assonantal stanzas like the one that degenerated into "Shandon" exhibited in Douglas Hyde's *Songs Ascribed to Raftery* (1903), with deft English imitations, as for instance:

> There's a lovely posy lives by the roadway
>> Deirdre was nowhere beside my joy,
> Nor Helen who boasted of conquests Trojan,
> For whom was roasted the town of Troy.

Try that again: "The <u>town</u> | <u>of</u> | <u>Troy</u>": "for a <u>wed</u> | <u>ding</u> | <u>day</u>": yes, it's close. A folk rhythm, then, known to Sassenachs in its "Bells of Shandon" debasement.

That he built this rhythm (and others) into speech after speech of *The Playboy* is indisputable. How he judged it we cannot know. Like much other Irish, it had been rendered banal already by English parody. A banality, then, to establish Christy's banality? A lilt, to endear? More likely, a token of how Christy and his da and Pegeen and the rest are bound into one community of lilting rogues.

Had he lived we'd know more of the drama he intuited: prose knitted by cross-rhythms insistent as any verse. He wrote but six plays, and in a brief time, 1902–1909, the last months of which were also taken up with dying. William Shakespeare's sixth play (of thirty-odd) was merely *Titus Andronicus*.

The sixth play of Synge was *Deirdre of the Sorrows,* which the indefatigable first-nighter Joseph Holloway thought "of little worth."

"The ruck of muck," he wrote in his 1910 diary; and "the loftiness of the theme was trailed in the mud." True, this Deirdre is a girl who can be short with the High King of Ireland and men comparably exalted. Her "Draw a little back with the squabbling of fools" is not a thing we'd hear from the Deirdre of Yeats, a poet's Queen, never less than lofty, even coquettishly lofty. Yet it hushes the stage for words she can speak in a low intent voice, and even spoken with no special emphasis they search the full register of Synge's rhetoric:

> DEIRDRE: Draw a little back with the squabbling of fools when I am broken
> up with misery. (*She turns round.*) I see the flames of Emain starting upward
> in the dark night; and because of me there will be weasels and wild cats
> crying on a lonely wall where there were queens and armies and red gold,
> the way there will be a story told of a ruined city and a raving king and a
> woman will be young for ever. (*She looks round.*) I see the trees naked and
> bare, and the moon shining. Little moon, little moon of Alban, it's lonesome
> you'll be this night, and tomorrow night, and long nights after, and you
> pacing the woods beyond Glen Laoi, looking every place for Deirdre and
> Naisi, the two lovers who slept so sweetly with each other.

"Raving," "naked," "slept with each other": with an effort one can grasp what it was dismayed Holloway. Yet there is precedent for such descents of diction. "A lass unparallel'd," wrote Shakespeare of his Cleopatra, in his one play to meld the subplot with the high plot and achieve this by language only. "Lass" is a low word. So is "dung":

> And it is great
> To do that thing that ends all other deeds,
> Which shackles accidents and bolts up change,
> Which sleeps, and never palates more the dung,
> The beggar's nurse, and Caesar's.

Wincers have not been lacking who'd emend "dung" to "dug." And what of "wretch," "fool," and "ass"?

> (*To an asp*) Come, thou mortal wretch,
> With thy sharp teeth this knot intrinsicate
> Of life at once untie. Poor venomous fool,
> Be angry, and dispatch. O, couldst thou speak,
> That I might hear thee call great Caesar ass,
> Unpolicied!

(The next words are "O Eastern star!") And Deirdre:

—I have put away sorrow like a shoe that is worn out and muddy, for it is I
have had a life that will be envied by great companies. It was not by a low
birth I made kings uneasy, and they sitting in the halls of Emain. It was not
a low thing to be chosen by Conchubor, who was wise, and Naisi had no
match for bravery. It is not a small thing to be rid of grey hairs, and the
loosening of the teeth. (*With a sort of triumph.*) It was the choice of lives we
had in the clear woods, and in the grave, we're safe, surely.

One more speech (". . . It is a cold place I must go to be with you, Naisi. . . .")
and she has pressed a knife into her heart. It seems beyond doubt that
Synge's model was the death-scene of Cleopatra, that he was not awed by
its challenge, and that transposing such effects of scale and grandeur from
Shakespeare's baroque Alexandria to a "Tent . . . with shabby skins and
benches" in barbaric Ireland was well within the grasp of a talent still
extending its scope as he sank toward death. If "grey hairs, and the loosening of the teeth" might be Nora Burke speaking, that is not because Synge
is still fixed amid his phrases of 1903. It is one note merely on a long scale
over which, in those last desperate months, he was gaining serene command.
The resources of the Synge of Deirdre, unglimpsed by the Synge of Nora
Burke and Pegeen Mike, include a new mastery of the single taut word: "It
was the choice of lives we had in the clear woods," where "clear" condenses
an outdoor starlit world, their one-time openness of vision, the freedom of
the woods as against Emain with red gold on the walls, a moment's decisive
clarity amid entanglements. Or test the ring of another understated phrase:
"It was not by a low birth I made kings uneasy. . . ." How finely indeter-
minate is "uneasy"!

There is language here of such originality that Synge would be dead
twenty years before anyone managed an articulate response to it. That was
William Empson, who saw in 1929 that such words as the following force
a critic to say something new:

DEIRDRE: . . . It should be a sweet thing to have what is best and richest, if it's
for a short space only.
NAISI: And we've a short space only to be triumphant and brave.

"The language here seems rich in implications; it certainly carries much
feeling and conveys a delicate sense of style. But if one thinks of the Roman
and mediaeval associations of *triumphant,* even of its normal use in English,
one feels a sort of unexplained warning that these are irrelevant; the word
here is a thin counter standing for a notion not fully translated out of Irish;

it is used to eke out that alien and sliding speech-rhythm, which puts no weight upon its single words."

Deirdre of the Sorrows is not a play Synge finished; Act II is especially thin, and no one can say what he would have done to it all in more months. In its provisional state it's still enough to show us how his conception of tragedy had progressed from the steady keening of *Riders to the Sea,* and his sense of language from the quick comic contrasts of *The Playboy.* Old Mahon's "It's Christy! by the stars of God! I'd know his way of spitting and he astride the moon" was minted by the same sensibility as "I have put away sorrow like a shoe that is worn out and muddy," but being comic it verges on mannerism, and the *Deirdre* speech is beyond mannerism. So is this:

DEIRDRE: Do not raise a hand to touch me.
CONCHUBOR: There are other hands to touch you. My fighters are set round in
   among the trees.
DEIRDRE: Who'll fight the grave, Conchubor, and it opened on a dark night?

It was soon a commonplace that Synge wrote such speeches with a mind absorbed by his own death. That he was dying all his short working life— indeed "dying chose the living world for text"—was a necessary part of the myth Yeats made of him. Romantic ritual has need of a stilled precursor: must canonize if need be even a Chatterton, pathetic faker and Words- worth's "marvelous boy." The complex role Wordsworths or Yeatses play includes obligation toward some void left by destiny, some body of unimag- inable things unsaid: what mute inglorious Miltons might have uttered, what sweeter unheard melodies were lost with Keats. Such compensation as the living can offer is all the more poignant in being forever insufficient, since what can replace unique individual power?

Though we can never test such a myth for truth, it is tempting to wonder how the Irish Renaissance would look had Synge lived, the Psalmist's span, into the 1940's, and had it been Yeats who was silenced instead, say by the nervous breakdown he suffered early in 1909. In losing much poetry, need- less to itemize, we should have gained a movement at whose center was a great dramatist, internationally acclaimed. What we have, *The Playboy* even, is 'prentice work; he found his vocation late, and had but six years for it.

His death left Yeats to create a myth of noble isolation in a Tower, and left the other pole of the Irish literary future at the disposal of a "lankylook- ing galoot" Synge had known in Paris, where, the hole being greater than the pants, he seldom took off his macintosh. That was James Joyce, 1902. Though Joyce, fresh out of college, argued heatedly that *Riders to the Sea* was too brief for canonical tragedy, he esteemed it enough to take trouble over an Italian translation the Synge estate wouldn't grant Triestinos leave to play. He even called Synge's art "more original than my own" (1907), and though he made Buck Mulligan mock at Synge—Shakespeare, says the Buck, is "the chap that writes like Synge"—in *Finnegans Wake* he slipped Synge's name into a list of Lord Mayors of Dublin, and in Trieste and Zurich and Paris sustained as did no one else in our century the principle that incessant labor and redrafting might elevate seeming trivia into greatness.

BERLITZ DAYS

O, triste, triste était mon âme.

VERLAINE

And trieste, ah trieste ate I my liver!

Finnegans Wake

James Joyce, B.A., taught English in Trieste, where he had found something else you could do with an Irish degree.

A degree led most young men one of three ways: toward law, the route his friend Con Curran had taken; toward medicine, like his friend Gogarty; or toward the priesthood. The first two entailed expense on a scale the Joyce family could no longer think of meeting, though even so Jim had dabbled in medicine, which proved not to be his cup of broth. As for the priesthood, its rule is that God chooses you, and though visions of an illuminated name, "The Rev. James A. Joyce, S.J.," had at one time swirled in his head, Jim grew convinced that whatever the Roman priesthood might be it had not been chosen for him.

He had been chosen instead by the Priesthood of Art, a notion not incompatible in those days with inkwells and low bohemia. In France lapsed Catholics staffed the Symbolist movement, questing for efficacious words of power. *Hoc est enim corpus meum* were words that claimed power to alter whatever reality underlay bread's unchanged appearances. Quite as potent might be, thought Stéphane Mallarmé, some fit words for the azure Nothing at the heart of everything in a world mysteriously destined to terminate in a Book. (*Tout, au monde, existe pour aboutir à un livre.*) Gazing on his inkwell, he saw it "crystalline as consciousness, with at bottom its drop of shadows pertaining to 'let there be something' " (*l'encrier, cristal comme un conscience, avec sa goutte, au fond, de ténèbres relatives à ce que quelque chose soit*). So the Penman of *Finnegans Wake* inhabits the Haunted Inkbottle.

In Paris Mallarmé had lived by teaching English. He had learned it in order to decipher inscriptions by Poe, an incanting bard whose very name was embedded in the syllables of "Poète." Less formally, and unpaid save by esteem, he taught with "inexhaustibly subtle speech" a way for his visitors to regard the universe: as a dream. (Likewise, remarked one of them, the sea is summed up by a murmur in a shell.) Arthur Symons had attended his Tuesday evening séances* at 87 rue de Rome, and is said to have taken Yeats there (useless: Mallarmé's French was subtle, Yeats's bad). It was Symons who filled Yeats's head with tidings of a new Sacred Book of the Arts: a conception the better calculated to arouse Yeats in that Mallarmé himself ascribed it to the Alchemists.

In November 1897, in *The Savoy,* Yeats published *The Tables of the Law,* a *fin-de-siècle* fantasy in which the monk-errant Owen Aherne, connoisseur of fine wines through which the light can pass to dye his long delicate fingers, has acquired the lost *Liber Inducens in Evangelium Aeternum* of Joachim de Flora, who prophesied the Kingdom of the Spirit triumphing over the dead letter. Its first part, *Fractura Tabularum,* the breaking of the tablets, invites adepts to invert the Mosaic commandments, and its second, *Lex Secreta,* the secret law, "describes the true inspiration of action, the only Eternal Evangel."

If this "Joachim" has been worded with the aid of Blake, a spirit more exclusive than Blake's has interfered too. For there exist a secret few, we learn, "elected not to live, but to reveal that secret substance of God which is colour and music and softness and a sweet odour." These have "no father but the Holy Spirit," and no midwife perhaps but Arthur Symons, or rather W. B. Yeats's misunderstanding of how Symons misunderstood the sayings of Mallarmé. Whatever its pedigree, by age nineteen James Joyce knew whole paragraphs of it by heart. It helped shape the conception of "Stephen Dedalus," whose purpose is "to live, to err, to fall, to triumph, to recreate life out of life." Stephen is defined in part by the 1890's, in part by being an Irish ex-Christian.

---

*Legend has accumulated around those *Mardis*; the Columbia *Dictionary of Modern European Literature* (1947; s.v. "Mallarmé") even lists T. S. Eliot among the postulants, notwithstanding that Mallarmé died when Eliot was ten.

Persisting in his concern for Sacred Books and their authors, Yeats scanned the horizons visible from the Tower he had rebuilt in the spirit of Axël. "Why are these strange souls born everywhere today?" he would be asking as late as 1922: he meant souls "with hearts that Christianity as shaped by history cannot satisfy." And:

> Why should we believe that religion can never bring round its antithesis? Is it true that our air is disturbed, as Mallarmé said, by "the trembling of the veil of the temple," or "that our whole age is seeking to bring forth a sacred book"? Some of us thought that book near towards the end of last century, but the tide sank again.

It was in the year Yeats dated those words that the firm of Shakespeare & Co., Paris, published a big blue book called *Ulysses,* in which a mocker modelled on Yeats's friend Oliver Gogarty mocks the freedom with which an earlier Yeats had identified sacred books: "The most beautiful book that has come out of our country in my time. One thinks of Homer." That is cruel in conflating two Yeatsian remarks, one of which had pertained to Lady Gregory's *Cuchulain of Muirthemne.* A book called *Ulysses,* though, yes, that does make you think of Homer, though there's no sign that Yeats ever thought it a candidate for sacredness.

But in 1905 *Ulysses* was seventeen years ahead. Back in Dublin Yeats was burbling of Sacred Books and rewriting yet again *The Shadowy Waters,* Oliver Gogarty was making ready to buy the kind of automobile you wore goggles to drive, Joseph Holloway's journal was accumulating reprobations of Synge's new play *The Well of the Saints* ("unpleasantly plain speech"; "mixture of lyric and dirt"). In Gaelic League classes patriots stumbled through Gaelic; in Dublin Castle authorities recruited spies. Easter was not to explode for eleven years.

In Trieste, amid a mixture of idealism and dirt, James A. Joyce, B.A., high in rented quarters he had scant prospect of paying for, worked on stories by night, taught Triestinos English by day. The girl who'd come with him from Dublin was pregnant.

He taught English according to the new Berlitz system, which departed from centuries of custom in forbidding a teacher to use any language in the students' hearing save the one they were learning. It was modelled on the fact that French children learn French by hearing French, not from discussions of French in a meta-tongue, and it forced him to confront anew, idiom by idiom, "this language, so familiar and so foreign."

—It is raining. You have brought an umbrella.

—??

—An um-brel-la.

—??

—(*pointing*): Um–brel–la.

With what banalities were his days not filled? "It is a fine day. It is not raining. You have not brought an umbrella. The cat sits on the mat. There is tea in the pot. This is a pot. There is tea in it. I shall pour you some tea." For this he earned nine and a half pence an hour, and priceless experience.

For what other writer has confronted English conversation like that, from the ground up? It is not by the intentions of speakers but by forms of words that much of its silence is filled, and dialogue contrived to tell facts to readers of stories is apt to be false dialogue. There is no sign that Joyce valued his Berlitz experience at the time. It brought in pennies. At night he could write.

Mrs Mooney was a butcher's daughter. She was a woman who was quite able to keep things to herself: a determined woman. Note the Berlitz discipline whereby the words that precede it help define "determined." *She had married her father's foreman and opened a butcher's shop near Spring Gardens.* Note the subject of both verbs. *But as soon as his father-in-law was dead Mr Mooney began to go to the devil. He drank, plundered the till, ran headlong into debt. . . . By fighting his wife in the presence of customers and by buying bad meat he ruined his business.* Note the order of these two items; scandal exceeds bad meat. And fifty monosyllables in eighty-one words.

Such were nuances Joyce could isolate in the heat of watching them elude beginners amid only the simplest constructions.

One thing seemed oddly clear: that the language of any Sacred Book of the Arts was destined to be English. Mallarmé had written a treatise on English words, *Les Mots anglais,* and Yeats's eye for symptomatic detail did not fail to note an English dictionary among the few books in the room of Paul Verlaine (who located in it, somehow, "Erysipelas"). Who now could cast a colder eye upon English than an Irishman with Jesuit training? Skeat's *Etymological Dictionary* dated from the very year of Joyce's birth, and he had read it in the National Library "by the hour."

His first published fiction (August 1904: he was still in Dublin) was an unsettling little story called "The Sisters." The names of the sisters were Nannie and Eliza and they had a brother, a priest, now dead upstairs.

Reading the story today in *Dubliners,* we may think to wonder why Joyce called it "The Sisters," so much is its narrator preoccupied with the dead man. Then paying heed to the sisters, we may notice that though Eliza talks incessantly, Nannie, who's so hardworking she's "wore out," says nothing whatsoever, and this may prompt us to remember the sisters in St. Luke's narrative (ch. x), one of whom, Martha, kept conspicuously busy while Mary (who had "chosen the better part") preferred divine talk.

In St. John's gospel (ch. xi) we encounter these sisters again. They have lost their brother Lazarus, but since their guest is the Messiah the ending is happy: Jesus calls him back from the grave. (Dubliners are not Bible-readers, but the words of recall rang out from pulpits annually. "Come forth, Lazarus!" went a Dublin joke; but "he came fifth, and lost the job.") Joyce's story ends like the joke. Near the end all talk stops for everyone to listen. "I too listened; but there was no sound in the house." This brother lies in his coffin unresurrected.

That is one way to commence a sacred book, by keeping your eye on another one. Synge too got themes by converting Biblical ones, and it may have been the unwanted resurrection in *The Shadow of the Glen* that prompted Joyce. Having met Synge and argued with him about dramaturgy in Paris in March 1903, he is unlikely to have missed the play's premiere on 8 October when they were both back in Dublin, and it is on record that he turned up when a new production was in rehearsal the next summer, just before he wrote "The Sisters."

"I am writing a series of epicleti—ten—for a paper," Joyce wrote to Con Curran of his plans at that stage, some time in mid-1904. With ten envisaged, it is no surprise if he turned to the New Testament for his prompt-book. Its themes were, by homiletic convention, reenacted all the time among Christian people: scales falling from eyes, faith moving mountains, assemblies in upper rooms: any preacher could tell you, and did tell every Sunday, how you'd recognize such things in the life around you. And we note that Joyce didn't say "stories," accounts of happenings; his word, *epicleti*, pertains to his clarifications of what clergy took it upon themselves to clarify.

Epicleti would be "invocations": in the Eastern rite, though no longer the Western, callings to the Holy Spirit, to come down and transubstantiate the ordinary. We should notice in passing that Joyce who knew no Greek would let himself be seen parading Greek words (most famously, *epiphany*) the way other young men showed off tags of Irish, from a language most of them were no wiser about. His Greek, though later Homeric, was scriptural at this stage, the Priest of the Eternal Imagination hewing close to the texts rival priests elucidated.

The "paper" he mentioned was *The Irish Homestead,* where his connection was the gentle AE. Its readers were interested in cooperative dairies, and in the issue of 13 August 1904 an early text of "The Sisters" competed with advertisements for cream separators and milk pumps. No one, we may safely guess, AE least of all, divined the story's model, in part because beginner's technique obscured it. The narrative progressed by flat statement:

> We sat downstairs in the little room behind the shop, my aunt and I and the two sisters. Nannie sat in a corner and said nothing, but her lips moved from speaker to speaker with a painfully intelligent motion. I said nothing either, being too young, but my aunt spoke a good deal, for she is a bit of a gossip—harmless.

In the version of "The Sisters" readers of *Dubliners* know, barely a sentence of this was left untouched from beginning to end; that paragraph for instance became,

> We blessed ourselves and came away. In the little room downstairs we found Eliza seated in his chair in state. I groped my way towards my usual chair in the corner while Nannie went to the sideboard and brought out a decanter of sherry and some wine-glasses. She set these on the table and invited us to take a little glass of wine. Then, at her sister's bidding, she poured out the sherry into the glasses and passed them to us. She pressed me to take some cream crackers also but I declined because I thought I would make too much noise eating them. She seemed to be somewhat disappointed at my refusal and went over quietly to the sofa where she sat down behind her sister. No one spoke: we all gazed at the empty fireplace.

This uncannily engages the reader's attention. "Eliza seated in his chair in state"—the chair her brother has vacated forever: while Nannie does the necessary work, Eliza has made the move toward dominance. It is she who bids her sister pour the sherry. Nannie always performs these practical actions, but Eliza never: something the story is no longer explicit about. Also the boy who had been explicitly "young" has become a lad self-conscious about the noise he'd make eating crackers. And emphasis on his gossipy aunt is withdrawn, to keep our attention on the talkative Eliza. We are left to notice these things—good Berlitz technique. Also, like the boy, we are made to feel that behind all that is perfectly explicit there is something we are not quite grasping.

We may guess at what went wrong with Father Flynn. He grasped that

God did not choose him—perhaps out of non-existence? And, prompted by the enigma of the title, we may even divine the story's scriptural model.

We need not. But if we do it gives us two narratives to compare. Of Luke's Mary and Joyce's Eliza, the word-oriented women, we may note that whereas the Bethany Mary "sat at Jesus' feet, and heard his word," the Dublin Eliza chatters; as for the Dublin Nannie, the one who plays the biblical Martha's part and keeps busy, she is not silent because occupied but because gone deaf (and "it would have been unseemly to have shouted at her"). There is no Messiah present of any description. And for counterpart to the center of St. John's story, when Jesus before he undertakes the miracle challenges the bereaved, "Believest thou this?" we have someone who (as the boy does not divine) some years ago lost all belief. Father Flynn was found "sitting up by himself in the dark in his confession-box, wide awake and laughing-like softly to himself." Later he would give the boy instruction, less in Jesus' way than in the way of the Scribes, with emphasis on "books as thick as the *Post Office Directory* and as closely written as the law notices in the newspaper, elucidating all these intricate questions." That was a touch Joyce added in the revising.

Had anyone in 1904 read "The Sisters" to its bottom, there would have been an outcry against the *Homestead* to rival the *Playboy* riots. But no one noticed, nor was it noticed either that the next story by "Stephen Daedalus" (10 September 1904) had for unwritten text "Follow me," words the gospels twelve times ascribe to Jesus. You'd follow Jesus to an ascetic life, but it's not to that life the sailor in "Eveline" has summoned an impressionable girl. What she has in mind is matrimony, meaning escape. What he has in mind . . . but we've no access to his mind.

Eveline Hill in the end does not follow this chap who calls himself "Frank": perhaps just as well for her if you ponder the improbability of a house await for a bride in Buenos Ayres (Joyce's twist on the "Hi Breasil" of Irish lore, a good place beyond the sea). When she doesn't follow he leaves anyway, hardly the act of a man who is claiming his bride. And like the rich youth (Matthew xix) who also declined to follow, Eveline sorrows and will think for the rest of her life that it was by her own fault she missed something grand.

In "After the Race," his next *Homestead* story (17 December 1904), "Stephen Daedalus" returned to the troubled Rich Young Man. Jimmy Doyle too at the end of his story is troubled, though not, like his scriptural prototype, on account of any injunction to distribute his heritage to the poor. No, he's remorseful after a meaningless night he has spent losing much of it at cards to other youths who are already rich. This is the least of the stories because most dependent on a prototype* the others permit you to miss. Joyce said he meant to rewrite it but lost interest.

After that his connection with the *Homestead* lapsed; not that implicit blasphemy was discerned, but there were letters of complaint. Readers of "Our Weekly Story" were accustomed to a positive note.

By the end of December, 1905, in Trieste, the "Epicleti—ten" had become twelve stories, soon afterward fourteen, by 1907 fifteen, that nobody would publish. A printer in London balked at the taboo word *bloody,* and at other details. The London publisher dropped out. Dublin next, where there was fuss about mention of pubs by name—might Davy Byrne sue? Also *bloody* still gave trouble. In 1910–1912 the same publisher (Maunsell's George Roberts) who was gathering Synge's *Works* into four volumes, shifts and all, dithered and temporized. Joyce travelled all the way to Dublin, to no avail. A Dublin printer who'd manufactured a thousand copies of the book invoked his saints and destroyed them, Joyce heard by fire though that was an Irish Fact (they'd been chopped). Back in Trieste, he responded to word of fire with *Gas from a Burner*, in which the printer explains:

> Ladies and gents, you are here assembled
> To hear how earth and heaven trembled. . . .
>
> .   .   .
>
> Who was it said: Resist not evil?
> I'll burn that book, so help me devil.
> I'll sing a psalm as I watch it burn
> And the ashes I'll keep in a one-handled† urn. . . .
> This very next lent I will unbare
> My penitent buttocks to the air . . .
> My Irish foreman from Bannockburn
> Shall dip his right hand in the urn
> And sign crisscross with reverent thumb
> *Memento homo* on my bum.

Memento homo: "Remember, man, that thou art mortal": the priest says this on Ash Wednesday, marking each penitent's forehead with a cross of sacred

---

*Richard Ellmann (*James Joyce,* 170) suggests another prototype, the victim of enchanted cards in "Red Hanrahan," a story Yeats had published the previous December. With Joyce all things are possible. But I'd guess that only in the grip of an extrinsic idea like transposing the Bible's Rich Young Man to Dublin would he have attempted a milieu he didn't know, the yachting set. He never did that again.

†Dublin euphemism for a chamberpot. Thus in *Ulysses* the loop of his akimbo arm gets Nelson on his monument called "the onehandled adulterer."

ashes. The ashes had been last year's Palm Sunday palms, which commemorated the branches strewn before the Messiah as he entered Jerusalem that last time, on an ass. Recipients of *Gas from a Burner* were free to divine how Joyce's last entry into Ireland's chief city had ended, *ut implerentur scripturae,* in what he deemed a crucifixion. He never returned.

Aside from "The Dead," an afterthought of 1907, the last two stories to be written were "Two Gallants," in which a man puts in time wandering the streets while another man is performing a seduction, and "A Little Cloud," in which a poet *manqué* confronts the kind of word-man who gets ahead. In these we may glimpse the author's first intimations of the Bloom and Stephen situations in *Ulysses.* Likewise we may catch in *Gas from a Burner* an early whiff of the big book's parodic manner, something it does not explicitly flaunt until the long, savagely travestied patriotic set-pieces of "Cyclops" proclaim the sacred commonplaces of men as self-righteous as Roberts's printer.

Large systems of attention are coming together. It was after "Two Gallants" and "A Little Cloud," at the end of September 1906, that he thought of a story to be called "Ulysses," about the Dublin Jew on the Clonliffe Road—Jim and his brother both knew him—who went by the name of Hunter and had a wife said to receive admirers.

If "Ulysses," as Joyce later reported, "never got any forrarder than the title," that may have been because it was overmuch like "Two Gallants" in its focus on a man putting in time, waiting. For it can't have been meant to encompass the events in the second half of the *Ulysses* we know. The title, what could that bring to mind save a wanderer awaited by a faithful wife? And the ironic point would have been, an *un*faithful wife. A story about a man adrift, attending to makeshift business, knowing he's being cuckolded, that's a *Dubliners* story, with "Ulysses" for a title. It encompasses the matter of seven consecutive episodes of *Ulysses,* "Calypso" to "Wandering Rocks," and given what later came of the conception we are unspeakably fortunate it never got written. When midway through "Wandering Rocks" we watch Bloom procuring for his wife the new book she's requested, moreover a piece of porn by which he's taken when he sees their life mirrored in it, we recognize the tang of a *Dubliners* ending. (The world exists to end in a book.)

With *Ulysses* growing somewhere in the back of his mind, Joyce went on teaching, went on trying to get *Dubliners* published, and labored to rework yet another book, of which earlier he had dashed off a thousand dispensable pages: the story of his own early life. This was ten years becoming *A Portrait of the Artist as a Young Man*, after which fiction in English would never be the same.

> Once upon a time and a very good time it was there was a moocow coming down along the road and this moocow that was coming down along the road met a nicens little boy named Baby Tuckoo. . . .
> His father told him that story: his father looked at him through a glass: he had a hairy face. . . .

In the first sentence, three words we've never read before: we absorb them. Then for "glass" we guess to read "monocle," a word Baby Tuckoo wouldn't know. And "hairy face" says "bearded," a decision we are put to the risk of making. We enjoy no position of privilege with a helpful author-cicerone at our side. We are Berlitz pupils, moving alert, inductively, substituting, comprehending. The English language is something this Irishman will have us *watch* as it's never been watched before. ("When you wet the bed first it is warm then it gets cold"; two hundred pages later the mind in creation is likened to "a fading coal": ponder that correlation.) For a page and a half we undergo a qualifying exam, until a row of asterisks inaugurates familiar narrative: "The wide playgrounds were swarming with boys. . . ."

In this five-parted book, his first extended unified composition, Joyce pressed his intuitions of mathematic form. On the second page a mocking vengeful chorus—

> *Apologise,*
> *Pull out his eyes,*
> *Pull out his eyes,*
> *Apologise.*

—pounds through Stephen's brain and silently diagrams on the page the *a-b-b-a* figure Greek rhetoricians called *chiasmus,* later exemplified by such expressions as "but her long fair hair was girlish, and girlish . . . was her face."

Chiasmus, though, is not confined to clauses. It is everywhere; the whole book is chiasmic, its left the mirror of its right, the even-numbered chapters, II and IV, set in correspondence with a vision of a woman at the end of each, and the diary fragments of the book's last pages reflecting the quick-cut glimpses of its first.

We may even wonder if such symmetry has a center. It has. The center falls midway among the four sermons which make up the middle part (of three) of the middle chapter (of five). What we find between the second and third of the sermons is exactly this:

> The preacher took a chainless watch from a pocket within his soutane and, having considered its dial for a moment in silence, placed it silently before him on the table.

Note "silence" and "silently"; note too a chiasmic pattern early in *Finnegans Wake,* which may be summarized,

1132 A.D. . . .
556 A.D. . . .
(Silent.)
556 A.D. . . .
1132 A.D. . . .

Note also that *Finnegans Wake*'s middle chapter (of seventeen) is 9, the "Mime," near the middle of which (page 244) we find

. . . silent. ii. . . .

What does all this mean?

We may guess what it means in the *Portrait,* at any rate. *A Portrait of the Artist as a Young Man* borrows its title from Rembrandt, who painted his numerous self-portraits with the aid of a mirror. So imagine, arrayed,

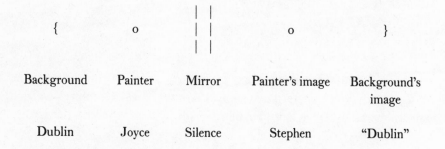

Background	Painter	Mirror	Painter's image	Background's image
Dublin	Joyce	Silence	Stephen	"Dublin"

Lo, chiasmus. The text places silence where Rembrandt's mirror is, because when the busy, sounding world ends in a book it passes through print's looking-glass into a silent domain. Any book is silent; the silence of a sacred book uncanny.

So reduced, chiasmus seems a feeble joke to have given the Fabulous Artificer so much trouble. But all jokes are feeble, sufficiently reduced; so,

Joyce would have us think, is the underlying structure of all we can know: a flaccidity of weltering coincidence, only arresting when enfleshed in rich meretricious multiplicity. The pun is mightier than the word.

By 1914 *Dubliners* was published, and *A Portrait of the Artist as a Young Man* was being serialized. Joyce had beaten out his exile and was uniting every wile he knew to tell at last the story of Ulysses, *sub specie temporis nostris*. When it was published in 1922, *Ulysses* was a new kind of book altogether, a Berlitz classroom between covers: a book from which we are systematically taught the skills we require to read it. The first response, shock, was like the shock you'd feel if you were suddenly put down where you hardly knew the language. In subsequent decades readers were learning how to learn. From Trieste, from Zurich, finally from Paris, the Irish Jesuits' most cunning pupil had silently made the literate world his classroom. The subject of study was the English Dean of Studies' native tongue.

MORE POINTS TO PONDER

... Dublin ... without doubt one of the most dirty cities in the kingdom. ...

Medical Press, 1907

Despite more than thirty years of activity by the Health Committee, the annual death rate in 1899 was higher than it had been in any year since 1880. At 33.6 per thousand living (only slightly below Calcutta's) it exceeded that of any large city in Europe or the United States. ...

JOSEPH O'BRIEN, *Dear Dirty Dublin,* 1982, p. 102

... streets that ... left the pedestrian's feet immersed in mud and horse drop- pings or his nostrils assailed by swirling clouds of dust and pulverized particles of macadam. ... Dublin generated twice as many tons of street sweepings per mile per year as even larger cities such as Edinburgh and Leeds. ...

O'BRIEN, p. 67

Enjoy a bath now: clean trough of water, cool enamel, the gentle tepid stream.

LEOPOLD BLOOM

In 1902 the collapse of a tenement in Townsend Street killed one person and injured others. What was embarrassing about this case was that the building was owned by Alderman O'Reilly of Trinity Ward, a member of the Health Committee.

O'BRIEN, p. 149

(. . . *In the course of its extension . . . numerous houses are razed to the ground. The inhabitants are lodged in barrels and boxes, all marked in red with the letters: L. B. Several paupers fall from a ladder. A part of the walls of Dublin, crowded with loyal sightseers, collapses.*)

THE SIGHTSEERS

(*Dying.*) *Morituri te salutant.* (*They die.*)

Ulysses

". . . room with two bedsteads occupied by a family of six, a bundle of straw on the floor where the husband slept, the wife ill with typhus fever, the little girl being treated for typhoid, the window overlooking a small yard covered in excrement. . . . the homes of men have become the living sepulchres of the people."

O'BRIEN, pp. 32–33

The Irishman's house is his coffin.

Ulysses

On the state of the Liffey we held an inquiry which showed that it is polluted to a fearful extent. . . . the water was at places so filthy as to cause almost instant death to fish. . . .

O'BRIEN, p. 19

Sir Charles Cameron rarely let the opportunity slip ... to decry the careless and filthy habits of those in the lowest class of tenement houses, maintaining that even when transplanted to new Corporation flats they continued to make improper use of the WC, using it as an ashpit, a fowlhouse, a receptacle for broken jampots, and so forth.

O'BRIEN, p. 135

Durtaigh disloigheal Reibeal aighris dogs.

MYLES NA GCOPALEEN

A DWINDLING GYRE

> Didn't it always exist the moon wasn't it
> always there as large as life and what did
> it ever mean only fantasy and delusion,
> Gorman, fantasy and delusion.
>
> SAMUEL BECKETT

It was over, Yeats was coming to think, and began to keep a journal: sticky paper for random flies. "To keep these notes natural and useful to me in my life I must keep one note from leading on to another. To do that is to surrender oneself to literature": so an early entry, January 1909.

And again, not quite a year after the *Playboy* rioting, "To oppose the new ill-breeding of Ireland, which may in a few years destroy all that has given Ireland a distinguished name in the world, . . . I can only set up a secondary or interior personality created by me out of the tradition of myself, and this personality (alas, to me only possible in my writings) must be always gracious and simple."

Calculation, calculation. This personality would need charm, enabled by "slight separation from immediate interests," charm being perhaps "an escape from mechanism." "So much of the world as is dominated by conflict of interests is a mechanism. The newspaper is the roar of the machine." Logic, he had written a few days earlier, "is a machine." When men argue, everything there is to say will be said by someone, and "the fool is as likely as the sage to speak the appropriate answer to any assertion." If an argument is forgotten, he added, someone will go home miserable.

The thoughts he heard around him seemed "made in some manufactory," "the creation of impersonal mechanism—of schools, of textbooks, of newspapers, these above all." "This ill-breeding of the mind is far more destructive than the mere bad manners that spits on the floor."

What he was watching was a growing exploitation of print, a growing print-mindedness among the faithful of every party. Daniel O'Connor had shouted to audiences of thousands, but nowadays to advance a political cause your first essential was control of a newspaper. Sinn Fein had its paper, the Gaelic League had its paper. Week by week they printed pretty much what they'd printed before, rearranged. The sole function of syntactic and onomastic resourcefulness was to keep two successive issues from being identical.

He had renounced a twenty years' dream: "In our age it is impossible to create, as I had dreamed, an heroic and passionate conception of life . . . and to make that conception the special dream of the Irish people." The Irish people, he said, "cry out for stones and vapour, pedantry and hysteria, rhetoric and sentiment."

As late as the third week of January, 1909, fully twenty years after they'd met, the thought came to him that Maud Gonne "never really understands my plans, or nature, or ideas." That was six years after she'd shocked him by marriage to "a clown," Major MacBride. Yeats was thirty-seven then. When he turned forty and admirers presented a Kelmscott Chaucer, he was making ready his own *Works*, eight volumes that were published at Stratford-on-Avon by the time he was forty-three. The volumes averaged 265 pages, and one held all his poems, three his plays, two apiece fictions and essays. A. H. Bullen printed 1060 sets. In Dublin, Maunsel & Co.'s estimate of the Irish demand prompted them to import perhaps 20.

The Collected Works as we might expect carried with it an odd look of finality. Romantic Poets, so to speak, die at forty if not earlier, and the *Works* contains but a dozen or so poems written after 1900, the latest a twelve-line lyric he'd published in October 1905, aged forty years and four months:

> Sweetheart, do not love too long:
> I loved long and long,
> And grew to be out of fashion
> Like an old song. . . .

That reads like a finale; and we should notice too how the autobiographical volumes he commenced writing in 1915 say nothing about his life after 1909 save for a coda on the Nobel Prize he received in 1923 for work done in his twenties and thirties. In 1909 Yeats had still thirty years to live and two-thirds of his poetry to write, but all that was, so to speak, posthumous.

He was content now to let casual readers suppose that *Poems (1895)* contained his essential canon. Endlessly revised, repeatedly reprinted, it comprised, as we've noted already, *The Wanderings of Oisin*; his two earliest plays, *The Countess Cathleen* and *The Land of Heart's Desire*; and the lyrics, including "Innisfree," which he'd written before he was thirty, in pre-Maud and post-Maud groupings, *Crossways* and *The Rose*. Sharp eyes will spot the absence of the 1899 *Wind Among the Reeds*.

This collection was being reissued as late as 1929, by which time both plays and many of the poems had been reworked almost beyond recognition. Again and again, amid the press of novel explorations, he revisits the terrain of that poet with his name, dead long ago, whose lines he alone has authority to alter.

> brawling of a sparrow
> The ~~quarrel of the sparrows~~ in the eaves,
>
> brilliant　　　　all the milky
> The ~~full round~~ moon and ~~the star-laden~~ sky,
>
> all that famous harmony of
> And ~~the loud song of the ever-singing~~ leaves
>
> blotted out man's image and his
> Had ~~hid away earth's old and weary~~ cry. . . .

—So his 1925 surgery to an 1892 poem. Is this ship the same ship, Greek sophists used to ask, seeing that each of its timbers has at some time been replaced? What does *The Countess Cathleen* we read today share with the one Yeats published in 1892, or with what James Joyce saw in 1899?

Through the Enchanted Forest of Yeats bibliography, phantom books glimmer and poems metamorphose. If some new mutation of *Poems (1895)* would suffice for the casual, the existence of the collector was not forgotten, and whoever wanted Yeats complete on his shelves required an astonishing number of books, revisions, rearrangings, regroupings, selections, limited and trade editions—some 200 in the poet's lifetime. There was even a publishing business in the family, the Dun Emer, later the Cuala* Press, edited by him and managed by his sister Lollie, that specialized in hand-set limited editions. It issued thirty of his books in his lifetime, in small runs

---

*Say "Coo-la." They took the name from the old barony where the place in Dundrum stood. "Dun Emer" was the Dún or Fort of Cuchulain's queen, whose interest in feminine handicrafts was notable.

(fifty to four hundred copies) before the machine-made trade editions came out of New York and London.

Through his Pollexfen ancestry—Sligo shipowners, his mother's people—he had a businessman's calculating blood, antithetic to the feckless charm of the Yeatses: of his father especially, who could paint better portraits than anyone but seldom managed to get money for them. Rumor had it in Dublin that W. B.'s ceremonial appearances at the Abbey were less for the purpose of extending a poet's benediction than for estimating the night's receipts, which he did by a rapid count of the empty seats when there were many people or the full ones when there were few. And they say that before the old theatre burned down the place they kept Willie's portrait in the lobby was where its unblinking eyes kept watch on the till. Bernard Shaw rightly called Dublin "that city of tedious and silly derision where men can do nothing but sneer," but Dublin was on to something.

One thing that brought on so much disenchantment was middle age. Another was the saturation in Irish realities that had commenced when he got thick with Lady Gregory and then with the National Theatre. Until then he had been able to dream such realities away, for confronting only as poetic myth. Mythologizing Cuchulain and Maeve and the sons of Usna, he'd mythologized the Irish people too.

Against O'Leary prescribing a duty to Ireland, against Maud Gonne urging strident Irish duties ceaselessly, as long ago as 1892 Yeats had defined his own compromise: to be Irish, yes, but not the way patriots expected. That was in "To Ireland in the Coming Times," a poem he'd written to accompany *The Countess Kathleen*:

> . . . *Nor may I less be counted one*
> *With Davis, Mangan, Ferguson,*
> *Because, to him who ponders well,*
> *My rhymes more than their rhyming tell*
> *Of things discovered in the deep,*
> *Where only body's laid asleep. . . .*

The year he wrote this he and Edwin J. Ellis were at work on their edition of Blake,* and his meter is the octosyllable Blake used for the gnomic rhymes of *Auguries of Innocence*, the same meter Yeats would revert to forty-

---

*Published in 1893, and often jeered at since for its claim that Blake was of Irish birth. But Yeats and Ellis could have found this stated in the 1854 edition of the *Encyclopaedia Britannica*, IV.153.

six years later for the companion-poem to this one, "Under Ben Bulben," where

> . . . sleepers wake and yet still dream,
> And when it's vanished still declare,
> With only bed and bedstead there,
> That heavens had opened. . . .

Ireland contained the English army's principal garrisons, partly for convenience, partly to admonish the Irish, and Blake, who in 1803 expelled a drunken English soldier from his garden, had impeccable credentials for guiding a bard whose mission was to guide Irish patriots. Moreover, Blake would have known what to say about Tom Davis and other patriot iterators of the obvious: very much what he did say of fashionable painters who were content to look but not to see:

Men think they can Copy Nature as Correctly as I copy Imagination; this they will find impossible, & all the Copies or Pretended Copiers of Nature, from Rembrandt to Reynolds, Prove that Nature becomes to its Victim nothing but Blots & Blurs. Why are Copiers of Nature Incorrect, while Copiers of Imagination are Correct? This is manifest to all.

A Copier of Nature was just what J. M. Synge had refused to be: hence the fracas. Elsewhere Blake outlined a hierarchy of Vision:

> Now I a fourfold vision see,
> And a fourfold vision is given to me;
> 'Tis fourfold in my supreme delight
> And threefold in soft Beulah's night
> And twofold always. May God us keep
> From single vision & Newton's sleep!

Single vision, that was the vision of Thomas Davis and Young Ireland, who could never see past some obsessive political fact. But,

> . . . things discovered in the deep,
> Where only body's laid asleep. . . .

—in those lines the twenty-seven-year-old Yeats made Blakean claims for what Dublin used to jeer at as Dreamy Willie's abstractedness: a-dream, yes, but no less effective a patriot than "Davis, Mangan, Ferguson," no less entitled to his country's gratitude. The work of the theatre he sponsored would be nothing less than the reconstitution of his country's imagination.

Lost in his dream of rural Ireland and faeries, he'd misjudged grey Dublin's theatre-goer. It was in the vicinity of the theatre now that day by day he could see how little effect any of his work was having. The man of print can believe, as did Pound for decades, in an ideal readership however small or scattered, a saving remnant to command a mighty posterity. The man of the playhouse knows differently.

Which plays filled houses, which emptied them, no one knew better than Yeats. Night by night he was there, counting. In the lobby no chill of public disappointment would escape him: lowered eyes, lowered voices. Nor could he evade the choric voice in his ear of this or that persistent ruminator, such a man for instance as Joseph Holloway.

We saw Holloway outside the Abbey the first night of the *Playboy* riots, the time he hissed "Blackguardism!" at Lady Gregory. He came back to *The Playboy* the next night, and the next, and *every* night, hating it. Grooved habit, not lust for a row, was what drew Holloway. All his long life (1861–1944) he had no other passion than the Dublin stage. Late every night he scribbled in his journal what he'd seen and heard: by the time he died, a hundred thousand pages, twenty-five million words: "one of the worst books ever written," say two men who've read it; "that donkey's detritus" in the phrase of Frank O'Connor; a thing of far more words than Yeats's lifelong production. All of it went to the groaning National Library. Also to the Library and to the Municipal Gallery went vanload after vanload of his pictures and playbills too, and playscripts, promptbooks, scrapbooks, letters from actors and playwrights: tons of stuff through which for years he'd had to clear pathways, and a heaping of which had collapsed his study table long since. If you'd been a comic playwright and wanted to put on stage a crank historian to make the pit shriek with delight, you might have invented Joseph Holloway. To improve your plot, you might make him the architect who'd supervised the conversion from morgue to playhouse of the Abbey he haunted. Yes, Holloway had done that too.

When his judgment is absolutely conventional, an articulate crank tells us much about convention. Holloway's almost innocent eye was the eye of Dublin, connected to a busy pen instead of a bitter tongue. It is he who preserves for us the telling banalities everyone relished but no one else recorded: three men side by side dozing off while W. B. Yeats chanted out to the National Literary Society his ideas on how drama ought to be presented (i.e. "Acting should not be acting but recitation of the old sing-song order"; is that common-sense paraphrase, or resolute refusal to understand what

Yeats was saying?). On other pages we may read of Yeats after *Cathleen ni Houlihan* holding forth "in his usual thumpty-thigh, monotonous, affected, preachy style," or Yeats during a Synge performance "wandering hither and thither in the gloom, now popping his head out from behind the curtains, and anon taking short spurts up and down the centre passage in the hall, ever restless, ever in evidence—but he did not make a speech so I forgave him." " 'Humbug,' thy name is Yeats" was one of his judgments, and he was at pains to write down what he heard people say about a "lovable," "simple" comedy called *The Country Dressmaker*: "There was nothing *Shadowy Waters* about it. . . . It was fine. We could understand it. . . ."

So much for expanding the imagination of the Gael, and Yeats slowly came to hate the denizens of "this unmannerly town": one reason he preferred to work at Coole. There were specific frustrations as well: in 1907, the dismal fuss about *The Playboy*, which demonstrated that vociferous people would not sit still long enough to grasp what it was they were seeing; in the same year, the death of John O'Leary; in 1905–1912, the row about the Lane Pictures; in 1909 the death of J. M. Synge, of Hodgkins' Disease, a lymphatic cancer so little accessible to lay understanding Yeats was able to believe his friend had died, like the Keats of legend, from sheer rejection. Since the *Autobiography* in effect concludes with 1909, it is as though the Yeats whose life it mythologizes had died the very year Synge did.

The story of the Lane Pictures offers reasons Yeats embraced, all the rest of his life, a chimerical aristocracy.

Hugh Lane—he'd been prominent at the *Playboy* uproar, a dark, moustachioed chucker-out of the obstreperous—was Lady Gregory's nephew, a picture-dealer in London, a money-maker born. In 1912 he offered a collection of Impressionist pictures to Dublin if Dublin would put up the gallery to house them, moreover the gallery he stipulated: built on a bridge in the Florentine way astride the Liffey, and according to a titled Englishman's design. Official Dublin saw better uses for money. Unofficial Dublin was hopelessly divided. Some liked the pictures but not the bridge. Some cared nothing about pictures but did not want the Liffey disfigured. Some found Manets and Monets silly: why not pictures like "those beautiful productions displayed in the windows of our city shops"? Some screamed blindly at "picture-dealers," at "log-rolling cranks and fanatics."

Tirelessly fitting archetypes, the mind of Yeats perceived a princely gesture, Italianate. It took him back five years.

In April 1907, just weeks after the *Playboy* obstreperousness, W. B. Yeats had been to Italy with the Gregorys, "making his peace," so a biographer puts it, "with the Renaissance, which hitherto he had distrusted as the period when unity gave way to multiplication." This was facile when he contrasted Urbino, Ferrara, Ravenna in their sunlight with grey Dublin's recently demonstrated knack for division. The guidebook myth was irresistible: *there* had been a unified civilization, artists (like Synge and himself), courtiers (like Lady Gregory), collaborating to lift the imaginations of the onion-sellers. That ought to have been their milieu: no ice, no greatcoated policemen, no louts with tin trumpets. "I might have lived," he would dream,

> Where every day my footfall should have lit
> In the green shadow of Ferrara wall;
> Or climbed among the images of the past—
> The unperturbed and courtly images—
> Evening and morning, the steep street of Urbino. . . .

And that fall, on returning to the flat streets and grey skies: "Three types of men have made all beautiful things": aristocracies made manners, country-men stories, artists the rest. What remains is the dreary lot who "prefer the stalk to the flower," and can neither create nor value creation. "Whatever they do or have must be a means to something else," so "painting and poetry exist that there may be instruction, and love that there may be children, and theatres that busy men may rest, and holidays that busy men may go on being busy." That affirmation of hierarchies had come four months after Italy, seven after *The Playboy*.

Behold now, five years later, Hugh Lane's lordly gesture; behold too a man of the local aristocracy, in real life a brewer who went by the name of Lord Ardilaun, shorting the Platonic circuit Yeats and courtly custom had designed: voicing reluctance to do more for the Lane gallery unless there was demonstrable "public demand." Demonstrable how? Why, by the extent of public subscription, something his accountant could gauge. In December Yeats dressed him down:

> You gave, but will not give again
> Until enough of Paudeen's pence
> By Biddy's halfpennies have lain
> To be "some sort of evidence," . . .

. . . evidence for the inconceivable, that "the blind and ignorant town" knows what is good for its spirit. Instructing ignorance is the duty of those who know better.

> What cared Duke Ercole, that bid
> His mummers to the market-place,
> What th' onion-sellers thought or did
> So that his Plautus set the pace
> For the Italian comedies? . . .

That (dated "December 1912") is a new note for Yeats: something para-phrasable, the voice lifted in remonstrance, neither crooning nor commun-ing with itself. He's learned from writing for the stage, which taught the difference between tushery with "yon"—

> How yon dog bays,
> And how the grey hen flutters in the coop.
> (*The Countess Kathleen*, 1892)

and the force of a simple question—

> What can have made the grey hen flutter so?
> (*The Countess Cathleen*, 1912)

Paraphrasable, yes, that remonstrance with Ardilaun; yet its full paraphrase turns out to be itself.

> Let Paudeens play at pitch and toss,
> Look up in the sun's eye and give
> What the exultant heart calls good
> That some new day may breed the best
> Because you gave, not what they would,
> But the right twigs for an eagle's nest!

You'll not improve any of that by plainer words or straighter sentences.

Writing verse so bare, so manifestly *spoken*, as by a Willie no parent or sibling had met, was not his only innovation. He did something else he'd never done before: he published it in *The Irish Times*: the loftiest letter-to-the-editor ever, in a Unionist paper too, not read by Paudeens. As well as Duke Ercole of Ferrara, it adduced Guidobaldo de Montefeltro of Urbino and Cosimo di Medici of Florence, fit monitors for a Dubliner born plain Arthur Guinness whose grandpa, they say, got accidental eminence when he let the hops burn brown.

For some years Yeats had been circling toward this decorum of untactful speech. Since 1906 he'd been reading Ben Jonson, whose schoolmaster

William Camden had taught him to map out his sense first in prose, and who could work verse so close to its prose bones that no prose reduction will yield anything plainer or shorter:

> Would'st thou heare, what man can say
> In a little? Reader, stay.
> Under-neath this stone doth lye
> As much beautie, as could dye:
> Which in life did harbour give
> To more vertue, than doth live. . . .

Yeats's longtime concern for the sinews of the sentence equipped him uniquely to profit by such an example, and no one since Jonson better manifests, at high moments, the Jonsonian virtue.

He'd taken note too of Jonson's resolutions to spend less time on plays:

> And since our Daintie age
>   Cannot endure reproofe,
> Make not thy selfe a Page,
> To that strumpet the Stage,
>   But sing high and aloofe,
> Safe from the wolves black jaw, and the dull Asses hoofe.

Dull asses with tin trumpets, that would comprise much. And again,

> Come leave the loathed Stage,
> And the more loathesome Age,
> Where pride and impudence in faction knit
> Usurpe the Chaire of wit:
> Inditing and arraigning every day
> Something they call a Play. . . .

We can hear the percussion of those rhymes in Yeats's lines of 1910:

> . . . My curse on plays
> That have to be set up in fifty ways,
> On the day's war with every knave and dolt,
> Theatre business, management of men. . . .

In 1912 that disenchantment with theatre was serving him, also that Jonsonian directness, also a depression over what the Lane fuss portended, the willingness of men who ought to have been leaders to follow mass opinion. In five poems the Cuala Press published in 1913 as *Poems Written in Discouragement* (eight pages, fifty copies, not for sale) he let his friends know about his sense of encroaching ignobility.

> What need you, being come to sense,
> But fumble in a greasy till
> And add the halfpence to the pence
> And prayer to shivering prayer, until
> You have dried the marrow from the bone?
> For men were born to pray and save:
> Romantic Ireland's dead and gone,
> It's with O'Leary in the grave.

That grows explicit. The people he had mentioned in 1907 who thought love existed that there might be children would be heeders of Catholic bishops, but his unemphatic prose cadence made it likely that the phrase would pass unnoticed. Now, the verse of 1912—"Add the halfpence to the pence / And prayer to shivering prayer"—is pretty direct about people counting Rosary decades. The urban Catholic mercantile class is his scorn's explicit target: such people as James Joyce depicted in "The Boarding House" ("Mrs Mooney was a butcher's daughter . . ."). They had come, or their parents had come, off the homesteads, out of the West; the wild life of Pegeen Mike they had left behind, the Galway knack for visions, the ripe Syngean speech. In Dublin they counted prayers, they counted cash, they calculated. (Mrs Mooney "counted all her cards again," and noting that it was seventeen minutes past eleven, "knew that she would have lots of time to have the matter out with Mr Doran and then catch short twelve* at Marlborough Street.")

These were folk Yeats would hate ever after, the betrayers of his vision, the "Base-born products of base beds" he would scorn as "unremembering" when he was seventy-three. He had no reason to remember himself that 1912, the year he'd conceived this passion, was the year of the local *Dubliners* fiasco, the year James Joyce left Ireland for the last time. (The year before that, "Flann O'Brien" was born in Tyrone, a desperate bog indeed they'll tell you in Dublin, and a wonder it is he made anything of himself.)

All hope, Yeats had decided, lay with the landed: Lady Gregory: the great houses, like the Penshurst Ben Jonson had celebrated. He too had celebrated Coole, that could breed "the lidless eye that loves the sun," and

---

*The noon Mass, short because Canon Law in those days required the priest to have fasted since midnight; frequented by people who wanted to get the Sunday obligation over in a hurry.

foster "a written speech / Wrought of high laughter, loveliness and ease."
Now his mind was confirmed in its flight to the West. In a few years he'd
have his own Tower there.

Like most Irish quarrels, the Lane wrangle went on nearly forever. When
Hugh Lane in disgust took his pictures off to London and lent them to the
National Gallery, Yeats saw an occasion to address the shade of Parnell,
back in town maybe to look at his monument ("I wonder if the builder has
been paid") and be confirmed in the unchanging ways of the Irish:

> A man
> Of your own passionate serving kind who had brought
> In his full hands what, had they only known,
> Had given their children's children loftier thought,
> Sweeter emotion, working in their veins
> Like gentle blood, has been driven from the place,
> And insult heaped upon him for his pains,
> And for his open-handedness, disgrace. . . .

Then Lane relented, and a codicil to his will bequeathed the pictures to
Ireland. After a torpedo sent down him and the *Lusitania,* the codicil turned
out to be unwitnessed. British lawyers were literalists: the first will stood.
Not until 1959, when everyone who'd cared was dead, did a scheme of
rotating loans to the Dublin Municipal Gallery lay the matter more or less
to rest. You'll search high and low through the polemics for a simple list of
what the pictures were.

So Synge was dead, and in the mind of Yeats Irish vulgarity now had more
force than English. In Dublin they were fierce logicians and newspaper-
readers. "Logic is a machine"; "The newspaper is the roar of the machine":
it was Blake who had taught him that terminology, at bottom anti-English
terminology, for were not her machines England's pride?

All through his Nationalist years, the O'Leary years, Ireland's boast had
been that she was unseduced by purseproud Albion's material glitter: the
steam engines, great bridges, steamships, trains and tunnels, the looms and
spinning jennies and iron fingers to make pins; everything that clicked or
glittered or moved on rails; the typesetting machines and steam presses that
mass-produced more reading-matter than could be good for anyone to read;
the drains and pumps, the belts and driveshafts, the dynamos and many
many thousand miles of copper wire. Yeats was indifferent to such ameni-

ties; when the BBC offered him a handsome wireless, he couldn't remember if he had electricity or not.

The tradition of disliking all this was aesthetic, derived from Ruskin and William Morris. One of Morris's gestures had been to print books by hand, on handmade paper; the Kelmscott Chaucer for instance Yeats received on his fortieth birthday, a book so ornate you couldn't read it. Fortunately, Morris tended to print books you'd already read.

The Cuala Press was different; it printed *new* books, very legibly. Its foreman, Emery Walker, had worked with Morris. Its equipment, like that of most of the private presses that commenced to proliferate after 1900, was picked up cheaply from a firm that had mechanized. As the Yeats family's First Edition Factory, it soon made no special cause of its handicraft methods; that was simply the way good things were done.

Yeats once dreamed of a sewing machine that perpetually smiled, then realized that it was Bernard Shaw. By 1909 his contempt for machines had become metaphorical, a contempt for mechanical minds. He no longer gave their Englishness much thought, nor despised through them the land where chimneys smoked. Meanwhile official Nationalist rage, which had always been abstract, grew fiercely so. Not the quality of English life, no, just the bare idea of English dominance: that was the thing to hate.

So the aesthetic protest against English taste was let lapse: against the taste of opulent insolent materialists. Could examples of all that glittering vulgarity have been placed inside a huge Irish-built metal coffin and sunk in the deepest Atlantic—steam engines, dynamos, electric chandeliers and miles of wiring, grand pianos, tubas and cricket bats, salvers, tureens and many thousand goblets, mechanical meat lockers, motorized spits and cavernous iron ovens—all that sent dramatically down among the fishes would have been at one time a gratifying symbol, but when it did happen the symbolism was lost.

A conjunction of timing went unnoticed as well. John Millington Synge had been dead just one week when, on 31 March 1909, Irish workers at Harland and Woolf's in Belfast put down the keel of the R.M.S. *Titanic*. On the night he died Lily Yeats saw a ship in a vision.

ARRAY! SURRECTION!

> Jesus, there's always some bloody clown
> or other kicking up a bloody murder about
> bloody nothing. Gob, it'd turn the porter
> sour in your guts, so it would.
>
> *Ulysses*

In the spring of 1916, *annus horribilis,* Yeats was in London, engaged on what he coyly described to his father as "a little play in which the characters wear masks designed by the painter, Dulac, it is an experiment and is to be played in Lady Cunard's drawing room." It was an effort to free his theatre from everything that had grown irksome and ignoble at the Abbey. He had conceived an imagined episode in the life of Cuchulain as it might have been enacted by *Noh* players in medieval Japan. "All imaginative art remains at a distance, and this distance, once chosen, must be firmly held against a pushing world." Tin trumpeters could simply be denied admittance.

The romantic story has been often told: Mary Fenollosa, attracted by certain work of Ezra Pound's in *Poetry,* making over to him her late husband's manuscripts and notebooks; Pound in the winter of 1913 extracting and arranging from the notes of Ernest Fenollosa English versions of a number of *Noh* plays, bits of Anglo-Irish diction seeping into his Imagist idiom from the powerful presence of Yeats in the same room; Yeats's work on *At the Hawk's Well,* an Irish play prompted by *Noh* plays; the discovery by Pound—in London!—of a real *Noh* actor, Michio Ito, who mimed, in masklike makeup, *The Guardian of the Well* at Lady Cunard's on 2 April 1916.

The young Cuchulain, in a mask "like an archaic Greek statue," was played by Harry Ainley, the same who'd attempted Usheen in the Yeats-Moore *Diarmuid and Grania* fifteen years before, that night of the Caoelte-Quilcher-Wheelchair confusion. In rehearsal he waved his arms "like a drowning kitten." The musicians were a trouble. One of them insisted on a guitar, which Dulac disguised with cardboard.

But they had Ito and his stern ways of moving, the marvel of this play. In a large but otherwise ordinary London room, Yeats recalled,

> There, where no studied lighting, no stage-picture made an artificial world, he was able, as he rose from the floor, where he had been sitting cross-legged, or as he threw out an arm, to recede from us into some more powerful life.

There is no better place to see Yeats catching just the detail that signifies, elusive locus of the transfer of energy. We'd cherish a like glimpse of Burbage's Hamlet.

They made no effort to be "real." "Realism . . . is the delight today of all those whose minds, educated alone by schoolmasters and newspapers, are without the memory of beauty and emotional subtlety." This says that education leads minds *away* from the conventions instinct approves; Pound has preserved Yeats's story of an old priest in a train, who denounced "ignorance . . . spreading every day from the schools": places where, Yeats would put it ten years later in a poem called "Among School Children," they learn

> . . . to cipher and to sing,
> To study reading-books and history,
> To cut and sew, be neat in everything
> In the best modern way. . . .

"Reading-books," that's a dead time's barbarous name for its books not fit to read. "History" so studied of course excludes Cuchulain, Deirdre, the Morrigu, Queen Maeve, all the racial past. And "to cipher and to sing" perverts Pythagoras, who taught us how music is mathematically based, but whose *mathematikē* was no more like shopkeepers' ciphering than his *mousikē*, something sacred to the Muses, was like mimicry of a sol-fa pitchpipe.

That same year (1926) Yeats would write his noble lines about the Soul:

> An aged man is but a paltry thing,
> A tattered cloak upon a stick, unless
> Soul clap its hands and sing, and louder sing

> For every tatter in its mortal dress,
> Nor is there singing school but studying
> Monuments of its own magnificence. . . .

The children in the classroom he'd walked into—it was at St. Otteran's School, Waterford, a Monday morning in February 1926*—were confronted by such a monument, William Butler Yeats, exponent of the soul's magnificence, who'd come in at the door like any other visitor. They did not "study" him, he was not their "singing school," and though he indulged a brief revery in their presence, there's no indication that any gesture of his arm or head allowed them to experience, as at a *Noh* play, the recession "into some more powerful life."

For the parallel with the *Noh* performances of 1916 is striking. Like Yeats into the schoolroom, the actors entered a London drawing room by the same door the guests had used, and you'd hardly have noticed anything unusual going on until a black cloth embroidered with a stylized gold hawk began to be ritually unfolded.

> I call to the eye of the mind
> A well long choked up and dry
> And boughs long stripped by the wind,
> And I call to the mind's eye
> Pallor of an ivory face,
> Its lofty dissolute air,
> A man climbing up to a place
> The salt sea wind has swept bare.

This old man has waited fifty years for the well to bubble (in 1916 Yeats was fifty-one). The young man who next enters—Cuchulain—is impatient for it to bubble. Anyone who drinks of it will live forever. The woman who guards the well is a woman of the *Sidhe*; her unworldly gaze entrances the old man, her dance enchants the young man; it is during their distraction

---

*I've not cluttered this exposition with the acknowledgment that Yeats was in fact much impressed with the Montessorian procedures at St. Otteran's, and praised them in a Senate speech on 24 March: see Donald Torchiana's fine essay in Jeffares and Cross, eds., *In Excited Revery*, 1965, 123–50. But "Among School Children" tugs the visit into its own mythology, and we'd best not let what is known of a certain occasion nudge us, as it does Torchiana (page 141), into finding neither irony nor mockery in the poem's first stanza. Time and again, as readers of Joyce are aware, what a writer's experiences were and what his works did with them can be almost unrecognizably different.

that the well flows and empties. The musicians then ceremonially refold the cloth. After thirty minutes our ambience is a drawing room once more, our company its people.

Though the first performances were imperfect—Cuchulain needed recasting, the musicians replacing—Yeats was exultant over his new theatre, made not of lights and flats but of sheer *presence*: a cloth, a mask, a drumbeat, an arousal, a dance. Frank O'Connor has noted an odd orientalism entwining the Abbey's fortunes from its start, and Yeats was easily persuaded that players strolling from town to town in Ireland, their few props in a knapsack, might recreate such a passion for the sacredness of *place* as he discerned in the exotica Pound was creating out of Fenollosa's scribble.

It was on the theatre of presence that he would draw to shape the poem about his presence in that Waterford classroom, 1926: Yeats, monument of unaging intellect, was *there* that morning; and if nothing much had happened save his own excitement, nothing much ever happens when or as it should. Any child who learned that miraculous water had flowed would learn it long afterward. The poem moves from the classroom to a vision summoned to the eye of the mind, and has its old man and young people, its ritual terminal dance, even a stanza (*v*) that recapitulates a stanza of the first song in the play. What can be taught? Can we ever make something go as we'd like, in the great world or in another's mind?

Only in art; or perhaps not even in art, not even with the royal audience of one's dreams. The Queen of England came to the second performance of *At the Hawk's Well*. Yeats was ready to feel "happier than Sophocles," and the Queen sent word back that she'd like things speeded up; she was "hoarse."

Still, it was all far from Dublin. Dublin?

In the play, first performed 2 April 1916, young Cuchulain ran off toward the clash of arms, and on 24 April, the day after Easter, Dublin blew up. Scheduled for Easter Sunday, by coincidence Shakespeare's birthday and the tercentenary of his death, this event had been delayed over organizational difficulties. By coincidence too, the Abbey had planned to open its spring season reviving *Cathleen ni Houlihan,* of all plays. "Do not make a great keening / When the graves have been dug tomorrow. . . ."

Many graves ensued, and much ruin. Joyce records the devastation wrought by the biscuit-tin the Citizen threw at Bloom—"the epicentre appears to have been that part of the metropolis which constitutes the Inn's Quay Ward and parish of St. Michan's"—not far, in fact, from the area that got shelled into ruins by a British gunboat* in the Liffey and British howitzers lobbing high explosive up what had been one of the finest avenues in Europe, Sackville Street, now called O'Connell. On its east side everything was blown open as far up as North Earl Street, on the west side half as much but quite enough. The post office walls stayed rubble for ten years. Dublin was one of the very first cities to experience what post-Nobel chemical science could do. German shelling of Arras and Ypres for two and a half years produced, so Bernard Shaw thought, but laughable results compared to a week's British achievement in Dublin. One abetment to its thoroughness was the looting of shops including toyshops by locals who started fires, another the rebel practice of firing on the firemen, who then sensibly withdrew and let things burn.

Joyce's famous hope, that Dublin if destroyed might be reconstituted from his writings, was voiced when the part of the city he then had Bloom traversing was already much destroyed. The office of the *Freeman's Journal,* setting of his "Aeolus" episode, was gone by the third day. He started "Cyclops"—the part of *Ulysses* given over to violent 1904 patriotism— while the wreckage patriotism could wreak was demonstrable.

His one-time Irish teacher, Patrick Pearse, had seized the post office with a tiny garrison. They ran up a new flag, green for Ireland, orange for Ulster, white for their unity, and from the post office steps Pearse read out a proclamation of the new Republic, Poblacht na hÉireann. It's unclear who heard him read, though legend preserves the relief of a bowler-hatted citizen who was prompt to urinate *al fresco,* shouting "now we have a Republic we can do what we like." And yet people think Joyce exaggerates.

Word may have filtered back to Zurich that the proclamation was in Irish, though it wasn't, since in "Circe" Bloom is made to unroll a paper and read solemnly, "Aleph Beth Ghimel Daleth Hagadah Tephilim Kosher Yom Kippur Hanukah Roschaschana Beni Brith Bar Mitzvah Mazzoth Askenazim Meshuggah Talith," producing just the effect a proclamation in Irish would have had on likely bystanders.

Patrick (Padraig) Pearse had made a cult of Cuchulain. In the post office he summoned (Yeats later said) "Cuchulain to his side." That is why, in Joyce's mocking rescript, a voice comes out of heaven calling to Ben Bloom Elijah; also why, in the lobby of the restored post office, you will find today a bronze Cuchulain. He is dying tied to a stake, the way the bronze-age Cuchulain died, upright: the way the Easter 1916 martyrs died when the

*So the Irish Fact, still affirmed. But the "gunboat *Helga*" was no more than an armed fishing vessel.

firing squads levelled their rifles. Being fused to its stake the figure has of course no buttocks, which makes an episode of Beckett's *Murphy,* Mr. Neary in desperation dashing his head against the buttocks ("such as they are") of Cuchulain in the post office, into metaphysical mockery.

Mockery, yes, that is the note of much literary response to the symbols of 1916, in part because the event through sheer incoherence contrived to mock so much of its own purpose. In a capital where eight decades' experience of the telephone has not yet fostered the habit of returning calls, they were ill-prepared to coordinate a nation-wide uprising in synchrony with the arrival of small arms by sea from Germany past the British blockade. If you can suppress thought of the pain, the bloodshed, all the spilt idealism, much of what's left is Keystone comedy. From confusion about the date no pilot boat in Tralee Bay met the German ship with the twenty thousand rifles, ten million rounds of ammunition, and ten machine guns; cornered by the Royal Navy, her captain scuttled her.* Nearby, where an expert was to have replaced the British wireless by a rebel station, his car took a wrong turn and drove off a pier, drowning three men of four including him. In Dublin, a Nationalist faction led by Eoin MacNeill, who long before had founded the Gaelic League and now thought he was Chief of Staff of what was called the Provisional Committee of the Irish Republican Brotherhood, held that the long-drilled Volunteers should march only in case of such urgent danger as an order of suppression, while a different faction, captained by the fanatic Pearse of the IRB's Military Council, had resolved on an Easter blood-sacrifice come what might. The factions kept their secrets from one another, and when Pearse ordered an uprising for Easter Sunday, the day the German guns were supposed to arrive, MacNeill published by paid advertisement in the *Sunday Independent* a countermanding order which did not forestall but gravely weakened an event Pearse simply rescheduled for Easter Monday, German arms or no. There was no chance at all, after that, of involving the rest of the country.

It is easy to see why the British authorities paid little attention to such clowns. They granted holiday leaves as usual, en masse, and their officers drifted off to the Kildare races. Easter Monday was much more than a "religious" occasion: it was what England calls a Bank Holiday. Hardly anyone noticed the contingent that marched into the post office and took charge of it. Later a fellow who'd not heard the Republic proclaimed and

---

*Connoisseurs will compare the exploit of Gen. Eoin O'Duffy, who, as John P. Roche tells it, "is famous in limited circles for raising a regiment to fight for France in the Spanish Civil War, but taking them to Cork when the ship was waiting at Limerick. Half his troops decided this was not the leadership they wanted and vanished."

also seemed not to notice all the rifles was to wander in and then wonder what the country was coming to when you couldn't buy a penny stamp in the post office itself. James Connolly, who was there, recounted that story a few minutes before the firing squad carried out his sentence. They shot him sitting because he was so wounded he could not stand.

Connolly was the last to die, and his death caused special horror; nobody had thought they'd shoot a crippled man. The executions proved a worse mistake than any the rebels made. Had the ringleaders simply been thrown into jail and kept there, noted W. B. Yeats's father, "Ireland would have pitied and loved and smiled at these men, knowing them to be mad fools. In the end they would have come to see that fools are the worst criminals." That is true; the populace were on the whole resentful of a gang who'd shut the city down all week and wrecked it to the extent of £2.5 million.

It was the horror of the executions, protracted over many days, that converted resentment and apathy into veneration of martyrdom. Fourteen were shot in Dublin, one hanged in Cork; back in England they also hanged Sir Roger Casement, who'd arranged the deal with Germany for the arms and then gotten captured when the submarine that put him ashore wasn't met. That made sixteen; they also condemned the Countess Markievicz (née Constance Gore-Booth of Lissadell, near Sligo) but didn't shoot her because she wasn't a man, and didn't shoot Eamon de Valera either, not wanting trouble with America where he was born. A man they did shoot was Maud Gonne's estranged husband, John MacBride. He declined a blindfold, having, he said, faced enemy rifles too often to need one now, and left the British to work out his meaning: that they'd missed one chance to kill him in South Africa, when he fought them at the side of the Boers.

Just as when the lads had rioted at *The Playboy*, W. B. Yeats happened to be out of the country. He was staying with Sir William Rothenstein, the painter, in Gloucester, and his first thoughts concerned the safety of Lady Gregory, in Galway. Sir William; Lady Augusta—these days Yeats kept exalted company. He also belonged to a club in Stephen's Green, where you could warm your person by the fire and your companion's heart with a gibe at the current fire-eaters, the mobilized boy scouts (Fianna) Con Markievicz gave her heart to, the pale-faced drillers with their wooden rifles, the fervid ungrammatical Irish-speakers: none of them O'Leary's kind of activist, and not an O'Leary among their leaders either: Catholic middle-class, most of them, counter-men, till-men.

Pearse he knew slightly: a schoolmaster. He knew Thomas MacDonagh a little better. MacDonagh, he wrote in his 1909 journal, seemed "a man with some literary faculty which will probably come to nothing through lack of culture and encouragement." MacDonagh was astute enough to notice that when you revived Gaelic, to the extent of making it the language of a Dublin newspaper, *An Claidheamh Soluis* ("The Sword of Light"), it got infected with the habits of journalism in a way inimical to its other use as preserving amber for Celtic civilization. What he'd come to believe in was not the urbanization of Irish, but what Synge too had wanted, an Irish literature written in English, out of the co-pressure of the two tongues. He left some agreeable poems.

> I once spent an evening in a village
> Where the people are all taken up with tillage . . .

Don't hunt for stresses, he counseled, read it like prose, slurring no syllables, and you'll come out right—

> All bent up double, a village of hobblers
> And slouchers and squatters, whether they straggle
> Up and down, or bend to haggle
> Over a counter, or bend at a plough,
> Or to dig with a spade, or to milk a cow. . . .

There's a pleasure in little plain words there, and a syntax artfully artless: the thirty-nine lines have just two sentences among them. It ends the way MacDonagh did:

> There came a man of a different gait—
> A man who neither slouched nor pattered,
> But planted his steps as if each step mattered;
> Yet walked down the middle of the street
> Not like the policeman on his beat,
> But like a man with nothing to do
> Except walk straight upright like me and you.

They shot him with his mother's rosary around his neck. The bullets destroyed just four beads of it.

The Rising had commenced on Easter Monday, 24 April; the executions were over by 12 May. On 11 May, writing to Lady Gregory, Yeats divulged a line for a poem on the victims: "Terrible beauty has been born again." (We may note that his first move on this grave occasion was toward the accredited pentameter.) "I had no idea," he added, "that any public event could so deeply move me." It wasn't long since he'd judged that on great occasions poets had best keep quiet, their office not to mediate public sentiment, no, to please "A young girl in the indolence of her youth, / Or an old man upon a winter's night." But that had pertained to the mere war in Europe. When he wrote on 23 May of "a world . . . swept away" he was brooding on events in Dublin. "I keep going over the past in my mind and wondering if I could have done anything to turn those young men in some other direction."

"Easter 1916," his first direct poetic *response* to a public event if we except a lugubrious exercise on the death of Parnell, is dated "25 September 1916," more than nineteen weeks after the final volley. "Terrible beauty has been born again" was a sentiment still at the heart of it, but he'd rethought that sententious pentameter, lowered his pitch to a casual-seeming three-stress line to recount casual encounters with the martyrs-designate:

> . . . I have passed with a nod of the head
> Or polite meaningless words,
> Or have lingered awhile and said
> Polite meaningless words,
> And thought before I had done
> Of a mocking tale or a gibe
> To please a companion
> Around the fire at the club . . .

—nerveless syntax onto which the great refrain will drop its iron portcullis:

> All changed, changed utterly:
> A terrible beauty is born.

A terr-i-ble beau-ty is born: never did Yeats devise a more imperative rhythmic summons: at what a distance from "Innisfree"! Noons a purple glow are no longer incanted; credit him now with the full force of his words, and notably of the perilous word "Beauty," by which he means nothing pre-Raphaelite, no, an edged bewilderment that's haunted his mind for five years, "beauty like a tightened bow," which he called "not natural in an age like this": beauty "terrible" as in the wildering Aphrodite he could hear of from his friend Ezra Pound, a man whom "*Kuthera deina,*" terrible beauty, would one day visit in a cell near Pisa. When Yeats conceived "Beauty like a tightened bow" it was perhaps a counter in the old game of lauding Maud Gonne, a tautening of Arthur Symons's "Modern Beauty" who said "I am the torch" and had been Helen, but what is wonderful in "Easter 1916" is how none of these worn aspects of "Beauty" comes to mind, not the Black Rose, *Roisin Dúbh*, nor even Cathleen ni Houlihan, that lethal crone with her "walk of a queen."

If the terrible beauty is "born," it is out of that bloody welter like Aphrodite out of sea-foam: the agonies of Easter Week were birth-pangs. Other writers would get around to asking whether actuality, in due time, long due, had not delivered rather little. Joyce heard one devious name throughout the next decade and called it "the devil era," while O'Casey mocked, "A terrible beauty is Borneo."

Yeats's poem, unembarrassed by dispiriting foresight, keeps part of its mind on its counted formalities: eighty lines, in four parts, arranged sixteen, twenty-four, sixteen, twenty-four, a symmetry hardly discernible till the Variorum Edition numbered all the lines. (Sixteen is for 1916; twenty-four is for the millennia of a Great Year.) It keeps an a-a-b-a symmetry also, the third part unique in lacking the famous refrain and in proposing the image of the stone in the stream, far from the city, amid moorhens and mounted men; such a stone is like stony fanaticism in troubling the flow of the natural. The poem locates its details like elements in a mobile, putting "Wherever green is worn" three lines from the end of part 4, to balance "where motley is worn," three lines from the end of part 1. Most spectacularly, it silhouettes anonymities, "this woman," "this man," "this other" in part 2, against the sunburst of part 4, where names start forth and the poet-mage takes charge:

> And what if excess of love
> Bewildered them till they died?
> I write it out in a verse—
> MacDonagh and MacBride
> And Connolly and Pearse
> Now and in time to be,
> Wherever green is worn,
> Are changed, changed utterly:
> A terrible beauty is born.

What it cost him to put MacBride's name in rhyming position we can only guess. But: "I write it out in a verse": that is the story we watched him enact with Synge: the poet who takes charge of what seems failure and transfigures it by his mention. This is his first assumption of such a role, so if "Easter 1916" is creating them for posterity it's creating their creator too. Unsurprisingly, the poem's first word is "I."

Having achieved this, he was four years publishing it; the twenty-five copies he had produced in London were for distribution to friends, and to guard the copyright. The world did not see it until *The New Statesman* (London) and *The Dial* (New York) printed it in the late autumn of 1920. Not till 1922 did he put it into a book meant for trade circulation.

By then he had taken several important steps. He had married (1917, Georgie Hyde-Lees, a cousin of Dorothy Shakespear Pound's; Ezra served as best man). He had ceased being a recurrent guest at Coole, but had not left the vicinity, having taken up symbolic residence in a square three-story tower near the Coole demesne. And aided by the Tower and by his wife's gift for automatic writing, he had commenced a new myth entirely, that of the poet in heroic isolation from affairs. If he wrote plays now, they were on the Japanese model he'd been investigating, with Pound's assistance, in the spring of 1916 when the Rising interrupted.

Today in Ireland "Easter" is apt to connote the Rising, not the Resurrection. "Tower" likewise connotes Yeats, not some Norman ruin. And "Yeats" everywhere connotes not what they gave him the Nobel Prize for in 1923, "The Lake Isle of Innisfree" and the early Abbey, but a difficult forceful diagrammatic starkness, of mummies, gyres, and shades, very Byzantine. Still, look at the pages of "The Book of Kells": is that decoration Byzantine, or Irish?

Born, he says, Good Friday 13, 1906, Sam Beckett by Easter 1916 was ten. In Zurich James Augustine Joyce, thirty-four, was digesting yet one more English rejection of *A Portrait of the Artist as a Young Man,* this one on behalf of Duckworth by Edward Garnett, who advised "pruning" and "pulling into shape." It needed "time and trouble spent on it": he'd spent only ten years. On 29 December it was finally published in New York.

Joyce had been an Irish pupil of Padraig Pearse's. He dropped out, he said, because Pearse thought it necessary to promote Irish by denigrating English as inexpressive. One of the inexpressive words was "thunder," for which the Irish is *tórnach,* if you like that. Later Joyce made up ten better ones, among them "bababadalgharaghtakamminarronnkonnbronntonner ronntuonnthunntrovarrhounawnskawntoohoohoordenenthurnuk!" "Thurnuk" is Irish getting in the last word and sounding like a hiccup.

In Cork a policeman's son, John Whelan, sixteen, had been watching forty or fifty local volunteers "fumble and stumble"—"rudely accoutered fellows, only a very few bearing rifles." His Irish teacher was drilling them. They looked shabby, absurd, awkward, unheroic, and when he heard of a rising in Dublin he was unexcited. Elsewhere in Cork Michael Frank

O'Donovan, twelve and a half, felt "horror that Irishmen could commit such a crime against England," but later picked up the Irish primer he'd thrown aside and "started trying to re-learn all that I had forgotten." A couple of years later, the two having met and neither with a place where the other could sit, they would walk round in the Cork rain, "sheltering in doors, talking literature." Later they were Sean O'Faolain and Frank O'Connor, stormy petrels of a future that never came. *The New Yorker* would buy their Irishness.

If we look behind their pseudonyms we see an X-ray of a time. "Frank O'Connor" used a made-up name to shield the friends and relatives bigots would savage because you'd published something. He'd seen Lennox Robinson forced out of a good job over what Lady Gregory rightly called "a storm in a chalice": priests fussing about a little piece of fiction. (Yeats's contribution to the melée, his poem "Leda and the Swan," didn't help at all.) The new name of "Sean O'Faolain" was a gesture of the patriotic era, simply "John Whelan" put back into native speech.

Of the native speech, O'Faolain at seventy-six said carefully that he was "glad to have known it." His wife, who was pouring the tea, he'd met long ago at an Irish summer school they went to in the full flush of nationalist fervor. There he had "dipped the tip of her ponytail in the inkwell and politely handed it forward to her." An erect blue-eyed gentleman, he'd be anybody's model of deportment whatever anarchy he might be committing. He thought Joyce overliterary. He did commend a story in *Dubliners,* I wish I could remember which.

Early in 1918 the titular master of Coole was shot down over Italy—by an erring Allied plane, it later turned out—and once again an event exacted of W. B. Yeats the best powers he could summon.

His first thoughts, beckoned by *Lycidas,* turned to Pastoral. He liked the outcome well enough to preserve it as "Shepherd and Goatherd," not well enough to put Robert Gregory's name atop it. "Goatherd" is himself, aged fifty-two, sometime poet, now scrutineer of "the road that the soul treads." "Shepherd" is someone like himself but younger, hence fresher, more impetuous. Preoccupied with beginning again and remembering the way a younger man with his name had begun before, he readily became two people, the Old Man and the Young Man of *At the Hawk's Well.* Self, self: he hardly knew how to work Gregory in.

For these public crises were coinciding with something unprecedented, the effort of a Romantic poet, dead at forty, to commence a second incarnation. The eight-volume *Works* he published at forty-three were a terminal moraine. Keats and Shelley had not lived as long, and Wordsworth should not have, nor Tennyson. Romanticism's premium on early experience entails a diminuendo as the shades close, and the poet who escapes tuberculosis or drowning must confront the fact that he has done his living. So by 1915 Yeats was reliving a former life, in fact writing his *Memoirs,* when the *Noh* unexpectedly gave him rebirth as a playwright. It is unsurprising that his first *Noh* play is preoccupied with two selves: himself now and in youth. He needed a unitive role, and we should glance at the possibility that it was Joyce who helped him find it, much as long ago, when he wrote "The Tables of the Law," he'd helped Joyce find Stephen Dedalus.

Between 2 February 1914 and 1 September 1915 the *Egoist* serialized in twenty-five installments *A Portrait of the Artist as a Young Man.* Pound saw to it that Yeats saw them, having enlisted Yeats in his campaign to get the penniless Joyce a grant from the Royal Literary Fund.* The only mention we know of is in a letter of 29 July 1915; but did Yeats at about this time pick up from the *Portrait* the sacerdotal model Stephen Dedalus proposes for art? A laying-on of consecrating hands by the priest of the eternal imagination, not altering the show of ordinary things but transforming them into food for the spirit: that, de-Romanized by the Yeatsian Magician, would yield the voice that says "I write it out in a verse," to transfigure the anticlimaxes of Easter 1916 into names for a litany "now and in time to be."

In "Shepherd and Goatherd," 1918, he was back to the two selves. That had been a March fumble. Mid-June brought a triumph. In his new incarnation he'd been rereading the English poets with other eyes than in boyhood. And in Abraham Cowley of all poets, a man on everyone's interdicted list since Samuel Johnson memorably savaged him and through him the Metaphysicals, Yeats found a model less hackneyed than *Lycidas:* the 1642 Ode on the Death of Cowley's college friend Mr. William Hervey, with its ingenious stanza that contracts itself into a couplet usable for reverie or qualification, preparatory to asserting a solemn close.

> . . . But happy Thou, ta'en from this frantick age,
> Where *Ignorance* and *Hypocrosie* does rage!
> A fitter *time* for Heav'n no soul ere chose,
>   The place now only free from those.
> There 'mongst the *Blest* thou does for ever shine,
>   And wheresoere thou casts thy view

*Yeats's efforts on behalf of the man who is supposed to have snubbed him were exemplary: *Letters,* 596–601. The benefit to Joyce was £75: in those days, several months' income.

> Upon that white and radiant crew,
> See'st not a Soul cloath'd with more *Light* than *Thine*.

We notice the short count of lines 4, 6, 7, where the voice can *insert* something: notice too how after a pair of eight-syllable lines the last pentameter can resonate like an alexandrine of Spenser's. Cowley has a rudimentary sense of what can be done here; it was Yeats's genius that he saw ceremonial possibilities. Listen:

> Some burn damp faggots, others may consume
> The entire combustible world in one small room
> As though dried straw, and if we turn about
> The bare chimney is gone black out
> Because the work had finished in that flare.
> Soldier, scholar, horseman, he,
> As 'twere all life's epitome.
> What made us dream that he could comb grey hair?

"The bare chimney is gone black out": what a tensely theatrical line!

This sample is atypical in one important way: it contains three sentences. Of the twelve stanzas in Yeats's Gregory Ode, all but three shape a single sentence each, a noble intricate ceremony of syntax, notable among them the great sentence he framed to commemorate "that enquiring man John Synge."

One stanza, one sentence: such would be Yeats's way in the major performances that distinguish his last twenty years: "Among School Children" for instance, "Prayer for my Daughter," "Coole Park and Ballylee." He may have been prompted by the Shelley of "Adonais," though Shelley's headlong assertiveness has little use for suspensions and qualifications, his sentences spliced with semicolons that might as well be full-stops. But Yeats, as in stanza 5 of "Nineteen Hundred and Nineteen," will design a labyrinth of predications to connect his opening pronoun with his climax:

> He who can read the signs, nor sink unmanned
> Into the half-deceit of some intoxicant
> For shallow wits; who knows no work can stand,
> Whether health, wealth or peace of mind were spent
> On master-work of intellect or hand,
> No honour leave its mighty monument,
> Has but one comfort left: all triumph would
> But break upon his ghostly solitude.

Despite its syntax of magisterial prose, that would be congested prose; the sentence needs the stanza, the measured lines set off by the rhymes and the off-rhymes, to guide an enquiring mind, an entrusting voice.

Observe one last thing. Most often starting from a dependent clause, such a sentence cannot pretend to be improvised as it makes its elaborate way among rhyming markers toward an unforeseeable, necessarily foreseen close where rhyme and syntax and thought are resolved together. It enacts there-fore a weighty deliberation, remote from the effects of spontaneity by which other modernists were seeking to counter Victorian indiscipline. That a line should "seem a moment's thought" had been Yeats's ambition once. No more; or not quite. And we can see why, except here and there in the earliest *Noh* plays he wrote with Pound at his elbow, free verse was of little use to him.

The elegy for Major Robert Gregory was his first triumph in this magis-terial manner. Having died as the spontaneous lyricist who'd "Cover it up with a lonely tune," Yeats is resurrected as the poet-mage of resolute concat-enated statement, modelled on a lyrical Augustanism that never was. And in a time of fierce local passions he has dropped "Davis, Mangan, Ferguson" to unite himself with an English tradition anterior to them, and with a European tradition embracing that. But for English Cowley, no Gregory Ode; but for Grecian Pindar, no Cowley.

Literary history has its own resurrections. In making the name of a minor Irish squire known everywhere among the literate, Yeats completed too something begun by a poet we had nearly forgotten save as a bone Johnson gnawed. Cowley, the last Metaphysical, was also the first Augustan, and when Yeats, at journey's end, dines (we trust habitually) "with Landor and with Donne"—Donne smiling with skeletal thought, Landor unforgetful of the moment it dawned on him (good God!) that the man he'd thrown from the window would smash the violets—let there be at that table a fourth poet, Abraham Cowley, to dream back over his hopes for Pindaric varia-tions, intricate built rhymes, and take satisfaction in the lofty rhyme Yeats, at his prompting, built for Robert Gregory.

> Always we'd have the new friend meet the old
> And we are hurt if either friend seem cold,
> And there is salt to lengthen out the smart
> In the affections of our heart,
> And quarrels are blown up upon that head;
> But not a friend that I would bring
> This night can set us quarrelling,
> For all that come into my mind are dead.

THE *ULYSSES* YEARS

"The book! The book!"

—*Apocryphal last words of Joyce's aunt.*

The Book of the Century, with some four thousand typographical errors ("unavoidable," said a note, "in the exceptional circumstances") appeared in Paris on 2 February 1922, the author's fortieth birthday and the last day in the life of John Butler Yeats Sr. They had met, possibly, once, on the strand, the time J.J. invoked Occam's Razor: if J.B.Y. said he was refusing a two-shilling loan because it would be squandered on drink, that was meaningless since J.B.Y. had also said he didn't have two shillings to lend, and was therefore adducing "the possible use of the non-existent." Seeing that its sole source is Oliver Gogarty, this tale is almost surely an Irish Fact, though its logic is plausibly Joycean.

Dr. Oliver St. John Gogarty (1878–1957) will be remembered as long as *Ulysses* is read, with always a footnote somewhere to explain that "Buck Mulligan," stately and plump, derives from him.

Who cares about A.E.C. Hodister today? Yet he was Conrad's Kurtz. The originals of characters in novels tend to be unnoticed, or when noticed forgotten. But not in Dublin, where gossip was quick to put it round that a big dirty book had Dr. G. in it. The victim roared his protest: "That bloody Joyce whom I kept in my youth has written a book you can read on all the lavatory walls of Dublin." Not the least of his afflictions was a gilded turd of a name. If "Buck" is an eighteenth-century honorific, "Mulligan" is slum-grubby: a low name indeed, Mulligan, a class of stew. To call your man "Buck Mulligan" is to liken him to a tramp who affects calling-cards.

"That bloody Joyce" is the splutter of an Irishman angry enough to sue. Bringing suit is the national catharsis; later Gogarty crucified naïve Paddy Kavanagh in the courts over a single ill-gauged jest in Paddy's memoir *The Green Fool,* having been himself brought to book by a man he libelled in a "memoir" of his own, an action memorable for the words his counsel applied to a twenty-two-year-old witness then domiciled in France, "the bawd and blasphemer from Paris": that was Sam Beckett.

Lawsuits sleep like serpents in *Ulysses*. Many years later the BBC wakened one of them, when it broadcast the "Hades" episode in all innocence and heard (to its heavy cost) from Reuben J. Dodd, Jr., who had not been aware before that his name was mentioned in a book. The counsel who won Dodd damages wrote Gogarty's biography.

But Gogarty could not sue Joyce because Joyce was not in Ireland. We should note that his permanent exile commenced with the publication of *Dubliners,* which had sent "Mr. Bartell D'Arcy" to a solicitor. If you insist on putting identifiable people in books you do well to stay out of town when the town is Dublin.

Being in a book, Buck Mulligan cannot change; he will walk the same treadmill of dead witticisms forever. Forever, as he drops his gown, he will mock the Tenth Station of the Cross, saying resignedly, "Mulligan is stripped of his garments"; forever, moving toward the door, he will say, wellnigh with sorrow, "And going forth he met Butterly," winking toward Simon Peter in St. Matthew's Gospel, who, going out, wept bitterly.

To have been immobilized like that was a great cross for mercurial Oliver Gogarty, who is changing perpetually whenever he can be caught sight of in history's kaleidoscope. By some accounts he was a third-rate poet and a first-rate surgeon, by other accounts the reverse. He is known to have successfully removed Yeats's tonsils, no joke with a fifty-five-year-old for a patient. He did it "with exuberant gaiety," and suggested the lines along which Yeats should conduct a dying speech. "The arch-mocker," George Moore wrote, "the author of all the jokes that enable us to live in Dublin." Of a surgeon enmired in a divorce case: "He made his reputation with his knife and lost it with his fork." Of a plunge into Liffey effluvia: "Not swimming, just going through the movements." Of Eamon de Valera: "A cross between a corpse and a cormorant." Versions of his limericks still pass from mouth to mouth:

> There was a young man from St. John's
> Who wanted to bugger the swans.
>   "Oh no!" said the porter,
>   "Oblige with my daughter;
> The swans are reserved for the dons."

"My masterpiece," he would say when it was quoted, mocking the intonation Yeats would affect when someone praised "Innisfree."

Yeats, who admired the Buck and ignored the Mulligan, thought Gogarty "one of the great lyric poets of our age," adducing in evidence an act that concerned swans:

> Twelve years ago Oliver Gogarty was captured by his enemies, imprisoned in a deserted house on the edge of the Liffey with every prospect of death. Pleading a natural necessity he got into the garden, plunged under a shower of revolver bullets and as he swam the ice-cold December stream promised it, should it land him in safety, two swans. I was present when he fulfilled that vow.

Anne Yeats, who was present too, has recalled Father being impressed "with the majesty of the occasion" while Gogarty swore and kicked at the wooden box the reserved swans were reluctant to emerge from. They eventually waddled Liffeywards.

"Ringsend" gives a measure of his lyric gift:

> I will live in Ringsend
> With a red-headed whore,
> And the fan-light gone in
> Where it lights the hall-door;
> And listen each night
> For her querulous shout,
> As at last she streels in
> And the pubs empty out.
> To soothe that wild breast
> With my old-fangled songs,
> Till she feels it redressed
> From inordinate wrongs,
> Imagined, outrageous,
> Preposterous wrongs,
> Till peace at last comes
> Will be all I will do,
> Where the little lamp blooms

Like a rose in the stew;
And up the back-garden
The sound comes to me
Of the lapsing, unsoilable,
Whispering sea.

The end of that compares well with any attempt to catch in English the sound of Homer's "*polyphloisboio thalasses.*" ("Ah, Dedalus, the Greeks," cries Buck Mulligan, "I must teach you. You must read them in the original." Later Joyce tackled *polyphloisboio* head on: "Polyfizzyboisterous.") Anapestic rhythm and adjectival cumulation—"Imagined, outrageous, preposterous wrongs"—tell us that Gogarty's been reading Swinburne; other verses of his bespeak a straw-hatted classicism like Housman's or Hilaire Belloc's. At his death *The Lancet* affirmed that his lyrics would be remembered "so long as there are men to quote them," which is true if you think about it.

Such a man wouldn't surprise you if he mummed a Mass with his shaving-bowl:

Stately,* plump Buck Mulligan came from the stairhead, bearing a bowl of lather on which a mirror and a razor lay crossed. A yellow dressinggown, ungirdled, was sustained gently behind him by the mild morning air. He held the bowl aloft and intoned:
—*Introibo ad altare Dei.*

But put him aside and heed the injunction of *Finnegans Wake*, "Wipe your glosses with what you know," including what you can learn from *Ulysses* itself, also from the *OED*.

As the book will soon be telling us, its Dublin is polarized between "The imperial British state" and the stewards of the cross. Sure enough, in the first sentence, "Stately" and "crossed," with twenty words marching between them.

That is one hint of many that James Joyce had his mind on a good deal more than impressions of Oliver St. John Gogarty. He had his mind on a taut cat's cradle of words, and if they conjure up a phantom Gogarty, that is virtually a side-effect. The Buck in the book resembles a hologram: three-

---

*The full-page *S* in the Vintage/Random House edition was the *art deco* touch of a 1934 designer and has no Joycean sanction.

dimensional, but close your hand and you're grasping nothing. The very words seem less obligated to him than to one another or to pedantries of usage.

"Stately, plump Buck Mulligan came from the stairhead . . .": by the inner criteria of *Ulysses* the Buck is "stately" in part because he isn't churchly, whatever his efforts at a parody-Mass. As for "plump," which we're often told Gogarty wasn't (though a 1909 postcard from Joyce mentions "Gogarty's fat back"), *Plump* (*adv.*) means "without hesitation or circuitous action," and nothing keeps both "stately" and "plump" from being adverbial, though if you opt for *Plump* (*adj.*), it need not as you may suppose say "obese," merely "no angularity of outline." It is perhaps relevant, or perhaps not, that its cognates include Dutch *plomp* (coarse, rude, clownish).

The *OED* in its four columns on *Plump* adverts several times to "the sound made by a solid body entering water," something Mulligan does at the end of the episode "Stately, plump" introduces. Just at that instant "plump" makes a second appearance: "His plump body plunged." Were you thinking perhaps those words are related? No, we got "plunge," via French, from Latin *plumbicare*, to heave the lead, whereas "plump," of Germanic ambience, is "prob. echoic, expressing a sound and action akin to those of *plop* (*v.*), but with more distinct expression of the liquid 'gulp' made by water when a body falls into it." Peeps at the *OED* in its moments of rapture are among the minor rewards of frequenting Joyce. He was himself a great dictionary-browser, reading Skeat "by the hour" in the library with the hissing gas (the same word, he'd have learned, as "chaos"*).

Do not for a moment suppose that Joyce came late to such practices. *Dubliners*, that seeming chapel of modest naturalism, will not let us forget what it is that fictions are made of: of language, as deciphered by ourselves. It does this whenever it reminds us (often) that only in cooperation with a context do we extricate narrative or description out of what we read. That is why each story can leave us with the sense that its world contains something we are not quite seeing; also why most of them contain a protagonist who must strain to comprehend what is going on around him. The boy in "The Sisters," Eveline, Little Chandler, Gabriel Conroy, all are frustrated by a reticence of signs. We too, every once in a while, may be given pause by some common word, discontinuous with what we think we understand.

Thus if "plump" and "plunge" are not related, neither are "mass," corporeal bulk, from Latin *massa*, a lump, and "Mass," the Eucharistic ceremony,

---

*This etymology pleased Beckett's Murphy, who dies of accidental gassing. "The gas went on in the w.c., excellent gas, superfine chaos. Soon his body was quiet."

from Latin *missa*, something sent (cf. "mission"). As early as "Eveline," the second story he wrote, we can find Joyce playing on such facts. He has his scared girl glimpsing "the black mass of the boat," and "black mass" was a phrase he of all men did not write inadvertently. "Black mass" says *missa*, "mass of the boat" says *massa*, and the point of this is to remind us that if we are visualizing a night scene at the North Wall, we're doing so at the promptings of words, half-unsure whether other promptings are relevant.

In "The Sisters" Old Cotter talks "of faints and worms," and what he is talking about is his beloved distillery, "faints" being the last leavings of the mash and "worms" the coiled pipes. Yet are not "faints" and "worms" right words to have found their way somehow into this story of death?

"North Richmond Street, being blind," commences "Araby," a story which ends with an opening of eyes: "Gazing up into the darkness I saw myself as a creature driven and derided by vanity . . .": never mind that "blind" of streets and "blind" of eyes are meanings hard to relate. (One etymological guess about "blind" streets is that they're cul-de-sacs into which you *blund*er.)

Lean on a *Dubliners* phrase and it dissolves into lexicography; yet *Dubliners* gives off the ring of firm naturalism, much like the kittens and apples created by God, whose matter has more empty space than substance, and whose substances under scrutiny dissolve into quarks. Quarks, by the way, got their name from *Finnegans Wake* because their namer, Murray Gell-Mann, a long-time *Wake* fan, remembered "Three quarks for Muster Mark" (*FW* 383), and the things (things?) he was naming come in threes. Joyce would have found "quark" in the *OED*, where it means to make a croaking sound, e.g. "Rooks cawing and quarking": just the word to be uttered by his chorus of seagulls. *In principio verbum*: press toward the material ultimate and come to an utterance.

The "realism" amid which *Ulysses* opens is still more an illusion than that of *Dubliners*, evoking as it does not even "reality" but the mannerisms of a turn-of-the-century novel, once taken by readers for "real," in which nothing done by anybody goes unchaperoned by a helpful adverb. Mulligan calls up "coarsely," covers the bowl "smartly," says something "sternly," something else "briskly," another thing "gaily." Stephen Dedalus follows all this "wearily." By retroaction, the pattern co-opts "Stately." This fistful of instances is from the first page. By 1960 the device Joyce was mocking had sufficiently ceased to beguile for literati to be playing a parlor game called "Swifties": " 'Open some windows,' commanded Tom, hotly"; " 'Are those nails sterilized?' asked Jesus, crossly"; " 'I've dropped my toothpaste,' said Tom, crestfallen."

By the third page "Mulligan" even turns "great searching eyes"—golly,

what a book—and not long afterward the convention of the "interior mono-
logue" (not the author's label but his critics') is permitting "Stephen Dedalus" to compose a paragraph-long set-piece in more time than is plausibly
available.* Time is as elastic in this episode as space (which permits an
impossible view of Bray Head from atop the Martello Tower in Sandycove),
though neither time nor space is mauled as vigorously as normal novelists,
inconscient, maul them. (Joyce jeered at George Moore for having characters look up a train time they'd have known the way they knew their
address.) Far from being verbal cinematography, the first episode of *Ulysses*
is busy mocking the mannerisms and faults of the English novel, preparatory to seventeen further episodes which deftly eschew those faults while
introducing their own peculiarities.

A peculiarity present from the beginning is the book's awareness of
numbers: how many people in a room, shillings in a ledger, even words in
a sentence. A recurrent number is 11; the first sentence has 2 x 11 words,
the third one (from "He" to "*dei*") has 11: as we become skilled navigators
we recognize 11 as a Ulyssean seamark. For in this book 11, the fresh start
after a decade, is the number for the two primary kinds of events, beginnings
and endings; and while sometimes it is specified, it sometimes lurks behind
a count of episodes or paragraphs or words. A sampling of elevens: Rudy
Bloom died 11 years ago, aged 11 days; Stephen's age is 2 x 11; "Marion
Bloom" has 11 letters and so has "Hugh E. Boylan," and the hour of their
tryst is set in the 11th episode; 11 paragraphs of entry and 11 of exit precede
and follow the 40 paragraphs of gestation in "Oxen of the Sun"; as late as
1919, when he conceived "Wandering Rocks," Joyce had meant the center
of the book to consist of 11 episodes. And in Joyce's final book, *Finnegans
Wake*, the last sentence-fragment circles toward a new beginning with just
11 words:† "A way a lone a last a loved a long the. . . ." The last sentence
of *Ulysses* you can't count since you can't tell where it starts.

"Ulysses," of course, is Mr. Leopold Bloom, whom we do not meet until
the book's fourth episode when time doubles back to 8 a.m. and starts over.
By now there is no question of fictional procedures mocked. In their place

---

*It is on pages 20–21 and runs from "The proud potent titles" to "their lances and their shields."
Saying it through takes about forty seconds, and the time in which we are to credit it passing
through Stephen's mind is the instant between two sentences spoken by Haines.

†The *Wake*'s recurrent riddle-number, 1132, is 4 x 283, the year of the death of Finn MacCool,
but it is also 11, the return-number, set beside 32, the feet-per-second-per-second number of the
Fall.

we have the book's own unique blend of minute observation, miraculous local brevity, deft interweaving of inner and outer process, to convince us that prose fiction, reputedly at home in the familiar, has never till now been astute enough to take the measure of how people spend most of their lives: cooking, dealing with hats, manipulating doorknobs, walking, musing. Homer described things ordinary in his day: how men beached a ship, greeted a priest, put on a helmet. His noble verse was the medium for that; the contrivances of *Ulysses* are comparably ceremonial, be the theme but the feeding of a cat. That is the first point of contact between Bloom and his prototype: the care for style we discern everywhere in the rendering, the refusal of language to be merely casual. "He watched the bristles shining wirily in the weak light as she tipped three times and licked lightly."

Mr. Bloom incarnates several things besides Homer's cunning wanderer. In particular, he is a walking figure of Nationalist rhetoric, which delighted in parallels between the Jews and the Irish. Both peoples yearned to repossess a little homeland; both, dispersed through the world, resisted assimilation; both claimed a racial unity (Celtic, Semitic); both guarded an ancient language (Irish, Hebrew); both rejoiced in a proud remote past when literacy was in the keeping of their scribes. Both had heard oppressors talk of a system of surnames adaptable to the bureaucracy's filing systems; German Jews for instance took names like Stone, Brook, Bird (Stein, Bach, Vogel) in response to such regulations as that of 1465, which the Irish managed to disregard. And as Jews beneath the foreman's whip made bricks for Egypt, so Irishmen on starvation wages laid the tracks along which England's trains rumbled. Paddy was routinely despised, like Ikey; but like the Jews in Egypt he took comfort in scoffing at the materialism of his oppressors. For both peoples the journey out of oppression had been long and bitter, impossible save for the special protection of God. And when Parnell died on what had seemed the eve of Home Rule, was that not like Moses dying in sight of a Promised Land he had nearly gained but was forbidden to enter?

Joyce's way with any system of thought was the one he had learned from the way of his Jesuit masters with Catholic doctrine: absolute undeviating literalness, which tended to shrink the domain of mystery to dimensions you could generally ignore. This is disconcertingly like the way of the parodist; scholastic theology can sometimes read like a parody of contemplative theology, demanding definitions and multiplying distinctions, in books that (like *Ulysses*) get very long.

Like mystery, belief can dwindle. It is clear for instance that Joyce used the doctrines of reincarnation you heard so much of in turn-of-the-century

Dublin. It is pointless to ask what he thought of them. Yeats believed in reincarnation; so did AE; so did Maud Gonne. This meant they had lived before and would live again, and it allowed Yeats to play his poet's game of imagining Maud had been "a woman Homer sung," the way he was singing her now. Joyce, though, having once arranged for Bloom to explain the word "metempsychosis" to Molly (and get it muddled with "metamorphosis"), reverts to the idea no more. To him the doctrine is no occasion for awe. His attention is on multiplying plausible correspondences by which the returned Ulysses can be recognized.

A few come readily to mind. Ulysses will be taller than the average citizen (Bloom is five foot nine and one-half, in a city where policemen—minimum height five-nine—were apt to look like giants), he will live at the highest point within the city's old boundaries, he will have a wife who is famous for her allure, there will be something Mediterranean about his looks. . . . Had Yeats set out to design a reborn Ulysses he might have drawn up a list like that, but he would also have made Ulysses produce an heroic *effect*, something Joyce does not do. No one mentions Bloom's stature, and we'd not be aware of it but for pondering a measurement introduced late in the book and inconspicuous amid much pedantry of detail. (Most readers miss it and think of Bloom as a little man.) No mention is made of the uphill climb getting to Eccles Street entails; you learn about that by visiting Dublin and walking. And if you'd gotten to number 7 Eccles Street before they wrecked it, you'd have confronted a row house anonymous like thousands of others, producing no more in the brick than in the book an effect in any way comparable to that of an Ithacan palace.

Likewise, in working out the parallel between Jew and Irishman, Joyce concentrates on ramifications, not on effects. If Nationalist rhetoric meant anything save empty exhortation to take heart, it meant that the ideal citizen of the New Ireland would be a Jew: someone like the Irish in many belauded ways, but also not a boozer, not a squanderer, not a brawler. These were implications the rhetoricians skipped over. They preferred their Jews in the Bible where they belonged, and did not take kindly to such people "coming over here to Ireland filling the country with bugs." (At the time of which Joyce was writing the number of Jews in Dublin was just about two thousand.)

Bloom, though, grows in stature throughout the day the big book chronicles. His emergence as a man to care about and ponder is among the greatest of literary miracles, seeing that we encounter it in a book so seemingly insistent on its own indifference to illusion, to "character" and "plot," to anything but schemes of formal consistency. By less than the halfway point the book seems wholly preoccupied for good with stylistic pastiche, yet already Leopold Bloom is so firmly established we cannot lose sight of him despite any pedantry of verbal system. He is what Joyce once famously promised, "the uncreated conscience of my race."

That the Book of Bloom derives a structure from the *Odyssey* is something by now well publicized. This implies that the *Odyssey* is Western man's pioneer novel, so in rewriting it *sub specie MCMIV*, Joyce undertook to take stock of what the art of narrative had been up to during twenty-seven intervening centuries. He concluded that it had done little more than contrive variations on Homer; thus *The Count of Monte Cristo*, with which Stephen Dedalus has a period of obsession in Chapter II of *A Portrait*, is unquestionably an *Odyssey* for adolescents.

Usually, the narrative mind of the West has concealed its indebtedness better than Dumas did. We can penetrate its tricks once we reflect that the *Odyssey*'s fantastic wanderings are optional. Its node requires just four main characters: absent father, avenging son, beset wife, usurper, and many stories are the story of these four.

Stephen in *Ulysses* fancies himself a second Hamlet, in ostentatious mourning and beset by impostors. Sure enough, *Hamlet* fits neatly into the pattern, an *Odyssey* told from the viewpoint of the son:

FATHER	SON	MOTHER	USURPER
Ulysses	Telemachus	Penelope	Suitors
The Ghost	Hamlet	Queen Gertrude	King Claudius
Si Dedalus	Stephen	Dead Mother	Mulligan

Leopold Bloom would fill this schema with different names:

Bloom	Little Rudy	Molly	Blazes Boylan

Back at number 7 Eccles Street, Molly and Boylan are singing the seduction duet from *Don Giovanni*, and Bloom has fantasies of breaking in upon them like the Stone Guest. That would be like Homer's slaughter of the suitors, since *Don Giovanni* is an *Odyssey* too, told from the viewpoint of the usurper.

Bloom and Stephen are enacting different but congruent scenarios, nightmares from which they are trying to awake. Stephen would like nothing better than to be quit of Si Dedalus's drunken improvidence, of his dead mother's importunities, of Mulligan's insolent exactions. He would like to escape altogether and start over, but that is one thing life does not permit. Bloom wishes he could get out of the cuckold's role in which this Dublin analogue of *Don Giovanni* has cast him, but that is a role from which there is no escape: once cuckolded, a cuckold always.

Late at night, though, at the cabman's shelter, Bloom conceives a brilliant plan which will in effect amalgamate the two plots. He will take Stephen home with him; Stephen can be his new son; Stephen's attractiveness can expunge Boylan from Molly's affections; under the Bloom roof Stephen can go on to a brilliant career; can even, wonder of wonders, perhaps marry sprightly Milly Bloom, the daughter to whom at this moment in Mullingar a medical student is paying alarming attention. Bloom's envisaged schema would be:

FATHER	SON	MOTHER	USURPER
Bloom	Stephen	Molly/Milly	Boylan/Student

This has a familiar shape: the shape of *Tom Jones* and of *Nicholas Nickleby*: the Picaresque Novel with a Happy Ending, an English specialty from Fielding's time till after Dickens's. In that novel, the bourgeois dream, many thousand times rewritten for 150 years, mankind is divided, like Quixote and Sancho, into two persons, the Picaro and the Benefactor. It is the bourgeois dream because it endows Sancho Panza with money and then brings him on stage to solve everything. Sancho Panza, it turns out, was all the time Ulysses in a clown's mask.

The story devotes itself to the picaro, the unattached homeless young man. He has adventures that seem endless but must end, in part because books must end, in part because life demands roots and rootless adventure has none. So they end when his father finds him: in some versions his long-lost natural father, in other versions simply a man of benevolence, a *social* father. And enfolded by his rescuer's benefactions, the young man faces happily toward triumphant marriage (End of the Story). So repeatedly did Victorian pens rescribble it, we are hardly excessive if we call this novel *the* novel, and it too we can think of as derived from the *Odyssey*: an *Odyssey* focussed, like *Hamlet*, on the wayward son.

As surely as the coming of the Benefactor at the end of the Victorian novel, the plan Bloom adumbrates would solve absolutely everything, not least Stephen's immediate problem, which is where to spend the night. It is easy to feel that Stephen needs taking in hand. Bloom will take him in hand. He needs, for a change, to be with someone who values him. Lord, how Bloom values him! Bloom will help him manage his money too, and incul-

cate regular hours and sound diet and bathing and self-regulation and . . .
the mind boggles. And Stephen quite sensibly says a prompt No Thank
You, and walks out of Bloom's universe and the book's.

Which is the end of an era: the English Novel so comprehensively, so
consummately Done that there has been (at last) no need for it to be done
again. *Ulysses* was one more unappreciated blow an Irishman struck for
Irish independence. Everywhere it co-opts the sacred. The great urban
novel in English ought to have been set in London. It is set in Dublin. Its
picaro ought to be a hearty spirited youth. He is morose and unwashed and
moreover an intellectual. Its benefactor ought to be smiling, affluent, quietly
top-drawer, epitome of the system that has structured classes so wisely. He
is Jewish, insecure, irregularly employed, cuckolded. It ought to end with
an affirmation of universal rightness. But because its picaro has walked off
the stage, it ends with a lonely man going to bed, and with the sleeplessness
of his lonely wife. And the whole has the variousness and the encyclopedic
finality of a sacred book.

Ireland strained in those years to bring forth a Sacred Book; Yeats used
to talk of "the Sacred Book of the Arts." Sacred Books are weighty, intricate, labyrinthine, vast arcane texts to annotate and ponder, filled with the
ethos and destiny of a people. When a Sacred Book for Ireland was at last
published (though bound in blue and white, the colors of Greece), the new
Free State did not even trouble to ban it. Any bookseller knew without
being told that it wasn't the sort of thing decent people would have around.
It mocked Senator Gogarty too; by 1923 "Buck Mulligan" was a Senator,
and so was W. B. Yeats.

Yeats never guessed that the book he took with him to the Tower to read
was a testament as arcane in its way as the *Vision* on which he was then
engaged. Of the first episode, where he apparently saw a cunning glass
which shadowed a phantom Gogarty, he murmured complimentary things
about "our Irish beauty and also our kind of strength," and detected "a cruel
playful mind like a great soft tiger cat," but he left the book unfinished.

George Moore, whose *Hail and Farewell* with its leitmotifs from Wagner
had pretensions toward being the national mock-epic, asked "How can one
plow through such stuff?" Bernard Shaw, who seems to have plowed through
the first episode anyhow, found in it "young men . . . drivelling in slack-
jawed blackguardism just as they were in 1870." ("Blackguardism" had
been Holloway's word for *The Playboy*.) Shaw hoped *Ulysses* might be
efficacious in Ireland, on the Irish principle of training a cat by rubbing its

nose in its filth; himself no incontinent cat, he'd been sampling excerpts in magazines, and declined to spend the price that was asked for the book.

Yeats, Moore, Shaw, none has a word about Bloom, which arouses suspicion that they didn't get beyond twenty pages. They saw what so many saw, simply a "novel," a mirror (bad news? whip the messenger), and were bemused in the old no-man's-land between the written word and the spoken. Joyce writes things you'd never *say*; yet in a pub you might say things you'd not want to see written. Himself, he saw no reason you might not arrange twenty-six letters into whatever patterns you wished. He used upper- and lower-case, also three fonts including italics and display capitals. The compositors (twenty-six of them, a numinous tally) were exacerbated by his handwriting, and the shop in Dijon suffered crises from a recurrent shortage of *w*, a letter the French do not use.

Milton's bookseller had recalled people who leafed through *Paradise Lost* and were puzzled to make out what was happening; it was for their benefit the author supplied prose summaries for the second edition. (Joyce did not, but abetted Stuart Gilbert's crib.) Non-buyers were also puzzled as to "why the poem rhymes not," provoking a great burst of Miltonic ferocity. Epochal books do puzzle, and *Ulysses* has affected our imagination of the world and of the written word more decisively than any book in English since *Paradise Lost*.

In "Circe," the long climax of *Ulysses*, Joyce brought onto the book's mental stage a definitively objectionable drama for people with a tradition of needing to have their plays protected from them by policemen. He may have thought he was sporting with the passions of a vanished time, but in February 1926 Abbey-goers once again demonstrated their old genius for getting upset.

What had been traduced this time was a cow just newly sanctified, the Easter Rebellion, which, if you believed Sean O'Casey's *The Plough and the Stars*, had drawn into its vortex patriots so insensitive they'd carry the Tricolor of Ireland into a pub. That was the outrage, that and a girl named Rosie Redmond who seemed to be making a living with her charms, and as everyone knew there were no prostitutes in Ireland, no more than there were snakes. (Though not many knew it there were snakes anyhow, Dr. Gogarty, who else, having turned some loose atop Featherbed Mountain to rebalance what St. Patrick had interfered with.)

All but the tin trumpets, the dismal scenario of 1907 was rerun, with modern improvements that included stink-bombs. There was the howling mob, hurling vegetables, shoes and chairs at the stage; there were the actors, playing once more in dumb-show; there were the police, now called Gardai, dragging hooligans out. There in the lobby stood the deathless Holloway, snarling at a man whose offense was not to have been offended:

—You have a filthy mind. There are no streetwalkers in Dublin.

—I was accosted by one only last night.

—There were none in Dublin till the Tommies brought them over.

There too on stage was W. B. Yeats once more—sixty now and his raven tresses turned white—to shout at the mob, "You have disgraced yourselves again." And was that Maud Gonne? That was Maud Gonne herself, black-gowned and silent as the sphinx in the theatre, speaker of bitter words against O'Casey in a public debate: "the colonel's daughter still," O'Casey thought, "never quite at ease with the crowd whose cheers she loved": bitter against "one who refused to make her dying dream his own." She had changed, changed utterly; and he pondered how Cathleen ni Houlihan could be an old snarly gob at times and an ignorant one too.

Her dying dream had been of limelit nobility, a Victorian and essentially an English dream. She was born (1866) in England, near the military base at Aldershot. She was given Tennysonian names, Edith Maud. No one at her christening likely knew of "Maud" as a degeneration of Irish "Maeve." "Come into the garden, Maud" will have been what fluted in her parents' ears, and while she was a little girl Tennyson was finishing *The Idylls of the King*. She would fret out her long life now till eighty-seven, maddened to the end by that dream, "To ride abroad, redressing human wrongs," esteemed as casually as any other ruin by people apt to think her finest hour had been in 1902 when she was Cathleen ni Houlihan in a white wig on a makeshift stage, summoning young men to their deaths.

O'Casey, though, was a portent: not Ascendancy like Synge and Yeats and the others, not rural nor western, but like Joyce Dublin-urban and lower-middle-class, though unlike Joyce Protestant and therefore exempt both from the Church and from the traumas of disengaging from the Church. By coincidence he'd been born (in 1880) just around the corner from Bloom's house of 1904. He of all men had authority to say that Maud Gonne, *pace* Yeats, could not have "hurled the little streets upon the great" because "her knowledge of the ways of little streets was scanty, interesting her only when they issued from their dim places headed by a green flag."

Born John Casey, later "Sean O'Cathasaigh" till that seemed an undue perplexity for scanners of Abbey programs, O'Casey had grown up in the little streets and their foul tenements, where the death rate exceeded Calcutta's. In his preliterate years, which bad eyesight prolonged till his teens, he'd picked up much Shakespeare and Boucicault by ear from a brother. Later with his nose touching the page he'd seemingly read everything there was. With scant money for books he may be the one man of the Revival who ever had to decide if *Paradise Lost* was worth stealing (yes). He wrote his first playscripts on sheets of mixed sizes, in an ink made by boiling the leads of indelible pencils his friends filched from offices. His clear gift was for inscribing talk that sang crazily, and he filled his pages with phonetic spellings to guide the actors syllable by syllable through acoustic wonders they'd forgotten or never experienced:

> FLUTHER (*more loudly*): Excited? Who's gettin' excited? There's no one gettin' excited. It would take something more than a thing like you to flutther a feather o' Fluther.

You could print that as free verse. And "flutther" takes note of a habit of aspiration, brought over from the Irish; an actor who'd trained his tongue out of such habits had better relearn. The man who expected to hear them distinguish "darlin'," "daarlin' " and "daaarlin' " ("That's a darlin' motto . . . a daaarlin' . . . motto!") had the lines going through his head like licks of jazz.

A duet or trio or quartet for Dublin voices is his unit of composition; they will even break into song from time to time.

> FLUTHER: Why d'ye take notice of him? If he seen you didn't, he'd say nothin' derogatory.
> PETER: I'll make him stop his laughin' an' leerin', jibin' an' jeerin' an' scarifyin' people with his cornerboy insinuations! . . . He's always thryin' to rouse me: if it's not a song, it's a whistle; if it isn't a whistle, it's a cough. But you can taunt an' taunt—I'm laughin' at you; he, hee, hee, hee, hee, heee!
> THE COVEY (*singing through the keyhole*):
> 　　　　Dear harp o' me counthry, in darkness I found thee,
> 　　　　The dark chain of silence had hung o'er thee long—
> PETER (*frantically*): Jasus, d'ye hear that? D'ye hear him soundin' forth his divil-souled song o' provocation?
> THE COVEY (*singing as before*):
> 　　　　When proudly, me own island harp, I unbound thee,
> 　　　　An' gave all thy chords to light, freedom an' song!
> PETER (*battering at door*): When I get out I'll do for you, I'll do for you!
> THE COVEY (*through the keyhole*): Cuckoo-oo!

Such is the texture of an episode; eight or ten such episodes make an act, getting somewhere though it's not always obvious where. The resemblance to music-hall turns was not missed and was disapproved by connoisseurs, uneasy in part because everyone was *laughing*, in part because somewhere offstage Sacred 1916 was supposed to be taking its course.

We can note how scrupulously O'Casey scores an episode's acoustic variables, not only the intonations but the idiom, which isn't Kiltartan quaintness but the tart stuff of urban experience. Though he was stylizing as much as Synge, he stylized what there were thousands to know firsthand. It all drew a class of people to the Abbey who'd never set foot there before. *Juno and the Paycock* (1924) had something unprecedented in the theatre's twenty-year history, an unscheduled second week, and crowds still turned away. So lackadaisical had normal attendance become, it was *Juno* that year kept the Abbey from going bankrupt.*

Much therefore was expected of *The Plough and the Stars*, despite details offensive to some of the actors. But the genteel were not having it. They possessed, as Sean O'Faolain would note later, a political status their *Playboy*-hating predecessors had not enjoyed, and they owed it, they thought, to the glorious rebellion, the myth of which therefore required to be cherished inviolate. A way of stating the offense is to remark that no one in O'Casey's foreground is emulating Cuchulain.

When Stephen Dedalus very late in the *Portrait* made "a sudden gesture of a revolutionary nature," he reflected later that he must have looked like a fellow throwing a handful of peas into the air. When the revolutionizing "Citizen" in Barney Kiernan's pub throws a biscuit-tin at Bloom, he may look like either a fellow throwing a bomb or Cuchulain (or Homer's Cyclops) hurling a boulder. The Cyclops was big and stupid and by this showing Cuchulain was too, so Patrick Pearse emulating Cuchulain's defeat was what Dubliners call a prize gawm. In a world where diplomats can summon gunboats, heroism is a futile piece of theatrics for a theatre where the spectators get killed too.

Joyce makes that kind of point by keeping his Cuchulain not in the foreground where Standish O'Grady kept him but in the background amid the clutter of subplots, and O'Casey did something very similar when he made his non-heroes occupy the forestage. The speech about fluttherin' a feather o' Fluther is delivered in a pub, through a window of which we occasionally see a tall man silhouetted. He is Padraic Pearse himself, haranguing gapers; to make sure we'd know him, O'Casey used excerpts from

---

*His popularity has not abated. Through 1978, the Abbey had sponsored 1,791 O'Casey performances, and his three Dublin plays, according to Robert Lowery, "rank 1-2-3 in the number of performances during the history of the Abbey."

actual Pearse orations, notably, to end with, the graveside panegyric on O'Donovan Rossa every 1916 patriot knew by heart: "They think that they have foreseen everything, think that they have provided against everything? but the fools, the fools, the fools! they have left us our Fenian dead, and while Ireland holds these graves, Ireland unfree shall never be at peace."

That class of talk makes people thirsty, so it's at the bar they deliver their choric commentary:

> FLUTHER: Jammed as I was in th' crowd, I listened to th' speeches pattherin' on th' people's head, like rain fallin' on th' corn; every derogatory thought went out o' me mind, an' I said to meself, 'You can die now, Fluther, for you've seen th' shadow-dhreams of th' past leppin' to life in th' bodies of livin' men that show, if we were without a titther o' courage for centuries, we're vice versa now!' Looka here. (*He stretches out his arm under Peter's face and rolls up his sleeve.*) The blood was BOILIN' in me veins!

We hear too from Mrs. Gogan, who is admiring the fancy uniform of a patriot:

> MRS. GOGAN (*drinking*): The Foresthers' is a gorgeous dhress! I don't think I've seen nicer, mind you, in a pantomime. . . . Th' loveliest part of th' dhress, I think, is th' ostrichess plume. . . . When yous are goin' along, an' I see them wavin' an' noddin' an' waggin', I seem to be lookin' at each of yous hangin' at th' end of a rope, your eyes bulgin' an' your legs twistin' an' jerkin', gaspin' an' gaspin' for breath while yous are thryin' to die for Ireland!

Though the scaffold has been Ireland's loftiest stage and no patriot would refuse its leading part, such fine evocations as O'Casey provides were not admired in 1926. A certain skepticism was detected. He was generally felt to have restaged patriotism's High Mass in the likes of a whorehouse and profaned rebellion's solemnities with clowning. One critic, though, thought that his intentions were high, had not shameless actors played for the laughs they could get from the simple folk the Abbey drew these days.

It is his solemn parts that jar now, especially when he saves them all for the end. The last set of *The Plough and the Stars* discloses a tenement loft with a cardgame in progress foreground, a coffin on kitchen chairs background, and visible through a bullet-pierced window Dublin's sky aflame afar. Minutes after the curtain goes up we shall learn in rapid succession about (1) the death of the tubercular girl (coffined), (2) the madness of

Nora Clitheroe (bereft), (3) the loss of her baby (miscarried), (4) the fate of her husband (killed in street fighting), and while still digesting these tidings we shall also witness (5) the violent end of Bessie Burgess (shot by mistake for a sniper). To three acts of peerless dialogue for his cast of temporizers, fanatics and poltroons, O'Casey seems to have affixed the last act of a different play about the roof of the universe falling in.

Nor was this a novel failing; it was a habit, quite as visible in *Shadow of a Gunman* (1923) and *Juno and the Paycock* (1924). "Faulty Construction" is a rubber stamp critics reach for. They also discuss whether "tragicomedy" be possible, as though *Waiting for Godot* did not settle that. But what wrenches these plays asunder is not some failure of structural intuition. It is a disparity between what O'Casey believed he should be telling his audiences and the way his gifts led him naturally. Like a wit with an obligation to preach hell-fire, he'd indulge his gifts till his conscience could rest no longer, which would be about twenty minutes before the last curtain.

His belief, approximately Marxist, was that the System generates ruin, in part because people do not pay it heed but sit around being comic while it pares its claws. His talent, though, was for writing comic dialogue. Sam Beckett, another Irish playwright with a Protestant conscience, saw a kind of play that could equilibrate this: one that honors "the principle of disintegration in even the most complacent solids, and activates it to their explosion." Here was "the principle of knockabout . . . on all its planes, from the furniture to the higher centres," and to Beckett it seemed Sean O'Casey's special daemon.

Though Beckett mentioned *Juno and the Paycock*, where much disintegration does duly emanate not from offstage but from events we see, his eye was on a one-act farce called *The End of the Beginning* which O'Casey published in 1934. By the end of *The End of the Beginning*, a title Winston Churchill appropriated at a time when his Empire was in a bad way, the clock is wrecked, jugs and windows and spectacles smashed, dishes ground to powder, hands and noses bleeding, the electricity fused, the storeroom shelves destroyed, inflammable oil spilled everywhere, and one of the characters pulled up the chimney by a cow at the far end of a rope: the principle of disintegration indeed. It all takes half an hour.

O'Casey did not build a full-length play round this principle till 1940, when *Purple Dust* destroyed at loving length every vestige of the Tudor mansion a pair of English zanies called Stoke and Poges have been so misguided as to try to resurrect in Ireland. They asked for the trouble by "Comin' over here . . . an' stickin' out their tongue at a race that's oldher

than themselves by a little like a thousand years, greater in their beginnin'
than they are in their prime; with us speakin' with ayse the mighty language
o' the world when they could barely gurgle a few sounds, sayin' the rest in
the movement of their fingers." Irish has not enjoyed a finer encomium.

This wonder is flawed by a tiresome presupposition that only working-
men talk sense, and on the way to it his conscience fissured much other
work. Even *The Plough and the Stars* had been guided in its resistance to
1916 less by a sense of the ridiculous (the comic writer's safe compass) than
by ideology. The title hints at this; it alludes to the blue banner of the Irish
Citizen Army with seven stars arrayed in the pattern Americans call the Big
Dipper but Irishmen the Plough. The Citizen Army had been founded to
protect strikers when Jim Larkin the orator was organizing Irish labor in
1908–1913, and its small knot of hardened adherents, among them O'Casey,
thought that the rival Irish Volunteers, Pearse's romantics who conducted
the Rising under their Tricolor, had made men die for irrelevance, Liberty
being empty if you weren't eating.

In *The Plough and the Stars* when "The Voice of the Man" (i.e. Pearse)
exhorts Ireland to welcome War, "The Covey," Pavlovian voice of Social-
ism, responds, "Dope, dope. There's only one war worth havin': th' war for
th' economic emancipation of th' proletariat." The author knows as well as
we do that this is recited by rote. Later O'Casey was less willing to concede
that opinions he favored could be voiced as mindlessly as opinions he abhorred.
His first lapse was the 1928 *Silver Tassie*, an "anti-war" play; he seems not
to have ever reflected how easy are anti-war statements. When the Abbey
rejected *The Tassie* he and Yeats exchanged well-publicized letters. Though
they both soon strayed into slam-bang irrelevance, Yeats had got it right at
the very start: "I am sad and discouraged. You have no subject." A conviction however passionate isn't a subject.

As the row continued Yeats drifted into proposing that all valid drama
approximated to *Noh*, O'Casey into asserting his right to do as he pleased.
He had already left for exile in England.

In 1934 the Abbey made amends and produced *The Silver Tassie*. It was
not a success. The Catholic Young Men's Society of Galway protested its
infringement of the canons of Christian reverence and human decency. The
Irish Catholic thought audiences should be kept away by law. *The Standard*
called W. B. Yeats, by then sixty-nine, "no literary leader for a Catholic
country." The President of the Gaelic League, no less, said the Abbey
should be abolished; he remembered having had to leave after one act of *The
Plough and the Stars*, from a fit of nausea. One of the directors of the Abbey,

even, preferred "Catholic cleanliness and wholesome entertainment in a theatre which our Catholic Government is subsidising": as, alas, since 1925 it had been, and what a Government.

From all the turbulence Yeats had removed himself to a vast symbolic distance. It was in 1917, the year after the Rising, that he bought the Tower at *Baile-ui-liath*, "the grey town," Ballylee, in the West near Gort. The noisy stream that flowed round its base plunged underground into *an soiléar*, "the cellar," seeking through caverns measureless to man the implacable Atlantic. But on the way there it resurfaced at Kinvara near Coole (*Cúil*, a niche, a place of retirement), where on a brief stretch above ground it spread into a lake swans came to. So its course enacted his enduring bond with the house he'd come to twenty years before, a homeless swan, to do much of his best work there, the place he'd given up being a constant guest at when at fifty-two he married at last.

In October 1916 he'd stood by the lake in Coole Park, counting swans, fifty-nine of them, brilliant creatures. The poem he made about that is a paradigm of his mature manner, sure in its modulations of intensity. It begins with the flattest syntax he could manage, mere copulas and abstractions:

> The trees are in their autumn beauty,
> The woodland paths are dry,
> Under October twilight the water
> Mirrors a still sky;
> Upon the brimming water among the stones
> Are nine-and-fifty swans.

"The trees are in their autumn beauty" is a nerveless line few teachers of Creative Writing would permit, but Yeats is long past their simplicities. He is enacting a whole theory of poetic deterioration, whereby that sort of abstraction overtakes you when age has drained the energy that made metaphors once. Wordsworth had sketched such a theory in the "Immortality" Ode, Coleridge in "Dejection." It is the High Romantic complaint; Poetry, it says, is the mind's joyous gift of leaping to meet immediate experience: a gift the young have by birthright: but men grow old. Yeats knows he is older now than ever a Romantic poet was who made a poem worth reading.

The Romantic élan rhymed with the flight of some bird: Shelley's skylark, Keats's nightingale, Wordsworth's springtime cuckoo, that bird went its own way. So too these swans:

> Unwearied still, lover by lover,
> They paddle in the cold
> Companionable streams or climb the air;
> Their hearts have not grown old;
> Passion or conquest, wander where they will,
> Attend upon them still.

"Thou wert not born for death, immortal bird . . ."—Keats and Yeats, a logician would tell us, entertain the same fallacy, that the immortality of the species gives any hint that one member's heart will not age. Swans only feel unwearied, if they do, because not one of them knows it will die; never mind the tradition that a dying swan sings its swan song.

There is a Yeats present, however, who is superior to the enervated Yeats in the poem, since he can supply at need such powerful words as make the swans "scatter wheeling in great broken rings / Upon their clamorous wings." And who is this superior Yeats? We shall be taught to call him the anti-self, master of "all / That I have handled least, least looked upon," someone precisely *un-natural*, a poet reconstituted by intent contrivance out of the relics of a poet who has aged away.

"The Wild Swans at Coole" heads a volume of the same title, a series of meditations about a universe with the fact of death in it (Gregory's death for one, and the death of Mabel Beardsley, its "Dying Lady"). Death need not be the worst that can happen. If "men improve with the years" it is only in worldly wisdom, a possession little usable by poets since no amount of it will make them indistinguishable from weather-worn marble statues or sixty-year-old smiling public men. The remedy, if you find you're alive at fifty, is to fashion an anti-self that shall wax as the dying self wanes. The place to do this work is the Tower, and in "The Phases of the Moon," a fine epistemological puzzle, two vagabonds created by the author recite the doctrine of the necessary anti-self, a doctrine they mean to withhold from him, while he in his tower writes the poem in which they recite it, and snuffs a lamp out at the end. Which Yeats wrote *that* poem? Set two mirrors face to face and conjure up an image they cast to and fro; did one of them originate it? Both? Neither?

In *The Wild Swans at Coole*, published in 1919, Yeats also addressed the possibility of the Romantic Long Poem in his time. The book is one intricate work made by arranging shorter ones, its arc stretching from swans anyone can see to "The Double Vision" only Michael Robartes can see, from Romantic Nature, indifferent, self-involved, to a supernature of stark iconic mysteries. The poet who constructed it so deliberately, in years when he saw Ezra

Pound so often, was participating in the twentieth-century Modernist adventure, of which a governing principle was the eloquence to be had by arranging discontinuities. In 1919 Pound began *Hugh Selwyn Mauberley*, another long poem made on such a principle; in 1922 T. S. Eliot would publish *The Waste Land*, a brief epic made of fragments, and by then Pound would have staked the rest of his life on a poem investigating how far the principle could be made to go: the sequence he called *The Cantos* and abandoned only when extreme age stopped him concentrating any longer. Yeats's "Meditations in Time of Civil War" and "Nineteen Hundred and Nineteen," two demonstrations of what sequencing can do when old-fashioned mastery like his shapes the components, were published in 1921 and 1923, just before *The Waste Land* and just after it.

In those years, and again like Pound and Eliot, he was appropriating literary history with both hands. He'd commenced this in 1918 when he found the stanza Cowley invented to commemorate Hervey and used it to commemorate Gregory. We should notice his willful timing. Since 1916 Irish Nationalist excoriation of England had been in crescendo, and, much as Allied musicians had dropped German music from their repertoire, so an Irish poet's elegy on an Irishman, though reversion to Ferguson or Mangan was unthinkable, at the very least might have employed an English form so neutral as to elude attention. Yeats did not do that, and he even called Gregory "our Sidney." A rebuke to provincialism is implied.

But of course he was also creating resonances between a twentieth-century elegy and a seventeenth, part of his regret for Gregory being regret for a sense of historical dignity mad Ireland had never possessed. In this his intercourse with the traditional resembles Eliot's, who in 1917 had written "Whispers of Immortality" in a meter reminiscent of Donne's "Extasie" and given it a title wryly adapted from Wordsworth.

Unlike Eliot, though, Yeats had no desire to install himself however obliquely in English literary tradition, understandable though that desire might be in an American. So having used Cowley's stanza in an Eliotic way, he proceeded to reuse it in his own way, ignoring its historical context and simply making it his own. The very next year he used it in "Prayer for my Daughter," to which its origins in elegy are wholly irrelevant. Thereafter, in Part II of "The Tower" and in "Byzantium," it is simply one of the many modes of eloquence possessed by William Butler Yeats.

He did something similar to, of all things, the sonnet. "Leda and the Swan," with its supernatural rapist, is a sonnet, acknowledging with irony the Petrarchan shape for Love's discontents. That is normal Modernist strategy, like Eliot using the Spenser "Prothalamion" to acknowledge sterile lusts. But so much for homage to origins: Yeats's next sonnet is "Meru," where there are no lovers but only naked hermits, and out of the fourteen-line music-box come the dissonances of apocalypse.

The stanza he found most use for was *ottava rima*, Italian by name and by origin; Boccaccio invented it, Tasso and Ariosto exploited its narrative speed, Byron in *Beppo* and *Don Juan* found uses for the raffishness he could affect by improvising its rhymes in rhyme-poor English, also for the insolent shrug he could get with the terminal couplet:

> What are the hopes of men? Old Egypt's King
>   Cheops erected the first Pyramid
> And largest, thinking it was just the thing
>   To keep his memory whole, and mummy hid;
> But somebody or other rummaging
>   Burglariously broke his coffin lid:
> Let not a monument give you or me hopes,
> Since not a pinch of dust remains of Cheops.

How this stanza came to Yeats's attention there is no telling, but evidently its Italian provenance struck him, since his first use of it was to give an Italian context to a meditation on great houses, their fountains, their gardens:

> What if the glory of escutcheoned doors,
> And buildings that a haughtier age designed,
> The pacing to and fro on polished floors
> Amid great chambers and long galleries, lined
> With famous portraits of our ancestors;
> What if those things the greatest of mankind
> Consider both to magnify, or to bless,
> But take our greatness with our bitterness?

That is no Irish house however lavish but a great Italian villa, and "the greatest of mankind" are the men of the Renaissance. And once more, having once used it so, he deprives the stanza of all traces of origin. It becomes the Yeats stanza, his normal recourse in forensic performance: the stanza of "Sailing to Byzantium," of "Among School Children," of the two Coole Park poems, of "The Gyres," "The Municipal Gallery Revisited," "The Circus Animals' Desertion." Its rhymes are an ebb and flow of inevitabilities, its last couplet a moment for vision to be arrested by statement, or reverie by the call of the particular.

*   *   *

When in the sequence called "Meditations in Time of Civil War" the Cicero-
nian opulence of "Ancestral Houses," glorying in its intricate sentences and
rhetorical questions, gives way to a paratactic poem called "My House," we
perceive one way he's using the Tower as emblem:

> An ancient bridge, and a more ancient tower,
> A farmhouse that is sheltered by its wall,
> An acre of stony ground,
> Where the symbolic rose can break in flower,
> Old ragged elms, old thorns innumerable,
> The sound of the rain or sound
> Of every wind that blows;
> The stilted water-hen
> Crossing stream again
> Scared by the splashing of a dozen cows; . . .

Water-hens, not peacocks, and an acre of stony ground to do for "flowering
lawns" and "planted hills"; no exultance moreover of long dependent clauses:
still, it's a Norman Tower, not L. Bloom's Eccles Street row-house, and
one of his props has come there with him, his symbolical Secret Rose from
1897. If all this is partly about giving up his old presumptive right to a
guest-room at Coole, it is more about the dwindled world of late middle
age, and even more about "the desolation of reality," notably the desolation
of the political scene that by 1921 had replaced Ascendancy dreams.

For while he was hammering together his tower of poetry, Ireland back
in Dublin was convulsed as never before. A summary should begin with a
fact often overlooked in summaries, that on 18 September 1914 King George
V had actually signed something like what Parnell had fought for, a Home
Rule Bill for Ireland. It had two provisos, unluckily: that it should not be
implemented till the end of the War with Germany, and that before it got
implemented something explicit, to be determined later, would have to be
done about Ulster, where Unionist (British-rule) sentiment had hardened
into a knot and was threatening rebellion.

Home Rule under the Crown was in no case enough for die-hard Fenians
(of whom Yeats was one by temperament if no longer by policy), not to
mention Home Rule for an Ireland lacking six of its thirty-two counties.
The Easter Rebellion of 1916 was an effort to forestall any such thing by
proclaiming a Republic.

Then to the sixteen executions of 1916 Britain was foolish enough to add
another outrage: conscription in 1918. Piaras Béaslaí, whom we last saw

spelling himself "Piaraos Beaslaoi" and being fined as a *Playboy* rioter, was
the publisher of a typical response:

> We must recognize that anyone, civilian or soldier, who assists . . . in this
> crime against us, merits no more consideration than a wild beast. . . . Thus the
> man who serves on an exemption tribunal, the doctor who treats soldiers or
> examines conscripts, the man who voluntarily surrenders when called for, . . .
> all these . . . must be shot or otherwise destroyed with the least possible delay.

This said Irishmen had a duty to kill Irishmen, and though within a month
the end of the war left its assumptions moot, it's a very grim tide-mark.
Watch.

War's end brought an election, and Sinn Fein was victorious, despite the
fact that many of its candidates were in jail. Having won, it implemented its
founder Griffith's old "Hungarian" Policy, the one the barfly gossips in
Ulysses suppose to have been drawn up by that second-generation Hungarian Leopold Bloom.* This called for a loose imitation of tactics Hungarian deputies had used against Austria in 1861: simply not recognizing the
Parliament the Irish members were supposedly being elected to. They'd
stay home (or in jail) and be members of something local: as it turned out,
the Abstentionist Parliament (*Dáil*: say "Doyle") which convened in Dublin
on 21 January 1919 with thirty-four of its sixty-nine members "Imprisoned
by the Foreigner," among them Griffith and de Valera. Though soon driven
underground, by August the Dáil was preempting British legal authority
by setting up informal courts of justice all over the island. In the process
they burned down the Customs House, Dublin's finest building, to get rid
of the Local Government Board it housed.

When he developed this scheme in 1904, Griffith had had in mind a
British-Irish association like that of Austro-Hungary. But an unforgettable
thing had happened since then: on the steps of the post office, Pearse had
proclaimed the Republic. The Dáil that met in 1919 could not but think of
itself as the first government of the Republic of Ireland, all thirty-two counties. To that end it commenced transforming Pearse's Volunteers of the
green, white and orange into the Army of the Irish Republic (IRA). Britain
sent in a mercenary counterforce, soon known, from their makeshift uniforms,
as the Black and Tans. Assassinations, reprisals, burnings, looting afflicted

---

*"He's a perverted jew, says Martin, from a place in Hungary and it was he drew up all the plans
according to the Hungarian system. We know that in the castle."—*Ulysses*, 337. This was believed
because Griffith was persistently rumored to have a Jewish advisor/ghostwriter. Joyce wrote th
episode in 1919, when the debacle wrought by the policy was apparent.

Dublin, Limerick and Cork. "Weasels fighting in a hole," was Yeats's bitter summation. Let us mock, he also wrote, the short-sighted great, wise and good; and mock mockers after that; "for we / traffic in mockery."

The next step was the negotiated treaty with England, providing for a Free State; the next was the Civil War of 1922–1923, between a government that was trying to implement the Treaty and a slice of the IRA to which it was unacceptable because (1) the separate status of Ulster was formalized, and (2) the Free State's separation from England was not total. The mystique of the Republic had taken lethal hold. In the Civil War some four thousand people died, including seventy-seven hostages executed by the pro-treaty government. Irishmen's duty to kill Irishmen had come home.

The Civil War surged round the country, and both sorts of troops turned up at the Tower door: the IRA "Irregulars," who blew up Yeats's bridge, and the Nationalists, whose name now meant pro-treaty. In the poem that records their visits Yeats finds himself unable to define his sympathies. He counts moor-hen chicks as he'd counted swans once, and retreats to "the cold snows of a dream."

In 1927 Yeats's health broke down: lung hemorrhages, high fever, nervous scatter, exhaustion. Thereafter he spent every winter on the Mediterranean, and kept alive and busy another twelve years. In 1928 he published *The Tower*, "the best book I have written." The next year *Poems, 1895* was republished yet again. In *The Tower* he said, "It is time that I wrote my will," and in a queer stubborn way those old Poems remained the heart of his legacy.

He commenced *The Tower* with "Sailing to Byzantium," bidding farewell to

> the young
> In one another's arms, birds in the trees
> —Those dying generations—

in words that remember

> Thou wast not born for death, immortal Bird!
> No hungry generations tread thee down . . .

and point forward to the Immortal Bird of Byzantium, "Of hammered gold and gold enamelling."

Once again, as in *The Wild Swans at Coole*, he has contrived to open a sequence by rewriting the Nightingale Ode of Keats; this time, though, he seems to have triumphed over the certainty that his emblematic birds will one day fly off forever. For the bird, whether swan, nightingale or jewelled artifact, is himself as Poet; and in his Byzantium of the mind he will sing to the "drowsy Emperor" without aging. Were there gold birds in historical Byzantium? "I have read somewhere . . . ," ran a characteristic note, and scholarship has plausibly pointed to Gibbon and the *Cambridge Mediaeval History*. Yeats omitted mention of the tale by Hans Christian Andersen, in which a clockwork bird's unaging unspontaneity makes the Emperor miserable, though it's closer than Byzantine minutiae to his theme, another Romantic theme, the cost of Art. For over this new homage to one Keats ode he has managed to lay the thematic structure of another: it is in the Ode on a Grecian Urn ("Bold Lover, never, never canst thou kiss") that Keats manages his precarious equilibrium between Art's "cold pastoral" and the transience of the senses. "She cannot fade, though thou hast not thy bliss."

Like the Tower, Byzantium is a place for bird or bard to enjoy indifference to what the emperor may be up to. That W. B. Yeats served in the Free State's Senate is nothing we'd divine from reading his poetry. By the time of the breakdown his *Autobiography* was written, his esoteric testament *A Vision* was published (1925; and not for the merely curious; it was limited to six hundred copies), and if as seemed likely *The Tower* was to be his last book, then it ended as a last book should:

> Such thought—such thought have I that hold it tight
> Till meditation master all its parts,
> Nothing can stay my glance
> Until that glance run in the world's despite
> To where the damned have howled away their hearts,
> Or where the blessed dance;
> Such thought, that in it bound
> I need no other thing,
> Wound in mind's wandering
> As mummies in the mummy-cloth are wound.

Nothing is more striking, in the manner he has perfected since 1916, than the way its accessible declaiming language, its eighteenth-century clarity of diction, serves purely private themes, makes purely esoteric proclamations: not what oft was thought, to which the poet brings new adequacy of expression; no: what ne'er was thought save by him, to which we bring our somewhat bedazzled assent: a conditional assent, in the midst of which we may wonder what it may mean, to believe such a thing as that some rough beast slouches anew toward Bethlehem. The symptoms of disintegration, yes, those we know; but what of Magnus Annus, of revelations from the Spiritus Mundi, of the gyres, of the affirmation that

> Death and life were not
> Till man made up the whole,
> Made lock, stock and barrel
> Out of his bitter soul,
> Aye, sun and moon and star, all . . . ?

For we may know how to trace such assertions to sources in Blake and elsewhere, but to hear them so downrightly asserted, to be expected to assent? We may choose to settle for being glad that Yeats knows.

So he withdrew, "wound in mind's wandering," into a world of supernal assertive clarity. It was in the Tower he had decided *Ulysses* was unreadable, and as he withdrew from the world where de Valera mattered, that "cross between a corpse and a cormorant," and from O'Casey's populous world, so too from Bloom's world of the obdurately physical. Swans were not feathered savages that could break your leg with a wing, not surly hissers in a box by Gogarty's feet, no, but pure emblems: "Another emblem there!" As for water, "What's water but the generated soul?" And his moon was the moon in a diagram from a sixpenny book of astrology. All this comports with his withdrawal out of strife-torn Ireland to a Tower which unlike the tower atop which *Ulysses* begins has little ascertainable history save the one he imagined for it. Joyce's Tower was one of a chain of squat coastal forts erected between ascertainable dates to keep out Napoleon's ships. But Thoor Ballylee? No one seems to know for sure who built it, or even in what century. Like the poetry Yeats commanded, its history begins with Yeats.

THE WAKE OF WAKES

On 8 December 1922, in Dublin, the Irregular firebrand Rory O'Connor
was an Irish victim of an Irish firing-squad: one of four hostages the pro-
treaty government ordered shot in reprisal for another shooting. A man at
whose wedding Rory O'Connor had been groomsman concurred in the, so
to speak, fratricidal decision.

On 20 March 1923, in Paris, James Joyce commenced his new book in
the middle, with a draft of "the 'Roderick O'Conor' fragment" (now pages
380–82 of *Finnegans Wake*).

Though that was a different O'Connor, the last High King of Ireland,
who surrendered to Henry II of England in 1175 back at the beginning of
the infamous Seven Centuries, it is difficult not to imagine some connection.
Still, you'll search those pages of Joyce's scripture in vain for any trace of
Rory less ambiguous than his surname. Later Joyce put the name Rory,
plainly spelled, on the very first page of his book; but which Rory is that?
For "Rory" is but a more phonetic way than "Roderick" of anglicizing the
Irish *Ruaidhrí* (pronounced "ruri," *u* as in "rule," *i* as in "machine"), and
the Rory O'Connor who was shot in 1922 would have been named for the
unfortunate High King, in his own time Ruaidhrí Ó Conchobhair, who was

embroiled in civil wars all through his aborted reign, saw even his son rise against him, and died, 1198, worn out, in a cloister. When he spoke his own name he said something like "Ruri O Conukher," and easing him into the history books as "Roderick O'Connor" was a piece of linguistic imperialism.

But what does it mean for that matter to say of the fragment Joyce drafted that it pertains to the last High King, though it seems to name him several times? As far as one can make out somebody after closing time (a pub-keeper?) is drinking up the leavings of every opened bottle in the place before he spins to his chair in a vertigo the words catch nicely—

> . . . one to do and one to dare,
> par by par, a peerless pair,
> ever here and over there,
> > with his
> fol the dee
> > oll the doo
> on the flure
> > of his feats
> and the feels
> > of the fumes
> in the wakes
> > of his ears
> our wineman from Barleyhome he just slumped to throne.

Well, when King Ruaidhrí submitted to Henry that was closing time on the kingship, so to speak, after which, a king in name only, he was years finishing off the dregs.

> *The Wild Man from Borneo has just come to town . . .*

—that nonsense song to be sure is a long way from the High King; but then so, in all but name, was his namesake Rory, whose best publicized exploit before he got himself executed was to seize the Four Courts in central Dublin with a gang of Irregulars and hold it against government bombardment for three days until 30 June 1922, when the flames forced him out. That was the Civil War's beginning. "The Wild Man from Borneo," yes indeed.

And if you page backward in *Finnegans Wake* from the fragment in question, you keep encountering modern hubbubs, for example,

> . . . You can't impose on frayshouters like os. Every tub here spucks his own
> fat. Hang coersion everyhow! And smotthermock Gramm's laws! But we're a

drippindhrue gayleague all at ones. In the buginning is the woid, in the muddle is the sounddance and thereinofter you're in the unbewised again, vund vulsyvolsy.

"Drippindhrue gayleague" looks like dripping hues/rues and gaiety and the Gaelic League but it seems to want to sound like *Tuigeann tú Gaedhealg* ("tigen tu gelg")—"Do you understand Irish?"; indeed you can't impose on frayshouters like us (free shouters? Free Staters? Shouters of the Fray?). "Gramm" says "Graham," Peel's Home Secretary, whose "Law" (1845) established secular colleges in Ireland which the bishops forbade the faithful to attend; as for Grimm's Laws, they were of course offensive in suggesting that Irish had anything to do with other European languages. The truculence beneath these sentences was still more explicit a few pages earlier:

> Guns.
> Keep backwards, please, because there was no good to gundy running up again. Guns. And it was written up in big capital. Guns. Saying never underrupt greatgrandgosterfosters! Guns. And whatever one did they said, the fourlings, that on no acounts you were not to. Guns.

Truly, "the boomomouths from their dupest dupes were in envery and anononously blowing great," as you'd believe without so much as noticing the behemoths of the deepest deeps, and with all that spatting and gunfire it's possible to credit that the fate of Rory O'Connor among others is entangled in these tangled pages after all.

So a good first approach to *Finnegans Wake* is to remember that Joyce commenced work on it when years of Irish violence had just ended, and the Free State had just come into precarious being. If its confusion is "imitative form," Ireland had been providing a good deal of confusion to imitate, much of it emanating from disputes about how to read documents, such as the Treaty itself or de Valera's notorious "document number two" on which the book plays at least seven times, something Dev said was in effect the same as the Treaty and yet dear God not the same because the oath it implied was not an oath. . . . "His own obsessive preoccupation with the meaning of words," writes an historian, "led [de Valera] into intricacies of speech where deputies found it hard to follow him," and there are even parts of the *Wake* that clear up a little if you imagine Dev writing them.

Back to O'Connor's name though: for it seems that in Ireland you cannot so much as bestow a name without making a statement. When they named the

Civil War Rory for the High King they equipped him with a destiny, so the choice of destinies is no wider than the choice of names. Joyce found this convenient, since homonymous actors could interchange roles. When the huge James Laughlin, now elder statesman of avant-garde publishing, appeared silhouetted in his Paris doorway, Joyce heard "Lochlann," a Norseman, and announced, "We two last met on the battlefield at Clontarf." (Brian Boru in 1014 defeated the Danes there.)

This is the principle on which Rory O'Connor can play King Roderick O'Connor (or perhaps vice versa). By extension, the pubkeeper who is the King of the Inn can play either of them, or be played by them; and the father of a family can play King or Pubkeeper, since any family is a repertory company. To enact all of history, many thousands of roles, we can do with a surprisingly small cast. In 1977, five men and two women at Radio Éireann were enough to enact any scene out of Joyce that was asked for by a script with thirty or forty parts in it.

In *Finnegans Wake* the casting principle is chiefly onomastic; not just Laughlin/Lochlann or O'Connor/O'Connor but *any* pair of homonyms can interchange roles. This hushed-up fact of linguistic experience is the basis of what is called the pun. It bespeaks something evidently true, that the world has far more phenomena crying to be named than any language has word-sized strings of phonemes, and the names get reused.

We have already seen Joyce taking note of "mass," a bulk, from *massa*, and "mass," divine service, from *missa*. English speakers having found it unimportant to distinguish these (for it's seldom indeed that perplexity would arise) they have ended up being, as people say, "the same word." This means that you find them both at the same place in the dictionary, along with an etymologist's note on the confusion. It was at one time fondly supposed that when etymology had settled the facts, English would disclose an order of truly Darwinian majesty, meanings ravelling by seamless process from root meanings, the sky for instance *blue* because a place from which the clouds had been *blown*. Such, when (as commonly) it can find them, are etymology's preferred themes; it delights to tell us that *spark* and *speak* are both scatterings as by a sower (cf. Latin *spargere*). But *blue* and *blow* turned out to be unrelated; and Joyce's browsings in the *Etymological Dictionary* of W. W. Skeat, published the year he was born, disclosed many a *mass* and *Mass*, many a *blind* eye and *blind* alley, many *faints* and *worms* Hamlet would not have discoursed of, to suggest that the cohesion of the English language might be nearly as illusory as that of the Irish Parliamentary Party.

There's an Irish word, *curcagh*, a swamp, from which they named a city that gets written Cork, and a Spanish word, *alcorque*, from which they named a substance we call cork, and when Frank O'Connor on a visit to Joyce in Paris asked what that picture was and was told "Cork," he next asked what its frame was, and was told "cork" again. Being an old-fashioned story-teller for whom words have chiefly instrumental interest, O'Connor thought Joyce was going out of his mind.

Or consider the sign you can see today at the foot of the path to the summit of Howth where Poldy and Molly lay in that memorable light amid the rhododendrons; it enjoins tourists not to Disturb the Blooms. Since it was surely put up by an official who'd no notion of making a joke, common sense thinks it amusing provided you don't take it seriously; but Joyce would have taken it seriously. Common sense supposes such confusions exceptional. Joyce thought otherwise.

He had scrutinized a sufficient number of words to be convinced that potential confusion was their norm. The miracle, in his opinion, lay in how readers ever know which sense to collect, and one thing *Finnegans Wake* is about is the seemingly insuperable difficulty of reading anything at all. His books abound everywhere with sly examples: as when he has Molly Bloom reading in bed a book that actually exists under the title *Ruby: a Novel Founded on the Life of a Circus Girl*. Joyce improved on this by renaming it *Ruby, the Pride of the Ring*, a name which, if we found it in *Finnegans Wake*, we'd not know whether to refer to circuses or to jewelry. He would have enjoyed the way Coleridge in *Kubla Khan* made the earth breathe "in short thick pants," not to mention the seemingly arithmetical import of a 1981 headline, "Pope Plans Talks to End Long Division."

Most puns are inadvertent; most go undetected thanks to context, which releases the appropriate meaning and hides the others. The word "Pope" creates for "Division" a context in Church history headline-writers feel safe in trusting. It would be hard for *The New Yorker* to prod us into finding "Pope Plans Talks to End Division" even faintly punny. But "Long" placed next to "Division" tugs it toward a classroom context the headline-writer ought perhaps to have noticed. We may guess that he'd spent so much of his day counting letters the words were losing their meaning, and when words have lost meaning you may be very fluent with them, as fluent as the narrator of the "Eumaeus" section of *Ulysses*, who tells us how Parnell "notoriously stuck to his guns to the last drop even when clothed in the mantle of adultery." If the inadvertent pun results from a word bringing to one context its affinities for another, then the paragraphs of "Eumaeus" work with inadvertent puns on a Homeric scale, the scale on which we speak instead of mixed metaphor. A mixed metaphor is a slow-motion pun.

> ... Mr Bloom being handicapped by the circumstance that one of the back buttons of his trousers had, to vary the timehonoured adage, gone the way of all buttons, though, entering thoroughly into the spirit of the thing, he heroically made light of the mischance. ...

Circumstances, we are to reflect, are things that stand around; *handicap*-money was once held hand-in-cap; *the way of all buttons* runs spookily parallel to *the way of all flesh*, evoking some Glasnevin Cemetery for buttons; *the spirit of the thing* is presumably the spirit that giveth life, not the letter that killeth; we find Ulysses doing all things, as befits a hero, *heroically*; and it was God who *made light*. To assemble all these elements with any decorum would take a composition on the scale of *Prometheus Unbound*. Here they coexist in one sentence as incongruously as six bridegrooms at one wedding.

When Joyce finished "Eumaeus" in early 1921 he was approaching the terrain of the *Wake* he'd start two years later. A Wake is a collective jollification. His *Wake* is a multiplicity of voices being misapprehended by a collectivity of ears. And such writing as offered precedent for "Eumaeus" is itself collective, resulting from a mass amnesia concerning normal ways for words to keep company. "Illiterate writers," observed Dr. Johnson, "will at one time or another, by public infatuation, rise into renown, who, not knowing the original import of words, will use them with colloquial licentiousness, confound distinction, and forget propriety." Such were the scribblers for Irish provincial newspapers who provided one model for the style of "Eumaeus," and "Eumaeus" in turn, where from end to end of every shapeless sentence the tropes wriggle in place like maggots, was one armature for the style of *Finnegans Wake*. Prune the Wakese from a Wakean sentence, even consult one of the author's unelaborated drafts, and you are apt to find a "Eumaeus" sentence, nerveless, meandering, only of interest when Joyce has later contrived to fill it with minute inappropriatenesses. You find, in short, a language that has died, but that like an unembalmed corpse is full of local life. The occasion calls for a wake.

Yeats used nobility, Joyce ignobility. From the remote Irish past Yeats chose the courtly Red Branch cycle, where we find the tales of Deirdre and Cuchulain. Joyce chose the plebeian (and stylistically degenerate) Fionn cycle, where we find the walloping exploits of *Fionn Mac Cumhail*, Finn MacCool. "Despite sentimental appraisals," writes Brendan O Hehir, "genuinely popular literature is usually defective in style, characterization, and psychology, and for a thousand years now *Fionn Mac Cumhail* has been the popular hero of the Gaelic-speaking peoples of Ireland, Scotland, and the Isle of Man." That is how he came to be Macpherson's "Fingal," his son Oisín Macpherson's "Ossian": something else by the way to attract Joyce, gratifying his parodist's zest for degeneration and fakery.

And to get the Resurrection Story he needed for a book of events that commenced with the Easter Rising, Joyce went not to the Gospels but to a song: moreover to a pseudo-Irish song, since "Finnegan's Wake" is not an Irish ballad at all but American stage-Irish, "The Popular Irish Song Sung by Mr. Dan Bryant, with Enthusiastic Applause," published in New York, 1864, "The Only Correct Edition." "To rise in the world he carried the hod" is a line that looks down at an Irishman in America, and the wink at his weakness—"With a love for the liquor poor Tim was born"—asks for answering winks from people who see Irishmen from without: the ones for instance who gave the Saturday-night limousine its Boston name, Paddy Wagon.

Like any hanged man's, Tim's fall entails a scaffold.

> One morning Tim was rather full,
>   His head felt heavy, which made him shake,
> He fell from the ladder and broke his skull;
>   So they carried him home his corpse to wake:
> They rolled him up in a nice clean sheet,
>   And laid him out upon the bed,
> With fourteen candles round his feet,
>   And a couple of dozen around his head.*

By the time our book is but seven paragraphs old it is supplying words and tune in closer paraphrase than *Ulysses* anywhere offers of the *Odyssey*.

> . . . wan warning Phill filt tippling full. His howd feeled heavy, his hoddit did shake. (There was a wall of course in erection.) Dimb! He stottered from the latter. Damb! He was dud. Dumb! . . .
>
> Sobs they sighdid at Fillagain's chrissormiss wake, all the hoolivans of the nation, prostrated in their consternation and their duodisimally profusive plethora of ululation. . . . They laid him brawdawn alanglast bed. With a bockalips of

---

*So the 1864 sheet music; but Joyce knew other versions which replaced the fourteen and twenty-four candles with a gallon of whiskey and a barrel of porter respectively.

finisky fore his feet. And a barrowload of guenesis hoer his head. Tee the tootal of the fluid hang the twoddle of the fuddled, O!

Other voices are lifted in other songs (notably *Phil the Fluter's Ball*: "With a toot on the flute and a twiddle on the fiddle, O!"), and a churchly voice is intoning of Genesis and Apocalypse, but the wake of Tim Finnegan is coming through more or less recognizably. He will come to life, as he does at the end of the ballad, when a splash of the whiskey that had been his downfall brings him up and roaring: "Bad luck till yer souls d'ye think I'm dead!" In Joyce, though, it's like the resurrections in Synge, unwanted: "Now be aisy, good Mr Finnimore, sir. And take your laysure like a god on pension and don't be walking abroad. Sure you'd only lose yourself in Healiopolis now. . . ." Heliopolis was where the phoenix burned; it was also what Dubliners called the Viceregal Lodge in Phoenix Park after Tim Healy became the Free State's Governor-General, when they weren't calling it Uncle Tim's Cabin.

Real wakes were not genteel, and fiendish ingenuity could go into diversifying them. If old rheumatic limbs had been tied out straight to make a decent-looking corpse, some trickster was apt to cut the ropes to make it sit up spontaneously. That is a mild specimen of what Seán Ó Súilleabháin lets us hear of in a book he blandly calls *Irish Wake Amusements*. There were other ways to fake a resurrection. "A rogue might hide himself under the bed on which the corpse was laid out and cause it to shake from side to side, frightening everybody. . . . Cards might be played on the bed where the body lay, or else on the corpse itself; and the corpse too would be given a hand of cards. A pipe was sometimes placed in its mouth, and occasionally it was taken on the floor to dance." Happening in on such a hooley you'd hardly know the dead from the living, who'd be conducting loud mock trials and mock weddings, tormenting the village simpleton, playing games so rowdy the furniture got broken, banging losers with a strap or ducking them in a cesspool, hurling potatoes, broken pipes and one another in a manner to gladden anthropologists. The Synod of Armagh censured this class of unseemliness in 1614, and the Synod of Maynooth was being incensed as late as 1927.

The real point of a wake game seems to have been the chance to skelp someone. Players got biffed who couldn't lift a chair by the leg with one hand, repeat the tonguetwister of the evening, or answer a riddle that might involve "the unusual use or pronunciation of certain words," something easy in Irish. Joyce's reader is often biffed too. There is a whole chapter of riddles, where the words are unusual indeed, as they are throughout the long book. Sometimes the page is reflecting a speaker's will to be difficult, sometimes garble and malapropism, sometimes your uncertainty what language you are hearing,* sometimes the effect of many voices raised at once. Wherever you open *Finnegans Wake*, it can look impenetrable. Half its words aren't in the dictionary, and not till we catch tunes are we cued toward words that are. By page 118, if we struggle that far, the text itself is assuring us that "it is not a miseffectual whyacinthinous riot of blots and blurs and bars and balls and hoops and wriggles and juxtaposed jottings linked by spurts of speed; it only looks as like it as damn it," and expressing on its own behalf the hope "that . . . things will begin to clear up in a bit one way or another in the next quarrel of an hour . . . as, stricly between ourselves, there is a limit to all things so this will never do."

There is Irish precedent in *A Tale of a Tub* commenting on its own unreadability. *All* books are more or less unreadable, and theologians are still trying to read the Bible. According to persistent Irish intuition, there is something essentially ridiculous about writing things down, even more about printing them, and especially about feeling any assurance that you can read them. What your eye can skim off a page is apt to be only what the page is ready to slough off, dead cuticle, gathered dust. The "Oxen of the Sun" episode in *Ulysses* offers skilled readers a large helping of what they can read very well, pages written in every existing English style, for instance Bunyan's—

But was young Boasthard's fear vanquished by Calmer's words? No, for he had in his bosom a spike named Bitterness which could not by words be done away. . . .

—which styles, in a chapter full of talk, have the odd effect of preventing us from hearing a single word that is said (what were Calmer Bloom's words?). These are followed by several pages which offer speech in all its immediacy, and we can't make head or tale of them because too many people are talking at once and the Narrator who ought to be keeping things sorted out seems to have shut up shop:

Silentium! Get a spurt on. Tention. Proceed to nearest canteen and there annex liquor stores. March! Tramp, tramp, the boys are (attitudes!) parching. Beer, beef, business, bibles, bulldogs, battleships, buggery and bishops. Whether on

*The 12 June 1982 *Irish Times* reported an incident in the Dáil where a speaker was switching tongues so fast the Irish-to-English translator found himself processing excellent English into less good English.

the scaffold high. Beerbeef trample the bibles. When for Irelandear. Trample the trampellers. Thunderation!

Accordingly, *Finnegans Wake* makes a policy of opposing voices (which we can't hear) to print (which is what we see), and our efforts to reconstitute the voices are complicated by the fact that, as at a wake or in a pub or the Dáil, a number are going on at once. Thus someone may be trying to tell an interminable story about a tailor and a hunchbacked Norwegian captain while others are being ribald about a wedding and a radio drones in the background.

> Welter focussed.
> Wind from the nordth. Warmer towards muffinbell, Lull.
> As our revelant Colunnfiller predicted in last mount's chattiry sermon, the allexpected depression over Schiumdinebbia, a bygger muster of veirying pre-cipitation and haralded by faugh sicknells, (hear kokkenhovens ekstras!) and umwalloped in an unusuable suite of clouds, having filthered through the middelhav of the same gorgers' kennel on its wage wealthwards and incur-sioned a sodden retch of low pleasure, missed in some parts but with lucal drizzles, the outlook for tomarry (Streamstress Mandig) beamed brider, his ability good.

The radio, immune to interruption, is forecasting tomorrow's weather (sudden rush of low pressure, outlook brighter, visibility good). "Kokkenhovens" and "bygger muster" (via Ibsen's *Bygmeister Solness*) are distortions produced by the proximity of the Norwegian captain, whose difficulties with the tailor cause "unusable suit of clothes" to fuse with something the announcer was saying about clouds. "Marry" and "bride" and "ability" (not to mention "low pleasure") register the jostle of another conversation entirely. Amid the din there is much mishearing; "charity" becomes "chattiry," and "last month's sermon" is "last mount's" by interference from the Sermon on the Mount. "Local" is "lucal" because the nearest town is Lucan, and "same gorger's kennel" is what a distraught ear makes of "St. George's Channel." Words are pulling every way at once, in search of enabling contexts.

And contexts need to be familiar, else all is Babel. For note that we can only read this passage because none of its elements is new. Staring at words that have never existed before despite their availability to any pixillated typist, we permit them to prompt well-known locutions that aren't there at all, and the result of this we call "understanding." It is Joyce's fascination with this process that prods him toward utterly dead set-pieces of affectation, as when an unctuous voice from the loudspeaker (for this wake has a radio) is inviting us to appreciate Music.

> We are now diffusing among our lovers of this sequence (to you! to you!) the dewfolded song of the naughtingels (Alys! Alysaloe!) from their sheltered positions, in rosescenery haydyng, on the heather side of waldalure, Mount Saint John's, Jinnyland, whither our allies winged by duskfoil from Moore-parque, swift sanctuary seeking, after Sunsink gang (Oiboe! Hitherzither! Almost dotty! I must dash!) to pour their peace in partial (floflo floreflorence), sweetishsad lightandgayle, twittwin twosingwoolow. Let everie sound of a pitch keep still in resonance, jemcrow, jackdaw, prime and secund with their terce that whoe betwides them, now full theorbe, now dulcifair, and when we press of pedal (sof!) pick out and vowelise your name. A mum. You pere Golazy, you mere Bare and you Bill Heeny, and you Smirky Dainty and, more beethoken, you wheckfoolthenairyans with all your badchthumpered peanas! We are gluckglucky in our being so far fortunate that, bark and bay duol with Man Goodfox inchimings having ceased to the moment, so allow the clinkars of our nocturnefield, night's sweetmoztheart, their Carmen Sylvae, my quest, my queen. Lou must wail to cool me airly! Coil me curly, warbler dear! May song it flourish (in the underwood), in chorush, long make it flourish (in the Nut, in the Nutsky) till thorush! Secret Hookup.

In this rite of exquisite silliness, the well-publicized song of the nightingale is being brought to us as a cultural event, adorned with the names of composers (Rossini, Haydn, Pergolesi, Meyerbeer, Bellini, Mercadante, Beethoven, Bach, Gluck, Mozart), with passing homage to Jenny Lind, the Swedish Nightingale ("Jinnyland . . . sweetishsad lightandgayle"), and to floflo floreflorence Nightingale herself. There are satellite birds (jemcrow, jackdaw), and oboe conscripts zither, dot pairs with dash, Swift with Moore Park, night sky (Nutsky) with Nut the Nile sky-goddess; toward the end massed choirs are singing "You must wake to call me early, call me early, mother dear" in counterpoint to a brass-lunged prayer for the King—

> Send him victorious,
> Happy and glorious,
> Long to reign over us . . .

—in short, the BBC's shutting-down ritual.

This is musical bric-à-brac in God's plenty, again recognizable (and the passage readable) to the extent that its components are reducible to dead lists whose members prompt their neighbors into visibility. "Let every sound of a pitch keep still in resonance" says "Let every son of a bitch keep still in reverence," reverence being defined as a state of being overwhelmed by this piece that passeth understanding, the only parts of which that we can read are the parts we have somehow read before.

There are quite specific ways in which these peculiarities are "Irish." In a 1979 lecture on "The Grammatical Structure of the Celtic Languages," the German phonetician Elmar Ternes made remark after remark which we can apply without modification to *Finnegans Wake*. "There is hardly a language in the world," he tells us, "for which the traditional concept of 'word' is so doubtful as for the Celtic languages." A word is something printed with spaces fore and aft, and that is about all you can safely say of it. "The word in Celtic is like a chameleon which changes its appearance according to its surroundings." It is "very loose, almost amorphous, and its shape can only be defined by analysing the sentence as a whole." The custom of inflecting about one word in three at the head as well as at the tail can defeat all dictionary-thumbers save the expert. So can the way verbs have of changing their conjugational rules according to the kind of clause they are embedded in: principal or subordinate, affirmative or negative, relative or temporal. The reader of Irish, in short, can't say what a given word *is* without referring to a good deal of context, and likewise the reader of *Finnegans Wake* soon learns that to puzzle over isolated words is to puzzle forever.

For we read *Finnegans Wake* by giving local association rein, letting "swift" link Moore Park with birds and the way they fly, or the welltempered scale join with a badtempered banger to produce, with Bach's aid, "badchthumpered peanas." We normally do the opposite; we normally read by shutting out irrelevance.

We next confront the fact that after forty-five years nobody knows for sure what *Finnegans Wake* is, so to speak, "about." *Ulysses* is the Book of Bloom, also a 1904 *Odyssey*. We can still say nothing that fundamental about the *Wake*.

That the two books are conspicuously different is only part of the story. They are not *that* different. We are confident about *Ulysses* thanks to a tradition of commentary, derived through loose apostolic succession from early books whose authors Joyce prompted. Though Joyce had the instincts of a Fenian conspirator, "conspiracy" is a misleading word to use. It is impossible to read with no idea *what* you are reading; no one in 1715 would have known what to make of Mr. Pope's *Iliad* who did not know it was translated from Homer, and numerous eighteenth-century poems would seem wholly chaotic did we not know what to expect of things we've been taught to call Pindaric Odes. Swift disoriented his readers by confusing the genre signals: critical tradition has taught us to call *Gulliver's Travels* and *A Modest Proposal* "satires," but new readers were led to think the former a travel-book, the latter a projector's pamphlet, and were increasingly vexed as they turned the pages and found these conventions getting less and less helpful, which was part of what Swift intended. And Joyce was Swift's Irish successor in subverting what an English tradition—this time "the novel"— leads readers to expect. Six decades later, *Ulysses* has in effect created its own genre.

The most evident tradition *Finnegans Wake* subverts is that of dictionary words in perspicuously consecutive sentences. True to form, from 1928 on, while drafts of his "Work in Progress" were appearing in periodicals, Joyce was organizing a campaign of reeducation, chiefly through articles published by friends in the Paris magazine *transition*. By the time the whole book was available in 1939 sophisticated readers were past that particular barrier: how far past, we may judge from the surprisingly coherent review Whitta- ker Chambers was able to write in a cover story for *Time*.

If critics still feel most comfortable explicating short units, that is because Joyce got no further with his promptings. He seems to have meant a young Swiss, Jacques Mercanton, to write the authorized overview, but by late 1939 Europe was once more upside down, by January 1941 James Joyce dead with Mercanton unprompted, and we are still describing *Finnegans Wake* the way the four blind men described the elephant: tail, trunk, flank, legs: "like a rope," "like a snake," "like a wall," "like a tree." One of its most expert living readers has been neither able to be satisfied that the book is all about Shakespeare, nor able to give the notion up.

That *Finnegans Wake* is a dream is one commonplace; so who is dream- ing? An answer may be, the book itself, though Professor Ellmann has Joyce telling "a friend" (unidentified) that it was the dream of old Finn MacCool, "lying in death beside the river Liffey and watching the history of Ireland and the world—past and future—flow through his mind like flotsam on the river of life."

That was likely one way he thought of it, but he also spoke to Eugene Jolas of "the story of this Chapelizod family," and these words ought to be weighed. The man whose mind was never far from the physical realities of tides and tramlines, whose seven years on his previous book had entailed so much care for physical coherence—deciding on a height and weight for Bloom, installing him in a house the Directory showed to be vacant—surely he was unlikely to have overnight let that order of things just slide? It seemed a natural assumption at one time that the characters of this night-book possessed, so to speak, daylight selves, recoverable, it was even thought, in part 4 of book III, when the sleepers seem to be temporarily awake and out of bed. Anyone who (like Edmund Wilson) tries to tell you that the dreamer's "real" name is Porter is clutching at a straw in III.4, where that name is used three times in eighteen lines (pages 560–61) and nowhere else. But this skeleton key proved unusable—III.4 is now thought to entail very deep sleep indeed—and commentators lost interest in an underlying "novel," indeed came to deem the very idea naïve.

For in France, meanwhile, intellectuals were undergoing one of their bouts of scorched-earth radicalism, of the sort inaugurated by Descartes when he wiped all previous systems out of his mind as the first step toward a new one. By the time Claude Lévi-Strauss, Roland Barthes and Jacques Derrida had reshaped the academy's canons of interpretation, bare dumb blind "text" lay dead for its readers to animate, readers so far as possible uninfluenced either by received (hence culture-bound) conventions—here Joyce would have approved—or by any hint of what the (equally culture-bound) author wanted—but here Joyce's assent would have been greatly qualified.

Though at present they shy away from close engagement, post-structuralists point to Joyce as a prime exhibit. Does not *Ulysses* itself enact the gradual encroachment of "textuality" upon representational narrative? It does; Joyce spent all his life generating "text" and was very knowing about how it gets written and read. So at present we hear that *Finnegans Wake* is pure "text," at the lowest estimate a sort of commentators' Rorschach, at the highest a massive vindication of post-structuralist theory. That's one quick way to make it uninteresting.

But by post-structuralist theory *all* books end to end are pure text, notably *Ulysses*, which however remains haunted by Leopold Bloom's remarkably substantial ghost, moving through a certain city in a certain year. Though the city in the book is a city of words, it corresponds so minutely to a city in Ireland that facts drawn from that city dovetail into the book even when the book does not mention them.

Fritz Senn has produced a minor but compelling example. As the "Ithaca" episode opens, something close to sheer textuality is informing us that Stephen and Bloom on their way from the cabman's shelter discussed among other topics "the influence of gaslight or the light of arc and glow-lamps on the growth of adjoining paraheliotropic trees." In the previous episode, in the cabman's shelter, Bloom and Stephen sit with the *Telegraph* spread out before them. That newspaper exists, and in its relevant issue, 16 June 1904,

Mr. Senn found on page 1, in the right-hand column that is before Bloom as he sits on Stephen's right, a tidbit on "queer things which happen to flowers when they are exposed to the electric light." So we can see what put one topic of conversation into Bloom's mind.

But (1) neither Bloom nor his mind has ever existed, except as a construct derived by us from *Ulysses*; that is not merely post-structuralist orthodoxy but received common sense about fiction. However, (2) the *Telegraph* article is not mentioned in *Ulysses*, so how does it put something into a mind that does not exist apart from *Ulysses*?

In planting something perhaps never to be discovered, perhaps for Mr. Senn to discover sixty years later, Joyce played an exhilarating game, uniquely Irish. Excluded as he felt from the English consensus ("The language in which we are speaking is his before it is mine"), he could knowingly toy with what English empiricism had long said was the root assumption of that English speciality the novel, the assumption that physical stimuli prompt mental processes; could toy too with the bully assumption that English bourgeois reality is so normative we needn't pause over the mere texts that point our minds toward it. But here's the stimulus *outside* the text, the response *inside* it. Joyce was teasing such readers as might some day come upon this Friday footprint; but let prophets of bare textuality too explain if they can how it's possible.

So we may want to reconsider the proposition that *Finnegans Wake* is the first great book to have locked extra-textual reality outside. Every once in a while a job of *Wake* annotation turns up sequences of stark extra-textual fact, as when Fritz Senn found Chapelizod houses and their addresses arrayed in obdurate sequence. When such substantialities poke through the fog they are apt to get discounted for lack of a governing plot. So let's suggest one.

We have seen that the book was begun just after the Troubles: Easter Rebellion, Black-and-Tan bloodshed, Civil War: a time of "executions" right and left. Gogarty thanked the swans who'd helped him narrowly escape being executed. Joyce's college friend Francis Sheehy-Skeffington had no swans on his side; he was trying to restrain looting and help the wounded when an insane British officer "executed" him the day after Easter Monday, 1916. Troops later broke into his house in vain quest of proof that his death had been justified. Such executions were performed by bullet, though in less accelerated times their provenance was the scaffold. Tim Finnegan when he fell was climbing a scaffold: "And people thinks you missed the scaffold. Of fell design."—*Finnegans Wake*, 621. And a wake presupposes a corpse.

May we be waking the corpse of someone executed during the Civil War?

May we be waking the corpse of someone executed during the Civil War? Not a firebrand like Rory O'Connor, but some man drawn into the business? Erskine Childers, whose uncle Hugh Culling Eardley Childers (1827–1896), nicknamed "Here Comes Everybody" (*Finnegans Wake*, 32), gave his initials to the book's eponymous hero HCE, was another executed hostage of 1922. Erskine Childers was English and had thrown in his lot with the Republicans; the excuse for shooting him was that (contrary to a recent edict) he owned a revolver. The reason may have been that Arthur Griffith and Kevin O'Higgins thought him especially irksome and dangerous. Childers was a skilled yachtsman, as witness his thriller, *The Riddle of the Sands* (1903), and his 1914 exploit running guns from Hamburg for his subsequent executioners.

In *Finnegans Wake*, an executed sailor perhaps, a foreigner? Not Childers, no, a Norwegian, a pubkeeper? It's worth considering.

Very briefly: he came to Dublin a seaman, married a tailor's daughter (perky, tiny), whom he'd met while ordering a suit from her father. (He needn't be a hunchback, despite the mixup with the story of the hunchback and the tailor.) With Anna, he settled down and opened a Chapelizod pub. There are two sons, a daughter. Some obscure misdemeanor involving girls and soldiers has done for him. (It need not make any sense. Skeffington's offense didn't, nor Childers's.) In a little place like Chapelizod the gossip is endless, likewise the misinformation. He's dead now; we've been "Waking" him.

Finnegans Wake may differ from *Ulysses* chiefly in this, that whereas in the earlier book Bloom occupies the foreground, reenacting unawares Odysseus' adventures, in the later book's universe it would be just as pertinent to say that Odysseus was enacting the adventures of Bloom. Rory O'Connor mimes King Roderick, King Roderick mimes the innkeeper, the innkeeper mimes Rory, round and round and crisscross: "mirror on mirror mirrored is all the show," wrote Yeats of something else, and in such a bewilderment of mirrors we can no longer say where the chain of reflections commences. "When Pearse summoned Cuchulain to his side" (Yeats again), did not Cuchulain also summon Pearse to that quicklimed grave at Kilmainham?

If indeed the Troubles impinging on a Chapelizod family make a twentieth-century face for the *Finnegans Wake* polyhedron, it will be their human note we hear in the book's finale, a plaintive woman's voice urging her husband to get up for a morning walk, then receding into reminiscence, then dropping into a void whence, as if dying, it circles back to start the *Wake* again. These pages, by common consent among Joyce's most moving, gain yet more poignancy if we imagine their words to be passing through the dormant mind of the widow, the morning after, trying not to awaken to awareness that her husband lies beside her no longer. Back down, then, like Cathleen ni Houlihan, into the endless turbulent uneasy sleep in which Ireland still contrives that "patriotic" enormity shall go forever unconfronted.

"Many a man has died for love of me," said Yeats's Cathleen; and after Maud Gonne spoke those words from a stage on 2 April 1902, a spectator recorded misgivings: should such plays be produced "unless one was prepared for people to go out to shoot and be shot"? Maybe Yeats wasn't prepared for that; but Maud Gonne was.

"Many a man has died for love of me": James Joyce first echoed those words in his story "The Dead," when Gretta Conroy lets her husband know what poor Michael Furey died of: "I think he died for me." He'd died of being hypnotized by her beauty: a delicate fellow who stood in the rain gazing up at her window, and caught his death. His memory stands between her and her husband now. It is Joyce's deepest lesson, that romantic illusion can always block off the real; his "poetic" passages mean that something is being evaded. Nor need the femme fatale be Captain Tommy Gonne's (tommy gun's!) English-born golden-haired daughter: just a lass out of Galway.

But for the muddled staffwork that postponed it to Monday, the birth date of the terrible beauty would have been, by Patrick Pearse's schedule, Easter Sunday, 23 April 1916. That Easter day was the birthday of William Shakespeare, and also, by numerological coincidence, the three-hundredth anniversary of his death. It is unsurprising that Shakespeare pervades *Finnegans Wake*. He ended where he began. Joyce may well have judged that habitable Ireland ended that week amid the illusion that it was beginning. He took a similar view of the ministry of Jesus. And *Finnegans Wake* in returning to its own beginning, its last fragment looped back to its uncapitalized opening, in being Joyce's last published fiction returns to his first, "The Sisters," that 1904 story of a resurrection that did not occur.

TWO ECCENTRICS

Contemporary Irish poets may be divided
into antiquarians and others, the former in
the majority, the latter kindly noticed by Mr.
W. B. Yeats as "the fish that lie gasping on
the shore," suggesting that they might at least
learn to expire with an air.

SAMUEL BECKETT, 1934

Beckett should have invented Paddy Kavanagh, born in Mucker, he said, parish of Inniskeen, County Monaghan, in a 1791 cabin with holes in the roof, son of a shoemaker who farmed on the side with three cows and six dozen hens but could never surpass four pigs since when a fifth was added one always died. The birth was in 1904, Bloomsyear, and Paddy grew an inch taller than Bloom: five feet ten and a half, 190 pounds, "great roots of hands," huge feet needing custom shoes, "a voice like coal sliding down a chute." "In his youth he easily carried sacks of barley weighing two hundred and fifty pounds." He smashed things unwittingly, having what he called "the destructive power of the poet": "My father told me, 'You broke everything on the farm except the crowbar. And you bent that.' " He lived a long decomposition, etherialized at intervals into poems. He called his autobiography *The Green Fool*.

As a youth near Mucker, God help him, he was composing in his head poems like this:

> I turn the lea-green down
> Gaily now,

And paint the meadow brown
With my plough.

       ʻ . .

Tranquillity walks with me
And no care.
O, the quiet ecstasy
Like a prayer.

I find a star-lovely art
In a dark sod.
Joy that is timeless! O heart
That knows God!

No wonder AE printed "Ploughman" in the *Irish Statesman*; it is such a poem as he'd gladly have written himself. "The dreams and visions in a peasant's heart on the hillside" were central to his deepest faith: peasants to whom (as Joyce makes him say in the library on Bloomsday) "the earth is not an exploitable ground but the living mother."

AE was the sweetest of Irishmen, a stronger claim than it sounds. Born George William Russell in Lurgan, County Armagh, just a few miles from Mucker, he came to Dublin in 1878, aged eleven, and met W. B. Yeats at an art school that otherwise had no special effect on either of them. In the paintings he made all his life you can't tell one tree from another, no fault to eyes that saw Art in emphatic vagueness. His poems too are luminously vague:

> . . . suddenly the veil was lifted.
> By a touch of fire awakened, in a moment caught and led
> Upward to the wondrous vision: through the star mists overhead
> Flare and flaunt the monstrous highlands: on the sapphire coast of night
> Fall the ghostly froth and fringes of the oceans of the light.

A canonical anecdote explains the origin of his famous pseudonym in a typographical error; he'd meant it to be "Aeon," a word he derived from the Primal Language—

A	—sound for God
AE	—is first divergence from A
Au sound	—continuity for a time
N	—change

"So Aeon would mean that the spirit would continue for a time and finally be absorbed into God again." The typesetter who got stuck at the second letter was certainly ignorant of the Primal Language and very likely did not understand either "the Rosicrucian view that every man is God," and destined to return to himself.*

AE had a practical head on him, though, and not even the vision he reported to Yeats in 1896, which located Ireland's imminent Messiah in "a little white-washed cottage" in Donegal or Sligo—"He is middleaged has a grey golden beard and hair (more golden than grey) face very delicate and absorbed. Eyes have a curious golden fire in them, broad forehead"—could interfere with his tireless organizing of cooperative dairies, or with his unique perception that writers whose claim to be the Messiah was minimal nevertheless needed to eat. AE did not withhold money even from the wastrel Joyce of 1904, and he instigated what became *Dubliners* by promising the young scoffer a pound apiece for stories he could publish in the cooperative dairymen's organ, the *Irish Homestead*. "You can sign any name you like as a pseudonym." Joyce used "Stephen Daedalus." It wasn't the Cuala Press but it was publication while it lasted. On the *Homestead*'s page, advertisements for dairy machinery occupied strategic locations; the text of "The Sisters" was fitted around them.

The author of "Ploughman" who knocked at AE's door in December 1931 did not resemble the Messiah of the vision any more than Joyce had. He resembled what he was, a country boy whose hob-nailed boots had walked him begging his bread all the fifty-five miles from Mucker to Dublin. AE had to regret not being able to feed him (the cook was out). His tooshort patched trousers exposed his shins as he sat, and it was clear to AE that "the dreams and visions in a peasant's heart on the hillside" would achieve fuller expression once the peasant's mind was furnished with words. So when Kavanagh tramped north again it was lugging sixty-odd pounds of AE's books, Emerson, Whitman, Browning, Hugo, Dostoyevsky. After AE's death in 1935 he reflected that "the only true friend of the Irish poets had passed." AE's generosity was practical: not the "soft-mouthed admiration" it's never hard to come by. Little though he wrote that's durable, the Irish Renaissance is unthinkable without him. He was never, like Yeats, an orchestrator of reputations, and in twenty-five years of editing he printed whatever caught his generous fancy.

Five years after that Kavanagh tried London; useless. In 1938, back in Ireland, he published *The Green Fool*, prose to charm the birds out of trees,

---

*Joyce understood it better; it underlies Stephen's babble in the brothel about "the greatest possible ellipse consistent with the ultimate return," and the solemn cadences that liken Bloom to Halley's comet, swinging to the extreme limit of his orbit and returning "an estranged avenger, a dark crusader" (*Ulysses*, pp. 505, 728).

all about his upgrowing in Mucker and his leaving. It was the one story he
ever had to tell, and he told it twice, the second time in 1947, less lyrically,
as *Tarry Flynn*. The first telling was unlucky; on that visit to Dublin, green
Paddy had knocked, it said, on Oliver Gogarty's door, and "mistook Gogarty's white-robed maid for his wife—or his mistress. I expected every poet to
have a spare wife." For these twenty words the stately buck hauled the
green fool into court and obtained £100 and the book's suppression. According
to Gogarty's later quips the real offense had been to imply that he was down
to one mistress.

Gogarty, it may be, was redirecting a kick the law had dealt him a year
or so previously, when a Jewish antique dealer he'd libelled in a fictionalized
memoir of his own, *As I Was Going Down Sackville Street*, collected £900,
in the process causing great pain to young Sam Beckett, resident in Paris,
called as witness for the plaintiff, mauled by counsel for the defense. (Beckett, it was suggested to the jury, spent his time writing such "blasphemous
and obscene" books as the monograph on "Marcel *Prowst*," and when asked
did he call himself Christian, Jew or Atheist he made scandal by answering
"None of the three.")

Barristers are among the best-dressed men in Dublin. Their specialty is
destroying the credibility of witnesses. How the crowd enjoys their theatrics! And how frequent these are. The expense of a lawsuit about a book
review was what closed down AE's *Irish Statesman* in 1930. Paddy Kavanagh's education was proceeding apace. That a suit correctly aimed might
bring in pounds by the hundred was an insight he tried applying some years
later, though with no luck.

By then he had moved to Dublin, where one evening in 1941 he
commenced a long poem called "The Great Hunger" and finished it in a
couple of days. (By pen of course; no typewriter in the place. That gave any
holograph copy the look of being "the original," and crafty Kavanagh later
made "originals" for many collectors.)

"The Great Hunger" was about the countryman's hunger not for food,
which tends to be adequate, but for anything else at all. Here are "the
dreams and visions in the peasant's heart on the hillside," as recorded by
one who was there:

> O he loved his mother
> Above all others.
> O he loved his ploughs
> And he loved his cows
> And his happiest dream

> Was to clean his arse
> With perennial grass
> On the bank of some summer stream;
> To smoke his pipe
> In some sheltered gripe
> In the middle of July—
> His face in a mist
> And two stones in his fist
> And an impotent worm on his thigh. . . .

That is his life and so is this:

> . . . His mother called down to him to look again
> And make sure that the hen-house was locked. His sister grunted in bed.
> The sound of a sow taking up a new position.
>
>   .   .   .
>
> The clock ticked on. Time passes.

Decade after decade of hopeless vacuous boredom, that is the life of the sacred peasantry of Ireland: not a Pegeen Mike among them nor a Christy Mahon, and no talk racy of the soil but only this:

> "A treble, full multiple odds. . . . That's flat porter . . .
> My turnips are destroyed with the blackguardly crows. . . .
> Another one. . . . No, you're wrong about that thing I was telling you. . . .
> Did you part with your filly, Jack? I heard that you sold her. . . ."

This isn't Kiltartanese and there were reprisals: not riots in theatres but two policemen in Kavanagh's flat—"Did you write that?" Dev's Vice Squad had heard about something anti-Irish. Ah yes, gyres had turned by 1942, and to be Irish now was to be like Yeats and Synge, those two onlookers.

> The world looks on
> And talks of the peasant:
> The peasant has no worries;
> In his little lyrical fields
> He ploughs and sows;
> He eats fresh food,
> He loves fresh women,
> He is his own master
> As it was in the Beginning

The simpleness of peasant life.
The birds that sing for him are eternal choirs,
Everywhere he walks there are flowers. . . .
He can talk to God as Moses and Isaiah talked—
The peasant who is only one remove from the beasts he drives.
The travellers stop their cars to gape over the green bank into his fields. . . .

. . .

The peasant is all virtues—let us salute him without irony
The peasant ploughman who is half a vegetable—

He sees no faeries, partakes of no Celtic Twilight. What had happened to the Kavanagh who wrote verses AE liked? For one thing, in Dublin he had to put up with talk about civilization rooted in the soil. Yeats had published a proud boast as recently as 1937:

John Synge, I and Augusta Gregory, thought
All that we did, all that we said or sang
Must come from contact with the soil, from that
Contact everything Antaeus-like grew strong.
We three alone in modern times had brought
Everything down to that sole test again,
Dream of the noble and the beggar-man.

So foreigners would like to believe, was Kavanagh's retort. The whole of modern Irish literature, he came to think, had been concocted for the delectation of foreigners, Englishmen and Americans chiefly. Yeats himself was but a new form of stage-Irishman, and the great Literary Renaissance had been "a thoroughgoing English-bred lie." A throne moreover was vacant; Yeats was dead.

In the south of France, on 28 January 1939, a Saturday, the moon just passing the half, William Butler Yeats had died, aged seventy-three. "It seems to me that I have found what I wanted," he had written twenty-four days earlier. "When I try to put it all in a phrase I say, 'Man can embody truth but he cannot know it.'" They laid him to temporary rest above Roquebrune, not far from Aubrey Beardsley's grave at Menton. It was not until 1948 that the corvette *Macha* (the old Irish Goddess of War) brought his remains to Galway harbor, whence they bumped to Sligo, past knots of schoolchildren standing mute with their teachers, over roads never built for a poet's gliding. Irish Fact has since penetrated every interstice of this ceremony. You will be told how the coffin was a substitute filled with stones, drunken sailors having let the original slide into the unplumbed Mediterranean; also how the *Macha* ran aground in Sligo harbor before being diverted to Galway, and how her load, whether stones or lead-encased bones, instantly broke the hearse's springs. Though his children remember nothing of any of this, Irish Fact has hold of one principle anyhow, that W. B. Yeats was never meant for the physical world.

"Reality" in 1934 he had called a "desolation." In 1938 his "Lapis Lazuli" removed men's troubles to a "tragic scene" for old Chinese sages to gaze on from their mountain. The mountain was something he could hold in his hands, a tooth-shaped chunk of deep blue-black lapis lazuli, perhaps a foot high. The Yeats family has it still. Carved sages the size of matchsticks gaze outward into our world from partway up its side.

> Every discoloration of the stone,
> Every accidental crack or dent,
> Seems a water-course or an avalanche,
> Or lofty slope where it still snows
> Though doubtless plum or cherry-branch
> Sweetens the little half-way house
> Those Chinamen climb towards, and I
> Delight to imagine them seated there;
> There, on the mountain and the sky,
> On all the tragic scene they stare.
> One asks for mournful melodies;
> Accomplished fingers begin to play.
> Their eyes mid many wrinkles, their eyes,
> Their ancient, glittering eyes, are gay.

Those eyes on those tiny figures are but horizontal slits in matchheads of stone, their wrinkles, their glitter, their gaiety all imparted by the beholder. Likewise imparted, so the poem implies, are the salon terrors of 1938: Hitler banging about, talk running on about bombs and civilian slaughter. These would vanish on the instant did the mind but change its theme. Their stuff is not the stuff of timeless reality, deep where the Gyres turn, the Cones and the Great Wheel. No, in the long view all the world's a stage: "There struts Hamlet, there is Lear, / That's Ophelia, that Cordelia."

The Friday after his death Dublin's three morning papers all published the testament he'd finished twenty-one weeks previously, "Under Ben Bulben," the poem with the terminal instructions about the gravestone.

Readers were to hear it spoken by his ghost: its portentous "Swear" echoes what the dead king in *Hamlet* uttered from beneath the stage, in the scene that ends, "The time is out of joint. . . ." He meant certain of the last poems to come after it, as though spoken by his ghost too, and his *Collected Poems* has been out of joint ever since its publisher opted for the facile drama that makes "Under Ben Bulben" an ending.

The time had been out of joint since the Easter Rising, when fanatics commenced to seize hold of the country: religious fanatics as it proved, technicians before long of a rigorous censorship, also fanatics for an abstract ideology of violence. Until six counties had been added to twenty-six, to make the sum a canonical thirty-two, neither they nor their descendants would ever rest. Their emblem, de Valera, would one day be accorded the distinction, uniquely his among modern heads of state, of an obituary in the *Biographical Memoirs of Fellows of the Royal Society* (1976) on account of his mathematical attainments (6 + 26 = 32). To compound an irony Yeats didn't live to confront, its author was J. L. Synge, F.R.S., distinguished mathematician and nephew of the playwright.*

In his late years Yeats was less estranged from fanatics than you'd think. The bond commenced with the fanatics of 1916, and when "Under Ben Bulben" proposes two ways of dying—

> Whether man die in his bed
> Or the rifle knocks him dead

—it affirms his common destiny with Pearse, Connolly and MacDonagh: to be thrust into racial memory by the gravediggers' spades. Their exultant mania too he can savor:

> You that Mitchel's prayer have heard,
> "Send war in our time, O Lord!"
> Know that when all words are said
> And a man is fighting mad,
> Something drops from eyes long blind,
> He completes his partial mind. . . .

"Mitchel's prayer" had restated the old equation, England's difficulty, Ireland's opportunity. An associate of Thomas Davis's who got fourteen years' trans-

---

*And we should suspend the pleasures of irony long enough to state that Dev's mathematical competence was considerable, and that the Dublin Institute for Advanced Studies he created was sufficiently well conceived to attract the likes of Schrödinger and Dirac. Its divisions are Celtic Studies, Theoretical Physics, and Cosmic Physics: things that require brains and paper, not equipment.

portation for urging armed risings, John Mitchel recorded in his *Jail Journal* a moment of ecstasy on hearing how the Czar's designs on Constantinople were threatening Britain's overland route to India. If the Czar kept pressing, soon England would be fighting Russia. "Czar, I bless thee. I kiss the hem of thy garment. I drink to thy health and longevity. Give us war in our time, O Lord!" (His prayer was answered by the Crimean War, of which Ireland made no special use.) It's an insouciant way Yeats has with a quotation. Mitchel's hopes were strategic. Yeats leads you to think they were adrenal.

"Poet and sculptor," he continues, "do the work"; the painter likewise. The work is at once religious and erotic:

> Bring the soul of man to God,
> Make him fill the cradles right.

Whatever the Pope may have intended, Michelangelo's Adam is an erotic masterpiece, "Profane perfection of mankind," and so much for the Irish Catholic censors. The "modish painter" (Picasso maybe?) shirks this great obligation; so, come to think of it, does Jack Yeats.

As for Irish poets, the word they must come to terms with is "trade." ("This sedentary trade," he'd called it a dozen years back.) It's work, work, work. Being "Celtic" is not enough.

> Irish poets, learn your trade,
> Sing whatever is well made,
> Scorn the sort now growing up
> All out of shape from toe to top,
> Their unremembering hearts and heads
> Base-born products of base beds.
> Sing the peasantry. . . .

"Products," what a word. And what a scornful sputter of *b*'s. These are the Catholic urban middle classes, Synge's "thick-necked ruck of fat-faced sweaty-headed swine," today's lords of the nation thanks to enfranchisement: the *Playboy* rioters enshrined in the Dáil. "Sing the peasantry" prescribes the classic antidote. In five years Kavanagh would be singing "The peasant ploughman who is half a vegetable." What Yeats never foresaw was that Ireland's future poets might come out of the Catholic peasantry, not to mention the Catholic middle class. And they'd see no way at all to obey his injunctions: would even find him an obstacle to get round. "Swear," intones the great ghost: like all ghosts impotent except to haunt.

* * *

"Oh Christ!" thinks the protagonist of *The Great Hunger*, "I am locked in a stable with pigs and cows for ever." (Christ had been *born* in a stable, but emerged.) Kavanagh later thought the poem excessive: "There is something wrong with a work of art, some kinetic vulgarity in it, when it is visible to policemen." What it omitted was the delight in daily particularity that animates *The Green Fool*. It is Kavanagh's *Dubliners*, and his misgivings were like the ones Joyce himself came to have about *Dubliners* ("I have been unnecessarily harsh. . . . I have not reproduced [Dublin's] ingenuous insularity and its hospitality. . . . I have not been just to its beauty . . .").

In *The Green Fool*, on the other hand, he had omitted from his account of a rural boyhood the one colossal fact on which *The Great Hunger* is built: the numbing futureless boredom which was all that Irish peasant culture had to offer its grown men. "A dreadful stage-Irish so-called autobiography," he later called that book. What was more, he had written it under "the evil aegis of the so-called Irish literary movement." He had been the classic naïf—a role to which he often had recourse—with no idea that his betters were not to be trusted, and the example of Yeats and Synge and Lady Gregory had misled him into "this stage-Irish lie."

In 1910 Synge's peasants were a needful corrective to the chromolithographed peasantry of Nationalist politics. By 1937 they were a bad model for a young writer. Synge's plays, like Shakespeare's, had become part of the world's imaginative heritage, undergoing no harm should somebody remark that *The Playboy* represents Mayo speech and customs about as reliably as *The Winter's Tale* represents seacoastless, bearless Bohemia. But that was not how the middle-aging Green Fool saw it. He had let himself be led astray, and his congregation of regulars at McDaid's pub heard him rail at Synge and Yeats. Like any writer who has inherited a convention no longer of use, like young Wordsworth for instance, he said he was after "Truth" and that the convention taught a lie. That was not true. *The Green Fool* is not stage-Irish, though it has its omissions, as what book has not?

Something he was confronting is well stated by Anthony Cronin: "Dublin is the administrative capital of a small country with a swollen civil service. It is also a University city twice over. Academics and civil servants are frequently of a literary bent, but they are rarely real writers. Dublin therefore contains some hundreds of uncreative literary men, most of them recruited from the provinces and liberated from provincial backgrounds of varying remoteness. . . ." It is no wonder Kavanagh, who'd left school for good at twelve, soon acquired the self-educated man's impotent feeling that all talk is blather, not excluding most of his own.

The best talk that could be mustered wasn't good enough. Print, then. He and his brother blew the brother's life savings on thirteen issues of a paper, *Kavanagh's Weekly* (1952). In slam-banging all of Ireland it did not fail to anthologize idiocies from the current press: "Mr. T. O'Deirg, Minister for Lands, said . . . that he thought it a pity that there was not now the close connection between the poets and the people such as existed fifty years ago. He hoped that one of the results of the meeting would be to revive popular poetry that would bring nationality to its bosom such as Ethna Carberry did in her time.—*The Irish Press*, March 2nd." Who was Ethna Carberry? Ah, that's the joke. Research discloses a poetess of that pseudonym, 1866–1902: a contemporary of Yeats's, utterly forgotten, but not by Mr. O'Deirg.

Also: "Regarding the question of erecting two public lavatories in the town . . . Mr. Cahill said—I don't know of any urban area with a ladies' and a gents' lavatory. You cannot have a low rate and go in for these high-brow schemes.—*The Tipperary Star*."

But collecting such things was no way for a poet to be spending his time, nor was suing *The Leader* over a hostile profile. (He made that attempt in 1954, asked £10,000, expected £500, got nothing, but thought highly enough of his performance under cross-examination to include the transcript in *Collected Pruse*.) By then he was committed to a wasteful business indeed, enacting his own legend. He was the public Thersites, and wrote lampoons in that role:

> . . . this is Heaven's high manna,
> God is good to Patrick Kavanagh . . .

> . . .

> In the pubs for seven years
> Men have given him their ears,
> Buying the essence of his heart
> With a porter-perfumed fart. . . .

At the age of fifty-odd, though, luck brought unexpected manna: a drastic illness, a pneumonectomy, months of just sitting and soaking up the welcome fact that he was alive. His passive mind in those months arranged its patterns into what he'd been wanting, a style he could think styleless:

> The important thing is not
> To imagine one ought
> Have something to say. . . .
>
>   .   .   .
>
> The only true teaching
> Subsists in watching
> Things move or just colour
> Without comment from the scholar.
> To look on is enough. . . .

That's so easy to say he had to brush against death to earn it, and easy to say proved uneasy indeed to do, also infrequent. The lines that safeguard his memory can be difficult to distinguish from *faux-naïf*. They include these:

CANAL BANK WALK

> Leafy-with-love banks and the green waters of the canal
> Pouring redemption for me, that I do
> The will of God, wallow in the habitual, the banal,
> Grow with nature again as before I grew. . . .
>
>   .   .   .
>
> O unworn world encapture me, encapture me in a web
> Of fabulous grass and eternal voices by a beech,
> Feed the gaping need of my senses, give me ad lib
> To pray unselfconsciously with overflowing speech. . . .

And most memorably, these:

> O commemorate me where there is water,
> Canal water preferably, so stilly
> Greeny at the heart of summer. Brother
> Commemorate me thus beautifully.
> Where by a lock Niagarously roars
> The falls for those who sit in the tremendous silence
> Of mid-July. No one will speak in prose
> Who finds his way to these Parnassian islands.
> A swan goes by head low with many apologies,
> Fantastic light looks through the eyes of bridges—
> And look! a barge comes bringing from Athy
> And other far-flung towns mythologies.

> O commemorate me with no hero-courageous
> Tomb—just a canal-bank seat for the passer-by.

"A backhanded catch," observes Darcy O'Brien, "the favorite winning by an easy neck." He adds that Kavanagh "got rid of a good deal in order to accomplish this sonnet: self-righteousness, self-pity, the temptation to take himself rather than life seriously." It's a quiet triumph, yes, of wise passiveness, just *acceptance*, acceptance even of poet's-corner diction like "stilly" and "greeny" when those are words that offer.

Alongside any page of Yeats at all the canal-bank poems seem unstable, awkward, amateurish. But so enclosed had accomplishment become, so circumscribed by the great accomplishers, Yeats mainly, that unpretentious word-by-word *gazing* could free younger writers, could suggest a domain W.B.Y. hadn't preempted. Seamus Heaney for one "acknowledges that reading Kavanagh made him think that he might have something to write about himself." That acknowledgment says much about the fix in which a poet as great as Yeats had managed to leave Anglo-Irish literature.

Kavanagh died in 1967 after maybe two decades of compulsive drinking: suicidal drinking, his friend Anthony Cronin thinks. So much energy expended in sixty-three years! And so little result: a personal legend, *The Great Hunger*, a few short poems, two memoirs; also a blurry vivid vision of the Grand Canal in south Dublin. His shade has a dedicated bench there now.

Kavanagh, whatever else, is a presence. By contrast, Austin Clarke (1896–1974), "generally considered the finest Irish poet of the generation after Yeats," is a wraith in all accounts of his era, not least because W.B.Y. helped will his non-existence. His contemporaries weave in and out of printed memoirs: not Clarke. They are themes for Dublin anecdote: not Clarke. Their names turn up in the lists that establish provenance: not Clarke's.

A few furtive and pathetic facts are accessible. He is said to have been, for example, the "Austin Ticklepenny" of Beckett's 1938 *roman à clef*, *Murphy*. Ticklepenny, whose card reads "Pot Poet," is a "creature" who "does not merit any particular description." He is off the booze when Murphy encounters him, works in a mental hospital, fears going mad, and writes verse "bulging with as many minor beauties from the gaelic pseudoturfy as could be sucked out of a mug of Beamish's porter." (Gogarty urged Clarke to sue, but Clarke judged *Murphy* so turgid few would read it.) And he was Kavanagh's instance of a poetaster: the "Paddy of the Celtic Mist" of "The Paddiad" for instance. And he has become the stock example of an Irish poet somewhat conspicuously omitted from the *Oxford Book of Modern Verse* Yeats edited in 1936, an imbalance emphasized by the inclusion of seventeen Gogarty lyrics. That may seem all the odder when we learn that in 1932 Yeats had named Austin Clarke a Founder Member of the Irish Academy of Letters, but Yeats had named him with a certain absence of conviction: "Should I make him an Academician?" he had asked Olivia Shakespear.

"I load myself with chains and try to get out of them," was Clarke's answer when Robert Frost asked what kind of poetry he wrote. The chains included Gaelic systems of assonance, which took, he said, "the clapper from the bell of rhyme."

"In simple patterns, the tonic word at the end of the line is supported by a vowel-rhyme in the middle of the next line. Unfortunately the internal patterns of assonance and consonance in Gaelic are so intricate they can only be suggested in another language." An example of a simple pattern is

> Summer delights the scholar
> With knowledge and reason.
> Who is happy in hedgerow
> Or meadow as he is? . . .

That is a pleasant game, Clarke learning the tricks, but "Martha Blake" has a weightier use for them:

> Before the day is everywhere
> And the timid warmth of sleep
> Is delicate on limb, she dares
> The silence of the street
> Until the double bells are thrown back
> For Mass and echoes bound
> In the chapel yard, O then her soul
> Makes bold in the arms of sound.

A mimetic bewilderment, this:

> bells | back | bound

and

> echoes | O | soul | bold

and the full-blooded rhyme,

> bound | sound

—clangor of assonance and consonance everywhere, the ear picking up delayed echoes, b_ack | M_ass | y_ard, as we come to terms with an extraordinary expression, "her soul makes bold in the arms of sound": this timid woman letting herself be ravished (yes) by piety's appurtenances the way acoustic virtuosity can ravish us. She is a victim of the religion that consoles her, and eight delicate stanzas explore her furtive refusal of her own sensuality. The poem ends:

> . . . So to begin the common day
> She needs a miracle,
> Knowing the safety of angels
> That see her home again.
> Yet ignorant of all the rest,
> The hidden grace that people
> Hurrying to business
> Look after in the street.

Here the pairings aren't acoustic but semantic: angels and people, home and street, see and look, a "miracle" and the deftly phrased "hidden grace": something which neither embraces nor altogether shuns a theological tradition of "grace": doesn't shun that tradition in the poem, no, but tends to shun it in Ireland of the unwelcomes, where good girls are taught that they must not heed being looked at. She is so far abstracted from Mediterranean awareness, she's ignorant alike of being seen and of the moving body they see: only aware of being seen to by angels.

Twenty-five years later "Martha Blake" acquired a bitter sequel, "Martha Blake at Fifty-One," twenty-four stanzas about the fate of the body she refused all her life. The last stanza:

> Unpitied, wasting with diarrhea
> And the constant strain,
> Poor child of Mary with one idea,
> She ruptured a small vein,
> Bled inwardly to jazz. No priest
> Came. She had been anointed
> Two days before, yet knew no peace:
> Her last breath, disappointed.

"Jazz," the vein throbbing to a heart's tempo, is perfection; and we note "idea" rhyming with "diarrhea" while "priest" fails to rhyme with "peace."

Austin Clarke's main themes are four: the Irish past, fragile, remote; the chill of religious restraints; outrageous things in the papers; the precariousness of his own reason. Since (as Yeats assured us) "manifold illusion" hoops

civilization's staves around an emptiness, such themes will threaten an insecure community, and Clarke's failure to be more heard of is explicable.
When you've picked your way into his packed, difficult verse you find
something you don't want to be told.

The verse is packed and evasive because it must achieve its air of control
without recourse to the declamatory tones of certainty. What it is certain of
is all nuance: that Ireland's religion thwarts, but not, for instance, that
Ireland "would be better without its religion." (Reflect that Ireland is
unimaginable without its religion.) Yeats's rhetorical certainties were more
easily come by, pertaining as they did to diagrammatic make-believe:

> Such thought—such thought have I that hold it tight
> Till meditation master all its parts,
> Nothing can stay my glance
> Until that glance run in the world's despite
> To where the damned have howled away their hearts,
> Or where the blessed dance;
> Such thought, that in it bound
> I need no other thing,
> Wound in mind's wandering
> As mummies in the mummy-cloth are wound.

Its "damned" and "blessed" being but components in a system of opposites,
that magniloquence has no place for a Martha Blake.

Our tongue's most consummate declaimer, Yeats could make someone as
scrupulous as Clarke feel tongue-tied. Clarke once heard AE say, "The old
man is talking to himself." He recalls the scene in AE's study:

> I saw behind him
> Gold-leafed, with their dark blue or olive bindings,
> The *Collected Poems* of William Butler Yeats,
> Macmillan'd in a row.
> I wondered were they
> A Purgatory the poet had ghosted from hatred,
> Incessant, inner circles, of repetition
> Systematised by metaphysics, late
> Excuse for fantasies, that never let him
> Be still when he became a man of letters,
> Discovered in old age the physical.
> "His lyrics are Saturnian rings illumined
> By colder fire."
> "What of our common ill?
> Do they explain it?"

> "If rhetoric can last,
> Then all that lonely, premeditated art must."

It is AE speaking of Saturnian rings and rhetoric, Austin Clarke asking about his constant theme, "our common ill." Dublin-born, raised a Catholic, slowly, quietly embittered to the point of a mid-life mental breakdown, he did not think his case was in any way special.

In an odd way he is Yeats's furtive shadow. His first work, published in 1917 at twenty-one, inaugurates, like *The Wanderings of Oisin*, a project of retelling the old stories: of Fionn, of Concobar, of Cuchulinn, of Maeve. That was why Beckett and Kavanagh dismissed him as antiquarian. The narratives halt, but there are rich splendid passages. He kept this up for a dozen years. Then, like the Yeats of *Responsibilities*, he moved to contemporary epigrams. Then *Night and Morning* (1938) commences a regime of bitter self-examination ("Martha Blake" is part of that). Then Yeats dies, and for seventeen years, save for theatre projects that entailed writing plays of his own and staging Yeats's, Austin Clarke is silent.

Too much should not be made of the coincidence between the death of Yeats and his long silence. The 1930's had been a dispiriting decade in Ireland: the decade of Dev's catless grin and silly censorship. One trouble with Dev was that he was running the same Free State he'd brought on a civil war to repudiate, and running it as a tightening theocracy. His court of no appeal was what he called the Plain People of Ireland, to whom he got access, he said, by gazing into his own inscrutable heart. And the gods were departing. Lady Gregory had been dead since 1932, Yeats was seldom in the country (and died in France); even AE left in despair in 1933, to die in England, and Gogarty in 1939, to die in New York. As for the Joyce of *Ulysses*, if anyone cared, he spent most of the decade adrift in the labyrinths of *Work in Progress*. The commencement of the 1939 war caught Sam Beckett in Ireland; he preferred, he said, "France at war to Ireland at peace," and "made it just in time." His "neutral" homeland underwent six years of isolate unreality. More minds than Austin Clarke's were disoriented.

Clarke's first poems since 1938 were privately printed in 1955. Their fierce directness recalls the Yeats of *Last Poems*, though without his susceptibility to a tune. No tune can lull a response to an orphanage fire:

> . . . smoke and faith on fire
> Can hide us from enquiry
> And trust in Providence
> Rid us of vain expense.

. . .

> Has not a Bishop declared
> That flame-wrapped babes are spared
> Our life-time of temptation?
> Leap, mind, in consolation
> For heart can only lodge
> Itself, plucked out by logic.
> Those children, charred in Cavan,
> Passed straight through Hell to Heaven.

A note informs us that sixty children perished, and that the local bishop did indeed say such a thing. We are a long way on from 1910, when preoccupation with the myth of the peasantry suffered literature to let such outrages pass unnoticed.

Two-thirds of Austin Clarke's *Collected Poems*—all but 195 pages of 547—came from the last nineteen years of his long life. They are wildly uneven, sometimes impenetrable, sometimes so evidently topical we long (Thomas Kinsella notes) for access to just the right clipping. Pricking the mind, their thorny language rewards. Yes, that's enigmatic.

"Thorny" is nearly the word for one aspect of Yeats's late language, the aspect Clarke had in mind when he wrote that Yeats "discovered in old age the physical." One thing W.B. discovered in old age was a hag named Crazy Jane, as physical as you please. He was sixty-four and just come through a devastating illness when she commenced to plague him. "Life returned to me as an impression of the uncontrollable energy and daring of the great creators," and Crazy Jane was nothing if not uncontrollable. In her most celebrated moment she told the Bishop to his face that "Love has pitched his mansion in / The place of excrement." If a mansion you can pitch is a glorious tent, that makes "mansion" all the more a biblical word, handed down from nomads, tent-people. "In my Father's house are many mansions," the Bishop would remember from John xiv.2. "Not excluding *that* one," Crazy Jane would rejoin.

She is a scandalous old body indeed, differing from the equally scandalous old bellows Maud Gonne in having no political notions whatever, unless the naked union of flesh with flesh counts as a political notion in Ireland, and it likely does. Union of soul with soul is conceivable too, and many poems worry at a single theme, whether that and the union of bodies can be expected to coincide. The Lady in "The Three Bushes" gives her soul, her Chambermaid in darkness gives her body, and the lover detects no differ-

ence. No more do the bushes that grow from their three graves, so inter-
twined that "now none living can / When they have plucked a rose there, /
Know where its roots began," which would seem to resolve the theme till
we reflect on the imperfect insight of bushes. Indeed so little is the poem
resolved that it reechoes itself through six appended Songs. The Lady's
Second Song restates the soul-body paradox:

> Soul must learn a love that is
> Proper to my breast,
> Limbs a love in common
> With every noble beast.
> If soul may look and body touch,
> Which is the more blest?

The Lord have mercy upon us, is the refrain. The Chambermaid on the other
hand knows what to think of spirits:

> From pleasure of the bed,
> Dull as a worm,
> His rod and its butting head
> Limp as a worm,
> His spirit that has fled
> Blind as a worm.

Sung as all of them are by interested parties, these six songs do not so much
resolve "The Three Bushes" as keep its themes echoing after the curtain
drops. In this they resemble the rhetorical questions on which Yeats liked
to end strong poems: "Did she put on his knowledge with his power?"
"How can we know the dancer from the dance?" "What rough beast . . .
Slouches towards Bethlehem to be born?" This device reflects his playwright's instinct for keeping the last speech from being the last word, and
none of his late personae should be ascribed the last word, not even the
Wild Old Wicked Man who refuses to agitate himself any further with
questions posed by his opposite number, "the old man in the skies."

> . . . But a coarse old man am I,
> I choose the second-best,
> I forget it all awhile
> Upon a woman's breast.

Not even the Yeats familiar from anthologies, the Yeats of *ottava rima* and
lofty composure, has the truly comprehensive say. Though after 1930 his

marmoreal utterances continue as they'd done since 1919—"The Gyres,"
"The Statues," "The Municipal Gallery Revisited"—many interleaved outbursts of wildness are there to warn us that the Old Man in the Tower may
not know everything. It is Crazy Jane's voice that speaks nearly the last
verse Yeats knowingly published, "Crazy Jane on the Mountain." She has
a vision to report: in a two-horse war-chariot,

> Great-bladdered Emer sat,
> Her violent man
> Cuchulain sat by her side;
> Thereupon,
> Propped upon my two knees,
> I kissed a stone;
> I lay stretched out in the dirt
> And I cried tears down.

That's stark and archaic and not anything the measures of "Sailing to
Byzantium" could accommodate. Stretched out in the dirt, it looks back
with less than satisfaction on a lifetime of poetic dealings with Cuchulain. If
this poem's first title, "Ireland after the Revolution," would prompt us to
ascribe Jane's tears to the disparity between Cuchulain and de Valera, certainly
a weeping matter, still its final title, less coercive, leaves us free to ponder a
key word, "violent," and to ask a question Yeats seems to have asked himself
repeatedly: had there not been something excessively genteel about all his
early practice: something Tennysonian, even? If the Free State shrank from
all thought of sexuality, had the poets—not least, himself—whose job had
been to shape its imagination not drawn back likewise? Dwelt excessively
on Beautiful Lofty Things? In the days of the *Playboy* riots, Miss Milligan
the poetess had pronounced the Yeats *Deirdre* of 1907 indecent, apparently
for having mentioned in passing "the tumult of the limbs." The Yeats of
1938 is willing to administer still grosser shocks to Miss Milligan's shade:

> . . . Down the mountain walls
> From where Pan's cavern is
> Intolerable music falls.
> Foul goat-head, brutal arm appear,
> Belly, shoulder, bum,
> Flash fishlike; nymphs and satyrs
> Copulate in the foam.

So much for marble Greece and the groves of Arcady. Would public Unity
of Being have been attainable had Yeats commanded that order of rhetorical

violence three decades ago? More likely, would someone not have broken his head?

Yet the Irish Church had not been part of his conscience the way it had been part of Austin Clarke's. Not having been driven nearly mad by its taboos on the physical, Yeats enjoyed to the end the luxury of posing soul-body questions the way whim took him, weighing them like a philosopher, dividing them among voices like a dramatist. Clarke, long tormented, had a different destiny, unexpectedly happy. Deep in his soul, by a process inaccessible to readers, much that had nagged him for decades was somehow placated, and could he have enjoyed a second lifetime we should have had wonderfully sensuous poems to enjoy.

Toward the end he returned to the heroic narratives from which he started. They have speed now, and their burden is joyously sexual. In the last one, "The Wooing of Becfola," the Queen of Diarmuid the High King returns joyous from an escapade that did not really occur ("All that had happened had lasted less than a minute"), and in the course of which she did not deceive him, no, yet had pleasure with a phantom youth on a Lake Isle we may want to connect with Innisfree. The last lines are perfectly edifying:

> Becfola quickly undressed,
> Lay down by her husband. He turned
> To her.
> "You took my good advice
> And now you are like a honey-bush.
> All May and murmur as if you had hid in
> A raid of kisses. Why is it, I wonder?"
> She felt his mounting warmth. She slid
> Under his arms with a lay sigh,
> Stretching her own. She heard the dawing
> In the elms outside and smiled.
> "Because
> My Dear, I am your obedient wife."

—as she is and has been; yet she knows what her mind has experienced. "The Wooing of Becfola" is a quick little flashing parable about the autonomy of the imagination. If any bishop has pronounced on it his words have escaped me, and surely escaped Austin Clarke, who was dead, a little short of seventy-seven, a few weeks after he wrote it.

THE MOCKER

... Hell goes round and round. In
shape it is circular and by nature it
is interminable, repetitive and very
nearly unbearable. . . .
... It is supposed to be very funny
but I don't know about that either.

BRIAN O'NOLAN

Brian Ó Nualláin was one thing he was entitled to call himself, though his
Civil Service checks were made out to O'Nolan, and when he heard Douglas
Hyde attempt the Gaelic they say he laughed himself half sick. *An Craoibhín
Aoibhin* had held the Chair of Modern Irish at U.C.D. since 1905, but he
was self-taught and this particular pupil was bilingual by birthright.

What else he was by birthright is not defined: an unrelenting rationalist
certainly whose reason could trickle down irrefragable from any wrong
premise, at times toward irascible action which distressed his friends, at
other times toward sheer crystalline nonsense which delighted his readers.
As an example of the first, we hear of his efforts to haul Kavanagh savagely
down by the ankles while the two of them were scrambling up the founda-
tions of Joyce's Tower* in Bloomsyear + 50, a reasonable action given
Kavanagh's offense, which was to have been the faster climber. There is
nothing like the syllogistic habit for giving rise to paranoid behavior. As an
example of the second, we may savor the following wonder, arrived at by an

---

*There is no metaphor in this sentence. It was a commemorative expedition, 16 June 1954, attested
to by a living witness.

identical but more protracted mental process. Its exposition requires four stages.

1. *Atomics*. "Did you never study atomics when you were a lad?" asked the Sergeant. . . . "Everything is composed of small particles of itself and they are flying around in concentric circles and arcs and segments and innumerable other geometrical figures too numerous to mention. . . . These diminutive gentlemen are called atoms."

2. *Identity*. "Now take a sheep," the Sergeant said. "What is a sheep only millions of little bits of sheepness whirling around and doing intricate convolutions inside the sheep? What else is it but that?"

3. *Perfusion*. "Do you know what takes place when you strike a bar of iron with a good coal hammer? . . . The bar will dissipate itself away by degrees if you persevere with the hard wallops. Some of the atoms of the bar will go into the hammer and the other half into the table or the stone or the particular article that is underneath the bottom of the bar."

4. *Upshot*. "The gross and net result of it is that people who spend most of their natural lives riding iron bicycles over the rocky roadsteads of this parish get their personalities mixed up with the personalities of their bicycle as a result of the interchanging of the atoms of each of them and you would be surprised at the number of people in these parts who nearly are half people and half bicycles."

Such a person is readily identified. "He will walk smartly always and never sit down and he will lean against the wall with his elbow out and stay like that all night in the kitchen instead of going to bed. If he walks too slowly or stops in the middle of the road he will fall down in a heap and will have to be lifted and set in motion again by some extraneous party."

At this point Dublin readers who may be reminded of folk they have observed shortly after closing time will be glad of the explanation. There is no one like our author for clearing up mysteries. Indeed he differs from Joyce partly in this, that whereas Joyce thought a mental cosmos implausible that did not contain saving undecidabilities, "Flann O'Brien" prefers to leave nothing unexplained at all. *The Third Policeman*, of which the bicycle passage is but a detail, is profuse in local ratiocinations as it spins an elaborate disorienting world, the larger coherences of which grow less and less graspable until the final pages when everything suddenly does cohere, into a map of hell.

The local precisions of this unique book include its expositions, spilling into long footnotes, of the physicist de Selby, who "did not recognize sleep as such, preferring to regard the phenomenon as a series of 'fits' and heart-attacks," judged darkness a pernicious substance and attempted to bottle it, taught that water, "if not abused," can achieve "absolute superiority," and underwent continual prosecution for water wastage. "At one hearing it was shown that he had used 9,000 gallons in one day," yet "none of the vast quantity of water drawn in ever left the house." This phenomenon was no doubt not unrelated to "the famous water-box, probably the most delicate and fragile instrument ever made by human hands," in the course of constructing which "de Selby is known to have smashed three heavy coal-hammers," whence a French thesis on "the importance of percussion in the de Selby dialectic." Though most of his experiments were extremely noisy, "no commentator has hazarded even a guess as to what was being hammered and for what purpose." De Selby himself taught that "hammering is anything but what it appears to be," a statement to be sure "not open to explicit refutation."

In Dublin today there is a de Selby Society, its condition of membership possession of a bicycle. More pertinently, the Dublin phone directory has a single de Selby listing, a quarrying firm in Tallaght. The noise of de Selby lorries crashing by loaded with stone is said to have interfered with Brian O'Nolan's sleep, a fact with which most of *The Third Policeman*'s de Selbiana is more or less obliquely connected. So one strand of the book is vengeful, in a mocking schoolboy way.

You were wondering what he was doing trying to sleep during truckers' working hours, and the answer to that is sleeping off the drink. His habit was to write his newspaper column in the very early morning, then put down Irish whiskey through the forenoon and early afternoon. "Like many thoroughgoing alcoholics," Anthony Cronin remembers, "he had an early bedtime and because of sleeplessness and morning thoughts and the jigs in general a very early rising."

Was it the drink was his ruin, or was it the column? For ruin is the word. So much promise has seldom accomplished so little. The promise showed early. A northerner like AE and Kavanagh, in fact born (1911) in County Tyrone, syllables which educated Dubliners are apt to enunciate with slow disdain, the bilingual O'Nolan did not go to school until the family settled in Dublin when he was twelve, but six years later was a freshman in Joyce's old university. His B.A. subjects were English, Irish and German, his Master's thesis was on Irish poetry. Classmates looked to him as the most brilliant fellow around.

At twenty-eight he rewarded their confidence with *At Swim-Two-Birds*, but that was 1939, a bad year for a comic novel to get noticed. Despite praise from Graham Greene it sank like a stone. Greene mentioned *Tristram Shandy* and *Ulysses*, but *At Swim-Two-Birds* resembled *Ulysses* chiefly in a

respect in which readers were apt to find *Ulysses* troublesome: in its demonstration that fiction can be reduced to an arbitrary game of great intricacy.

It conducts this demonstration with unflagging zest. The book's
construction, boxes-within-boxes, would need to be explicated with diagrams.
To speak of an author (a college student) writing a book about an author
whose characters commence to turn the tables by writing a book about him,
is to utter but a first approximation. Also the book the student is writing is
the book we are reading, and it has three beginnings and three endings. It
is postulated moreover that characters in books resemble domestic employ-
ees in requiring food and sleep, a reason for the characters of Dermot Trellis,
author, to arrange for a book in which Trellis will be a character and be put
on trial for sundry acts of negligence amounting to cruelty:

> The next witness was a short-horn cow who was escorted by a black-liveried
> attendant from a cloakroom marked LADIES at the rear of the hall. . . . Udder
> and dewlap aswing in the rhythm of her motion, she shambled forward to the
> witness-box, turning her great eyes slowly about the court in a melancholy but
> respectful manner. . . .
> State your name. . . .
> That is a thing I have never attained, replied the cow. Her voice was low
> and guttural and of a quality not normally associated with the female mammalia.
> Are you acquainted with the accused?
> Yes.
> Socially or professionally?
> Professionally.
> Have your relations with him been satisfactory?
> By no means.
> State the circumstances of your relations with him.
> In a work entitled—pleonastically, indeed—*The Closed Cloister*, I was engaged
> to discharge my natural functions in a field. My milking was not attended to
> with regularity. When not in advanced pregnancy, a cow will suffer extreme
> discomfort if not milked at least once in twenty-four hours. On six occasions
> during the currency of the work referred to, I was left without attention for
> very long periods.
> You suffered pain?
> Intense pain.

That gives you part of the flavor, though it does not adequately represent
the offhand economy of the sentences, the command of parodic dialects, or
the structural topology that can keep in motion characters as widely assorted
as Finn MacCool and the boys of the Circle N Ranch, Irishtown, without
any look of rambling. The whole of Irish literature is somehow here, includ-

ing the potboilers Dublin readers really preferred. Though mention of *Ulysses* and *Tristram Shandy* was excessive, it is hard to know what other comparisons Graham Greene might have adduced. No talent of just this quality had been on display in English before. Not the least of its merits is innate self-restraint: no sentence longer than it needs to be, no violating of any self-imposed convention. If *At Swim-Two-Birds* was a prolonged college joke, the ability it demonstrated seemed to promise a masterpiece.

Then in 1940 O'Nolan had very bad luck. He finished a new book, which the publisher of *At Swim-Two-Birds* turned down. And he commenced a funny column in the *Irish Times*. For twenty-five years the column used him up.

Mr. Cronin again: "Brian became somehow fixed at a time of brilliant promise and pyrotechnical display, unable to shake off the reputation for prodigious cleverness he had early acquired. This reputation was transplanted from the hothouse confines of U.C.D. to the equally pernicious atmosphere of intimately acquainted Dublin. His humour became the currency of its denizens, the mode of his column their manner of response. . . . And by a curious but inevitable inversion he became their creation. . . . The fate of the licensed jester had befallen him. He existed in and through the response and understanding of his audience." His public nom-de-plume, "Myles," was even the name by which friends addressed him. He wore a wide-brimmed black hat and a dark gaberdine and looked like a gangster crossed with a tiny priest, his pallid face "ageless in a childish but experienced way." A great future lay behind him.

It did indeed, since the novel that got turned down in 1940 was *The Third Policeman*, unpublished until 1967, a year after he'd died. For a book that turns out to be about a dead man, that has an eerie rightness. But what had happened to it, really? After the first rejection he seems not to have tried to get anyone else to take it. From time to time he would complain about his entrapment in mediocrity, his need to have more to his name than daily ephemera, and talk of getting away to write a novel. Why did he not produce *The Third Policeman* from its drawer? You hear the theory that he'd lost it. That is unconvincing, since some of its pages, including the bicycle fantasia, got used verbatim to eke out an inferior novel he published in 1964. It's possible to guess that he was somehow scared of it.

For *The Third Policeman*, written in his thirtieth year, is his one serious book, and not only did he not publish it, he spent the rest of his life going back from it, not forward. It is about a man with no name moving round one tight bizarre circle forever, not a bad summary as it happened of how O'Nolan's life would be after 1940. To finance the one thing he cares for, the publication of his *De Selby Index*, this autodidact has connived at murder and is in a hell indistinguishable from rural Ireland save for the unfailingly magical weather and the strangeness that emanates from a police-station. But this hell is constructed according to the mad doctrines of de Selby. It is a *comic* hell, devilless and Godless. Was that what worried O'Nolan? Later he fumigated a much milder book with a dedication to his Guardian Angel, whom he bade remember that he was "only fooling."

At Swim-Two-Birds is a preternaturally gifted undergraduate's jape. *The Third Policeman* is a unique mature minor novel. And he locked it away like something compromising. He wrote acidulous blather for the city's most respectable paper. For eighteen years he held a civil-service job. He was respectably married and lived in the suburbs. Girls and what they represented were "abhorrent to him." Let the Kavanaghs rant and rage, let the Behans booze; for him, only serious slow drinking, self-destruction decade by decade, a respectable Dublin suicide. Under the black hat, Martha Blake? A Martha Blake suppressing a terrible knowledge?

Martha Blake, except for those outbursts of terrier-like rage, which he often sublimated in the column. It was the premise of the column that the sole sane and educated man in Dublin, Myles na gCopaleen, lived surrounded by gawms and omadhauns, not to mention people who could believe the *Irish Times* editorials that were printed next to the column, and the statements of the civil servants whom Brian O'Nolan saw close-up every day. To sustain this fiction, O'Nolan, alias Myles, divided himself into allotropic personalities whose common skill was command of the knife-edge sentence. On Spring, for instance:

> I notice these days that the Green Isle is getting greener. Delightful ulcerations resembling buds pit the branches of our trees, clumpy daffodils can be seen on the upland lawn. . . . Time will run on smoother till Favonius reinspire the frozen Meade and clothe in fresh attire the lily and rose that have not sown nor spun. Curse it, my mind races back to my Heidelberg days. Sonya and Lili. And Magda. And Ernst Smutz, Georg Geier, Theodor Winklemann, Efrem Zimbalist, Otto Grün. . . . Ich hab' mein Herz / in Heidelberg verloren. . . . Tumpty tumpty tum.
>
> THE PLAIN PEOPLE OF IRELAND: Isn't the German very like the Irish? Very guttural and so on?
>
> MYSELF: Yes.
>
> THE PLAIN PEOPLE OF IRELAND: People do say that the German language and the Irish language is very guttural tongues.
>
> MYSELF: Yes.
>
> THE PLAIN PEOPLE OF IRELAND: The sounds is all guttural do you understand.

MYSELF: Yes.

THE PLAIN PEOPLE OF IRELAND: Very guttural languages the pair of them the Gaelic and the German.

It's not fanciful, behind that, to hear his despair.

Or behind this:

I tried to get it many a time. O many a time.

Well I never could see any harm in it.

I seen it in a shop once on the quays, hadn't any money on me at the time and when I came back to look for it a week later bedamn but it was gone. And I never seen it in a shop since.

Well, I can't see what all the fuss was about.

You read it, did you?

I couldn't see any harm at all in it there was nothing in it.

I tried to get it many a time meself . . .

There's no harm in it at all.

Many's a time I promised meself I'd look that up and get it.

Nothing at all that anybody could object to, not a thing in it from the first page to the last.

It's banned, o' course.

Not a thing in it that anybody could object to, NO HARM AT ALL IN IT, nothing at all anywhere in the whole thing.

O indeed many's a time I tried to get it meself.

Three days a week; five days a week. Often at great length, and often in Irish, which (he savagely knew) half his readers couldn't read. Or he'd torment them by modulating from English cliché into Latin:

How are heights?
Great. (How's yourself?)

How are great heights reached?
Pardon me. ATTAINED. By soaring, of course.

Whom may we expect (with proper coaching) to soar to great heights?
Certain promising youngsters. . . .

What is the unit of measurement applied generally to commodities or articles which are available in gigantic quantities?

The oodle. . . .

Quid dicerent Dublin Transport Company?
Falsus in uno, falsus in omnibus.

Quis custodiet ipsos custodes?
Mulieres eorum.

Which omnibus line is best augured?
Fortuna favet 40 Bus.

—Day after day after day. The column was at its most magisterial in war-time, six years of Irish solipsism during which Myles's schemes for making jam out of used electricity or concocting emergency supplies of midnight oil—in general his knack for rigging up alternate universes—had a kind of derived plausibility.

The one book he published in the forties was *An Béal Bocht* (1941), a send-up of the cult of rural Irish, translated after his death as *The Poor Mouth*. After he'd retired from or been forced out of the civil service he did manage a couple more: *The Hard Life, The Dalkey Archive*. The former attempts a *funny* rescription of turn-of-the-century lower-middle-class life, something he and his readers knew chiefly from *Dubliners*. He bitterly dubbed it "this misterpiece," dedicated "to Graham Greene, whose own forms of gloom I admire." In one chapter, a papal audience, he is in his best form. The latter is a tired hodge-podge of recycled stuff with one splendid new sub-theme: James Joyce alive in the fifties and living quietly in Skerries. The two books show how obsessed O'Nolan had become with U.C.D.'s other famous liter-ary graduate, the man everyone used to think he ought to have equalled.

The Joyce of *The Dalkey Archive* wrote a small collection of "Dublin characteristics," also some unsigned pamphlets for the Catholic Truth Soci-ety, notably on matrimony. That is all. The rest consists of spurious attrib-utions. He is especially horrified by mention of *Ulysses*, a vile thing he had nothing to do with: various hangers-out in Paris scribbled sections for the price of a drink, and it was his name, alas, that got put to it. There is no bottom to human wickedness. And now he is experiencing a late vocation. His fond hope is to be admitted into the Jesuit order at last. That proves more than can be managed, but the Jesuits do accommodate him as far as they can. He is granted the privilege of mending the Reverend Fathers' underclothes. It's impossible to miss the revenge of "Flann O'Brien." How dare U.C.D.'s black sheep have achieved all that fame?

And how dare "Flann O'Brien" have tried to suppress his own great book? Neither Joyce nor he ever surpassed the nested ingenuity of its contrivances, the insidious taut language to make anything at all seem plausible, or the unforced beauty of such episodes as our man's dialogue with his soul, when, not knowing he's already dead, he supposes he's about to be hanged:

> *You know, of course, that I will be leaving you soon?*
> That is the usual arrangement.
> *. . . You have no idea where you are going . . . when all this is over?*
> No, none.
> *Nor have I. I do not know, or do not remember, what happens to the like of me in these circumstances. Sometimes I think that I might become part of . . . the world, if you understand me?*
> I know.
> *I mean—the wind, you know. Part of that. Or the spirit of the scenery in some beautiful place like the Lakes of Killarney, the inside meaning of it if you understand me.*
> I do.
> *Or perhaps something to do with the sea. "The light that never was on sea or land, the peasant's hope and the poet's dream." A big wave in mid-ocean, for instance, it is a very lonely and spiritual thing. Part of that.*
> I understand you.
> *Or the smell of a flower, even.*

"A very lonely and spiritual thing"—that phrase has been minted by the Irish aspective, it has on it the signature of Myles, the same who on the first page of his first book had achieved so idiosyncratic a construction as "The Pooka MacPhellimey, a member of the devil class . . . ," and it lets us glimpse lyric emotions he never disclosed again. There was much, after 1940, that he never did do again, save enact furtive details of *The Third Policeman*. Toward the end Dublin gossip even has him suffering an amputated leg, like the nameless man in the book (though he merely broke it). He died, aged fifty-four, on April Fool's Day, 1966.

THE TERMINATOR

I suppose this—might seem strange—
this—what shall I say—this what I
have said—yes—were it not ... that
all seems strange. (*Pause.*) Most strange.
(*Pause.*) Never any change. (*Pause.*) And
more and more strange.

Happy Days

Not bottled for export, Myles during the war years was a bitter antic conscience, exclusively Dublin's. In the post-war decades Sam Beckett became the world's. Irish claustrophobia spread itself round a planet on which there was no longer any place to hide. More than one counterculture infant of the sixties was awaited nine months and then christened "Godot." Such as have survived to the eighties are ambulant footnotes.

The name "Godot" haunts. In a play written in French, it contains as though by accident the English word "God," the way "sor" ("Good mornin', sor") sounds the Irish for "louse." In the English version of the play it preserves the French accentuation, not heavy on the first syllable but light, from a language you accent evenly like Irish. Godot is part of the name of a Paris street; spelled Godeau, it is the name of a French bicycle racer; spelled I do not know how, the name of an Air France pilot in whose care Beckett once had the misfortune to cross the Channel. "Le capitaine Godot vous accorde des bienvenues," came the voice on the intercom. At Heathrow an ashen Beckett required an immediate drink.

Such is by common consent the authenticity of his bleak vision, he has been translated into every language that comes to mind. Himself, is he part of French literature, or part of English? Not part of Irish, certainly. Like his master Joyce, he belongs to International Modernism, though the word "Modernism" in his case retains too strident a sound of willful daring. He is "modern" in this precise sense, that everywhere he is recognized as a contemporary. There are said to have been few performances of *Godot* to equal one staged by the prisoners in San Quentin, where Sartre's *No Exit* would have seemed like, well, playacting. "Nothing to be done. . . ." "Rien à faire." "Nichts zu tun." Like the "Who's there?" that opens *Hamlet*, that opening line is indifferent to idiom. So, unlike the rest of *Hamlet*, are its successors.

This universality, though, has local roots, in the Ireland of the running-down of the Revival. Beckett's good fortune was to come in late, when the shaping enthusiasms seemed quaint and remote and how Mayo peasants should behave on stage was no longer an urgent issue. By 1926, to a lad of twenty, it was not *The Plough and the Stars* that was abnormal but the archaic passions he saw mobilized against it.

He was a baby in Foxrock, near Dublin, in 1906, when W. B. Yeats was in his forty-first year. So around Easter 1916 he turned ten, and at the height of the Civil War he was sixteen. Far from tempting him, like boys just slightly older, O'Connor or O'Faolain, with a romantic choice of sides, that whole frenzied story was little more than a turbulence in the background of his adolescent years. Between his eleventh and his twenty-first years, a walk up O'Connell Street took him past the untended wreckage of the post office. If you cast a cold eye on that, what it emblematized was demolition, not glory.

Being Protestant also immunized him from those passions; they had become Sinn Fein, IRA, hence *Catholic* passions. He belonged to what was left of the old Ascendancy, which, as you choose to put it, was left out, or stayed aloof.

The family's middle-class comfort, in a house where bells summoned servants, had exceptional features too. Unlike the Yeatses and the Joyces, the Becketts did not belong to the obsolescent landowner class, condemned to watch their fortunes dwindle. Nor, like the Synges and Gogartys, were they prosperous from public role-playing: doctor, lawyer, Protestant bishop. Sam's attendance at the best schools—Portora Royal, Trinity—was underwritten by the immutable powers of arithmetic, used by his father in an arcane unspectacular skill, quantity surveying, i.e. preparing estimates of materials on which contractors could base their bids. Many Beckett characters share a passion for calculation.

Also, he came in late on the story of public entertainment. Joyce grew up
on decadent opera, a passion in his time. Yeats helped found the Abbey,
another passion and a hotbed of passions. But when Beckett was at Trinity
in the twenties the Abbey had competition from the cinemas: from Chaplin,
the tramp; from Keaton, for whom, long after, he wrote a screenplay; from
Laurel and Hardy, in whose queer universe is rooted Didi and Gogo's
inexplicable friendship, bluster protecting bemused incompetence. They
also provided emblematic bowler hats.

He attended the Abbey too, no longer a cause but one alternative to the
cinema: a shabby place north of the river: a declining Abbey, something
O'Casey kept solvent. Correspondingly, Beckett's plays assume a small theatre, and work best when the audience is sparse. The old Abbey that was
burned in 1951 had eccentric sight-lines and could seat some five hundred.
The Théâtre Babylone where Godot first failed to appear was less pretentious even than that.

It was at the old Abbey that Beckett saw all of Synge, the tenement plays
of O'Casey, some pseudo-*Noh* of Yeats. His homages to these abound.
O'Casey's dramaturgy of disintegration we've already heard him commend.
When Winnie in *Happy Days* says "I call to the eye of the mind . . . ," she is
repeating the first line of *At the Hawk's Well*. The minimal set of *Godot*—
one pathetic tree—recalls the *Noh* set Yeats had players create by doing no
more than unfold and fold a cloth.

And Yeats had anticipated a discovery Beckett greatly exploits, how little,
in an intimate place, actors need to *do*, and how powerful can be that little.
Ito, Yeats wrote, had been able "as he rose from the floor, where he had
been sitting cross-legged, or as he threw out an arm, to recede from us into
some more powerful life." So Winnie, immobilized, can invoke some less
powerless life by no more than her ceremony of opening a parasol, and when
her parasol bursts into flames, to the anguish of fire marshals in every city
where the play is performed, a higher life has plainly intervened. As for
Hamm in *Endgame*, the ritual for disclosing him seems derived from the
Yeatsian cloth. He seems kept on stage on his chair perpetually, under a
sheet lest he grow dusty. Before each new performance Clov uncovers him,
at the end covers him again; and Hamm's own first act, once uncovered, is
to remove in turn the handkerchief that covers his blind face.

More fundamental things could be learned from Synge. "Who else but
John Millington Synge?" was Beckett's response in 1972 to a question
about playwrights he'd learned from. Undistracted by the questions that

absorbed Synge's first viewers and colleagues— idiom, verisimilitude—he learned to be Synge's successor, the only one.

Synge died when Beckett was three, not yet having attained the age (forty-two) at which Beckett would write *En Attendant Godot*, and had possibly not come to isolate his own principal innovations. *The Shadow of the Glen* had introduced to the stage and to the Irish imagination the eloquent tramp who became Beckett's specialty. (That play got jeered at as "French.") In *The Well of the Saints* he showed how two actors, old and battered and blind, could hold an audience by scarcely moving from where they sit. That was a special gratification for Yeats, who had been so exasperated by actors' restlessness he longed, he said, to imprison them in barrels. "The barrels, I thought, might be on castors, so that I could shove them about with a pole when the action required it." That's in the October 1902 *Samhain*, a sixpenny review of the Irish Dramatic Movement. Had Beckett heard of it, when he put Nagg and Nell in *Endgame* into barrels? Or devised the pole, increasingly long and eventually fitted with wheels, that comes in from the wings in *Act Without Words #2* to wake up players who sleep? If he hadn't, the coincidence is wonderful.

The claustrophobic set of *Riders to the Sea* was another innovation, unremarked in the early days amid fuss about getting authentic Aran Island pampooties to put on the actresses' feet. In that play all we see is confined to a little bare room that shuts out the great violent world of the sea and the horses. Everything of importance to the play has happened previously or happens elsewhere, to be brought into this room by the vivid words. Greek drama has been adduced in precedent, but the Greeks with their music and spectacle and choric dancing never entrusted so much dramatic leverage to so little visible movement, so little variety. This principle leads from Synge's world straight into Beckett's: to *Embers* for instance, a play for radio that confines the whole of a novelistic plot and subplot within the head of a man who sits talking, talking, to drown out the sound of the sea and the sound of the remembered voices of the dead. All that confronts us, in this tour de force of expressive monotony, is the wreckage of a story, a wrecked life, wrecked words:

> Stories, stories, years and years of stories, till the need came on me, for someone, to be with me, anyone, a stranger, to talk to, imagine he hears me, years of that, and then, now for someone who . . . knew me, in the old days, anyone, to be with me, imagine he hears me, what I am, now.

And we know, of course, that that is Beckett, not Synge.

For where he differs markedly from Synge is in his concern for the stony resonances of utterly simple words. Here Synge was a prisoner of history, like so many who have aspired to renovate the drama in English and suppose that the way to resume its glories is through verse or some usage equally patterned. He aspired to a rhetoric of formal rhythm and exotic diction like Shakespeare's. It was to that end, and not for "realism," that he devised a stage language with the help of Irish idioms, in that unique cultural moment when literate men, as though first looking into Chapman's Homer, were discovering a national treasure in the speech of the Irish West. It takes skillful voices indeed to render his tunes. Badly spoken, they will cross the footlights as "Synge-song," and it's easy to speak them badly. Willie Fay remembers how Synge, though he knew how he meant them to sound, could never say them properly himself. He simply coached and corrected skilled professionals. Blank verse gives similar trouble, whether Shakespeare's or that of *The Countess Cathleen*. Yeats was decades achieving a verse you need not intone or declaim but can simply *speak*.

Beckett trusts his actors less than Synge did, his repetitive patterns more. "Finished, it's finished, nearly finished, it must be nearly finished"—Clov's first words in *Endgame* exert their power if spoken, as they should be, in a monotone. Let no thespian saw the air with his hand, thus, nor even speak the speech trippingly on the tongue.

He has parts for thespians, though: the Pozzo who sprays his throat with an atomizer before reciting his encomium to the sunset; the prince of players, Hamm, whose opening words are "Me to play," whose closing ones include "Our revels now are ended," and who reminded the British drama critic Harold Hobson of "a toppled Prospero." It should not be forgotten that in his Trinity years the greatest actor in Ireland was available for study, the man who had been all his life perfecting for the ages an orotund nobility: William Butler Yeats. He still made his ceremonious appearances at the Abbey, to count the house, to confer the touch of the poet.

Those were still the years of Yeatsian dominion, when O'Casey could be denied production of *The Silver Tassie* with a wave of the tyrannic hand. The Hamm who asks "Can there be misery . . . loftier than mine?" the inescapable presence who will allow no escape from his domain, seems studied from him; is not "lofty" a Yeatsian word? In Beckett's last Irish years the Great Founder was in the Senate and in the Tower, pacing upon the battlements, preoccupied with horoscopes and historical geometries, arranging lives and events into lunar patterns that bespoke an inevitability of rude decline, spinning his stories of beautiful lofty things which were artfully cadenced stories of his own past. He seems incapable of an uninteresting sentence.

But they are solipsistic stories. Nowhere in the *Autobiography* he worked on in the twenties does W. B. Yeats for instance *name* his brother Jack, though he mentions "my brother" a few times. We need information extraneous to the book we're reading to know that "my brother" refers to Ireland's greatest painter.

Jack Yeats too was by way of being a playwright, and when W. B. was entoiled in *The Shadowy Waters*, with its Formorians and its Pirates and its harp that takes fire like Winnie's umbrella, J. B. was issuing seagoing plays of his own that resemble a sardonic critique of all that. In 1901 Elkin Mathews, whose list would later include Joyce's *Chamber Music* and the first books of Ezra Pound, published Jack B. Yeats's *James Flaunty, or, The Terror of the Western Seas*, and in 1903 *The Treasure of the Garden*, also *The Scourge of the Gulph, or, Fierce Revenge*. As you'd guess from the titles, there are aesthetic claims these don't make, and staging them never depended on Frank and Willie Fay. You were to cut out the paper actors and mount them on cardboard, the paper scenery likewise, and in a little box, by lamplight, push the colored figures around while you mouthed such lines as "Turn your eyes to the stern windows, James Flaunty. Do you see his body swinging there?" Is that a theatre for children, or for the mind? It's less high-falutin' anyhow than

> . . . love is made
> Imperishable fire under the boughs
> Of chrysoberyl and beryl and chrysolite
> And chrysoprase and ruby and sardonyx.

The Yeats whose path would cross Beckett's several times was not W. B. but Jack, a painting by whom he owned and cherished. Their vision is not altogether dissimilar. Nothing, said Sam's dying Malone, is more real than nothing; and Jack ended *The Scourge of the Gulf* with a hollow enigma: "An empty skull, a black box, a dead skipper! Have I done anything or nothing?"

In Paris in 1928 he promptly commenced frequenting James Joyce, another man who worked all his life with what he had taken out of Ireland. Having left earlier (October 1904), Joyce was unimpressed with the theatre. The Abbey was not to open until December, and what preceded it bespoke chiefly ignominious ignobility. The Lower Camden Street hall where Joyce saw *In the Shadow of the Glen* rehearsed on 10 June had (Willie Fay recalled) a leaking roof, "a stage so small you couldn't swing a kitten," and an entrance hall crowded with the overflow stocks of a grocer on the left and a butcher on the right. You got in by slithering between crates of eggs and carcasses of beef. "Ye told me Mr. Yeats was queer," said one old lady, "but this is the queerest theatre that ever I saw." In those days "a race of clodhoppers" was a judgment that came readily to Joyce, and a National Theatre might have been ensconced in such quarters for the express purpose of confirming him. One indication that he saw *The Shadowy Waters* in January 1904 is that the "Brideship and Gulls" sequence of *Finnegans Wake* seems conceived in mockery of it. Joyce could cast a very cold eye.

He cherished more miscellaneous Dublin bric-à-brac: street sounds, toilet bowls in a plumber's window, a man who always walked on the outside of lampposts, the pedestrian obstacle (a manhole cover) that still rises above pavement level on the south side of Eccles Street.

Odder things linked in his mind. Day by day in 1895, a white-bearded man in a top hat could be glimpsed at the Westland Row end of College Park behind Trinity, attempting to get off the ground on batlike wings amid which he was fitted in a harness, upright. This was George Francis Fitzgerald, FRS, Professor of Physics, discoverer of the Fitzgerald Contraction that shortens you in the direction you are travelling, an effect not appreciable till you can measure your velocity in substantial fractions of that of light. Thanks to this piece of space-time headiness, Professor Fitzgerald is part of the history of relativity. He is not, however, part of the history of flight, since the greatest elevation he attained was six inches. But if (as seems probable when you think how word of queer sights gets round Dublin) one of the faces one day at the College Park railings was that of thirteen-year-old Jim Joyce, then the imprint of tophatted George Francis Fitzgerald, fabulous artificer, would-be hawklike man, may be just discernible on the margins of literature. It was the next year, in Latin class, that Joyce read the story of Daedalus in Ovid, to recognize, as he later would on a vast scale, a Dubliner reenacting a classical myth.

Another thing he seems to have remembered is how his first fiction, "The Sisters," had looked in AE's paper, machine-set paragraphs fitted above a half-page ad for Effektiv milk pumps and Alfalaval cream separators. At Dundrum the Cuala Press was preparing elegant little hand-set volumes in 14-point Caslon, and within a few years W. B. Yeats had brought into the Cuala series every Irish writer he thought worth notice: himself, AE, Lionel Johnson (Irish by courtesy), John Eglinton, Lady Gregory, Katharine Tynan,

Synge, even Lord Dunsany. The conspicuous omission was *Chamber Music*, by James A. Joyce, eventually issued in London by Elkin Mathews with "an open pianner" on the frontispiece.

On the last page of *Finnegans Wake* ("O bitter ending!") Joyce recapitulates his previous beginnings and endings: the "Yes" of *Ulysses* is conspicuous, the "old father" of *A Portrait*, the terminal cold of *Dubliners*. Near the top of the page the date 1904 is encoded—"my cold mad feary father," MCM*vier*. Further down "my leaves have drifted from me. All. But one clings still. I'll bear it one me. To remind me of." These are printed leaves as well as treeleaves on the river, and adjacent to them is "Avelaval": the *Ave atque vale* of Catullus (and Moore) entangled with the cream separator's name that *Irish Homestead* page of 1904 had displayed so prominently. In such style had dear dirty Dublin launched a master, much as it launched its glorious dramatic movement in a hall guarded by hanging sides of beef for W. B. Yeats of the pince-nez to push his way past.

> The years like great black oxen tread the world,
> And God the herdsman goads them on behind,
> And I am broken by their passing feet.

"Every syllable can be explained," Beckett recalls Joyce claiming. The way of the explainer must be to disengage Dublin trivia (advertisements, a cuckolded Jew, a tophatted professor) from classical entanglements (*Ave atque vale*, Homeric exploits, Daedalus). So it is with all dreams of nobility; they are entangled. The splendid lines of *The Countess* are not separable from Maud Gonne's shrill fanaticisms, nor the bizarre alert beauty of *The Third Policeman* from quarry lorries rumbling out of Tallaght.

Nor can the great Revival be disentangled from the simple fact that its originators—Yeats, Hyde, Lady Gregory, Synge—were Ascendancy Protestants, a minority inside a minor land, merely (Shaw said) "John Bull's Other Island." Their node of loyalty should have been John Bull. But, Romantics all, they cherished the Romantic dream, Shelley's dream, liberty: in their land, as it proved, an Irish Bull, not John. Yet none of them could disengage from the entanglements of origin.

Minds cannot dream away into disengagement. Beckett has said nothing would bring him back to Dublin; it is also told of Beckett that when others count sheep, he brings on dreams by playing over in his mind the nine holes of the golf course at Carrickmines, near Foxrock. Whether or not this commends the course is not certain. The one thing certain of Beckett is that he is not Irish as Irishness is defined today by the Free State. He is willing to be the last Anglo-Irishman, of the austere tradition of Protestant professional culture: "the people of Burke and Grattan," free to refuse. Unlike Joyce's his very agnosticism is Protestant; Nothing, like the Quark, comes in distinct flavors.

When Beckett fled the island of "formless spawning fury," he took his language away with him to *save* it: partly, to save it from the aftermath of the Revival. His fancy was that this could be achieved if he kept it aloof from Irish and crossed it with something as tough as French. *Watt*, which he wrote in English, simulates a translation from the French; its Dublin tram makes a "facultative" stop (*un arrêt facultatif*). No Irish movement has ever won Beckett's allegiance: certainly, though he is a lifelong athlete, nothing sponsored by the Gaelic Athletic Association. At Trinity he played the English game, to such effect he is likely the only Nobel laureate to be listed in the cricketer's Bible, Wisden's.

If the Literary Movement was started by the Anglo-Irishman Yeats, then the Anglo-Irishman Beckett terminates it, not least in his self-condemnation to works minimal and more minimal. What goes on now in Ireland is a different story.

In sight of Ben Bulben, Yeats from the grave addresses horsemen exclusively: no tourists in chartered buses, no Paddys afoot. Horsemen are neither to ponder their mortality nor to involve themselves in the busyness of this world. Perhaps because mounted visitors to Drumcliffe are scarce, the injunction goes unheeded.

As so often in his life, Yeats in death contrives to obliterate a tradition in the act of subsuming it. Who now remembers the past voices that are summoned and rejected by his gravestone's imperious words?

There was a collective voice the Christian dead used to assume, Church Latin on a stone to bid travellers pause, in countless epitaphs that commenced, *Siste, viator*. "Siste": stay, linger, ponder: ponder on the fact of death. I have died, so shall you; be admonished. Thus, on many thousand stones, the voice of Christian death; and in 1745 Jonathan Swift's single voice presumed to defy that voice. *Abi, viator*, Swift says from his plaque in St. Patrick's, *et imitare si poteris*: . . . get moving, traveller, and imitate if you can. . . . Let the late Dean's savage indignation infect you, and like him perform public acts on behalf of fuller human life.

Yeats follows Swift's example of imperiousness. The lines in "Under Ben Bulben" that lead up to the epitaph make that much explicit.

> . . . On limestone quarried near the spot
> By his command these words are cut . . .

"By his command" is the voice of a man who expects to be obeyed, being dead. The way that voice envisions advantages in death is worldly, not Christian. It says, "I am no longer the diffident poseur who came to Coole Park, the 'one that ruffled in a manly pose / For all his timid heart'; no, in death, having wholly assumed my imperious anti-self, I shall effect it that these words shall be cut in the world where the living are."

But if he will not have our meditations swoon into death the Christian way, neither are we to esteem like Swift the involvements of living. Elsewhere his book has told us that "Death and life were not / Till man made up the whole." Therefore:

> Cast a cold eye
> On life, on death.
> Horseman, pass by.

That is his hard-won minimalism, his epitome of many hundred wonderful pages: his last lordly rebuff of all the Irish rebuffs his work on behalf of Ireland underwent. He had aspired, with the aid of the Abbey, to win his countrymen into what he called Unity of Being, but they got (and get) bitterer pleasure out of division, the courtroom still the theatre of their pleasure, the ambush the recourse of their plot construction, a fine explosion their ecstasy of climax. "Shattered glass and toppling masonry," wrote Joyce; improved explosives now permit local rains of blood and severed limbs. As in the Western World of Synge's imagination, a murderer can still get idolized.

Meanwhile official Ireland has commemorated W. B. Yeats the best way bankers know how, by putting his engraved likeness on the Republic's £20 notes. Foreknowledge of that would have gratified the Pollexfens, those tough Sligo shipowners who thought their Susan might have made a luckier match than J.B.Y., failed barrister, failed painter. There's a Yeats Summer School in Sligo, and in Dublin the Tourist Board (Board of the Welcomes, *Bord Fáilte*) has discovered a good thing in Joyce.

From Stephen's Green, Marjorie Fitzgibbon's fine bronze head of the fabulous artificer broods toward a door across the street, the door that closed behind Stephen Dedalus when he entered the old University to hear the Dean of Studies say *home, Christ, ale, master* in a tongue that would be alien always. A plaque by the door claims distinction for the place, citing three names, one of them Irish: John Henry Newman, first Rector; Gerard Manley Hopkins, Professor of Greek; James Augustine Joyce, Student. American Express paid for the bronze head. Reciprocally, Joyce pilgrims buy Travellers' Cheques.

Some years ago a Joyce pilgrim from Berkeley, California located and identified the birthplace of Leopold Bloom. It is at 52 Clanbrassil St. Upper, where a few Jewish names are still discernible on shops nearby. Thereafter a scripture in *Ulysses* cried out for fulfillment: "That the house in which he was born be ornamented with a commemorative tablet." The argument against commemorating a fictional character was countered with the post office statue of Cuchulain, who is surely less well documented than Bloom, and in June 1982, at the height of the Joyce Centennial doings, a blue Bord Fáilte tablet was unveiled. The ceremony drew a small crowd and stirred the tongues of neighbors, who were instantly telling a delighted press that the scholars had as usual got the wrong house. "The Blooms didn't live there at all," said one old lady; "they lived down that way." So Irish Facts multiply still, and it's fair to say that Dublin remains obsessed with the writers it doesn't read. One Trinity undergraduate told a pressman the inside truth, that it was all an American cod, the books being unreadable. Not even of *A Portrait* could she make head or tail. She didn't say what she was doing at Trinity.

One way or another they're obsessed too with the North, and they've lost the battle for Irish. Nameplates blossom with the words of multinational commerce: "UNILOKomotive (European Division) (Local Office)." Whatever that is, it's on O'Connell Street, near the post office with its bronze Cuchulain. At an adjacent McDonald's the counter-girl wears her nametag: Emer: Cuchulain's queen. If you recover an heroic past, then face the fact that you'll have it splattered all around you. Recover Irish: it will be mispronounced, mocked, co-opted for slogans, forgotten. Recover the mystique of the lost land and the Four Green Fields: your fanatics will make a routine of blowing up babies in their efforts to reclaim the lost fraction of the fourth. That nightmare has not begun to be awakened from.

Impart literacy; people may read. Worry about what may get read; hire censors to block it. And the lot of the censor is to stall between fools.

Forty years ago prominent Irish writers tended to be defined by their banned books. Beckett turned the tables; enraged by bans, he banned his plays in Ireland. There is logic, yes, logic, behind every public proposition in the unfortunate country, behind every action however perverse it looks. The famous "smile and tear" are camouflage, thin as the publicized green on the chill North Atlantic rock maps now call Eire. The weather on that rock breeds a race of dissident logicians, Mylesians. Myles is their unacknowledged legislator. From premises chosen at whim ("Do you know what it is? Do you know what I'm going to tell you?") the Plain People of Ireland will argue you off the face of the Erse.

Though logic, Yeats knew, is a machine, and machines seize up.

Perverse likewise meanwhile, defying their nation's perversity which deems the written word (when you come down to it) unnatural, Yeats, Synge, Joyce and Beckett somehow defined themselves: four of the foremost bookmen of their century in a language that less than a hundred years ago there seemed strong reasons to extirpate from Ireland.

NOTES

The following editions are cited throughout:

YEATS

Autobiography: W. B. Yeats, *Autobiography*, Collier paperback, 1965.

Memoirs: W. B. Yeats, *Memoirs*, ed. Donoghue, 1972.

Variorum Plays: Alspach, ed., *The Variorum Edition of the Plays of W. B. Yeats*, 1966. (I used the third printing. The main text in all printings is dismayingly corrupt.)

Variorum Poems: Allt and Alspach, eds., *The Variorum Edition of the Poems of W. B. Yeats*, 1957.

Letters: A. Wade, ed., *The Letters of W. B. Yeats*, 1955.

Other Yeats references are to standard Macmillan editions except where specified.

JOYCE

Ulysses: James Joyce, *Ulysses*, Random House, 1961; Vintage paperback has identical pagination. All other Joyce page references are to Penguin editions.

All references to the Ellmann biography of Joyce are to the first (1959) printing. A revised edition was announced for the centenary year; I had not seen it when this book went to press.

SYNGE

All references are by volume and page to the four-volume Oxford edition of Synge's *Works*, ed. Robin Skelton, Alan Price, and Ann Saddlemyer, 1962–1968. This was out of print as *A Colder Eye* went to press, but a reprint had been promised by Colin Smythe.

WARNING

4   "a different church": the Chapel of Ease, Roundtown. Vivien Igoe, "A Cab at the Door," in *Ireland of the Welcomes*, May–June 1982, 8, and private communication. His given names appear as "Jacobus Augustinus."

5   "proving he is alive": See Swift's pamphlets against the astrologer Partridge.

5   "Mr. Hunter": see Joyce, *Selected Letters*, 286 for Clonliffe Road, 112 for the first intimation of the story.

6   "Boylan with impatience," "That's the bucko," "Tipping her": *Ulysses*, 267, 319, 274.

6   "a cuckold": Richard Ellmann, *James Joyce*, 1959, 238.

7   Gogarty's broadcast on Joyce. See the transcript in W. R. Rodgers, *Irish Literary Portraits*, 1972, 24–25.

7   "remembered to the pound": J. F. Byrne, *The Silent Years*, 1953, 157.

8   "How, demands Byrne": Byrne, 158.

8   "insinuating, upflowing," "carved out of a turnip": *Autobiography*, 283, 271.

8   "pants": *Autobiography*, 271.

10 "Interview": Maria Jolas, ed., *A James Joyce Yearbook*, Paris, 1949. Mme. Jolas has assured me it was among J.J.'s papers, and Prof. John V. Kelleher is convinced (on "O'Brien"'s authority and others') that "O'Brien" wrote it; and how these allegations are to be combined is unclear. The man Prof. Kelleher suggested might have taken the ms. to Paris denies having done so. Though I quoted it myself in 1956 (*Dublin's Joyce*) I now judge it too vivid to be true: what a miraculously accurate transcriber, for those days before tape! Prof. Ellmann alludes (759) to questions J.J. had his friends put to J.S.J. during the 1920's, but such notes on these as I've seen are bare fact-lists.

10 "The unfacts": Joyce, *Finnegans Wake*, 57.

10 "clear solution," "Dublin toper": *A Tale of a Tub*, of course, and *Ulysses*, 341.

THE THREE PROVINCES

16 "moralist with a corncob": chapter heading in Wyndham Lewis, *Men Without Art*, 1936.

16 "a roof for Thoor Ballylee": Frank Tuohy, *Yeats*, 1976, 172.

17 "shorthand for sociologies": for a lucid exposition, see Conor Cruise O'Brien, *States of Ireland*, 1972 (rev. ed. 1974).

17 "public opinion defined": thank you, Joe Sobran.

A BAG OF CATS

James Kilroy, *The "Playboy" Riots*, 1971, a hundred pages of contemporary reports, is the one indispensable source-book. My notes nowhere cite it, only because I'd not know where citations should begin and end.

19 "Tin trumpets": Lady Gregory, *Our Irish Theatre*, 1913, 112–13.

19 "greatcoats": shown in contemporary cartoons of the event.

20 "bad language": Gregory, 133.

20 "Don't strike me": Synge, *Works*, IV, 73.

20 "cut in rehearsal": Gregory, 133–34.

20 "making mighty kisses": Synge, *Works*, IV, 149.

21 "What good'd be my life-time": Synge, *Works*, IV, 165.

21 "Pegeen I'm seeking only": Synge, *Works*, IV, 167.

21 "Holloway": Robert Hogan and Michael J. O'Neill, eds., *Joseph Holloway's Abbey Theatre: A Selection from His Unpublished Journal*, 1967, 81. See also David H. Greene and Edward M. Stephens, *J. M. Synge, 1871–1909*, 1959, 237–38.

23 "Yeats had pointed out": in *Samhain*, December 1904, 7.

23 Note: "Fay's account": W. G. Fay and Catherine Carswell, *The Fays of the Abbey Theatre*, 1935, 214–15.
27 "large umbrella": George Moore, *Hail and Farewell*, repr. 1976, 188.
27 "He was alone": Joyce, *A Portrait of the Artist as a Young Man*, 226.
28 "from his head only": *Autobiography*, 356.
28 "Constrained, arraigned": "The Double Vision of Michael Robartes," *Variorum Poems*, 382.
28 "leave the theatre": Denis Johnston, *Dramatic Works*, 1977, I, 8.
30 "Joyce records": *Ulysses*, 542.
30 "Bend down": *Variorum Plays*, 163. These are lines Joyce has Stephen remember in *A Portrait*.
30 "Have I not seen": "A Prayer for My Daughter," *Variorum Poems*, 405.
31 "Yeats phrased": *Autobiography*, 278–79.
31 "In using what I considered": *Autobiography*, 279.
32 "Lady Gregory had given them": Gregory, 113.
34 "Some blasted little theatre": see "Song of a Shift," in *Drums Under the Windows*, vol. 3 of O'Casey's autobiography.
35 "Lady Gregory had made the mistake": Gregory, 114.
37 "thick as blackberries": Holloway, quoted by Greene and Stephens, 246.
39 "bag of cats": Joyce, *Dubliners*, 132–33.
40 "the height of a table": Gregory, 171.
40 "drive the vile thing": Gregory, 180.
40 "hell-inspired ingenuity": Gregory, 190.
40 "threw a good many potatoes": Gregory, 204.
41 "Nothing was thrown": Gregory, 219.
41 "demoralize a monastery": Gregory, 227.
41 "Not while the curtain was up": Gregory, 229.
41 "shot off a shovel": *Ulysses*, 345.

A TALE OF A POT

43 "no mastery of speech" and other Yeats citations: from the Notes to his *Plays in Prose and Verse*, 1922, reprinted in *Variorum Plays*, 254.
43 "stony silence": Willie Fay's account is in W. G. Fay and Catherine Carswell, *The Fays of the Abbey Theatre*, 1935, 127–29. Students of the Irish Fact will want to compare Yeats's brief version, *Variorum Plays*, 254.
44 "notorious Irishman": Oscar Wilde, of course. See "The Decay of Lying," antepenultimate paragraph.
44 "I sigh over the pig": for his contribution to the Coinage Committee's report (1928) see Donald R. Pearce, ed., *The Senate Speeches of W. B. Yeats*, 1960, or Brian Cleeve, ed., *W. B. Yeats and the Designing of Ireland's Coinage*, 1972. Cleeve reproduces the lost pig on p. 14.
45 "pragmatical pig": "Blood and the Moon," *Variorum Poems*, 480; first printed in Ezra Pound's *The Exile* (Spring 1928), the same year the Dublin Stationery Office published *Coinage of Saorstát Éireann*. This poem records the suspicion that every modern nation is "half dead at the top," to which Pound responded from the Pisan stockade, "My dear William B.Y. your 1/2 was too moderate" (*The Cantos of Ezra Pound*, 1970, LXXIX, 487). The presence of coinage in both poets' minds, Pound's programmatically, Yeats's accidentally, makes a pleasant historical rhyme.
45 "laughing *Ceres*": Pope's Epistle IV (to Burlington), ll. 173–76.
46 "nettles wave": "Coole Park, 1929," *Variorum Poems*, 489.
47 "roofless ruin": "Meditations in Time of Civil War," *Variorum Poems*, 423.
47 "violent bitter man": "Ancestral Houses," *Variorum Poems*, 418.

48   "leaves whirling on the road": Yeats's note to "The Hosting of the Sidhe," *Variorum Poems*, 800.

48   "And if any gaze": "The Hosting of the Sidhe," *Variorum Poems*, 141.

48   "likeness of a newspaper": "The Devil," in Yeats, *The Celtic Twilight*, repr. 1962, 59.

THE CONQUEST OF ENGLISH

49   "the language": Joyce, *A Portrait of the Artist as a Young Man*, 189.

50   "used to complain": recorded in Ford Madox Ford, *Joseph Conrad: A Personal Remembrance*, 1924, 229.

50   "sentimental and self-pitying": Anthony Burgess, *Joysprick*, 1973, 27.

50   "He feels the inferiority": *Joysprick*, 28.

51   "barrel-staves": J. C. Beckett, *The Making of Modern Ireland*, 1966, 28–29. There was military clearance indeed, but it's only part of the story.

52   "my own music": *Autobiography*, 103.

52   "instantly admired": details from the Hone biography of Yeats, 1943, ch. iii, 7; xiii, 5; xviii, 4.

52   Note: "reading Thoreau": *Autobiography*, 47

53   "infarm the audience": many sources, e.g. R. F. Rattray, "A Day with Yeats," in E. H. Mikhail, ed., *W. B. Yeats: Interviews and Recollections*, 1977, I, 157.

53   "bulgar in your bowels": Joyce, *Finnegans Wake*, 563.

54   "it darkles": Joyce, *Finnegans Wake*, 244.

54   "I don't envy yeh": O'Casey, "Dublin's Gods and Half-Gods," in *Inishfallen, Fare Thee Well*, 1949.

54   "wind in the chimney": *The Cantos of Ezra Pound*, 1970, LXXXIII, 533–34.

54   "What's riches": Yeats, "The Peacock," *Variorum Poems*, 310.

55   "nearly all Wordsworth": Canto LXXXIII, 534, where we learn that W.B.Y. preferred "Ennemosor on witches."

55   "*animosity*": Introduction to Marianne Moore's *Selected Poems*, 1936.

56   "Irishman's house": *Ulysses*, 110.

56   "Hohohohohome": *Ulysses*, 607.

57   "fish, flesh and fowl": "Sailing to Byzantium," *Variorum Poems*, 407.

57   "Calvary's turbulence": "The Magi," *Variorum Poems*, 318.

57   "tingling stars": in "Morte d'Arthur."

57   "witty Aristotle": see "The Holy Office." in Richard Ellman, *James Joyce*, 172.

58   "fight," "logic": "An Irish Airman Foresees his Death" and "Sixteen Dead Men," *Variorum Poems*, 328, 395.

58   "passionate intensity" *et seq.*: in order, "The Second Coming," "Prayer for My Daughter" (twice), "Byzantium," "In Memory of Major Robert Gregory," *Variorum Poems*, 402, 403–4, 498, 325.

60   "Clean," "Tully": *Ulysses*, 55, 394.

61   "So Thursday": *Ulysses*, 396.

THE LORE OF IRISH

62   "Hyde was reporting": in "The Necessity for De-Anglicising Ireland," contained in *The Revival of Irish Literature*, London, 1894, 117–61; see the long footnote on 137–38.

63   "census-takers": figures from F.S.L. Lyons, *Ireland Since the Famine*, rev. ed. 1973, 88.

63   "nobody did anything in Irish": Moore, *Hail and Farewell*, repr. 1976, 55.

64   "Synge's text": the following paragraphs draw on Declan Kiberd, *Synge and the Irish Language*, 1979, 19–23, and letters from John V. Kelleher.

65 "at bottom abominable": W. B. Stanford and R. B. McDowell, *Mahaffy: A Biography of an Anglo-Irishman*, 108.

65 "silly or indecent": *Mahaffy*, 104.

65 "great-bladdered Emer": "Crazy Jane on the Mountain," *Variorum Poems*, 628.

65 "two thousand octavo pages": cited by Lady Gregory, *Cuchulain of Muirthemne*, 267. "five hundred to a thousand printed volumes": Aodh de Blácam, *Gaelic Literature Surveyed*, 1929, xi.

66 "Kinsella version": in Thomas Kinsella, *The Tain*, 1969, 8–20. Lady Gregory's is in *Cuchulain of Muirthemne*.

66 Note: "real Gaelic ballads": see Derick S. Thomson, *The Gaelic Sources of Macpherson's "Ossian,"* Aberdeen University Studies, No. 130, 1952.

67 "Ferguson": quoted from Padraic Colum's little selection, *The Poems of Samuel Ferguson*, 1963, 85, 70, 64.

67 "Yeats twice rewrote": *Variorum Poems*, 550. The main versions are 1922 (for a revision of *The Pot of Broth*) and 1935 (in *A Full Moon in March*).

68 "Brown tells us": Malcolm Brown, *The Politics of Irish Literature*, 1972, 316. Brown exaggerates little when he numbers "The Fairy Thorn" among "the immortal lyrics of the English language" (60).

68 *"Irish Fireside"*: Yeats, *Uncollected Prose*, I, 82–83.

68 "their best music": Brown, *Politics of Irish Literature*, 316, 407, citing Austin Clarke, *Poetry in Modern Ireland*, 1951, 15.

69 "Max Beerbohm caricature": often reproduced, e.g. in Mac Liammóir and Boland, *W. B. Yeats and His World*, 1971, 65.

69 "Then all at once": Standish O'Grady, *The Coming of Cuculain*, 1894, ch. 1.

69 "AE recalled": in his "Introduction" to an undated Dublin reprint of O'Grady's *The Coming of Cuculain*, x. The "Introduction" can be dated pretty closely: after O'Grady's death in May 1928 but before the book came to Johns Hopkins late in 1930. So AE was about sixty-two when he fanned up this old glow.

70 "Paradise of pretenders": *Ulysses*, 45.

70 "Wisha, faith": opening sentence of "Biddy the Matchmaker," in *Some Strange Experiences of Kitty the Hare*, circulated with a straight face, God help them, by the normally responsible Mercier Press, Dublin and Cork, 1981.

71 "Moore describes": *Hail and Farewell*, 238.

71 "Mala Néfin": Hyde, *Love Songs of Connacht*, 9.

71 "'Tis the cause of this song": *Love Songs of Connacht*, 75–77.

72 "mountain stream," "coming of a new power": Yeats, *Uncollected Prose*, I, 293; Yeats, *Explorations*, 93.

72 "I shall not die": *Love Songs of Connacht*, 138–39.

73 "O woman": see, e.g., John Montague, ed., *The Book of Irish Verse*, 1974, 107.

73 "Muses' blade": see "Coole Park, 1929," *Variorum Poems*, 489.

74 "valuable exposition": Maire Cruise O'Brien, "The Two Languages," in *Conor Cruise O'Brien Introduces Ireland*, 1969, 43–60: an otherwise touristy book, not without lore.

75 "Sean O'Casey": both examples from Act II of *The Plough and the Stars*, in *Collected Plays*, 1949, I, 200, 201.

75 Note: "Pepys and Jane Austen": Thomas MacDonagh cited them in *Literature in Ireland*, 1916, 11. George Moore has similar observations in *Hail and Farewell*, 551.

76 "Synge's": all from *In the Shadow of the Glen*, but the mannerism is everywhere in Synge.

77 "Moore thought": *Hail and Farewell*, 549–51. "It consists of no more than a dozen turns of speech, dropped into pages of English so ordinary, that redeemed from these phrases it might appear in any newspaper without attracting attention."

77   "a Falcon": Gerard Manley Hopkins, "The Windhover."

78   "on verbs": D. D. Paige, ed., *The Letters of Ezra Pound*, #95, dated June 1916. For more on Fenollosa see my *The Pound Era*, 1971, 223–29 and 289–91.

78   "Pound divulged": in *Confucius to Cummings*, 1964, 327.

79   "sentence of Tennyson's": from *The Holy Grail*.

79   "THE FISH": *Variorum Poems*, 146.

81   "All that was sung": "Parnell's Funeral," *Variorum Poems*, 542.

IRISH WORDS

82   "Hamlet": Brendan O Hehir, *A Gaelic Lexicon for Finnegans Wake*, 1967, 387.

83   "Hill of the Lark": example from Mr. Séan Golden.

83   "Latin *devotus*": Aodh de Blácam, *Gaelic Literature Surveyed*, repr. 1973, 4.

83   "*fadó*": pointed out by Conor Johnston.

84   "Dolphin's Barn": lore from Séan Golden.

84   "the bannocks": Joyce, *Finnegans Wake*, 53.

84   "mhuith peisth": Joyce, *Finnegans Wake*, 91, unriddled by O Hehir, *A Gaelic Lexicon*, 62.

84   "Boildoyle": Joyce, *Finnegans Wake*, 17.

85   "At the Abbey Theatre": *Variorum Poems*, 264.

85   "I copied": note to his 1895 *Poems; Variorum Poems*, 840–41.

85   "Lady Gregory's spelling": note to his 1933 *Collected Poems; Variorum Poems*, 840.

85   "Clooth-na-Bare": in "The Hosting of the Sidhe," *Variorum Poems*, 140. The poem dates from 1893.

86   "Is it not brave": *Tamburlaine*, what else?

87   "Baile and Aillinn": *Variorum Poems*, 189.

87   "names of the demons": *Variorum Poems*, 52.

YOUNG YEATS

90   "He has come": George Moore, *Hail and Farewell*, repr. 1976, 244.

90   "Carpets muffled": Frank Tuohy, *Yeats*, 1976, 138.

90   "malicious account": *Hail and Farewell*, 187.

91   "tomb of Shakespeare": Frank Tuohy, *Yeats*, 1976, 136. In *Hail and Farewell*, 209–10, Moore has himself reflecting on a Yeats "no longer able to appreciate anything but literary values." "The heart of Yeats seemed to me to have died ten years ago [i.e. about 1891]; the last of it probably went into the composition of *The Countess Cathleen*."

91   "Yeats had told": *Uncollected Prose*, I, 267 ff.

93   "Shelley could write": example from Eric Havelock, *The Literate Revolution in Greece*, 1982, 20.

93   "Yeats tells it": *Variorum Poems*, 410.

93   "Hyde's translation": in Douglas Hyde, *Songs Ascribed to Raftery*, 1903, 331–35. My transcription ignores the typographic system by which Hyde mapped the assonances of the Irish.

93   "A girl arose": "The Sorrow of Love," *Variorum Poems*, 120.

94   "Professor Havelock": *The Literate Revolution in Greece*, 58.

95   "dishevelled": "Who Goes With Fergus?," *Variorum Poems*, 125; originally a song in *The Countess Kathleen* (1892).

95   "Bloom left": according to Joyce's chronological notes (reproduced by John Henry Raleigh in *The Chronicle of Leopold and Molly Bloom*, 1977, 3), Bloom left school in 1880. Whether Joyce knew he'd arranged this near-miss is uncertain. The details of Yeats's biography were not in print at the time, but then Dublin knowledge is independent of print.

95   "held his own": William M. Murphy, *Prodigal Father: The Life of John Butler Yeats*, 129.

96 "duel of song (I.1, 1–100)": *Variorum Poems*, 645–48.

96 Patmore on Crashaw, quoted in *The Verse in English of Richard Crashaw*, 1949, 16.

96 "lily, chilly": *Variorum Poems*, 647.

97 "Romantic Ireland": the refrain of "September 1913," *Variorum Poems*, 289.

97 "Roman coin," "Beautiful Lofty Things": *Memoirs*, 42; *Variorum Poems*, 577. For a clarifying account of Yeats and O'Leary see Murphy, *Prodigal Father*, 140–46.

97 "genius": John Malcolm Brown, *The Politics of Irish Literature*, 1972, 314.

97 "first published prose": Yeats, *Uncollected Prose*, I, 81–87.

97 "last essay": Allan Wade, *A Bibliography of the Writings of W. B. Yeats*, 3rd ed., 1968, 23.

97 "Thomas Davis": quotations from *The Poems of Thomas Davis*, a New York printing (1854) to raise expatriate consciousness. "The West's Asleep," 37–38; "Tipperary," 31–33; "Celts and Saxons," 53–56.

98 "ten thousand copies": Frank Tuohy, *Yeats*.

99 "planet Neptune": *Uncollected Prose*, I, 333.

99 Note: "The Erne": Colin Meir, *The Ballads and Songs of W. B. Yeats*, 1974, 35, says this is quoted by Yeats but does not say where.

100 "stands on the highest pavement": see T. S. Eliot, "La Figlia che Piange," written 1910.

100 "came to call": Murphy, *Prodigal Father*, 160, and Yeats, *Memoirs*, 40–43. His version in *Autobiography*, 82, is much condensed to fit that book's perspectives.

100 "elaborate paragraph": *Memoirs*, 40.

101 "Mona Lisa": e.g. in Walter Pater, *The Renaissance*, ed. Donald L. Hill, 1980, 98–99.

101 "akin to lines Swinburne wrote": Samuel Chew's suggestion, adduced in Hill's notes to *The Renaissance*, 380. The Swinburne is in *Rosamond*, scene 1.

101 "touch of the artist,'"first spoken words,": *Ulysses*, 235, 65.

101 "five feet ten": Nancy Cardozo, *Lucky Eyes and a High Heart: The Life of Maud Gonne*, 1978, 27.

102 "Pet monkey": Yeats, *Letters*, 1955, 108, reporting to John O'Leary.

102 "hating the Shepherdess": Yeats, *Letters*, 106.

102 "Did that play": "The Man and the Echo" (1939), *Variorum Poems*, 632.

102 "Who dreamed": "The Rose of the World," *Variorum Poems*, 111.

102 Note: "She recorded": Murphy, *Prodigal Father*, 172.

103 "old bellows": "A Prayer for My Daughter," *Variorum Poems*, 405.

103 "walked the cliff paths," "Yes," "nannygoat": *Memoirs*, 46; the scene is wonderfully evoked in Benedict Kiely's story, "A Ball of Malt and Madame Butterfly"; *Ulysses*, 783, 176.

103 "white birds": *Variorum Poems*, 121.

103 "drunken, vainglorious": "Easter 1916," *Variorum Poems*, 393.

104 "There is a thicket": *Letters*, 106 (31 Jan. 1889, to Katharine Tynan).

104 "Lay of Oisin": Russell K. Alspach identified this and other sources in *PMLA*, LVIII: 849–66. The trouble to which he was put reflects something Yeats did all his life: mentioning peripheral sources and being evasive about a primary one. He was unhappy to think that people might collate his words with those in the books he'd had open.

105 "three incompatible things": *Letters*, 111.

105 "Vain gaiety": "The Circus Animals' Desertion," *Variorum Poems*, 629.

105 "Antaeus-like": "The Municipal Gallery Revisited" (1937), *Variorum Poems*, 603.

105 "I hear my soul": *Variorum Poems*, 45.

106 "holding down": *Ulysses*, 9.

106 "Fergus": *Variorum Plays*, 52–54, the 1892 text, the only one that contains the song. Thereafter readers had to seek it among Yeats's Poems, as in *Variorum Poems*, 125.

107 "William Empson": see his *Seven Types of Ambiguity*, rev. ed., 1947, 187–90.

107 "God and God's mother": the first (1892) text: *Variorum Plays*, 16.

108   "Bow down": "The Rose of the World," *Variorum Poems*, 112.

108   "O Colleens": "The Lover Speaks to the Hearers of His Song in Coming Days," *Variorum Poems*, 173; I cite the earliest version of 1896. Later he had the decency to change the "Colleens" to "women," and "Maurya [Mary] of the wounded heart" to the brisker "Attorney of Lost Souls."

109   "Impetuous heart": *Variorum Plays*, 129, where, incredibly, "lonely" is misprinted "lovely."

109   "At the grey round": in "The Dreaming of the Bones," *Variorum Plays*, 776.

109   "the poet's exact time-sense": *Variorum Plays*, 1008.

109   "I said": "Adam's Curse," *Variorum Poems*, 204.

110   "burst into Moore's bedroom": *Hail and Farewell*, 248.

110   "French draft": *Hail and Farewell*, 250–54.

110   "literary lunatics": *Hail and Farewell*, 254.

111   "Matheson Lang": in his autobiography, *Mr. Wu Looks Back*, 1940, 48. I've made typographic corrections in quoting. And my thanks to Richard J. Finneran for providing the item.

111   "surviving typescript": printed in *Variorum Plays*, 1168–1222.

111   "We have reformed": quoted by the editor in *Hail and Farewell*, 1976, 752.

112   "Bloom told 'Thank you'": *Ulysses*, 650.

112   "Stephen Dedalus": in the disquisition on aesthetics, *A Portrait of the Artist as a Young Man*, ch. v.

112   "our national epic": *Ulysses*, 192, where Stephen overhears someone (AE or John Eglinton?) say "Moore is the man for it." Moore certainly conceived *Hail and Farewell*, with its title from Catullus, on a (mock) epic scale.

THE LIVING WORLD FOR TEXT

113   "The only truth": Synge, *Works*, III, 168

113   "highest figure": Synge, *Works*, III, 223.

114   "On a given census day": Nancy Scheper-Hughes, *Saints, Scholars, and Schizophrenics*, 1979, 65.

114   "She did what was right": Synge, *Works*, III, 165.

115   "Where nobody": *Variorum Plays*, 184.

116   "Thus do the spirits": *Variorum Plays*, 210.

116   "experiments": George Mills Harper, *Yeats's Golden Dawn*, 1974, 7.

117   "Denis Johnston": in his *Synge*, 1965, 14.

117   "the grouse, and the owls": Synge, *Works*, III, 57.

117   "It's a queer thing": Synge, *Works*, III, 51–3.

118   "detail Synge struck out": Synge, *Works*, III, 56.

118   "not be sitting": Synge, *Works*, III, 57.

118   "Adieu, sweet Angus": Synge, *Works*, I, 38.

118   "Under the Moon": *Variorum Poems*, 209.

118   "a quiet man": Synge, *Works*, III, 59.

118   "The man I had a love for:" Synge, *Works*, I, 80.

119   "I have met an old vagrant": Synge, *Works*, II, 195.

119   "naturally a nomad": Synge, *Works*, II, 195.

119   "waiting these days": Synge, *Works*, IV, 59.

120   "The stars are out": Synge, *Works*, IV, 211.

121   "ungodly ruck": writing to Stephen MacKenna; D. H. Greene and Edward M. Stephens, *J. M. Synge, 1871–1909*, 1959, 264.

121   "his attempts": "In Memory of Major Robert Gregory," "Coole Park, 1929," "The Municipal Gallery Revisited," *Variorum Poems*, 324, 489, 603.

121   "I knew the stars": Synge, *Works*, I, 32.

121   "My arms are round you": Synge, *Works*, I, 47.

122   "The ordinary student of drama": Yeats, *Essays and Introductions*, 304.

122   "but the more hated": Yeats, *Essays and Introductions*, 310.

123   "Practical movements": *Memoirs*, 247.

124   "John Synge, I and Augusta Gregory": "The Municipal Gallery Revisited," *Variorum Poems*, 603.

124   "shamrock," "wolfhound": Jeanne Sheehy, *The Rediscovery of Ireland's Past*, 1980, 10–13.

125   "J. M. Synge and the Ireland of His Time," Yeats, *Essays and Introductions*, 311–42; first published by the Cuala Press, 1911, 350 copies.

125   "One evening in 1912": *Memoirs*, 263.

125   "And that enquiring man": "In Memory of Major Robert Gregory," *Variorum Poems*, 324.

126   "Give up Paris": Yeats, *Essays and Introductions*, 299.

126   "where men must reap": Synge, *Works*, III, 64.

126   "have a peace": Synge, *Works*, II, 162.

126   "total of four and a half months": Greene and Stephens, 76.

126   "I have been sitting": Synge, *Works*, II, 48.

126   "Frenchmen and Danes and Germans": Synge, *Works*, II, 60.

126   "Walking about with two sticks": Synge, *Works*, II, 57.

127   "a curious dreaminess": Greene and Stephens, 121.

127   "Willie Fay would ask": W. G. Fay and Catherine Carswell, *The Fays of the Abbey Theatre*, 1935, 139.

128   "each keystroke": information on the Blickensderfer's foibles from typewriter expert Donald Sutherland, relayed by Mr. Barry Ahearn.

128   "good day's work": Greene and Stephens, 266.

128   "too full": Thomas MacDonagh, *Literature in Ireland*, 1916, 48.

128   "I work always with a typewriter": Synge, *Works*, IV, xxxii–xxxiii.

128   "notebook draft": this reconstruction follows that of David H. Greene, in Thomas R. Whitaker, ed., *Twentieth Century Interpretations of "The Playboy of the Western World,"* 1969, 100–1, with further details gleaned from Synge, *Works*, IV.

128   "flourish from a letter": Greene and Stephens, 103.

129   "Six yards of stuff": Synge, *Works*, IV, 57.

129   "stripped itself": Synge, *Works*, IV, 166.

129   "the old story": Declan Kiberd, *Synge and the Irish Language*, 1979, 118.

129   "It's a power": Synge, *Works*, III, 111.

130   "poor fellow would get drunk": Synge, *Works*, IV, 123.

130   "you'd see him": Synge, *Works*, IV, 123.

130   "a walking terror": Synge, *Works*, IV, 101.

130   "Weren't you off racing": Synge, *Works*, IV, 161.

131   "his journal recalls": Greene and Stephens, 168.

131   "old boatman's lament": Synge, *Works*, II, 305.

131   "But we'll come round him": Synge, *Works*, I, 57.

132   "Yeats was told": Yeats, *Essays and Introductions*, 338.

132   "about a Connaught man": Synge, *Works*, II, 95.

132   "Synge reflected": Synge, *Works*, II, 95.

132   "in Act I we should see": outline in Synge, *Works*, IV, 295.

133   "Yeats explained": *Uncollected Prose*, II, 400.

133   "With that the sun came out": Synge, *Works*, IV, 103.

134   "Prof. Henn": in the Notes to his 1963 edition of the Plays.

135   "The blessing of God": Synge, *Works*, IV, 151.

135   "What's that": Synge, *Works*, IV, 141.

136   "It's a fright": Synge, *Works*, IV, 137.

136   "as metaphysical as he pleased": *Autobiography*, 218.

136   "Did you ever hear tell": Synge, *Works*, IV, 133.

137   "With what rare gold": Synge, *Works*, I, 117.

137   "Yeats noted": Yeats, *Essays and Introductions*, 300.

137   "Ten thousand blessings": Synge, *Works*, IV, 173.

139   "The ruck of muck": Hogan and O'Neill, eds., *Joseph Holloway's Abbey Theatre*, 1967, 133.

140   "Draw a little back": Synge, *Works*, IV, 267.

141   "rich in implications": William Empson, *Seven Types of Ambiguity*, 1930, 2nd ed., 1947, 5; see also 38–42 for further response to Synge's language. Writing fifty years before Declan Kiberd, Empson was especially acute in guessing at notions "not fully translated out of Irish" beneath Synge's most magical effects.

142   "Do not raise": Synge, *Works*, IV, 265.

142   "nervous breakdown": *Memoirs*, 140.

142   "lankylooking galoot": *Ulysses*, 109. For a photo of the 1902 Joyce in a macintosh in Paris see Richard Ellmann, *James Joyce*, 1959, facing page 81.

143   "more original": Ellmann, 276.

143   "list of Lord Mayors": Joyce, *Finnegans Wake*, 549, line 3; see Roland McHugh, *Annotations to Finnegans Wake*, 1980, 549.

BERLITZ DAYS

145   "in a Book": "Le Livre, Instrument Spirituel"; see Anthony Hartley, ed., *Mallarmé*, 1965, 189.

145   "his inkwell": quoted in Hartley's Introduction, xxii; I've retouched the translation to point up an echo of Genesis I.3, "Que la lumière soit."

145   "sea is summed up": This was Georges Rodenbach, quoted by Hartley, xv.

145   *"The Tables of the Law"*: reprinted in Yeats, *Mythologies*, 1959; it had first appeared in book form in June 1904.

146   "Why are these strange souls": *Autobiography*, 210.

146   "most beautiful book": *Ulysses*, 216.

147   *"Mrs Mooney"*: opening of Joyce, "The Boarding House," *Dubliners*, 61.

147   "English dictionary": *Autobiography*, 229.

147   "by the hour": Joyce, *Stephen Hero*, 26.

147   "still in Dublin": the first version appeared in the 13 August 1904 *Irish Homestead*. Don Gifford reproduces its text in *Joyce Annotated*, 1982, 289–93.

148   "Dublin joke": remembered by Leopold Bloom; *Ulysses*, 105.

148   "on record": in Holloway's journal for 10 June 1904: Hogan and O'Neill, eds., *Joseph Holloway's Abbey Theatre*, 1967, 40.

148   "I am writing": Joyce, *Selected Letters*, 22.

152   "thought of a story": *Selected Letters*, 112.

153   "whole book chiasmic": As Hans Walter Gabler discovered. See his "The Seven Lost Years" in Staley and Benstock, eds., *Approaches to Joyce's Portrait*, 1976, 25–60.

154   "chiasmic pattern": *Finnegans Wake*, 13–14.

A DWINDLING GYRE

159   "To keep these notes": *Memoirs*, 139.

159   "To oppose": *Memoirs*, 142.

159   "So much of the world": *Memoirs*, 142.

159   "Logic a machine": *Memoirs*, 139.
160   "ill-breeding of the mind": *Memoirs*, 140.
160   "In our age it is impossible": *Memoirs*, 185.
160   "never really understands": *Memoirs*, 141.
160   "a clown": her "kisses to a clown" spurred an epigram he never published, *Memoirs*, 145.
160   "Sweetheart, do not love": *Variorum Poems*, 211.
161   "brawling of a sparrow": "The Sorrow of Love," *Variorum Poems*, 119–20.
161   "Dun Emer," "Cuala": for the story see W. M. Murphy, *Prodigal Father*, 1978, 240–42 and 334.
162   "city of tedious and silly derision": quoted in W. M. Murphy, *Prodigal Father*, 244.
162   Note: "Blake of Irish birth": I've not seen this Encyclopaedia article, for word of which I'm indebted to J. E. and M. L. Grant of the University of Iowa.
163   "sleepers wake": *Variorum Poems*, 639.
163   "Men think they can Copy": G. Keynes, ed., *Poetry and Prose of William Blake*, 1941, 623.
163   "fourfold vision": Blake, *Poetry and Prose*, 861–62.
164   "worst books": all Holloway details from the prefatory matter to Robert Hogan and Michael J. O'Neill, eds., *Joseph Holloway's Abbey Theatre*, 1967—an exquisitely culled selection.
164   "preserves for us": *Joseph Holloway's Abbey Theatre*, 5, 27, 28, 87, 94–95.
165   "this unmannerly town": *Variorum Poems*, 351.
165   "those beautiful productions": Joseph Hone, *W. B. Yeats*, 1971, 270.
166   "making his peace": Joseph Hone, *W. B. Yeats*, 221.
166   "I might have lived": "The People," *Variorum Poems*, 352.
166   "Three types": "Poetry and Tradition," in Yeats, *Essays and Introductions*, 251. It is dated "August 1907."
167   "you gave": "To a Wealthy Man . . . ," *Variorum Poems*, 287.
167   "Since 1906": *Letters*, 478; 21 Sept. 1906, "I am deep in Ben Jonson."
168   "Would'st thou heare": Ben Jonson, "Epitaph on Elizabeth, L.H."
168   "And since": Ben Jonson, "An Ode. To Himselfe."
168   "Come leave": Ben Jonson, "Ode to Himselfe."
168   "My curse": "The Fascination of What's Difficult," *Variorum Poems*, 260.
169   "five poems": "To a Wealthy Man . . . ," "September 1913," "To a Friend Whose Work Has Come to Nothing," "Paudeen," "To a Shade," *Variorum Poems*, 287–92.
169   "What need you": "September 1913," *Variorum Poems*, 289.
169   "counted all her cards," "knew that she would have": Joyce, *Dubliners*, 65, 64.
169   "Base-born": "Under Ben Bulben," *Variorum Poems*, 639.
169   "lidless eye": "Upon a House Shaken by the Land Agitation," *Variorum Poems*, 264. Date, 1910.
170   "A man": "To a Shade," *Variorum Poems*, 292.

ARRAY! SURRECTION!

172   "a little play": *Letters*, 607.
172   "remains at a distance": "Certain Noble Plays of Japan" (April 1916), in Yeats, *Essays and Introductions*, 224.
172   "English versions": published in Pound's *Noh, or Accomplishment*, 1917; but Yeats in effect had preempted them for Irishry the previous year, when the Cuala Press published selections with his introduction: *Certain Noble Plays of Japan*, September 16, 1916, 350 copies. And "Noble" is of course his adjective.
173   "archaic Greek statue," "drowning kitten": *Letters*, 610, 609.
173   "no studied lighting": Yeats, *Essays and Introductions*, 224.
173   "Pound has preserved": in *The Cantos*, 1970, CI, 725.

173 "Among School Children": *Variorum Poems*, 443,

173 "An aged man": "Sailing to Byzantium," *Variorum Poems*, 407.

174 "I call to the eye": *Variorum Plays*, 399.

175 "imperfect": *Letters*, 611. "We shall not do it again until June, in order to get rid of Ainley and the musicians. The music Beecham says is good, but one cannot discuss anything with a feud between Dulac and a stupid musician at every rehearsal."

175 "O'Connor has noted": *My Father's Son*, 1968, last sentence of ch. 18.

175 "sacredness of *place*": Yeats, *Essays and Introductions*, 232, 236.

175 "happier than Sophocles," "hoarse": *Letters*, 610; Hone, 302.

175 "blew up": for a detailed analytic account of the Rising that confronts most questions of fact and principle, see F.S.L. Lyons, *Ireland Since the Famine*, rev. 1973, Part III, ch. 1–3. Roger McHugh's *Dublin 1916*, 1966, repr. with illustrations 1976, is a collection of firsthand testimonies. Ulick O'Connor's *A Terrible Beauty*, 1975, embeds the story, with details you'll find nowhere else, in a short narrative running from Parnell to "Bloody Sunday," 1920.

175 "the epicentre": *Ulysses*, 344.

176 "on its east side": F. O. Dwyer, *Lost Dublin*, 1981, 16.

176 "Bernard Shaw thought": quoted in McHugh, *Dublin 1916*, 360.

176 "Joyce's famous hope": Frank Budgen, *James Joyce and the Making of Ulysses*, 1972, 69.

176 "*Freeman's Journal*": McHugh, *Dublin 1916*, 59.

176 "prompt to urinate": O'Connor, *A Terrible Beauty*, 76.

176 "Bloom made to unroll": *Ulysses*, 487.

176 "summoned Cuchulain": "The Statues," *Variorum Poems*, 611.

176 "voice out of heaven": *Ulysses*, 345.

177 "episode of *Murphy*": Samuel Beckett, *Murphy*, 42.

177 "From confusion": Lyons, *Ireland Since the Famine*, 350–52; "wireless expert," 356.

177 Note: "John P. Roche tells it": *National Review*, 11 June 1982, 717.

178 "Connolly recounted": O'Connor, *A Terrible Beauty*, 89.

178 "Ireland would have pitied": W. M. Murphy, *Prodigal Father*, 1978, 453.

178 "2.5 million": Lyons, *Ireland Since the Famine*, 802, note 12.

178 "1909 journal": Yeats, *Memoirs*, 177–78.

179 "he counseled": Thomas MacDonagh, *Literature in Ireland*, 1916, 69. For the poem see John Montague, *The Book of Irish Verse*, 1974, 245.

179 "mother's rosary": McHugh, *Dublin 1916*, 263.

179 "to Lady Gregory": *Letters*, 613.

180 "A young girl": "On Being Asked for a War Poem," *Variorum Poems*, 359.

180 "world swept away": *Letters*, 614.

180 "Easter 1916": *Variorum Poems*, 391.

180 "lugubrious exercise": "Mourn—and Then Onward!"; he never collected it but its ghost mocks his in *Variorum Poems*, 737.

180 "beauty like a tightened bow": "No Second Troy," *Variorum Poems*, 256.

180 "*Kuthera deina*": Pound, *The Cantos*, 1970, 511; a classical sentiment if not a classical phrase.

181 "devil era": Joyce, *Finnegans Wake*, 473.

181 "beauty is Borneo": O'Casey, *Inishfallen, Fare Thee Well*, chapter heading.

182 "pruning": Richard Ellmann, *James Joyce*, 1959, 416–17.

182 "dropped out": Ellmann, *James Joyce*, 62.

182 "ten better ones": Joyce, *Finnegans Wake*, 3, 23, 44, 90, 113, 257, 314, 332, 414, 424. They've 1001 letters among them.

182 "fumble and stumble": Sean O'Faolain, *Vive Moi!*, 1964, 130.

183 "horror": Frank O'Connor, *An Only Child*, 1961, 154.

183 "sheltering in doors": O'Faolain, *Vive Moi!*, 169.

183   "storm in a chalice": Frank O'Connor, *My Father's Son*, 1968, ch. 2.

183   "dipped the tip": O'Faolain, *Vive Moi!*, 135.

183   "Shepherd and Goatherd": *Variorum Poems*, 338.

185   "Some burn": "In Memory of Major Robert Gregory," *Variorum Poems*, 323–28.

185   "He who can read": *Variorum Poems*, 429.

THE *ULYSSES* YEARS

187   "Occam's Razor": W. M. Murphy, *Prodigal Father*, 1978, 247, and Richard Ellmann, 1959, *James Joyce*, 179.

187   "That bloody Joyce": quoted in J. B. Lyons, *James Joyce and Medicine*, 1973, 68.

188   "stripped," "met": *Ulysses*, 16, 17. Peter's bitter weeping is in Matthew xxvi. 75.

188   "Yeats's tonsils": Joseph Hone, *W. B. Yeats*, 1971, 332.

188   "George Moore wrote": *Hail and Farewell*, repr. 1976, 354.

189   "young man from St. John's": Richard Cave supplies this version in his edition of Moore's *Hail and Farewell*, 725. There are also laundered rescriptions.

189   "one of the great lyric poets": W.B.Y.'s Introduction to *The Oxford Book of Modern Verse*, 1936.

189   "majesty of the occasion": Miss Anne Yeats in conversation, May 1975.

189   "Ringsend": *The Collected Poems of Oliver St. John Gogarty*, 1954, 102.

190   "Polyfizzyboisterous": Joyce, *Finnegans Wake*, 547.

190   "Wipe your glosses": Joyce, *Finnegans Wake*, 304, note 3.

190   "imperial British state": *Ulysses*, 20.

191   "Gogarty's fat back": quoted by J. B. Lyons, *James Joyce and Medicine*, 67.

192   "guess about 'blind' ": Eric Partridge's, in *Origins*.

193   "jeered at George Moore": *Letters*, II, 71.

194   "He watched the bristles": *Ulysses*, 56.

194   "Jews and Irish": credit for discovering this particular base for the conception of *Ulysses* belongs to Herbert Howarth; see his *The Irish Writers*, 1958, 24–25, 259–60.

194   "such regulations": Douglas Hyde, *A Literary History of Ireland*, 1899, 609.

195   "measurement": *Ulysses*, 668, where Bloom climbing over a railing "lowered his body gradually by its length of five feet nine inches and a half."

195   "coming over here": *Ulysses*, 323.

198   Yeats, Moore: Richard Ellmann, 545, 543.

198   "blackguardism": Sylvia Beach, *Shakespeare and Company*, 1959, 52.

200   "You have a filthy mind": quoted from Lady Gregory's *Journals* by David Krause, *Sean O'Casey: The Man and His Work*, 1975, 339.

200   "the colonel's daughter" and other phrases hereabouts: Sean O'Casey, *Inishfallen Fare Thee Well*, 1949, chapter called "The Temple Entered."

200   "To ride abroad": Tennyson, *Guinivere*.

200   "hurled the little streets": "No Second Troy," *Variorum Poems*, 256.

200   "Born John Casey": biographical details from Krause, ch. 1.

201   "Who's gettin' excited?": O'Casey, *Collected Plays*, I, 1949, 208–9.

201   "darlin' motto": O'Casey, *Collected Plays*, I, 88.

201   "Why d'ye take notice": O'Casey, *Collected Plays*, I, 174–75.

202   "Sean O'Faolain would note": in *The Bell* in 1953; quoted at length by Krause, 44–45.

202   Note: "Robert Lowery": I take this information from a review (*James Joyce Quarterly*, XIX.2: 201) of *Sean O'Casey Centenary Essays*, which I've not seen.

203   "They think": delivered in 1915; quoted in Roger McHugh, *Dublin 1916*, 1966, 397. O'Casey's version (*The Plough and the Stars*, II) is virtually identical. Another source for the

words of the Man in the Window was Pearse's 1913 essay "The Coming Revolution"; see
F.S.L. Lyons, *Ireland Since the Famine*, rev. 1973, 336–37.

203   "Jammed as I was": O'Casey, *Collected Plays*, I, 195.

203   ". . . a gorgeous dhress": O'Casey, *Collected Plays*, I, 199.

203   "One critic": Andrew Malone, in the *Dublin Magazine*, March 1925, quoted by Krause, 81.

204   "Sam Beckett": in a review of O'Casey's *Windfalls* in *Bookman*, December 1934.

204   *"The End of the Beginning"*: O'Casey, *Collected Plays*, I, 263–92.

205   "Dope, dope": O'Casey, *Collected Plays*, 203.

205   "I am sad and discouraged": for the correspondence see Krause, 101–5 and 348–49.

205   "infringement of the canons": responses cited from Krause, 129.

206   "The trees": "The Wild Swans at Coole," *Variorum Poems*, 322.

207   "all that I have handled least": "Ego Dominus Tuus," *Variorum Poems*, 367.

207   "men improve with the years": *Variorum Poems*, 329.

209   "What are the hopes of men?": Byron, *Don Juan*, I, ccxix.

209   "first use of it": I'm not sure of this. "Ancestral Houses" and the opening of "Nineteen
Hundred and Nineteen," where we find *ottava rima* again, belong to long poems that shared
time on his worktable. But I'd guess that "Ancestral Houses" occupied him first.

209   "What if the glory": "Ancestral Houses," *Variorum Poems*, 418.

210   "An ancient bridge": "My House," *Variorum Poems*, 419.

210   "desolation of reality": from "Meru," *Variorum Poems*, 563.

210   "two provisos": Lyons, 311.

211   "We must recognize": Quoted in Lyons, 397. Though published by Béaslaí in his *An t
Oglách*, it was written by Ernest Blythe, later Minister of Finance in Cosgrave's 1923 cabinet.

211   "thirty-four of its sixty-nine": Lyons, 400.

211   "Weasels": *Variorum Poems*, 429.

212   "traffic in mockery": *Variorum Poems*, 432.

212   "some four thousand": Lyons, 468.

212   "poem that records": "Meditations in Time of Civil War, v," *Variorum Poems*, 423–24.

212   "best book I have written": *Letters*, 742.

212   "time that I wrote my will": *Variorum Poems*, 414.

213   "scholarship": T. L. Dume, "Yeats' Golden Tree and Birds in the Byzantine Poems," *Modern
Language Notes*, LXVII: 404–7.

213   "Such thought": *Variorum Poems*, 474.

214   "Death and life were not": *Variorum Poems*, 415.

214   "Another emblem," "What's water": *Variorum Poems*, 490.

THE WAKE OF WAKES

215   "Rory O'Connor": see F.S.L. Lyons, *Ireland Since the Famine*, rev. 1973, 467.

215   "20 March 1923": date from Richard Ellmann, *James Joyce*, 1959, 801.

216   "one to do": Joyce, *Finnegans Wake*, 382, rearranged on the page to guide newcomers. Here
as elsewhere I quote the final versions, not the drafts. What Joyce drafted in 1923 is lost, but
for something pretty close to it see David Hayman, *A First-Draft Version of Finnegans Wake*,
1963, 203–4.

216   "You can't impose": *Finnegans Wake*, 378.

217   "secular colleges": J. C. Beckett, *The Making of Modern Ireland*, 1966, 329–31.

217   "Guns": Joyce, *Finnegans Wake*, 368.

217   "the boomomouths": Joyce, *Finnegans Wake*, 367.

217   "seven times": page and line numbers of Joyce, *Finnegans Wake*: 358.30, 369.24, 386.20,
390.29, 482.20, 528.33, 619.19. For more on "document number two" see Lyons 448–49.

217   "obsessive preoccupation": Lyons, 442.

218 "huge James Laughlin": he told me this story in 1980.

218 "*blue, blown*": this etymology for "blue" was suggested in Charles Richardson's 1839 *Dictionary of the English Language*.

219 "stuck to his guns": *Ulysses*, 654.

219 "inadvertent pun": the next few pages plagiarize freely from my article "The Jokes at the Wake," *Massachusetts Review*, XXII.4 (1981): 722–33.

220 "Illiterate writers": Johnson, Preface to the *Dictionary*.

220 "scribblers for provincial newspapers": such as the *Kilkenny People* Bloom consults in the National Library (*Ulysses*, 200). This suggestion, which I've not had the resources to verify, came from Mr. Anthony Cronin.

220 "plebeian, degenerate": see Brendan O Hehir, *A Gaelic Lexicon for Finnegans Wake*, 1967, 419–22.

221 "wan warning": Joyce, *Finnegans Wake*, 6.

222 "Now be aisy": Joyce, *Finnegans Wake*, 24.

222 "A rogue": Seán Ó Súilleabháin, *Irish Wake Amusements*, 67. The Joyce people seem not to have happened on this book, the author's translation from his 1961 Irish original: Mercier Press, Dublin and Cork, 1967.

222 "unusual use of words": Ó Súilleabháin, 32.

223 "young Boasthard's fear": *Ulysses*, 395.

223 "*Silentium!*": *Ulysses*, 424–25.

224 "Welter focussed": *Finnegans Wake*, 324.

225 "We are now diffusing": *Finnegans Wake*, 359–60.

226 "Elmar Ternes": paper published in *The Canadian Journal of Irish Studies*, VI (1980): 50–73. The parts of interest here are excerpted in Robert O'Driscoll, ed., *The Celtic Consciousness*, 1982, 69–78.

226 "early books": Stuart Gilbert, *James Joyce's Ulysses*, 1930, and Frank Budgen, *James Joyce and the Making of Ulysses*, 1934.

226 "Mr. Pope's *Iliad*": I have lifted much of this paragraph from my own book *Ulysses*, 1980, 3.

227 "Jacques Mercanton": Richard Ellmann, 723.

227 "lying in death": Richard Ellmann, 559.

227 "story of this Chapelizod family": Eugene Jolas, "My Friend James Joyce," in S. Givens, ed., *James Joyce: Two Decades of Criticism*, 1948, 11.

228 "Fritz Senn": in *James Joyce Quarterly*, XIX.2 (1982): 177–78.

228 "Chapelizod houses": reported by Fritz Senn in *A Wake Newslitter*, VIII.1: 88–89.

229 "insane British officer": Lyons, 373, a good summary. For a much more detailed narrative by Skeffington's widow, see Roger McHugh, *Dublin 1916*, 1976, 276–88. It was she, by the way, who ten years later led the attack on *The Plough and the Stars*.

230 "mirror on mirror": "The Statues," *Variorum Poems*, 610: by no means a "source" for *Finnegans Wake*, since it wasn't published until March 1939.

231 "a spectator": that was Stephen MacKenna; see Nancy Cardozo, *Lucky Eyes and a High Heart: The Life of Maud Gonne*, 1978, 220.

231 "Shakespeare pervades": see Adaline Glasheen, *Third Census of Finnegans Wake*, 1977, 260: "To my mind, Shakespeare (man, works) is the matrix of FW . . . ."

TWO ECCENTRICS

232 "Mucker" and "the holes" from Kavanagh's *The Green Fool*, 1938, ch. 1; "1791 cabin" from Darcy O'Brien, *Patrick Kavanagh*, 1975, 30. Anyone who reads O'Brien's little book will perceive my indebtedness to it.

232   "great roots of hands" and other quoted phrases from O'Brien, 16; the custom shoes specified by Anthony Cronin, *Dead as Doornails*, 1976, 125.

232   "destructive power": Cronin, 171.

232   "I turn the lea-green down": "Ploughman," in Kavanagh, *Collected Poems*, 1972, 3. For "the origin of my ploughman ecstasy," see *The Green Fool*, ch. 28.

233   "dreams and visions": *Ulysses*, 186–87.

233   "Primal Language": see Herbert Howarth, *The Irish Writers*, 1958, 178. Like his whole book, Howarth's chapter on AE can be recommended without reservation.

234   "Ireland's imminent Messiah": Howarth, 174.

234   "the wastrel Joyce": Richard Ellmann, *James Joyce*, 1959; for the money, 184; for the *Homestead* commission, 169.

234   "knocked at AE's door": *The Green Fool*, ch. 29.

235   "down to one mistress": O'Brien, 29.

235   "Jewish antique dealer": J. B. Lyons, *Oliver St. John Gogarty*, 1980, 182–94.

235   "lawsuit about a book review": Howarth, 167. It was a book of Gaelic songs.

235   "one evening in 1941": O'Brien, 21–22.

235   "O he loved his mother": Kavanagh, *Collected Poems*, 37.

237   "John Synge, I": "The Municipal Gallery Revisited," *Variorum Poems*, 603.

237   "English-bred lie": O'Brien, 23.

237   "found what I wanted": Yeats, *Letters*, 922.

238   "desolation of reality": "Meru," *Variorum Poems*, 563.

238   "Every discoloration": *Variorum Poems*, 567.

239   *"Hamlet"*: I.v.149 ff.

240   "Czar, I bless thee": John Mitchel, *Jail Journal*, Dublin, n.d., 358.

241   "kinetic vulgarity": Kavanagh, *Collected Poems*, xiv.

241   "unnecessarily harsh": Joyce, *Selected Letters*, 109–10. The date is 25 September 1906. He had written all of *Dubliners* save "The Dead."

241   "dreadful stage-Irish": Kavanagh's comments on *The Green Fool* are from his 1963 "Self Portrait," *Collected Pruse*, 1973, 13. No, "Pruse" is not a misprint.

241   "seacoastless, bearless": see *The Winter's Tale*, III.iii, which opens on "the seacoast" of Bohemia (with "deserts" specified) and ends "(*Exit, pursued by a bear.*)"

241   "Dublin is the administrative capital": Cronin, 95.

242   "Mr. T. O'Deirg": *Kavanagh's Weekly*, 12 April 1952, 6.

242   "Heaven's high manna": "Bank Holiday," Kavanagh, *Collected Poems*, 100.

243   "The important thing": "Is," Kavanagh, *Collected Poems*, 154.

244   "O commemorate me": "Lines Written on a Seat on the Grand Canal, Dublin, 'Erected to the Memory of Mrs Dermot O'Brien,' " Kavanagh, *Collected Poems*, 150.

243   "A backhanded catch": O'Brien, 62.

244   "Heaney acknowledges": O'Brien, 67.

244   "generally considered": Thomas Kinsella, in Robert Hogan, ed., *Dictionary of Irish Literature*, 1979, 157. And Kinsella's opinion carries weight.

244   "Pot Poet": Samuel Beckett, *Murphy*, 1938, 84.

244   "bulging with minor beauties": *Murphy*, 89.

244   "Gogarty urged Clarke to sue": Lyons, *Gogarty*, 1980, 232.

244   "Paddy of the Celtic Mist": Kavanagh, *Collected Poems*, 90. For the identification, O'Brien, 45–46.

244   "Founder Member," "Should I?": *Letters*, 801, 795.

245   "I load myself with chains": quoted in Thomas Kinsella, Introduction to Clarke's *Selected Poems*, 1976, xi.

245   "the clapper from the bell": Clarke's note in a 1928 collection, see Clarke, *Selected Poems*, 190.

245   "Summer delights the scholar": Clarke, *Selected Poems*, 5.

245   "Before the day": Clarke, *Selected Poems*, 18.

246   "Unpitied, wasting": Clarke, *Selected Poems*, 59.

246   "manifold illusion": "Meru," *Variorum Poems*, 563.

247   "Such thought": "All Souls' Night," *Variorum Poems*, 474.

249   "Life returned": *Variorum Poems*, 831.

250   "now none living": *Variorum Poems*, 571.

250   "Soul must learn": *Variorum Poems*, 573.

250   "From pleasure of the bed": *Variorum Poems*, 575.

250   "But a coarse old man": *Variorum Poems*, 590.

251   "Crazy Jane on the Mountain": *Variorum Poems*, 628.

251   "Down the mountain walls": "News for the Delphic Oracle," *Variorum Poems*, 612.

252   " Becfola quickly undressed": Clarke, *Collected Poems*, 1976, 543.

THE MOCKER

253   "haul Kavanagh": Anthony Cronin, *Dead as Doornails*, 1976, 124–25.

254   "Did you never study atomics?": Flann O'Brien, *The Third Policeman*, 1967, 84–85.

254–55   "de Selby": cited phrases from *The Third Policeman*, 166, 146, 144.

255   "Like many alcoholics": Cronin, 116.

255   "A northerner": for the drab facts of his life, see Anne Clissmann, *Flann O'Brien: A Critical Introduction to his Writing*, 1975, 1–37.

256   "The next witness": Flann O'Brien, *At Swim-Two-Birds*, 1960, 294.

257   "Brian became fixed": Cronin, 111.

258   "a much milder book": *The Dalkey Archive*, 1964.

258   "I notice these days": *The Best of Myles*, 1968, 104.

259   "I tried": *The Best of Myles*, 99.

259   "How are heights?": conflated from *The Best of Myles*, 213 and 217.

261   *"You know, of course"*: *The Third Policeman*, 161.

THE TERMINATOR

262   "Le capitaine Godot": anecdote from Mr. John Calder.

264   "as he rose": Yeats, *Mythologies*, 224.

264   "Who else": from Mr. James Knowlson, *viva voce*. See Mr. Knowlson's "Beckett and John Millington Synge" in James Knowlson and John Pilling, *Frescoes of the Skull: the Later Prose and Drama of Samuel Beckett*, 1979, 259–74, which I came upon after this chapter had been drafted. It has pointed me to additional details.

265   "special gratification": Knowlson quotes Yeats, "An Introduction for My Plays," 1937: "It was certainly a day of triumph when the first act of *The Well of the Saints* held its audience, though the two chief persons sat side by side under a stone cross from start to finish."

266   "Willie Fay remembers": W. G. Fay and Catherine Carswell, *The Fays of the Abbey Theatre*, 1935, 138.

267   "Turn your eyes": Robin Skelton, ed., *The Collected Plays of Jack B. Yeats*, 1971, 45.

267   "Imperishable fire": *The Shadowy Waters*, 1900 version, *Variorum Poems*, 765.

268   "Joyce saw": his presence is recorded in *Joseph Holloway's Abbey Theatre*, 1967, 40.

268   "Willie Fay recalled": Fay and Carswell, 125–26.

268   "man in a top hat": Liam Byrne, *History of Aviation in Ireland*, 1980, 28–9.

268   "the next year": Bruce Bradley, S.J., *James Joyce's Schooldays*, 1982, 129.

269   "open pianner": Richard Ellmann, *James Joyce*, 1959, 241.

269   "The years": ending of *The Countess Cathleen*, Yeats, *Variorum Plays*, 169. Joyce quoted these lines in the *Portrait*.

269   "told of Beckett": by Michael Beausang, in "L'Exil du Samuel Beckett," *Critique*, #421–22, (1982): 563.

270   "formless spawning fury": Yeats, "The Statues," *Variorum Poems*, 611.

271   "one that ruffled": "Coole Park, 1929," *Variorum Poems*, 488.

271   "Death and life": "The Tower," *Variorum Poems*, 415.

272   "a Joyce pilgrim": Prof. John Henry Raleigh. See *James Joyce Quarterly*, VIII.2: 131.

272   "That the house": *Ulysses*, 479.

INDEX

DATE DUE